**THE UNIVERSITY OF
WINCHESTER**

**Martial Rose Library
Tel: 01962 827306**

To be returned on or before the day marked above, subject to recall.

Discipline and Desire

Surveillance Technologies in Performance

———— ❧ ————

ELISE MORRISON

University of Michigan Press
Ann Arbor

Published in the United States of America by the
University of Michigan Press
Manufactured in the United States of America
⊗ Printed on acid-free paper

2019   2018   2017   2016   4   3   2   1

A CIP catalog record for this book is available from the British Library.

ISBN: 978-0-472-07326-9 (hardcover : alk. paper)
ISBN: 978-0-472-05326-1 (paperback : alk. paper)
ISBN: 978-0-472-12236-3 (e-book)

For Bohan and Josephine,
who watch and are watched over

Acknowledgments

There are many people to thank for their support, insight, and encouragement throughout the development of this book. Mentors, teachers, students, editors, reviewers, friends, colleagues, and family (often overlapping in categories) have helped sustain and inspire me in early, late, and enduring stages of research, discussion, writing, and rewriting. In particular, I am indebted to the generous mentorship of Joseph Roach, who, as Principle Investigator of the Mellon-funded Interdisciplinary Performance Studies at Yale, provided me with the funding, time, space, and intellectual community I needed as I turned the dissertation into this book. Deep gratitude is also due to Rebecca Schneider, Professor of Theater and Performance Studies at Brown University, who guided my work when this book was a dissertation and has continued to offer motivation and support. I am so grateful to the kind and astute LeAnn Fields of University of Michigan Press, who, along with Christopher Dreyer and his production team and the resourceful Kelly Kerwin at the Yale School of Drama, helped produce this book. I wish also to thank my many students at Brown, Harvard, and Yale whose questions, arguments, and creative projects have helped shape my own. These and many more academic colleagues, mentors, and friends deserve recognition and gratitude: the members of the Performance Studies Working Group at Yale; my fellow postdocs at Yale, especially Dominika Laster and Mary Isbell; my academic family at Brown, Rebecca Schneider, Patricia Ybarra, John Emigh, Paige McGinely, Michelle Carriger, Molly Flynn, Christine

Mok, Andrew Starner, Lindsay Goss, Christian DuComb, Hans Vermy, Christine Evans, Ken Prestininzi, and Pannill Camp; and the many many more who have fed my thinking over the years at annual conferences of the American Society for Theatre Research (ASTR), Performance Studies international (PSi), Association for Theatre in Higher Education (ATHE), and other gatherings around the globe, Jennifer Parker-Starbuck, Sarah Bay-Cheng, James Harding, Donovan Sherman, Lindsay Brandon-Hunter, and Linsey Bostwick, to begin a list with no end.

I am greatly indebted to the artists whose work I discuss in this book; without their creativity, bravery, and generosity, this book could not exist. From witnessing inspirational performances to conversations at conferences, theaters, and galleries to providing images of their work, I have benefited greatly from the generosity and openness of so many of these surveillance artists. It is my hope that this book furthers their causes and careers.

And finally, I am eternally grateful to my family for their steadfast encouragement patience, and love: my father and mother, Clint Morrison and Nancy Rosenberger; my brother and sister, Ted and Laura Morrison; my husband, Brian Samas; my stepdaughter, Sabrina Samas; and my children, Bohan and Josephine, who have come into being alongside this work.

Contents

Introduction

Surveilling the Scene

————— ⚘ —————

On September 16, 2012, approximately one hundred posters advertising a New York Police Department (NYPD) armed drone program appeared on the sides of pay phone kiosks in several busy districts of midtown Manhattan. The posters featured silhouettes of a man, woman, and child running in terror from a missile let loose by a military drone flying above; in the corner, an official-looking NYPD seal hovered next to the sinister slogan "NYPD Drones: Protection When You Least Expect It."[1] The alarming placards were soon denounced as a hoax, as NYPD officials rushed to deny the existence of any such program. In the weeks that followed, as the NYPD sought out the identity and whereabouts of the perpetrator of the guerrilla street art campaign, visual artist Essam Attia released an anonymous video online, which explained the goals of this satirical but nonetheless alarming poster campaign. Voice disguised and face hidden in shadow, Attia stated that he had designed and installed the posters in response to recent revisions to the Federal Aviation Administration (FAA) regulations concerning the use of unmanned aerial vehicles (UAVs), commonly called drones, within domestic airspace. The new regulations, which had been approved by the US Congress in March 2012, permitted the use of drones for purposes of domestic law enforcement and environmental research, among other public safety and commercial pursuits. Attia, who had served as a geospatial analyst in the US

Fig. 1. Essam Attia's drone poster, 2012. (Photograph by Jason Shelowitz.)

military and was deployed in Iraq, said that he knew too much about the destructive power of military drone strikes to feel comfortable with the prospect of UAVs being used by law enforcement units and other civilian programs in the United States. Timing his subversive posters to appear a few days before the United Nations General Assembly was to convene, Attia aimed "to create a conversation about the deployment of drones in American airspace. We have to remember that right now, internationally, they are being used to kill people. They're armed: they shoot missiles. We're fighting an illegal war in Pakistan and no one seems to want to talk about it."[2] In the weeks after his posters hit the streets, Attia was arrested and charged with multiple felonies, including grand larceny and forgery.[3] In response to Attia's street art campaign, the NYPD firmly denied any active use of drones, but it remained noticeably silent regarding any future plans to actively employ them.

The media storm over Attia's performative activism revealed the high stakes and sensitive nature of the form and content of his critique. Activism in the public sphere has always invited controversy, particularly when it targets authoritarian forces, such as the NYPD. Attia's tactics added

insult to injury by engaging the theatrical tactic of fakery, a radical politics of (mis)identification in which the ontological ground of sociopolitical signification is shown to be less stable and trustworthy than we have
been anxiously led to believe. Using tactics of impersonation and forgery, Attia used the signs of authority (the NYPD logo, font, and name) to
stage a critical fiction on the public thoroughfares of New York City. The
imagery of his poster was laden with cultural symbolism; the outlines of
the man, woman, and child suggested a civilian nuclear family that, with
its attendant associations of security and prosperity, was under threat
of becoming a victim of the very state that was supposed to protect it.
Though fake and distinctly dystopic, his theatrical tableau teetered on
the edge of two very real and unnerving truths: first, that US military
drone strikes have been responsible for the deaths of thousands of civilians in Iraq, Afghanistan, and several other Middle Eastern and Central
Asian countries over the previous decade and a half; and, second, that
the recent changes to FAA regulations have invited these remotely controlled instruments of aerial surveillance and lethal weaponry into US
civilian life.

Surveillance Technologies in Performance

Although the dramatic scene portrayed by Attia was uniquely contemporary, the plot was far from new. Drones and the debates they are raising
were preceded by a host of other surveillance technologies that have
made their way from military arenas into the everyday interfaces of civilian life. Global Positioning System (GPS) locative media, closed-circuit
television (CCTV) cameras, radio frequency identification (RFID) tags,
facial recognition technology, medical ultrasounds, the Internet, mobile
communication devices, and countless other technologies firmly embedded in civilian life all originated as tools for military operations.[4] The
term *surveillance society* was first coined by sociologist Gary T. Marx in
1985 to describe the already rapidly increasing permeation of state and
military technologies of surveillance into the social and cultural spheres
of civilians around the world.[5] As drones are introduced into environmental research, consumer delivery services, amateur and professional
cinematography, border control, and local law enforcement departments, we are perched once again on a familiar razor's edge. On one
side, the risks of increased state discipline and corporate control threat-
en to cut into the privacy, personal freedoms, and information security

of groups and individuals around the world; on the other, the benefits of increased efficiency, safety, communication, mobility, economic growth, and entertainment staunch these wounds.

As digital technologies, so many of which are functionally undergirded by technologies of surveillance, have become more and more deeply integrated into our social, political, and economic lives, our relationship with surveillance as a concept and reality has become increasingly ambivalent. Today surveillance technologies are routinely used in overtly disciplinary projects, for military intelligence and offensives, counterterrorism efforts, border security, domestic law enforcement, and corporate oversight of employees and products; they are also present in social applications that are, at least on the surface, less about discipline than about our desires as consumers and social actors. Surveillance technologies facilitate online banking and commerce, locative media on our computers and smart phones, reality television programs, and social networking sites such as Facebook and Twitter. Within this "soft cage" of surveillance society, user-consumers of digital technologies are encouraged (if not required) to participate in surveillance society simply by showing up for work, communicating with friends and colleagues, traveling, and shopping.[6] While much of the population benefits from participatory surveillance, the model of discipline by participation poses risks that are more or less substantial depending on one's economic, medical, and citizenship status. Based on surveillance of personal data, or dataveillance, some individuals will be preapproved for car loans, given priority service through help centers online or over the phone, or fast-tracked through immigration and customs, while others encounter prohibitively high interest rates, increased scrutiny by law enforcement, or impermeable national borders.[7]

Debates over the risks and benefits of surveillance technologies have accompanied their adoption in both the civilian and military spheres, taking place in mainstream news and entertainment media, as well as the growing academic field of surveillance studies. Privacy has long served as the primary watchword hurled against comprehensive surveillance conducted in the name of national security;[8] such concerns were only intensified by the 2013 revelations of former security contractor Edward Snowden regarding the startling breadth and depth of the surveillance being conducted by the National Security Administration (NSA) on everyone from Gmail users to heads of state of foreign powers. At the same time, surveillance theorists concerned with the racial, gendered, and economic privilege that the term *privacy* implies have argued that "privacy is a limited lens for thinking about surveillance, since it is a right not granted equally to all."[9] Critical discourses of surveillance have thus expanded to include concerns over differential treatment of individuals and groups based on demographics and economic status, as well as on uneven access to legal recourse. As military research engines such as the Defense Advanced Research Projects Agency (DARPA) and state surveillance entities such as the NSA have contracted with the rapidly growing industry of private sector research and development, the field of surveillance studies has become rightly concerned with the increased *privatization* of surveillance. Surveillance activists and academics have worked to analyze and expose these often shadowy and ethically dubious partnerships among the private sector, state, and military-industrial complex, as well as the profit-driven interests they represent.[10]

Despite the prevalence of surveillance as a topic of fascination and debate in mainstream media and academia, however, opportunities to critically reflect on, and, more importantly, to imagine and rehearse alternative, creative responses to living in a rapidly expanding surveillance society have been harder to find. It is the argument of this book that such opportunities are being created through a growing genre of performance based arts activism, which I am calling "surveillance art and performance." This book explores the wide variety of ways in which artists and activists have tactically utilized technologies of surveillance to create new and different ways of interacting with and understanding contemporary surveillance technologies. I explain the important yet largely overlooked role of surveillance artists within contemporary surveillance society, arguing that surveillance art generates creative and critical alternatives to dominant, mainstream applications of surveillance technologies rather than simply reacting against them.

For example, in addition to Attia's project, described above, a number of artist-activists appropriated drone technologies as a means of imagining alternative uses for the UAVs in the year following passage of the FAA drone legislation. In 2012, artist-activists Angel Nevarez and Alex Rivera built an online project called *Lowdrone* that sought to counter the use of drones by the civilian, nongovernmental organization American Border Control, a conservative vigilante group that takes it upon itself to police the US-Mexico border using drones and other aircraft. Nevarez and Rivera decided to use consumer-level drone technology to facilitate transgressive border crossings instead. To do so, they positioned a drone on the US-Mexico border between Tijuana and Southern California, and linked its controls to a website through which users could log on and fly the drone over the fence that marks the border and back again.[11] *Lowdrone* is part of a constellation of politically radical appropriations of commercially available surveillance technologies that intervene in dominant modes of surveillance and disciplinary ideologies along the heavily surveilled US-Mexico border. For the *Transborder Immigrant Tool* project, Ricardo Dominguez, a professor at the University of California, San Diego, along with members of Electronic Disturbance Theatre (EDT) and his b.a.n.g. lab at UCSD, bought inexpensive Motorola cell phones and retooled them to become mobile GPS devices that could help Mexican immigrants safely cross the US-Mexico border.[12] As such projects show, drones or smart phones can be used for both normative and subversive political purposes; by extension, they suggest that our position as users, consumers, and subjects of surveillance technologies can likewise become radically ambivalent and open to revision.

Other examples of performative, transgressive in(ter)ventions abound throughout the book. From Steve Mann's wearable "sousveillance" technologies, Jill Magid's "surveillance shoe," and Wafaa Bilal's *3rdi* to James Bridle's *Drone Shadows*, Zach Blas's *Facial Weaponization Suite*, Mona Hatoum's *Deep Throat*, and Hasan Elahi's *Tracking Transcience*, the field of surveillance art is rapidly growing in diversity, scope, and scale. In the last several decades, artists and activists such as these have employed drones, CCTV cameras, GPS tracking systems, medical surveillance equipment, and a host of other commercially available surveillance technologies as representational tools with which to reflect and reimagine the social and political landscape of contemporary surveillance. Throughout the book I examine the tactics and processes by means of which surveillance artists and activists make visible—and thus available for scrutiny and revision—the risks posed by surveillance technologies in social and political spheres, as well as their inventive proposals for the alternative uses to which these technologies can be put.

Surveillance as Performance

A principal goal of this book is to introduce the reader to a wide range of surveillance artists and their performance works and to establish the genre of surveillance art more centrally within performance studies, surveillance studies, and the field of digital media and performance. At the same time, I am keenly aware that the field of surveillance art and activism is rapidly developing and will quickly outstrip any attempt to catalog its contents. Although I have made an effort to include a diversity of artists and account for the breadth of work that has been created over the past several decades, this book is not intended to be a comprehensive catalog of surveillance art. I employ examples of contemporary surveillance art in order to identify prevalent trends, themes, and tactics that are shaping the form as it moves forward in the twenty-first century. I contextualize this emergent lexicon of tactics used by surveillance artists by showing how they have been influenced and inspired by the work of twentieth-century feminist theorists and practitioners, avant-garde theater artists, cultural theorists, social activists, and amateur hobbyists, as well as by rapid technological developments in surveillance and the post–9/11 political climate. In doing so, I aim to provide a taxonomy and analytical framework for surveillance art that can aid the diverse pursuits of practitioners, scholars, teachers, students, activists, and hobbyists interested in critical and creative uses of surveillance technologies.

My study places surveillance art in the context of the increasingly robust genre of intermedial and digital performance.[13] While experimentation with emergent media in spaces of performance is by no means a new phenomenon, particularly rapid techno-social changes in the late twentieth and early twenty-first centuries lend an increased sense of urgency to the study of intermedial performance, as contemporary artists integrate new technologies and forms of information exchange into theatrical space at greater rates every year.[14] Following Steve Dixon's definition of *digital performance* as "performance works where computer technologies play a key role rather than a subsidiary one in content, techniques, aesthetics, or delivery forms,"[15] I consider surveillance art to be performances or installations in which surveillance technologies are central to their production, design, content, aesthetics, and/or reception.

Within this framework, I think through similarities and distinctions between surveillance technologies as tools of performance versus the ways in which these technologies function performatively in everyday life. Just as the moniker of digital performance could be applied to processes of everyday Internet communication, as these "constitute digital palimpsests of Erving Goffman's notions of performative presentations of the self . . . within the proscenium arch of the computer monitor,"[16] so, too, could surveillance in everyday life be said to constitute a form of performance in which subjects are disciplined, however subtly, into desired models of usership and citizenship. Cultural theorists and surveillance analysts/designers alike have used performance as a conceptual model through which to explain and analyze emergent forms of discipline within contemporary life. Terms such as *performance prediction, performance modeling, performance analytics,* and *total performance* are increasingly common descriptors in both scholarship and the marketing of surveillance technologies. In these instances, *performance* functions as a euphemism for the efficacy of a surveillance system or for the behavior that a system might monitor or predict or, as James Harding has argued, as a classification of risk management that serves to protect and increase the profit margins of private companies that take part in the growing surveillance industry.[17] Pointing to such usages in contemporary culture more broadly, performance theorist Jon McKenzie has argued that "performance" should be thought of as the new model for discipline, as the neoliberal subject is tracked, evaluated, and reproduced across increasingly linked spheres of work and leisure in everyday life.[18] Indeed, studying the performative aspects of surveillance is valuable not only for the purposes of defining new models of discipline and participation but also as a means of analyzing the forms of labor of "actors" on either side of surveillance interfaces. As Mark Andrejevic has argued, the integration of surveillance technologies into widespread systems of digital communication and entertainment has, through the promise of democratic interactivity, compelled users, consumers, and spectators into willingly performing "the work of being watched."[19] Harding also suggests that attention to the performative dimensions of surveillance technologies can reveal the ideological motivations of those that produce and employ them: "Find out how those technologies perform; find out what kind of information they deliver and how the information is sorted; and, you'll have a pretty good idea of whose interests they ultimately serve. Seldom if ever do they simply serve the interests of police officers monitoring CCTV screens."[20] This line of thinking led Harding to suggest that "the pivotal question for artist-activists—for politically inspired artists—who are concerned with the larger implications of an increasingly pervasive surveillance society is not how performance might counter surveillance but rather how the technologies of surveillance perform."[21]

An understanding of the performative and theatrical dimensions of surveillance technologies as they function in everyday life is integral to analyzing the tactics and effects of surveillance artists. I spend a good deal of time thinking through the performative aspects of surveillance in chapter 1. At the same time, I insist on the value of identifying and analyzing the performance-based techniques that surveillance artists have employed to counter dominant models of surveillance and to create alternative, resistant methods of using surveillance technologies. I have found that there is a significant difference between surveillance within a field of everyday interaction and the work of artists who reframe techniques and technologies of surveillance within "extra-daily" spaces of performance.[22] Staging works on street corners and online websites, in political protests and academic conferences, as well as in more traditional spaces of theatrical performance and installation art enables surveillance artists to present in distilled form pressing techno-cultural quandaries and ethical questions of the digital information age. To explain the cultural import of staging new media within theatrical space, performance scholar Jennifer Parker-Starbuck has argued that *cyborg theatre*, her term for performances that investigate the effects of multimedia technologies on the body, functions as a vital cultural laboratory, "a staging ground, a rehearsal for existing and inevitable mergings between bodies and technologies, . . . a space for trying things out, for introducing old ideas anew, for developing what hasn't been able to be articulated in other forms."[23]

The importance of using theatrical spaces as cultural laboratories in which to illuminate cultural habits of representation and to rehearse alternative models of participation is especially great in the case of surveillance. Techniques and technologies of surveillance, particularly as they are developed to chart the evolving terrain of the Internet and biometric technologies, have brought with them new layers of complexity with regard to issues of agency, (dis)empowerment, identity, participation, discipline, and desire. Characterized by processes that require self-disclosure as a means of participation, digital culture mirrors recent shifts in the operations of surveillance, wherein the centralized, optical, architectural system of panoptic discipline has given way to more dispersed, (in)dividualized, virtual, and algorithmic modes of control.[24] Contemporary disciplinary surveillance, enacted most visibly through CCTV networks installed in public and semipublic spaces but also less visibly through biometric and data-driven surveillance, functions in tandem with neoliberal ideology in which the individual is reframed as a commodity, a set of assets that must be produced, managed, and marketed. Consumer-based surveillance systems have thus increasingly been employed to track and predict—and in so doing, produce—desire. Desires for convenience, social visibility, individualized care, health management, and advertising, as well as, fomented by the post-9/11 culture of anxious national (in)security, a desire for discipline, have been fueled and shaped by the expansion of surveillance technologies into commercial and social arenas. Aided by social and corporate systems of communication and commerce, user-friendly social surveillance interfaces such as Facebook and Twitter provide opportunities for self-fashioning, social organization, and advertising; at the same time, these participatory interfaces facilitate the collection of masses of personal data on each user by state and corporate entities.[25] As Andrejevic has summarized, within structures of participatory surveillance, the burden of responsibility falls on "citizen-subjects," who must "take on the challenges of self-management and risk avoidance through forms of monitoring and rationalization associated with capitalist enterprise culture." This arrangement produces a "redoubling of the panoptic model whereby the subjects of the panoptic gaze come to take on some of the responsibilities not just of monitoring themselves, but of keeping track of one another."[26] At the same time, the integration of biometric surveillance and predictive analytics into law enforcement programs, such as Chicago's Virtual Shield, have raised concerns over racial profiling and racially motivated violence, as social assumptions and prejudices are programmed into the algorithms used to sort and analyze "at-risk" populations.[27] All of this is to say that contemporary social subjects are placed in a complicated position with regard to surveillance: we are at once producers, consumers, products, and subjects of surveillance across a range of interfaces and spaces of daily life.

Theatrical performance, as a discipline historically dedicated to the representation of a range of identities, conflicting intentions, and affective experiences of power and disempowerment, is well suited as a medium through which to examine these complexities of contemporary surveillance society. Drawing on my background as a theater artist and scholar, I approach surveillance as an essentially theatrical medium—that is, a representational practice in which bodies, objects, and gestures within a given frame function on both material and symbolic levels, simultaneously referencing and holding up for critical inspection their material or ideological referents from the everyday social world.[28] When staged within traditional theater spaces, street performances, or virtual spaces online, surveillance technologies function metonymically, appearing not only as functional sociopolitical objects but also as signs and symptoms of cultural ideologies of discipline and desire. My approach analyzes surveillance as a representational instrument that, like film, television, photography, and theater, produces—even as it is produced by—cultural norms, from gendered identities and political ideologies to aesthetic habits of representation and reception. In *Loving Big Brother: Performance, Privacy, and Surveillance Space* (2004), an invaluable precedent to the work of this book, John McGrath argued that performances or installations that (re-)create a space of surveillance provoke audiences to *experience* rather than simply *perceive* or *conceive of* surveillance, thereby allowing more radical openings within habitual understandings of surveillance.[29] This, McGrath argues, is the value of "performative space," wherein audience members can feel their "own bodily and psychic relation to the distortions of normative space enacted by surveillance technologies."[30] Hailed as user-consumer-subjects by a range of surveillance technologies in everyday life, audiences of surveillance art and performance are invited instead into a critical spectatorship, prompted to interact with surveillance technologies in new and different ways and to examine anew their habitual relationships with the matrix of discipline and desire in contemporary surveillance society.

Theatricality in Surveillance Art: Creating Critical Spectators

As surveillance art is largely concerned with illuminating the risks and complexities of surveillance society for audiences that are by and large habituated to living within it, surveillance artists have frequently taken a materialist approach in their representational strategies.[31] As the feminist performance theorist Jill Dolan wrote in *The Feminist Spectator as Critic*, a materialist approach helps artists and activists to "denaturalize the psychological identification processes implicit in representation," so that "when the representational apparatus is foregrounded, its once mystified ideology becomes clear."[32] Surveillance artists working in the materialist vein stage familiar techniques and technologies of surveillance in such a way as to draw critical attention to the norms and habits that produce and maintain them and, in some cases, to re-produce them with different social and political intent. The influential artist-activist group Critical Art Ensemble (CAE) has articulated such a strategy to enable artists, performers, and amateur engineers to expose and disrupt state and corporate information networks. As CAE puts it, "digital resistance" through "tactical media" challenges "the existing semiotic regime by replicating and redeploying it in a manner that offers participants in the projects a new way of seeing, understanding, and . . . interacting with a given system."[33] By strategically appropriating and reinterpreting the symbols and practices of dominant surveillance systems, amateur engineers and artists can expose capitalist, neoliberal interests driving such systems while simultaneously building alternative, resistant models.

The terms *recombinant theatre* and *theatre of information* were coined by CAE to describe such strategies of performative repetition and revision.[34] Attia's posters illustrate the tactic of recombinant theater, as he circulated what CAE would call "bad copies" of official information. In essence, bad copies "use elements from the emerging theatre of information and its attendant technologies" to build resistant models of alternative information flow and participation.[35] These performances of false information or unruly expertise can disrupt the truth value of corporate and semiprivatized channels of information and throw into question the ethical validity of standard practices of surveillance. Although Attia's posters were false in their claims, they nonetheless succeeded performatively. They thrust the specter of armed NYPD drones into the public thoroughfares of New York City in order to stimulate public debate over the ethics of such a prospect.

As CAE's deployment of the term *theatre* suggests, the slippery relationship between reality and fiction characteristic of theatrical representation can productively destabilize the truth claims of evidence, data, and information that prop up surveillance society. Throughout the book, I focus on the ways in which theatrical performance, as a representational apparatus in which audiences are accustomed to suspending their disbelief, can defamiliarize scenes of surveillance that have become so familiar and normalized as to escape critical recognition.[36] Through aesthetic tactics of defamiliarization—or the "alienation effect," as Bertolt Brecht described it—surveillance artists strive to create "critical spectators" of surveillance culture: user-consumer-participants who can more clearly see, evaluate, and respond to the forces of discipline and desire exerted on them by surveillance technologies in political, economic, and social arenas.

I therefore argue that the role of theatricality within surveillance art is valuable not only as a means of helping audiences see anew the real world sociopolitical conditions of surveillance but also for its capacity to rehearse alternative ways of viewing and being viewed by technologies of surveillance. Projects such as *Lowdrone* and the *Transborder Immigrant Tool* provide tools with which audiences can rehearse alternative methods of participating in surveillance society. For years the well-known Surveillance Camera Players (SCP) has created public performances on city streets that reimagine physical and psychological relationships between passersby and publicly installed surveillance cameras. Its performances not only make visible the often ignored techno-human interface between surveillance cameras and passersby in urban centers, but they also suggest alternative uses for these interfaces, using the security cameras as a potential means of two-way communication and empathetic relationships rather than only one-way discipline. As such, surveillance artists can theatrically represent aspects of contemporary surveillance society in such a way as to offer audiences valuable opportunities to begin to reconfigure the habitual blind spots, norms, and hierarchies that have come to be entrenched within everyday disciplinary interfaces.

Through the Looking Glass:
 Constructions of Gender under Surveillance

There is a particular blind spot in cultural studies of surveillance when it comes to gender and gendered identity as it is produced and reinforced through surveillance. Even while surveillance technologies are commonly figured as masculine instruments of patriarchal power and protection, often referred to as "the Man" or "Big Brother," the gendered and gendering gaze of surveillance has largely been overlooked in cultural analyses of surveillance. Thus far, when "difference" has been addressed within surveillance studies, there has been a tendency to pay attention to issues of racial profiling and economic discrimination in state and corporate surveillance rather than gender dynamics. While attention to race and class under surveillance remains vital, there has been a lack of consideration of surveillance as a "technology of gender" with important ramifications in the formation of gendered identity and representations of gender difference. Until quite recently, very few surveillance theorists had addressed gender imbalances within processes of looking and being looked at in surveillance society, and even fewer had theorized the relationship between conventions of gendered representation in visual culture and gendered habits of watching and being watched in surveillance society. More frequently surveillance theorists have fundamentally misread gender in the context of surveillance, claiming that surveillance has an equalizing effect with regard to gender difference because, as surveillance theorist David Lyon put it, surveillance "exposes men to an uncomfortable degree of scrutiny . . . all too familiar to women."[37] Such perspectives overlook historical imbalances between gendered experiences of looking and being looked at and rather blithely transpose the visual objectification of women to all subjects of surveillance.

However, feminist theory and practice has much to say to surveillance scholarship. Over the last half century many feminist practitioners and scholars have specialized in defining and critiquing imbalances of power maintained through conventions of looking and being looked at in film, theater, and other representational media—conventions that film theorist Laura Mulvey termed the "determining male gaze" of visual culture.[38] Where the disciplinary gaze of surveillance is replicated through the panoptic guard tower and its contemporary analogs—a process by which the subject of surveillance internalizes the visible but unverifiable specter of discipline—feminist theorists following Mulvey have long argued that patriarchal ideology is replicated and internalized through codified practices of looking and being looked at in mainstream visual media. These representational strategies have tended to figure the female body as "given to be looked at" and the male body as "given to look." This would suggest that, rather than leveling the playing field, the politics of visual surveillance doubly objectifies the female form. Criticism of cultural gender norms offered by more recent queer and feminist scholars likewise illuminate and problematize normalizing tendencies of contemporary surveillance practices, particularly biometrics, in which the individual body is rendered into even more easily normalized code.

Fortunately, there is evidence of growing attention to significant intersections between constructions and experiences of gender, sexuality, and surveillance. In her article "Video Surveillance, Gender, and the Safety of Public Urban Space: 'Peeping Tom' Goes High Tech?" (2002), Hille Koskela compared gendered violence and fear to voyeuristic uses of surveillance, exposing shared ground between cultural models of the desirous voyeur "Peeping Tom" and the protective disciplinarian "Big Brother" within urban surveillance systems.[39] In *Loving Big Brother*, McGrath examined the effects of the disciplinary gaze on expressions of homosexual desire in public space. Using contemporary surveillance as a vehicle to extend Freudian pathological diagnoses of homosexuality, McGrath astutely explored the capacity of "surveillance sex"—by which he means sex caught on or performed for surveillance cameras—to expose the gaze of surveillance as an agent not only of discipline but also of voyeuristic pleasure, homosexual narcissism, and "perverse" desire.[40] A 2009 special issue of *Surveillance & Society* focused on "Gender, Sexuality and Surveillance" took up the issue more broadly. In the editorial that opened the special issue, coeditors Kirstie Ball, Nicola Green, Hille Koskela, and David J. Phillips declared, "Surveillance studies needs Gender and Sexuality," explaining that "the political economies, methods, outcomes, and profound normalizing tendencies associated with surveillance are deeply amenable to critiques informed by theories of gender and sexuality."[41] They argued that, when read in light of historical constructions and treatments of the gendered body and sexual preference, maxims of contemporary surveillance such as "if you have nothing to hide, you have nothing to fear" reinforce a white, masculine, heteronormative bias. For women, racial minorities, and sexually marginalized groups (e.g., LGBTQ), the hidden is often equated with shame (in the case of women's bodies in particular) or criminalization (e.g., gay sex or transgendered bodies).[42] Shoshana Amielle Magnet's *When Biometrics Fail: Gender, Race, and the Technology of Identity* (2011) probed the problematic designs and outcomes of biometric surveillance; even as biometric technologies are increasingly employed by state and corporate entities to classify and control marginalized, vulnerable populations, these systems have been shown to have the highest rates of failure in classifying women, people of color, and people with disabilities.[43] And, most recently, Rachel Dubrofsky and Magnet published an edited volume, *Feminist Surveillance Studies* (2015), within which a diversity of authors demonstrated the need for surveillance studies to consider issues of discrimination, privilege, invisibility, hypervisibility, and mediatized representation through the lenses of feminist, gender, and queer studies. From what contributor Rachel Hall called "feminine heterosexual acquiescence to the new surveillance technologies," such as Transportation Security Administration (TSA) airport security scans, to Dubrofsky and Megan Wood's study of social perceptions of authenticity, agency, and self-representation within the Twitter profiles of female celebrities, that volume makes clear the value of a feminist approach to surveillance studies.[44]

This book adds to the growing conversation on gender and surveillance a detailed examination of how feminist theater and performance strategies are being mobilized to critique and reimagine surveillance society. I look not only at what feminist scholarship from media and film studies can add to surveillance discourse regarding histories of visual objectification and the vulnerabilities experienced by women and sexual minorities, but also at the strategies used by feminist performers and art makers to critique and create alternatives to these cultural practices. I argue that feminist performance theory and practice, particularly the materialist feminist movement articulated by theorists such as Dolan and Elin Diamond, provide valuable tactical precedents for the work of contemporary surveillance artists.[45] To this end, I look at the work of performance artists who interrogate surveillance as an apparatus that, like Hollywood cinema, encodes normalized ideologies of gender and sexual desire through a carefully produced and regulated relationship between image and spectator. Take, for example, the New York–based artist Jill Magid's piece *Monitoring Desire*. For this performance art piece the artist attached a wireless surveillance camera to a set of pointy stiletto heels and aimed the camera up her short skirt; as she walked, the camera captured images of her legs and glimpses of her underwear that were projected onto screens throughout the performance space.[46] Magid's reconstructed vision of surveillance overtly figured the surveillance camera as a "peeping Tom" actively involved in producing representations of Magid's body as a fetishized figure of male sexual fantasy. At the same time, the camera appended to her black stiletto heel with leather straps was framed as a classic visual fetish of sadomasochistic desire. Magid's framework, which I discuss in more detail in chapter 4, provocatively suggests that surveillance technologies are at once fetishizing and fetishized technologies and that the gaze of surveillance is far from gender neutral.

Works such as this, which make visible the often obscured sexual politics embedded in practices of surveillance, resonate with well-theorized feminist performance strategies. Following a history of what Rebecca Schneider has called feminist "explicit body performance," Magid and other feminist surveillance artists produce performances that "mak[e] explicit the haunting effects of naturalization" and knowledge production.[47] In doing so, they shed light on cultural blind spots that assume that surveillant gazes within institutions of medicine, education, and incarceration, among others, are gender neutral and outside the matrix of sexual desire. At the same time, using their own bodies as both canvas and subject, form and content, surveillance artists such as Magid enact a distinctly feminist form of investigating and representing the female body. Fueled by a desire to create an alternative, resistant economy of looking and being looked at, knowing and being known, they reimagine the agential possibilities for women within the gendered landscape of surveillance.

The cultural effects of such work are important for both surveillance and feminist studies. Feminist surveillance artists often seek to build coalitions of creative resistance and critique in an era sometimes (and problematically, to my mind) dubbed "postfeminist." As Dubrofsky and Magnet write in their introduction to *Feminist Surveillance Studies*, the urgency of coalition building across difference has only become greater in the digital age: "A feminist approach to surveillance studies argues for a reimagining of collective responses to the violence of state scrutiny . . . and asks how we might make our communities safer while continuing to refuse surveillance practices."[48] The artists I discuss in this book bring much needed attention to state, commercial, and social surveillance systems and the particular pressures these place on women and sexual, racial, and ethnic minorities.[49]

In order to counter the habitual exclusion of gender as a category of analysis in surveillance studies, I have maintained a feminist framework throughout the book. I argue that many surveillance artworks, while they do not all display explicit allegiances to feminism, are implicitly in conversation with feminist approaches to defining, critiquing, and building alternatives to a disciplinary gaze in visual culture. In looking at works that explicitly stage surveillance as a technology of gender and sexuality, as I do in chapter 4, I deliberately stage a return to "second-wave" feminist discourses in order to examine surveillance as a representational medium that, like mainstream film, television, photography, and theater, is part and parcel to norms and habits of visual culture. I draw also on third-wave and techno-feminist discourses to bring important questions about (dis)embodiment, liveness, and cyborgian subject positions to bear on surveillance society and art.[50] Throughout the book I address the question of what it means to define and deploy "third-wave" feminist strategies, which have been difficult to thematize, in part because of a notable resistance among this generation of feminists to claim a unifying agenda, and also because third wavers have tended to embrace seemingly conflicting representations of female sexuality and participatory social surveillance media.[51] Although I use the terms *second wave* and *third wave* as a convenient shorthand with which to group theorists and trends in feminist discourse, I strive overall to move beyond the rather restrictive "wave" model, with its implications that certain feminist discourses rise, crash, and then recede into the past. Inspired by Ednie Kaeh Garrison's reformulation of the historicization of feminist discourse, I instead think of surveillance art as engaging various "wavelengths" of feminist discourse and practice, which reach us, not as peaks and troughs that can be graphed on a timeline, but instead as radio waves, dispersing across time and space in an ongoing transmission.[52]

Performativity of Surveillance

A particularly significant feminist frequency that has guided my analysis of surveillance art more broadly is gender theorist Judith Butler's notion of "performativity," which I use to construct a theory of the "performativity of surveillance." Butler used the term to describe cultural processes of bodily discipline as well as "the possibility of a different sort of repeating, in the breaking or subversive repetition" of the performance of gender.[53] Insofar as one's gender is performative—that is, expressed through repeated, and potentially revised series of behaviors, gestures, clothing choices, and uses of language—so, too, is our relationship with contemporary surveillance technologies. We learn to express our gender identity through codified acts and representational apparatuses such as film, theater, and television, in what Teresa de Lauretis has called "technologies of gender."[54] In a similar way, the functional and symbolic aspects of surveillance society are the tools with which our relationships with disciplinary and desire-based systems of state and commercial surveillance are expressed, reinforced, and revised. If surveillance is a performative act, then dominant ideologies that govern mainstream models of discipline stand to be challenged and reconfigured by "subversive repetition[s] of that style," giving way to a broader range of perspectives, interactions, and desires.[55]

Butler's significant assertions about the performativity of gendered identity resonate with a rarely emphasized aspect of Jeremy Bentham's panoptic principle. In addition to the principles of visibility and unverifiability, which Foucault argued were the cornerstones of panoptic discipline, Bentham stated that "anyone" must be able to occupy the overseer position in the prison's central guard tower.[56] While, according to Foucault, this foundational principle was intended by Bentham to be a means by which the panoptic schema could be distributed across the social body, Butler's notion of performativity raises the possibility that the invitation to "anyone" to become a panoptic watcher introduces a radical and unruly element to the otherwise carefully controlled disciplinary institution. If anyone—implying a diversity of subject positions, intentionalities, and histories—can occupy the central guard tower, then there is potential for a different kind of looking, a different kind of repeating in the deployment of the disciplinary gaze of surveillance. Media theorists such as CAE and David Brin have similarly argued that the participation of amateurs using surveillance technologies and networks is important in combating imbalances of power that result from often invisible partnerships between state and corporate surveillance analysts.[57] This is not to say that the view of "anyone" is necessarily critical or resistant to dominant models of discipline, nor that historically marginalized or disenfranchised persons would easily be granted access to such a viewpoint. Amateur "anyones" may just as easily use everyday surveillance interfaces in ways that reinforce rather than challenge institutionalized systems of power-knowledge. By and large, amateur participation in popular software systems such as Facebook or Twitter ultimately contributes to corporate projects of data gathering and commercial marketing. At the same time, recent sizable social movements, such as Occupy Wall Street and its many regional counterparts in 2011–12 and the Arab Spring revolutions of 2010–11, illustrate the ability of motivated amateurs to effectively use mainstream social software systems toward politically subversive ends.

The genre of surveillance art can, to a large degree, be characterized by performative, politically disruptive appropriations of the position of the panoptic "anyone." Stepping into the metaphorical central guard tower, surveillance artists and activists take up, with a critical difference, the operations of the disciplinary gaze in surveillance, replacing that gaze with a mischievous, transformative second glance. As revisionary in(ter)ventions such as *Lowdrone* or *Monitoring Desire* evidence, technologies of surveillance can also be used toward politically disruptive and socially critical ends. I thus frequently describe the work of surveillance artists as "user *un*friendly," as their efforts should be distinguished not only from disciplinary uses of surveillance technologies but also from the mainstream models of participation that are guided by "user-friendly" interfaces that are largely complicit with state and corporate interests.[58]

Rescripting Surveillance: Surveillance Art as Resistant Spatial Practice

As a means of organizing and analyzing the critical and creative works that have been produced by surveillance artists thus far, I have found it useful to focus on spatial categories. Space works well as an organizing principle and conceptual framework through which to analyze artistic approaches to ongoing and emergent trends in surveillance for several reasons. Definitions of and divisions among public, private, semipublic and virtual spaces, however blurry, are foundational to debates over the regulation and operations of surveillance in contemporary life. Moreover, a spatial approach to surveillance can effectively address multiple layers of contemporary experiences of surveillance. It does not disavow the continued power of a panoptic model of discipline in which a centralized power watches over the masses within a given institutional, civic, or national space; though outdated in many ways, panopticism continues to function within many institutional spaces and continues to dominate much of the public imaginary of surveillance, even as the dictatorial image of "Big Brother" has splintered into diverse orders of "little brothers."[59] At the same time, a spatial reading of surveillance makes room for new models of dispersed, networked "synoptic" surveillance, participatory surveillance, and surveillance as lived experience.[60]

Thinking of surveillance art as a spatial practice invites valuable interlocutors in cultural theory: to write about surveillance, spatial practice, and resistant performances inevitably invokes the work of Michel de Certeau: "Seeing Manhattan from the 110th floor of the World Trade Center . . ." It is difficult to read the opening lines of de Certeau's well-known essay "Walking in the City" without noting the loss of this particular vantage point, and remembering the steep price that was paid for standing in such a place at a particular point in time.[61] His poetic descriptions of an "Icarian fall" back into the "dark space" of the pedestrian world of the streets below easily becomes tangled in mediatized memories of the horrific events of September 11, 2001. So, too, must the works of surveillance art in this book be related to this watershed event in our recent cultural history. As so many books on surveillance society have noted, the accelerating pace of both technological development and public acceptance of surveillance in the twenty-first century stem largely and unavoidably from that spectacular act of terror. Indeed, the changing shape of surveillance society can be measured, in many ways, through the absented architecture and theatrical acts of that day: the towering World Trade Center (WTC) served, among many other things, as a symbol of panopticism, "a gigantic rhetoric of excess in both expenditure and production" that was "only the most monumental figure of Western urban development."[62] The terrorist attacks reified the symbolic power of such a visible target while at the same time deploying a spatial rhetoric that effectively destroyed the notion that panoptic power was absolute or impenetrable.

Examining these symbolic-material aspects of the event in relation to theater and performance history, Richard Schechner boldly investigated 9/11 as a work of avant-garde art.[63] Noting that manifestos of destruction also characterized the avant-garde theater and art movements of the early twentieth century, he recalled strategies of representation that deliberately collapsed boundaries between high art and commodity culture, such as Marcel Duchamp's urinal or Andy Warhol's soup cans, as well as futurist manifestos that reimagined war as great artistic expression. Schechner argued that, similarly, "[T]he reporting-fictionalizing of 9/11, including the broadcasting and rebroadcasting of iconic images of the explosions, fires, destruction, aftermath, and war, constitutes . . . a presentation of events as objects d'art."[64] From the timing of the attacks, which gave the media time to record and comment on the second attack live during the morning news cycle, to the ensuing media assault on the fears of the American public, the events of 9/11 were as spectacular, performative, and symbolic as they were devastatingly material. These rituals of patriotism, national mourning, and vengeance, which rapidly took center stage in the days and months after September 11, 2001, "do not make the 9/11 attacks and the Iraq war art, but they come very close to the melodramatic form of the serial."[65] Although he admits to finding the position ethically reprehensible, Schechner confesses a sense of awe over a single act that changed world history, for "what (other) art act has done that?"[66]

Without becoming too entangled in the gravitational pull of this cultural tragedy, I explore the dark symmetry between the dramatic events of 9/11 and the rapid proliferation of surveillance technologies—from airport body scans to unmanned aerial vehicles—that have followed in military, state, commercial, and artistic arenas. I argue that avant-garde art and performance likewise provide political and aesthetic models for surveillance artists as they respond to the long aftermath of 9/11, as well as more recent watershed moments in surveillance history such as Edward Snowden's revelations of 2013.

Returning to de Certeau, I theorize surveillance art and performance as "resistant spatial practices." Juxtaposing the view from atop the WTC against the less visible spatial practice of walking the streets of the city far below, de Certeau theorized the everyday practice of walking as a resistant practice that eludes visual capture by hegemonic systems of surveillance. Although Foucault argued that there is no space outside systems of discipline, as institutionalized spaces work together to discipline individuals that move within and between them (school, factory, military, hospital, home, what Louis Althusser called ideological state apparatuses),[67] de Certeau insisted on the existence of spatial practices that operate *beneath* and among the disciplinary organization of space.[68] He asked, "But what *spatial practices* correspond, in the area where discipline is manipulated, to these apparatuses that produce a disciplinary space? In the collective mode of administration and an individual mode of reappropriation . . . spatial practices in fact secretly structure the determining conditions of social life."[69] He found resistant spatial practices in "these multiform, resistant, tricky and stubborn procedures that elude discipline without being outside the field in which it is exercised."[70]

De Certeau's theorization of resistant spatial practices effectively describes the work of many surveillance artists. They necessarily capitalize on the ubiquity and commercial availability of surveillance technologies, while at the same time rescripting their use value toward politically critical, disruptive, and imaginative ends. At the same time, just as Foucault's theory of panoptic surveillance has been challenged and updated by virtually every surveillance theorist of the last two decades, so, too, must be de Certeau's theorization of spatial practices.[71] In the long shadow of the "gone but not forgotten" WTC towers, debates continue to play out over the role of surveillance in contemporary society and its impact on individual agency, mobility, and the practice of daily life. The positions that de Certeau compares—the voyeur versus the walker—have become more entangled, less easy to separate. The practice of walking now involves user-friendly GPS tracking software embedded in cell phones and linked through satellites; social software applications through which one might arrange to meet a friend at a corner café also trace and record the meanderings of ordinary practitioners as they move about the city streets and alleyways. Beyond physical streets and pedestrian traffic, much of contemporary surveillance society locates itself in the virtual realm of the Internet, extending de Certeau's characterization of pedestrian practices to the invisible yet indelible operations of online commerce, communications, tracking, and hacking. This is to say that contemporary surveillance technologies supply both a totalizing map and a renegade spatial practice: they support systems of hegemonic discipline and control, while simultaneously supplying fissures through which alternative uses, perspectives, and desires can be practiced.

These paradigmatic shifts in the way we conceive of and experience space under and through surveillance require us to ask additional, different questions. For example, recent cultural theorists have added to the study of spatial practices important questions of mobility and access. Who gets to move within and between these spaces and toward what ends? What are the politics of mobility and access, and how do they play out across differences in race, class, and gender? How do technologies of surveillance facilitate, prohibit, and force mobility across and within borders of nations, institutions, city streets, and virtual interfaces? In my considerations of mobility in relation to surveillance culture and art, I have thus looked to what mobility studies scholars have termed a "new mobility paradigm" in which mobility is seen as an "uneven resource" that is made available in very different ways to different people according to their race, gender, nationality, physical dis/ability, and economic status.[72] I draw also on the emergent field of "neogeography" studies, which examines the ways in which neogeographic technologies such as Google Maps and geotagged photographs on Instagram can serve as tactical platforms that can empower marginalized users to share knowledge, organize socially and politically, and build expressive aesthetic performances.[73] Throughout the book I examine the ways in which artists approach surveillance technologies as tools that on one hand produce and maintain vast disparities across individual experiences of mobility, visibility, and agency and on the other provide the representational means with which to "rescript" habitual behaviors toward subversive, critical ends.

In pursuing this line of thinking, I have found it illuminating to think of surveillance technologies as what Robin Bernstein called "scriptive things." Scriptive things, like playscripts, do not denote singular or rigid interpretations but rather invite a range of interactions and usages: "[A] script is a dynamic substance that deeply influences but does not entirely determine live performances, which vary according to agential individuals' visions, impulses, resistances, revisions, and management of unexpected disruptions."[74] Considering surveillance technologies as scriptive things makes room for the wide range of uses to which they are put by a diversity of "agential individuals"—from engineers, lawmakers, and police officers to artists, activists, and hackers. As Bernstein wrote, "[T]o describe elements of material culture as 'scripting' actions is not to suggest that things possess agency or that people lack it, but instead to propose that agency emerges through constant engagement with the stuff of our lives."[75] As theater, performance, and digital media artists experiment with the political and aesthetic capabilities of surveillance technologies they create important and often radical reinterpretations of the form and function of surveillance in public space. For example, Austrian filmmaker Manu Luksch's "Manifesto for CCTV Filmmakers" (2006) boldly reinterpreted the legal script of Britain's Data Protection Act. Luksch reframed the document as a manual for filmmaking, suggesting that, since the footage captured by the comprehensive network of CCTV cameras in the United Kingdom legally belongs in part to the subjects of that surveillance, it is fair game for artistic re-presentation.[76] As I discuss in chapter 5, Luksch's film *Faceless* (2007), which was made in accordance with her manifesto, succeeds not only in appropriating CCTV cameras for aesthetic purposes but also in disrupting cultural expectations of criminality and terrorism that we have come to associate with surveillance footage. As urban geographer Amy Siciliano has argued, the film "gleans its CCTV footage from banal experiences and mundane spaces of the city, and in doing so, counters the tendency of this media to reify social relations. The film prompts us to ask why we now *expect* the sensational and in whose interests such expectations serve."[77]

I thus read surveillance technologies as historically conditioned, scriptive things that, by virtue of their cultural familiarity and expressive properties, prompt certain behaviors, interactions, and sentiments from people. I have found that surveillance "scripts" carry over from everyday life into "extradaily" or "performative" spaces with equal (or even greater) potency. Within a space of performance (be it in a proscenium theater or on a street corner), artists and audience members are prompted to pay increased attention to the symbolic value of objects; thus the representational power of surveillance technologies and their scriptedness often becomes even more apparent and malleable, open for critique and revision. As McGrath, drawing on his experiences as a theater director, observed, surveillance technologies onstage or in a gallery not only remind audiences of their appearance in everyday life but also serve to "re-enliven that space with a sense of agency and choice."[78] When encountering surveillance technologies within a frame of performance, the act of spectating, witnessing, or even of simply passing by becomes an agential choice that has the potential to rehearse new interpretations of surveillant scripts and the ways in which they shape the "stuff of our lives."

In approaching surveillance technologies as scriptive things, I follow Bernstein's eloquent directive: "[T]o read things as scripts is to coax the archive into divulging the repertoire."[79] Surveillance technologies are typically employed to not only record but also influence behavior and thereby produce a repertoire. As a medium of representation, surveillance has as one of its foundational tenets an obsession with archival remains; surveillance techniques and technologies aim to capture bits of visual, aural, or biometric "remains" that can serve as stable pieces of evidence in the future. Following performance theorists and practitioners who have challenged the historical privileging of archive over repertoire and material evidence over embodied memory in the production and analysis of history, I assert that surveillance art and performance trouble long-standing cultural assumptions that surveillance produces stable evidence. Surveillance artists make visible the archival drive of surveillance and work to enrich and redirect its repertoire.

What Lies Ahead

In order to map the performative in(ter)ventions being constructed by surveillance artists, I have organized the following chapters according to spatial categories—that is, according to the surveilled spaces in and across which surveillance artists stage their interventions: stages, streets, screens, sex, skin, and skies. These spaces (or, in the case of "sex" and "skin," conceptual spaces) represent spheres of everyday life and extra-daily performance in which surveillance technologies have become prominent as technologies of representation used by state and corporate entities as well as by artist-activists. There is, inevitably, overlap between spaces: screenal performances may take place on the street; gender-focused interventions, addressed in chapter 4 ("Sex"), share tactics and goals with body-focused artworks that I have grouped under the category "Skin" (chapter 5); and drone artworks fly over and through skies, stages, screens, and streets. Each chapter is comprised of a series of case studies organized according to common tactics and/or goals. I chose this strategy in order to simultaneously document many of the most notable surveillance artworks made in recent decades, while at the same time identifying trends within the genre as a whole. In this way, the book extends in two directions at once: I reach backward to provide a retrospective of the genre so far and, based on these examples, begin to establish a tactical taxonomy of the genre that can assist artists, critics, scholars, and other interested parties in moving surveillance art and performance forward in coming years. That said, I have ordered the chapters according to a loose temporal logic. Chapter 1 ("Stages") reaches the farthest back in history, as I mine several centuries of theatrical history in order to construct a theory of the theatricality of surveillance. Through several case studies in which surveillance technologies are "remediated" through theatrical performance, I argue that surveillance theater productions highlight significant resonances between representational strategies in surveillance and theater. By theatricalizing surveillance-based practices, artists can interrogate habits of representation and reception in both theater and surveillance and use each medium to illuminate and challenge assumptions about truth, pretense, reality, and evidence in the other.

Next, chapter 2 ("Streets") focuses on, among other performance artists who work in public space, the Surveillance Camera Players (SCP), whose performances in the streets and thoroughfares of New York City throughout the 1990s and early 2000s were among the earliest and most visible of the contemporary surveillance art movement. Works by Jill Magid, Hannah Price, and the Yes Men likewise utilized theatrical methods to draw attention to normalized blind spots in quotidian interfaces of surveillance and to explore possibilities for affective expression and interactivity available through publicly installed surveillance cameras. In chapter 3 ("Screens"), I examine links between early-twenty-first-century advances in digital technologies and shifts in participatory, user-driven surveillance across a range of screenal interfaces. I have termed these spaces of performance "the screen," not only because the artists in this chapter tend to stage their critiques of surveillance through screenal interfaces—Internet browser windows, cell phones, video games, CCTV monitors, personal blogs, and so on—but also for the metaphorical import of the term. Principles of surveillance, from panoptic discipline to dispersed, participatory societies of control, are expressed through the dual nature of "screening," which can mean either to display or to hide. Screenal surveillance artists such as Steve Mann, the Institute for Applied Autonomy, Ricardo Dominguez, Blast Theory, Hasan Elahi, and Wafaa Bilal critique hypervisible and invisible aspects of contemporary surveillance, particularly as they effect the mobility, access, and personal, political, or economic freedoms afforded to different individuals through preprogrammed software interfaces.

Linearity then gives way to topical focuses in chapters 4 ("Sex") and 5 ("Skin"), both of which function more metonymically than spatially. In chapter 4, I analyze surveillance as an apparatus that, like Hollywood cinema, encodes normalized ideologies of gender, sexuality, discipline, and desire through a carefully produced and regulated relationship between image and spectator. Jill Magid, Mona Hatoum, Giles Walker, and Janet Cardiff, among others, elucidate the notion of a sexual gaze of surveillance and make visible its impacts on practices of viewing and being viewed. Chapter 5 looks at the ways in which individuals are represented, controlled, and in some cases reembodied through biometric surveillance systems that collect and analyze their corporeal and informational data. Zach Blas, Adam Harvey, Manu Luksch, Leo Selvaggio, and Wafaa Bilal, among others, have utilized "skin" as a stage on which to explore issues of identity, privacy, prediction, and profiling in surveillance society and to explore and expose incongruences between the digital self and lived self.

In chapter 6 ("Skies"), I focus on the recent and controversial popularity of UAVs, or drones, as remote-controlled tools of contemporary warfare, commercial enterprise, and civilian leisure pursuits. The range of drone artworks that have thus far emerged is broad, as artists experimenting with drone technologies have taken various positions in relation to the opportunities and drawbacks of these remote flying devices—from political outrage to creative defense and aesthetic experimentation to new models of empathy and interconnectivity. As public opinion, ethical debates, and legal regulations for drone use are still in their infancy, drone art pieces provide valuable fodder for the burgeoning public discourse over drones and contemporary surveillance more broadly.

A final note on space. Surveillance society now has an undeniably global reach. The majority of the surveillance artworks in this book have been staged by artists working in the western military superpowers of the United States and United Kingdom. These countries have continued to stand, for better or worse, on the vanguard of developing and adopting surveillance technologies in both the military and civilian arenas. At the same time, they have remained comparatively open to political and artistic expression, protest, and dissent, in contrast to other countries that utilize similarly high levels of surveillance; as a result, the greatest volume of surveillance artworks have come thus far from artists working in these countries. That said, I have made an effort to examine the work of surveillance artists who operate beyond these borders: projects by Ricardo Dominguez and Coco Fusco bring us to the US-Mexico border; James Bridle, Josh Begley, and Wafaa Bilal draw attention to the brutal reality of drone strikes in Iraq, Syria, and Afghanistan; and the Polish theater group Theater of the Eighth Day recalls the repression of Soviet era surveillance from behind the "Iron Curtain."

It is my hope that artists from around the world will continue to be inspired and permitted to use surveillance technologies to build resistant spatial practices. As surveillance technologies become smaller, smarter, and more mobile, at once more dispersed and interconnected, and, perhaps most worryingly of all, more routine and familiar, the need to critique and reimagine solutions to local injustices and global imbalances of power is only growing. I am hopeful that this book will function as inspiration and invitation to "anyone"—students, instructors, amateur artists, and burgeoning activists—to participate in surveillance society on their own critical, ethical, and creative terms.

CHAPTER 1

Stages

———— ⚘ ————

Four members of the Polish theater group Theater of the Eighth Day
took their places on a simple wooden stage, perching on stools in front
of microphones and music stands. A triptych of projection screens stood
upstage behind them, showing images of the now aged actors from the
1960s and 1970s. In the photos they were young university students, long
haired and first discovering their passion for performance and political
activism. With hair now white or peppered gray, the actors read aloud
from their own letters and diary entries from the early days of their work
together, recalling the inspiration they found in Jerzy Grotowski's performance methods and the student-led protests of 1968. They recalled
their excitement at forming a "band-full of people who still think the
world can be set right through theater."[1] They intermittently reenacted
excerpts from early productions and played footage from several of their
original performances, highly physical, improvisatory theater works that
had responded directly to the social and political movements unfolding
around them.

The company members' trek down memory lane was driven by far
more than nostalgia, however. Beyond their personal written records,
the majority of the texts and photographs used in the performance were
taken from surveillance files that the Polish secret police had compiled
on these theater makers during the decades-long reign of the Polish
United Workers Party (PUWP). Under the Soviet-influenced communist
regime in Poland, which held power from 1948 to 1989, the group had

Fig. 2. Tadeusz Janiszewski and Marcin Kęszycki in *The Files*, Theater of the Eighth Day, 2009. (Photograph by Theater of the Eighth Day.)

been placed under routine surveillance, as secret police of the communist Politburo followed their daily movements, attended their performances, and even worked as embedded informants within the group. At especially intense moments, members were denied the right to perform, travel, or even exist as a theater group. Despite the oppressive and sometimes violent disciplinary conditions they faced, the members of Theater of the Eighth Day had continued to perform behind the Iron Curtain, becoming leaders of the underground theater movement in Poland and internationally.

In keeping with their reputation as politically engaged theater makers, these artists began work on *The Files* in 2007 after a truth and reconciliation committee in Poland permitted individuals to request access to surveillance documents compiled on them by the secret police. Again using their political landscape as source material, they created "a sardonic docudrama on their art as seen through the eyes of a totalitarian regime."[2] Without disavowing the serious effects that the surveillance had on their lives and art making, they found a good deal of humor in the surveillance records. With a mixture of disbelief and scorn in their delivery, they invited their audience to laugh with them over the absurdity of the code names that each member was given in the secret police files. As one company member mockingly observed, the reports were records of the absurdity of the political climate of the time, "written in stilted bureaucratic language and laced with communist mumbo-jumbo."[3] Clearly amused to hear how the "Secret Associates" (SA) had rebranded their performances and postshow discussions as counterstate strategies, the actors took some pride in the admission of one SA report that efforts to infiltrate the group with informants posing as members were failing due to the fact that "the commune is not only hard to infiltrate, but has the effect of conversion to a revolutionary viewpoint."[4] At other points, the performers abandoned words altogether, representing the exhausting acrobatics of life in a surveillance state through tragicomic slapstick routines.

Despite the delight they took in their theatrics, the actors imparted the darkness of those days. Their derision of the secret police's perspective on their art making was haunted by the high cost of the surveillance and political and artistic oppression they endured. Although the SA's reports on their performances could be read as clumsy, ill-informed theatrical reviews, the passages imparted the frightening amount of power that the communist regime held over artistic and political expression at that time in Poland. The government's assessments of the theater group's aesthetic choices, however ridiculous, had served as very real means of criminalizing the group's activities, leading to an official prohibition on its right to "exist" at all.[5] Behind their droll accounts of accusations by the secret police that the group members were arrogant, prone to alcoholic binges, and used extremely vulgar language lurked the very real consequences of these assessments.

The performance that emerged was a hybrid history, as the members' own memories and manifestos were interlaced with the viewpoint of a totalitarian regime bent on controlling and even eradicating the group's political and artistic work. One of the founding members and co-creator-performer in *The Files*, Ewa Wojciak, wrote about the complexities of revisiting their past through the gaze of the secret police. On one hand, it was an opportunity to take stock of and celebrate their formation as theater artists in the face of political adversity. On the other, the process of looking back was chilling: "We look at it all from a distance now. It seems that we have found a way out of the totalitarian maze, but its memories still terrify us, even if they amuse us sometimes, and at other times sound like a warning."[6]

As Wojciak put it, this piece of surveillance theater did more than excavate the personal histories of its members; it sounded a broader warning about the potentially dangerous interplay between political surveillance and artistic expression. Even though historical circumstances and personal details made *The Files* unique, clashes between personal freedoms, artistic expression, and state surveillance are by no means a thing of the past. As evidenced by Edward Snowden's exposure of the National Security Agency (NSA) mass surveillance projects, routine surveillance by governments on their own citizens has become both easier to perform and easier to hide in the digital age, and it is being practiced in even the most democratic countries around the world.

As illustrated by *The Files*, theatrical performance provides a particularly potent lens through which to consider the interplay of truth and fiction, reality and representation, and competing subjective accounts of the past within the politics of surveillance. In recent years, a growing number of theater artists have responded to rapidly increasing surveillance techniques and technologies by integrating them into their work as subjects of inquiry and tools of theatrical representation. This chapter focuses on the practice of staging technologies of surveillance in theatrical productions. Like *The Files*, many surveillance theater pieces use theatrical methods of representation to make visible the mechanisms and impacts of state and corporate surveillance on everyday life and art making. Moreover, staging techniques and technologies within theatrical frames can reveal a rich and historical interplay between theatrical performance and surveillance. Surveillance theater works can thus interrogate aesthetic, as well as disciplinary, capabilities of surveillance technologies and bring to light disciplinary habits of seeing and being seen within theatrical performance.

Staging surveillance technologies within theatrical space—a process known as "remediation," discussed in depth in the following section—raises important questions about historical and contemporary relationships between theater and surveillance. How do paradigms of theater and surveillance resemble each other, and where do they diverge? Is all theater a form of surveillance? What can we learn about the ways in which theatrical models of representation and reception depend on disciplinary ideologies? And, perhaps more significant, how and to what end is surveillance theatrical? What fictions within cultural conceptions of surveillance can be brought to light when viewed through a theatrical frame? In my analysis of surveillance theater, I examine remediation, the representation of one medium within another, as a representational tactic that makes visible similarities and divergences between practices of representation in surveillance and theater. Tracing the methods and effects of remediation within several surveillance theater productions, I argue that this genre of performance can be a significant mode of artistic and political intervention (1) because surveillance theater can productively unsettle habits of voyeuristic spectatorship induced by theatrical histories of realism; and (2) because surveillance theater can trouble the common claim that surveillance technologies provide objective evidence by framing surveillance *evidence* within theatrical *fictions*. That is, by bringing surveillance technologies into traditional theater spaces, surveillance theater artists not only ask their audiences to reflect on disciplinary processes of watching in surveillance society, but they also bring questions of watching and being watched to bear on habitual methods of representation and reception in theater.

Remediation in Surveillance Theater: Evidence and Fiction

Remediation, a term coined by cultural theorists Jay David Bolter and Richard Grusin to describe "the representation of one medium in another,"[7] is a useful concept with which to elucidate the various means by which artists have repurposed surveillance techniques and technologies for theatrical productions. Understanding remediation as a tactic that is at once aesthetic and political helps clarify the mutual pressures that surveillance and theater exert on each other in surveillance theater productions. Through this term, I evaluate what audiences can learn about surveillance when viewing it through a theatrical frame as opposed to the space of the everyday; conversely, I also investigate how surveillant media can be used to defamiliarize habits of theatrical spectatorship and suggest new modes of interactivity and political action within spaces of performance.

Bolter and Grusin argued that representational practices have always emerged through processes of remediation: photography remediated perspectival painting; film remediated stage production and photography; and television remediated film, vaudeville, and radio.[8] As they put it, "what is new about new media comes from the particular ways in which they refashion older media and the ways in which older media refashion themselves to answer the challenges of new media."[9] However, remediation is not simply a developmental process in which new media replace old. Theater in particular has long served as a means of remediating emergent media. Performance and media theorists such as Steve Dixon and Greg Giesekam have persuasively argued that theater, throughout its rich and varied history, has functioned as an open and malleable platform on which artists and audiences can experiment with and reflect on new technologies of representation, communication, and information exchange.[10]

A brief look at an earlier moment in history illustrates how theater has served as a site of remediation through which audiences and practitioners could learn about emergent visual technologies of capture and evidence. In "Performing Remediation: Minstrelsy, Photography, and the Octoroon," Adam Sonstegard used Dion Boucicault's *The Octoroon* (1859) to look at the process by which "one medium, a stage performance . . . participated in constructing another medium, photography."[11] Late in the complicated plot of the melodrama, a portrait camera of the type that would have been fairly recently introduced into the lives of mid-nineteenth-century audiences, supplied evidence that a murder had been perpetrated by the play's villain. The photographic plate was introduced at a key moment in the play's fourth act, providing stable evidence of guilt, innocence, good, and evil in a world that was otherwise deeply troubled by shifting power dynamics and hotly debated legal approaches to and definitions of race, class, and gender.[12] The incriminating photograph had been taken accidentally by a Native American character, a "savage" who, the play implies, would not have been versed in any prior cultural knowledge of camera operations or photographic representation. This narrative positioned photography—and, in particular, candid photography—as part of a natural, intuitive order that could supply objective truth and concrete evidence. In the deeply racialized world of the play the Native American's word would almost certainly not have stood up as reliable evidence of guilt or innocence; however, the camera trumped that racial bias with its seemingly neutral eye, providing irrefutable proof of guilt and innocence.

Sonstegard contextualized the overlapping media of stage performance and photography in the historical moment of the production's debut, arguing that the remediation of photography in the highly popular melodrama was a means by which Boucicault instructed his nineteenth-century audiences in the surveillant and evidentiary capabilities of photography: "The play represents an important historical moment, at which Americans first moved toward naturalizing photography's role in surveillance. . . . Boucicault and the theatrical players had to coach audiences in 1859 to accept photography's role in resolving the conflict of this play."[13] The lucky accident of the Native American's encounter with the camera not only showed audiences the ease with which it could be operated (even a "savage" could do it), but it importantly framed the evidentiary power of candid photography. Elucidating a historical trajectory similar to Sonstegard's, John Tagg has argued that the medium of photography, and in particular candid photography, was central to the construction of surveillance as productive of stable and irrefutable evidence. Whereas portraiture involved carefully held poses, in which the subject of the photograph could attempt to hide certain aspects of his or her nature, surreptitious photography would yield truths that could not be hidden.[14] The onstage camera in *The Octoroon* thus functioned as more than a convenient deus ex machina in the play's plot. It served more broadly as an instructive device that taught early audiences of the play about the power of candid photography—and the truth-telling eye of the camera—in policing criminality and other socially improper behaviors.

Just as *The Octoroon* functioned as a cultural instruction manual, "coaching" mid-nineteenth-century audiences in the evidentiary function of photography, so, too, do contemporary surveillance theater productions ask audiences to reflect on emergent surveillance techniques and technologies. In Simon McBurney's *Measure for Measure* (2004) and the Builders Association's *Super Vision* (2006), surveillance technologies functioned as part of the theatrical mise-en-scène for the purposes of making visible sociopolitical conditions of contemporary surveillance. McBurney employed live feed and recorded video on the stage of the Royal National Theatre to infuse the Shakespearean drama with the contemporary politics of hypersurveilled London.[15] The Builders Association overlaid interactive systems of digital commerce, communication, and travel to focus on the "data trails" of three characters caught in the changing conditions of a "post-private" society.[16] In the Wax Factory's *Quartet v. 4.0* (2010), Juggernaut Theatre's *Oh What War* (2008), Mia Rovegno's *Tartuffe* (2010), theatre two point oh #'s *Surveillance* (2008), Big Picture Group's *True + False* (2007), TEAM's *Architecting* (2009), David Commander's *Oakwood Apartments* (2012), and M. Lamar's *Surveillance Project and the Black Psyche* (2014), among others, CCTV cameras were present onstage as part of the theatrical set and properties, emerging at key moments to develop the narrative and/or mediate the audience's viewpoint concerning the onstage characters.

By and large, surveillance theater productions such as these urge their audiences to reflect on, analyze, and critique the cultural impacts of surveillance in contemporary life. In her analysis of Commander's

Oakwood Apartments, in which he used several small, live-feed cameras positioned above a miniature set to narrate the experiences of residents living in a doomed apartment complex, Sarah Bay-Cheng observed that

> the scale of Commander's tiny apartments and our position peering down into the residents' intimate lives remind us that surveillance technology holds particular dangers for vulnerable communities. . . . As the embodiment of disposable people, these discarded objects stand in for populations vulnerable both to a superior peering gaze and to an insidious surveillance from within their own walls. While this interior view might seem to provide them with a way to communicate to the outside world, Commander's performance suggests that it may be only one more form of exploitation.[17]

The form of remediation in such performances can be thought of as "instructive" in that it provides a "remedial" education that reminds audiences to look again and more closely at the real world referents of the onstage surveillance technologies. As users, consumers, and subjects of the surveillance technologies that weave through our daily lives, many of us have become so habituated to living with surveillance that, like students who have forgotten long division, we may need to be reminded of the ideological underpinnings of surveillance society. Functioning as creative teachers in a remedial class, surveillance artists can thus use theatrical narratives and performative scenarios to make visible political ideologies and conditions that have led to increased invasions of privacy and uneven levels of scrutiny that exacerbate social divisions based on race, gender, sexuality, nationality, and economic class.

Other surveillance theater pieces go further in their efforts to explore the formal impacts that surveillance and theater as representational media can have on one another. Rather than telling stories *about* the oppressive effects of surveillance, theater artists can also tell stories *with* surveillance technologies, thereby exposing and interrupting habits of representation and reception that perpetuate disciplinary aspects of both surveillance and theater. In this second mode of remediation, which I call *formalist remediation* in reference to strategies of defamiliarization practiced by Marxist materialist/Russian formalist artists and theorists such as Viktor Shlovsky and Bertolt Brecht,[18] surveillance and theater become formal counterpoints that can highlight and unsettle cultural assumptions about truth, evidence, power, and discipline in the other. As in any established art form, codified modes of representation and reception have become less visible within both theater and surveillance, concealing ideological biases that construct (and are constructed by) them. Norms such as who gets to watch whom, which bodies are put on display, and how and by whom behaviors are represented and assessed construct the power dynamics and ideologies of both surveillance and theater. Through the practice of formalist remediation, conventions of watching and being watched can be effectively overlaid in such a way as to defamiliarize and make newly visible such habits—and their attendant ideologies—in each paradigm. By placing everyday processes of surveillance within the frame of more recognizable media of representation (such as film, theater, or video games), the representational codes of surveillance can be defamiliarized and made to appear new and strange so that disciplinary ideologies beneath them can become open to critique and revision. Conversely, when used as a tool of narrative representation, surveillance technologies can unsettle long-running habits of passive spectatorship induced by theatrical histories of realism.

Although it functioned primarily as an instructive, cautionary tale about the hardships of theatrical expression in the face of totalitarian surveillance, *The Files* involved elements of formalist remediation. In the performance, the reports of the secret police were reframed as theatrical reviews, ephemera from long-past performances. By reading the political documents as theatrical reviews, which are known to be matters of opinion, the ideological biases of the "reviewers" (aka secret service agents) became more apparent. At the same time, when viewed as surveillance data, the performances of Theater of the Eighth Day in the 1970s and 1980s were made visible as acts of political dissidence and powerful threats to the communist regime. The production thus set the capabilities of both surveillance and theatre to chronicle history in productive tension. The surveillance data recorded by the secret police were set against the group members' own memories and reenactments of their earlier performances. *The Files* destabilized the validity of state surveillance as a means of securing evidence or accurately representing the past, instead presenting theatrical reenactment as a modality more effective in bringing the past to life. In contrast, the archival remains of totalitarian surveillance seemed to be a dry, faulty, and biased means of reconstructing the past.

Deep explorations of the formal pressures that the representational mediums surveillance and theater can exert on each other have been rare thus far. Two other surveillance theater pieces, *Contains Violence* (2008) and *Point Blank* (2009), likewise utilized formalist remediation as a tactic to unsettle habits of spectatorship, storytelling, and evaluating evidence. Before turning to close analyses of these productions, however, it will be useful to think further about the histories and cultural habits that have shaped our conceptions of theater and surveillance.

Policing the Intersection: Is Theater Surveillance?
Is Surveillance Theatrical?

There are notable similarities between the histories of surveillance and theater. Each medium has been shaped around practices of watching and being watched, carefully calibrated visibilities and invisibilities, and the power dynamics that attend each of these arrangements. *Surveillance*, which literally means "watching from above," is constructed according to the architecture of who is watching whom. Historically, this has implied a unidirectional, disciplinary gaze in surveillance, a gaze that has been most famously theorized by cultural theorist Michel Foucault in his analysis of Jeremy Bentham's 1791 prison design known as the Panopticon. Resonances between theatricality and surveillance were evident from the inception of panopticism. Indeed, panopticism itself emerged through a remediation of surveillance and theater. Bentham imagined the bodies of the prisoners strategically displayed and presented as "given to be seen," not unlike actors onstage, while the guards were concealed within the tower (like the darkened auditorium), "given to see" but not necessarily to be seen. Foucault, writing about Bentham's description of the backlit cells that circled around a central guard tower, likened the architecture of the Panopticon to "so many small theatres."[19]

The panoptic principle, which has been heralded as the dominant model for modern surveillance systems, has expanded and changed over the course of the twentieth and early twenty-first centuries. At its root, however, contemporary surveillance still depends on the hierarchy of certain bodies watching other bodies—whether it is the few watching the many, as in the panoptic model, or the many watching the many, as in David Lyon's concept of the synopticon.[20] Whether practiced in a prison, on city streets, or through the Internet, surveillance functions as a means of policing permissible behavior through a strategic balance of visibility and invisibility. In many of his writings, Foucault described the interplay of visibity and invisibility as central to operations of power in a range of institutions of sociopolitical discipline.[21] As Tagg has summarized Foucault's arguments about the tendency of power to obscure its own operations while displaying its seemingly comprehensive presence, "Power in the West is that which displays itself most and hides itself best."[22] As a result, social subjects may not recognize the ideologies and structures of discipline that condition them to into "proper" social behaviors.[23]

In theater, which has functioned in many cultures and time periods as an ideological state apparatus (ISA), power is likewise expressed through practices of watching and being watched. John McGrath has gone so far as to describe theater directing as a form of surveillance, suggesting that the two practices have come to share a great deal of cultural common ground. In *Loving Big Brother*, McGrath astutely links director-dominated avant-garde theater groups in the twentieth century to a growing cultural acceptance of sociopolitical surveillance. Citing artists such as Bertolt Brecht, Robert Wilson, Jerzy Grotowski, Tadeusz Kantor, Anne Bogart, Liz LeCompte, and founding members of Mabou Mines, McGrath argues that "the dominant cultural fantasies of surveillance—the protecting eye or controlling Big Brother—equate in many ways with the fetishized figure of the twentieth-century theatre director, controlling events from which he or she is absent through the creation of a structure that necessitates and depends upon continued obedience."[24] In theater practices that cross centuries and cultures, the "best" seat in the house has been reserved for either gods or members of the royal family. These practices of hierarchized viewing came to be embedded and normalized within theater architecture and naturalized in theater-going behavior, as persons of political, economic, and religious power were graced with the most advantageous view of the stage and actors.[25] While this kind of royal treatment is by no means transhistorical, similar traditions continue today as regional theaters, Broadway houses, and West End theaters feature great disparities in ticket prices based on the best view of and proximity to the stage.

Not unlike a political regime interpreting surveillance data on its citizens, theatrical representations of "the real" have long been influenced by the social, economic, and political stature of the watcher. Marilyn Frye, in *The Politics of Reality*, links the etymology of the word *reality* to the political power of granting legitimation within fields as diverse as law, property, citizenship, and the theatrical arts: "Real in Spanish means royal. Real property is that which is proper to the king. Reality is that which pertains to the one in power, is that over which he has power, is his domain, his estate, is proper to him. . . . *To be real is to be visible to the king*."[26] Indeed, throughout history theater artists have often had to gain the right to perform by the permission of a royal governing body;

subject matter or identities that might threaten the material or ideological control of a governing body would not be permitted to perform.[27] The interplay of visibility and invisibility in theater thus has a disciplinary purpose. Theatrical representation has been used to express historically contingent moralities and models of that which *should* or *should not* be seen or recognized, both onstage and in the everyday world. This is to say that as much as theater has been a space for experimenting with transgressive or utopian desires, it has also been a site of ideological discipline wherein legal, social, and bodily behaviors have been policed, punished, or rendered invisible.

In sum, surveillance and theater are both disciplinary institutions determined by sociopolitical ideologies and reflective of economic hierarchies. For both theater and surveillance, political power is expressed not only according to the hierarchical relationship of *who is watching whom* but also through a carefully balanced matrix of *visibility* and *invisibility*. The Panoptic guard tower, placed prominently in the center of the complex, could be viewed from anywhere within the prison, thus displaying the site/sight of power without ever showing the actual embodied presence of the surveillance guard. In contrast to the distinctly visible bodies of the surveilled inmates, the actual gaze of surveillance was designed to be hidden and *unverifiable* at any one point in time.[28] The subject of panoptic surveillance, realizing any infraction might be punished if observed by the visible but unverifiable surveilling gaze, would begin to discipline him- or herself, thus internalizing the aims and ideology of the presumed authoritarian gaze.

Although the panoptic principle and Foucault's theorization of a disciplinary society have received necessary and valuable revisions by Delueze, Lyon, and other contemporary cultural scholars,[29] the *unverifiability* of panopticism remains central to the function of contemporary CCTV surveillance systems in urban streets and shops. Surveillance cameras (or notifications about them) tend to be conspicuously displayed, yet it is rarely evident whether or not surveillance is being practiced in real time, if at all. On the Internet, users may be aware that their browsing histories and metadata are being recorded, but they do not know if and when that information will be perused by law enforcement agencies. The power of surveillance depends, in both historic and contemporary surveillance systems, on the strategic display of *symbols* of being watched, so that subjects of surveillance—be they inmates in a panoptic prison or contemporary shoppers in a store with CCTV cameras—are always aware of the disciplinary systems in place around them, even while they are never sure if they are being watched in real time.

In theatrical practices, the stakes of *(in)visibility* and *(un)verifiability* are somewhat different than in surveillance, but they are just as powerful and ingrained. Traditions of representation and reception in realist theater such as the "fourth wall," stage lighting, and darkened auditoriums date back to the influential writings of encyclopedist Denis Diderot in the eighteenth century.[30] These conventions of seeing and (not) being seen in dramatic realism came into common practice at the end of the nineteenth and beginning of the twentieth century under directors and writers such as Constantin Stanislavski, Anton Chekhov, and Henrik Ibsen, and such practices continue to be familiar to audiences of mainstream theater today. Deeply ingrained behavioral habits entail quiet attention from a largely invisible and passive audience, a shared understanding of the imaginary fourth wall that sets the audience outside of the narrative frame, and the "suspension of disbelief" that marks the borders between everyday reality and fictional theatrical space. As cell phones and other digital accessories have come to be among the expected personal effects of theatergoers in recent decades, our attempts as practitioners and audience members to silence these technologies in order to avoid the potential disruptions they could stage indicate that contemporary theater audiences, at least within more traditional theater productions, continue to cooperate according to habits of seeming invisibility.

The concept of *unverifiability* is also present, though in a more complicated fashion, within practices of theatrical spectatorship. Elements of realist theater that are made visible, such as actors' bodies, props, and set pieces, stand not only as themselves but also as symbols of events, gestures, and conditions of the "real world" outside the theater. The real world referents are themselves indexes of cultural histories and ideologies, made legible through the theatrical frame. The theatergoer participates in a layered leap that combines perception and imagination, as he or she invests in objects, bodies, and events that are simultaneously real and representational, material and abstract, actual and fictitious. The relationship between reality and representation in theatrical performance is thus unverifiable in a similar way to the construction of the gaze of power in the panoptic principle.

There are also significant differences between the cultural histories of surveillance and theater that reveal how the two practices have been constructed in direct opposition to each other. Whereas prison inmates or "ordinary practitioners" of surveillance are given to *not see* certain aspects of surveillance in public space, theater audience members have been disciplined to *see double.* In the theater, spectators watch actors and stage objects that perform both *as* and *in excess of* themselves. As performance theorist Peggy Phelan put it:

> In moving from the grammar of words to the grammar of the body, one moves from the realm of metaphor to the realm of metonymy. . . . Metaphor works to secure a vertical hierarchy of value and is reproductive; it works by erasing dissimilarity and negating difference; it turns two into one. Metonymy is additive and associative; it works to secure a horizontal axis of contiguity and displacement. . . . In performance, the body is metonymic of self, of character, of voice, of "presence."[31]

Within the metonymic processes of theatrical representation and reception, the stage object or body of the performer is doubled by the referent that it ghosts and can simultaneously never fully become. For all their concrete materiality, hypervisible markers of theater—actors, sets, props—remain, to some degree, slippery and multiple, as their status as representational objects oscillates among sign, referent, and material reality onstage. Theatrical representation thus depends on an awareness of the unseen—the unseen hands of laborers and designers, as well as the unseen spaces, actions, histories, and ideologies that shape and haunt the visible aspects of a performance.[32] But, unlike surveillance, which seeks to securely link bodies and objects to their social signs, theater and live performance requires bodies and objects to remain unstable, able to shift between and beyond the materiality they appear to be and the sign to which they refer. In contrast to cultural understandings of surveillance as stable and evidentiary, theatrical representations come into being in the present, again and again, never as entirely fixed meanings or contained, singular narratives but rather as performances that admit to "the impossibility of securing the Real."[33] This "impossible" relationship with "the real" has fueled historical debates and disputes over the reliability of facts or evidence presented within a theatrical context, driving antitheatrical polemics as well as staunch defenses of live performance.[34]

In contrast, "securing the real" is, ostensibly, the central purpose of dominant surveillance systems. Surveillance systems are understood to produce secure and reliable versions of events or situations, and to provide stable evidence and seal the past into a cauterized story from a particular point of view. The idea that truth and evidence are stable products of technological methods of capture has been produced and supported through a binary that contrasts objective reality with self-conscious and subjective representation. Candid or surreptitious photographs or video—images captured when a subject is unaware of being watched—have been historically constructed as indexes of *stable evidence* and the *real*, whereas posed portraits or performances have been understood as *theatrical* or *false* in their self-consciousness. Personal cameras, which became all the rage in the decades following the debut of *The Octoroon*, discussed above, were marketed as a technology that, due to its "immediate" method of capture, preserved and represented essential and irrefutable truths.[35] As cameras became smaller and more affordable, their capacity to capture candid moments rapidly became part of their cultural appeal. Capturing a candid moment with a camera came to stand as a modernist conception of reality.[36]

In the cultural imaginary of the late nineteenth and early twentieth centuries, consciously constructed poses, a foundational aspect of theatricality, served as a counterpoint against which to establish the stability and truth value of surreptitious photography. Awareness of the gaze of a camera was thought to interpellate the subject of the photograph into artificial, consciously constructed social poses, not unlike an actor on the stage. Posing seemed to indicate a subject's awareness of his or her audience and the frame of representation through which he or she was being seen, thereby providing the opportunity to strategically show or hide certain aspects of his or her character. In contrast, surreptitious or candid photography captured an unguarded moment and therefore supposedly avoided the self-consciousness and inauthenticity of the pose. The subject of the photograph, not knowing he or she was being watched let alone being captured by a photographic lens, would not have time or reason to contrive a pose, and would thereby be revealed in a truer state of being. Surreptitious photography—and its offshoots, spy photography and surveillance—thus came to be positively aligned with stable, irrefutable evidence through an explicit disavowal of the theatricality of consciously constructed posed photographs. Contemporary surveillance has continued along this trajectory, as the collection of biometric information and metadata, discussed in chapter 5, has further promoted the truth value of surveillance techniques that bypass an individual's subjective self-representation.

However, as many performance theorists have argued, to align photographic documentation with truth and theatrical performance with falsity produces a faulty and dangerous binary. Notable theorists of visual culture and performance, such as Joseph Roach, Diana Taylor, Kaja Silverman, and Rebecca Schneider, among many others, have insisted that tropes of theatrical representation—such as the self-conscious pose—should not be dismissed as either purely ephemeral or essentially false. Instead, they argue that the pose, gesture, and stories offered by a performer can function as a register of embodied history in which experience, memory, and tradition are passed along and *re-membered* through a process of body to body transmission and embodied memory. Rather than aligning historical accuracy with the production of stable, archived documents, these theorists read performances as rich and valid modes of recording and telling history. This perspective is particularly important as a means of validating a multiplicity of perspectives that might not have recourse to or the support of archival records and technologies of capture. Thus, as in *The Files*, theatrical, embodied histories can stand, slip, and move in excess of a singular, dominating history or narrative.

Reading performances as evidence is not necessarily a simple or comfortable task. Performance theorist Nicholas Ridout has described the slipperiness of theatricality as a kind of "queasiness," an exciting anxiety caused by a fundamental insecurity and instability in the exchange between representation and reception, between bodies onstage and bodies in the audience.[37] Ridout attributed this queasiness to audience members' encounter with themselves as spectating subjects, an observation that is particularly germane to the interactive performance conditions of *Point Blank*, as well as the Shunt Collective's *Contains Violence*, which I analyze in the following sections. As Ridout put it, theater "turns the spectator into an audience that thinks too much of itself, that exposes itself somehow to its own gaze, that puts itself, improperly, upon the stage, in place of the work that was supposed to have transcended such categories altogether."[38] In other words, just as panoptic prisoners internalize the disciplinary gaze from the guard tower to the extent that they police themselves, theater conditions spectators to see themselves as witnesses, voyeurs, or adjudicators that are at once produced by—even as they in some way produce—the onstage action they watch.

While aligning a theater with a panoptic prison might make us queasy for any number of reasons, there is a particularly productive uncertainty that can come from examining surveillance through a theatrical framework of representation and reception. If we take a moment to reflect constructions of theatricality back onto surveillant media, we can see that surveillance systems are fundamentally theatrical. The panoptic guard tower, or CCTV camera, functions as a symbol of visual surveillance, producing a form of disciplinary power that is based less on the material reality of being watched than on the interplay between the *sign* of visual surveillance and its implied disciplinary threat. Surveillance technologies in everyday settings, as in theater, function metonymically—a photographic or data record in surveillance, like an actor or prop in theater, can be thought of as simultaneously indexical and material—a photograph is both the place/time represented in the image and the piece of photographic paper itself (or the digitally rendered image). In contrast to theater, however, the relationship between the material record and the past event it indexes has, in the rhetoric of surveillance, been historically produced as stable.

Staging surveillance data within a theatrical frame of representation can thus productively destabilize—make queasy—cultural habituations to equating surveillance with archival knowledge, dominant history, and singular truth. Edit Kaldor's *Point Blank* (2009) demonstrates how theatrical representation and reception can challenge the evidentiary status of surveillance while at the same time producing alternative methods of measuring truth. Using one mode of visual representation (theater) to destabilize another (surreptitious photography), Kaldor utilizes the slippery and unstable relationship between the real and the representational that has been historically associated with the concept of theatricality in order to reframe and challenge cultural assumptions about the truth value of surveillance.

Evidence Fail: Pointing at the Blank

Edit Kaldor's *Point Blank*, billed by PS122 in New York as "the definitive spy-ware performance," staged a young woman's systematic search for the meaning of life through the high-powered zoom lens of her camera.[39] The show began with the nineteen-year-old Nada explaining her interactive research project to her audience, a group I was fortunate to be among one evening in November 2008 as the piece toured New York. Speaking with a laid-back, scientific detachment, Nada told us that she had spent the last few years traveling through a range of European and American cities and taking surreptitious photographs of intimate, everyday moments in strangers' lives. At the beginning of the show, Nada demonstrated the powerful capacity of her 200× zoom lens for the audience, showing how she could easily capture the facial expressions of a couple arguing on a balcony of a high rise roughly a quarter mile away. She explained that the distance allowed her to remain invisible so as to avoid influencing the candid reality of her subjects' behavior with the presence of her gaze. Armed with this powerful zoom lens she could surreptitiously capture detailed visual data that could serve as pieces of evidence of "what you really look like when you think no one is watching." She was confident that these photographs, if properly interpreted, would yield answers about the kind of life that would make her happiest. Her name itself a synonym for blankness, Nada felt that her previously unformed life was about to take shape as she entered her twenties. As she moved forward into adulthood, she wanted to avoid the chaos of an unexamined life governed by chance. Approaching human behavior as a social scientist or private detective, Nada believed that "everything in life was a possible clue" and therefore sought to objectively and (covertly) research her options.

For this, she needed our help. Over the next ninety minutes, Nada said, she needed our help to analyze the contents of her sprawling database of spy photographs—numbering over seventy-five thousand and growing daily—in order to deduce the secret of a life worth living. My fellow audience members and I, disarmed by her candor, soon found ourselves actively participating in the performance, working as impromptu surveillance analysts to interpret her photographs. At Nada's prompting, we attempted to autopsy the images and organize them according to qualities of life. We found evidence of "happiness," "loneliness," and, most terrifyingly, "blankness," Nada's term for the look of someone who has lost their way in life, one who is helplessly caught in chaos. While exact meanings of the glances and gestures in the photographs often defied clear interpretation or group consensus, Nada's analytical categories slowly grew as we labored to read the secrets of a "good life" that the surreptitious photographs supposedly held.

Presented as a project that progressed with each evening's audience, Nada told us that tonight she was searching the photographs for clues that would help her to decide whether it was better to live alone or with a partner. Her questions seemed at first to be nothing more or less than typical of anyone emerging into adulthood. "How much time should I spend alone?" "Do couples get bored living together?" "What does it look like to wake up alone, sleep alone, clean the fridge and kitchen alone, cry alone, eat alone?" Her debates over how best to spend her days and nights were entertaining but relatively benign. She was drawn to an

Fig. 3. Edit Kaldor's *Point Blank*, 2007. (Photograph by Erin Baiano.)

apartment with an artsy garden in which she could entertain creative friends, but beyond that her aspirations were vague and rather ordinary.

However, this glaze of normalcy masked the more provocative and political undercurrent of the piece. As Nada explained at the top of the show, the zoom lens was central to her project because it allowed her to get as close as possible without the danger of discovery. Maintaining a surreptitious vantage point would, she insisted, yield some kind of special insight. Nada's assumption that candid photographs could produce universal truths harkens back to the long history of social and political surveillance photography referenced above. From the Mass Observation movement of the 1930s to *Candid Camera* to *Enemy of the State*, layers of cultural training had prepared the audience well for Nada's assignment. Though some hesitated before answering Nada's question about which snapshot portrayed someone we "should trust," we all chuckled when we unanimously agreed as a group that we would not get in a car with the pale, skinny guy who, with tinted sunglasses and a moustache, resembled a young Charles Manson. In another instance, a palpable shudder went through the entire audience as a series of candid photographs showed a couple locked in a tearful shouting match. The ease with which my fellow audience members and I concurred in our analyses of many of Nada's candid photographs revealed common cultural assumptions about the evidence that such photographs provide.

Gathered as we were in a theater, a space in which we were accustomed to suspending our disbelief, doubts about the facticity of the pictures also lurked in the wings. Midway through the performance, an older man seated in front of me asked Nada about a photograph of a couple entangled in a particularly goofy way on a park bench: had she posed the seemingly candid photograph? The room went silent for a moment, until Nada smiled and shrugged, dodging his question with nonchalance: "Hey, this zoom lens is not a fake." The room erupted in the most nervous laughter of the night.

By shifting the focus back onto the technology of capture, Nada sidestepped the deeper question that was at the heart of *Point Blank*, the question that made us all titter and shift uncomfortably in our seats. Nada's surreptitious photographs referenced sociopolitical models of evidence and truth, and yet their status as props within the theater production resonated with debates over truth and falsity that have long haunted practices of theatrical representation. *Point Blank* reanimated cultural histories from the last century that have produced *theatricality* and *evidence* as oppositional terms—historical discourses that set up theatricality as a measure of self-consciousness and falsity in order to construct surreptitious or candid photography as a marker of stable evidence and truth.

Flip as Nada's attitude was, her logic and actions bore the weight of over a century of cultural understandings of photography, as well as ongoing discourses in performance and media studies surrounding theatricality, artifice, reality, and evidence. As I have argued, objects and bodies in theater and live performance are unverifiable, shifting between and beyond the materiality they appear to possess and the sign to which they refer. In contrast, contemporary and historic rhetoric surrounding photography and surveillance has posited that candid or surreptitious photographs are indexes of stable evidence and "the real." In the (largely positivist) political and cultural history of photography outlined briefly above, the photograph has stood as an accurate, trustworthy representation of that which it portrays. The stakes of remediation in the case of *Point Blank* were grounded in this complicated cultural territory, in which theatricality and evidence were produced (but often failed) as oppositional terms. Nada's reliance on her surreptitious photographs to scientifically determine her life path drew on long-standing cultural taxonomies that link truth to candid photography. As she aimed to find concrete answers to ineffable questions in life, she turned, naturally it would seem, to the culturally constructed truth value of surreptitious photographs. However, Nada's attachment to the truth value of her surreptitious photographs, as well as our willingness to participate in her process, was in itself theatrical. Cleverly set within a theatrical frame, neither her stories, her photos, nor our interpretations of them could be entirely trusted as stable. The theatricality of the production—Nada's direct address of the audience and Kaldor, the director, sitting onstage as Nada's photo-database assistant—existed in tension with the presentation of the photographs as untheatrical, unstaged. Rather than reifying the evidentiary status of surreptitious photography, the theatricality of *Point Blank* radically unsettled the logic underpinning surveillance and evidence. While Nada pointed out various emotional expressions in the photos, Kaldor's production pointed to something much deeper that was under scrutiny: the status of surveillance photographs as containers of stable, universal truth.

As much as I have valorized the destabilizing effects of Kaldor's formalist remediation of surveillance, I would be remiss in overlooking the significant political risks to undermining the facticity of visual evidence. Even while visual evidence can be faked, there are many instances in which candid photographs or videos have served as valuable evidence in bringing to justice abuses of power or political violence. Many activist groups routinely employ cameras, smart phones, and other recording devices to document atrocities, abuses, and injustices that occur around the world. Within theatrical performances as well, photographs can serve as a means of anchoring satirical or fictional narratives in serious political realities. American playwright Branden Jacob-Jenkins used this strategy in *An Octoroon* (2013), his radical deconstruction of Boucicault's *The Octoroon*. Amid a dizzying array of theatrical tricks, including a deliberately overblown melodramatic style, white and black actors donning black-, red-, yellow-, and whiteface, and both Jacob-Jenkins and Boucicault appearing as characters that debate the differences between their time periods and representational strategies, a photograph of a real lynching was introduced onstage.[40] In the 2014 Soho Repertory Theater production, directed by Sarah Benson, the hysterical theatricality of the production ground to a halt in that moment, as the actors and audience were confronted with what Roland Barthes called "the *necessarily* real thing which has been placed before the lens."[41] The historic photograph of the lynching of two young black men in Indiana in 1930 was projected across the entire proscenium stage, standing for many long minutes in stark contrast to the highly theatrical efforts to impart the violence, danger, and racism portrayed in the play.

This somber moment powerfully expressed the importance of the evidentiary capabilities of photography. As Barthes argued, the facticity of the photographic referent is insistent in its claim upon the present: "[I]n Photography I can never deny that *the thing has been there.* There is a superimposition there: of reality and of the past."[42] In *An Octoroon* the hypertheatrical labor of playing at violence paled in comparison with the harsh reminder of the real suffering and death evidenced by the lynching photograph. In that case the unavoidable reality of the photograph served as a sobering counterpoint to the exaggerated theatrics of the onstage representation. The contrast between the restless, shifting metonymic bodies onstage and the arresting effect of the photograph made palpable the extent to which cultural representations of race and racism in contemporary America remain haunted by the unresolved traumas of slavery and lynching and the violent history of racism.

Among other queasy, uncomfortable realities, this moment powerfully asserted that, despite dueling conceptions of theatricality and photographic evidence, there need not be a disavowal of the capacity for truth telling in either surveillance or theater. Instead, surveillance data and real photographs staged within theatrical productions can establish a middle ground between perspectives, somewhere between the convictions of nineteenth-century positivist thinkers, who aligned photography with science, evidence, and the law, and antitheatrical biases in which bodies in performance are dismissed as unreliable and subjective. In an interview about the documentary style used in *The Files,* Ewa Wojciak insisted, "One has to believe in the point of positivistic work. Romanticism in art, life, and politics is good as long as it is liable to some control and distance. Then, it gives some intellectual effects. Everything that can be observed from outside can always gain a more interesting form."[43] When viewed as media of representation, surveillance and theater can both be utilized as a means of producing documentary evidence that can, in turn, be viewed and analyzed from a spectatorial position. Wojciak argued that reading the surveillance records written by secret service agents aloud let the documents to stand on their own, as evidence of their own history, which could be judged anew in each performance by each audience. For the performers, too, the documentary texts provided stable records of history that could, at the same time, be assessed, held at a distance. As she put it, "The reading allows for preserving the narrator of the text. An actor has to trust him. He or she has to be close but cannot escape into him. Using his words, we cannot create another character out of him, a theatrical hero. One has to stop in time."[44]

To "stop in time" is to be caught between analysis and identification, objective distance and subjective intimacy. It is to enter a suspended moment in which, to reference Rebecca Schneider's analysis of theatrical reenactment, spectators can "touch time" through a theatrical embodiment of history; such (re)enactments rigorously explore but refuse to pin down what did, did not, or may have occurred, providing accounts that are "not exactly real" but at the same time not *not* real.[45] Viewing *An Octoroon*, audience members were confronted with the stumbling block of the *real* historical photograph of racial violence, presented not only as evidence of actual historical acts but also as a live artifact that continues to script and rescript racial relations and dialogues in America today. Together with the performers, spectators "touched" (and were touched by) the discomfort and violence that had, in fact, been there all along through the other, more satirical antics of the play. These moments demonstrated the representational power of the archival documents, while at the same time loosening their grip on singular historic narrative. Sharing the stage with the lynching photograph or the secret police surveillance notes, the actors' bodies, voices, and theatrical labor asserted themselves as forms of cultural evidence, and as symptoms and effects of similar historical forces that produced the archival remains.

The unsettling, tense undercurrent of doubt in *Point Blank* likewise produced an ambivalent relationship between spectators and performer, theatrical frame and photographic record. As an audience member, I was caught in a curiously confused position, unsure whether or not Nada's vast store of photographs were indeed *real* surreptitious photos of strangers or if some or all of them had been faked. And yet, what would it mean if they were faked? They were real photographs taken with a real digital camera, and a nice one at that. But were the subjects actually strangers? Did they really not know they were being photographed? The photographs certainly read as products of surveillance, shot from high angles, obscured by curtains and branches, their subjects caught in awkwardly intimate moments. But this could have been a rhetorical strategy of Kaldor's, posed in such a way as to make the photos appear genuinely candid. And how much did it matter, anyway? Would knowing have changed the blend of empathy and judgment with which my fellow audience members and I approached the photographs Nada showed us?

In the end, I was grateful for the uncertainty, the questions that remained unanswered. Regardless of whether the scenes in the photographs had been staged to appear candid or were really unposed, the murky territory between truth and falsity gave the piece its political edge. By setting her performance in the indeterminate, shadowy ground between the real and the representational, between photography's truth and theatricality's falsity, Kaldor cast surveillance data into a kind of doubt and mysticism historically reserved for theatrical production. In effect *Point Blank* was firing blanks—fake theatrical bullets—at the construct of surreptitious photographic evidence and the stability of any form of documentary representation. In partnership with the fictional (though real, embodied) Nada, Kaldor remediated the conceit of surreptitious photography, submitting the evidentiary claim of candid snapshots to the slipperiness of theatrical representation.

The answers for which Nada desperately searched in her huge collection of photographs pointedly showed themselves to be ever evasive; indeed, they were paper tigers set up to frustrate rather than reveal. In their place, however, a different kind of evidence emerged. The blanks kicked back against the unreliability of theater, as Kaldor created a scenario in which we produced our own archive of desire. My fellow audience members and I responded viscerally to the photographs Nada asked us to categorize, emitting groans of recognition when viewing pictures of unhappy couples and lonely people, spontaneous laughter at photos of joyful moments, and spirited debate over where to place more ambiguous scenes within Nada's database. Even while the slipperiness of the theatrical frame destabilized the status of the photographs as inarguable proof, the time we spent together looking at pictures of other people's lives produced a record of our desire to find truth within the theater, contradictory and contingent as it may have been.

After ninety minutes of struggling to find trustworthy answers in the candid photographs, Nada closed down the performance with an exhausted gesture to the light board operator. "That's enough for today," she said. "I'll begin again here tomorrow." Leaving the theater, I saw the actress who had played Nada standing on the street, wielding her trusty camera. She pointed her powerful zoom lens at a couple whose backs were turned, walking briskly away in the winter night. I recognized the woman's laugh and man's bald head from the seats in front of me in the theater that evening. I gasped in spite of myself, and turned to look at "Nada." Would these two be analyzed in tomorrow night's show? She smiled conspiratorially and gave a slight shrug, as if to say, "Wouldn't you do the same?" I smiled back, strangely thrilled to be standing with her in this overlapping space between theatrical fiction and everyday life. As I began the journey back into my own life I listened for the telltale click of the camera that would secure my place in Nada's archive of human lifestyles. What answers would I yield? What questions? Surveillance, theater, photography, and everyday life blurred in that moment. Despite my scholarly determination to trace the diverse cultural histories of each, I was, and often continue to be, caught by the overlapping and interconnected desires of surveillance and theater to catch and hold, if only for a moment, a glimpse of something that feels real.

Doing Violence to the Theatrical Container

The uneasy thrill and queasy self-consciousness of watching and being watched also looms large in the Shunt Collective's production of *Contains Violence* (2008). Utilizing the destabilizing power of remediation toward ends that differ from those of the productions discussed so far, creator David Rosenberg employed technologies of surveillance as interactive tools—weapons, we might say—with which to expose and challenge habits of passivity within traditional theatrical spectatorship. In the spring of 2008, the Lyric Hammersmith Theatre in London hosted the Shunt Collective's site-specific production.[46] Audiences of the event were presented with a peculiar request: arrive at dusk, wear gloves, and get ready for an evening of rooftop espionage. Upon arrival, the audience members were ushered onto the rooftop terrace of the Lyric Hammersmith, seated under the darkening sky on the edge of the balcony, and outfitted with a set of in-ear microphones and high-powered binoculars. A uniform-clad officer brusquely ordered them to use their individually issued surveillance equipment to follow a drama that would take place several hundred yards away, across a busy commercial street in a newly built, five-story, glass-fronted office building.

As the drama across the street unfolded, the lighted rooms revealed a disillusioned office worker typing a letter of resignation, a bubbly male coworker watering ornamental plants, and, several floors below, a woman in a neck brace and polka-dot dress sashaying around a photocopier and talking heatedly on her mobile phone. Over the hour-plus performance, the audience members had to piece together the suspenseful Hitchcockian narrative through the clues they gathered via their binoculars and specially calibrated earphones. Like amateur detectives, they had to draw connections between a fragmented series of sounds and

Fig. 4. The "audience" in David Rosenberg's *Contains Violence*, Lyric Hammersmith Theatre, London, 2008. (Photograph by Susanne Deitz.)

gestures that ranged from environmental sounds of typing, phones ringing, paper crackling, water pouring, and mundane office conversation to obscene and threatening phone calls, a passionate embrace, choice inner thoughts narrated by the characters, and a dramatically bloody murder.

While the elements of rooftop espionage created a sense of mischievous role-play, the performance conditions of *Contains Violence* more seriously challenged several ingrained habits of spectatorship in mainstream realist theater. By supplying his audience members with surveillant earpieces and binoculars, Rosenberg insisted that they become viscerally aware of their own habits of spectatorship and theatergoing, as well as their embedded assumptions about popular representations of surveillance. He did so using three central strategies. First, by outfitting audience members with familiar symbols of surveillance he recast habitually passive theater spectators as rooftop spies, activating their dramatic participation within the fictional narrative of surveillance and violence he had staged. Second, he destabilized their relationship with the fictional

Fig. 5. Simon Kane and Nigel Barrett in David Rosenberg's *Contains Violence*, Lyric Hammersmith Theatre, London, 2008. (Photograph by Susanne Deitz.)

realm of theater by placing them on the blurry border between the theatrical and the everyday. Third, he disoriented their visual and aural intake of the theatrical event itself with powerful zoom lenses and specially calibrated earphones. These subtle but powerful modifications defamiliarized the expectations and habits of theater spectatorship, making them reemerge as new and strange to themselves.

The dramatic narrative of *Contains Violence* received mixed reviews, as critics were unenthused about the rather mundane murder plot; nevertheless, audience members and critics at large blogged enthusiastically about Rosenberg's bold integration of surveillance technologies into their theatergoing experience. Heralded with popular culture references such as "*The Office* meets *Rear Window*," every online response and review that I read reflected indisputable fascination with the innovative formal elements of the show.

There's something gratifyingly unusual about being marshalled out on to a London roof terrace by surly, burly men with walkie-talkies, collecting binoculars and headphones . . . on the way and settling down to watch a play unfold in the windows of an office block across the road. How bizarre! How artfully creepy![47]

Susannah Clap, in an online *Guardian* review, noted the rare and valuable opportunity the piece provided, writing, "[T]he inside-outsideness sets you up to look quite differently at your surroundings—which is not something *The Importance of Being Earnest* will usually help you do."[48]

In other words, what made *Contains Violence* exciting or revolutionary was that it used a familiar cultural fantasy of surveillance (in this case, rooftop spying) to create a new experience of theatrical spectatorship. Giving audiences such an opportunity was, in fact, part of Rosenberg's foundational goal. He created *Contains Violence* as part of a two-year fellowship he had been awarded "to research techniques that 'facilitate participation and methods of empowering the audience.'"[49] In this piece, he fostered audience participation by giving theatergoers the chance to play at classic, old-fashioned surveillance—a model of surveillance that satisfyingly echoed popular representations of surveillance in films, TV shows, and news events but one that everyday social subjects rarely have the opportunity to embody without fear of being labelled a peeping tom. As one audience member shared on a blog, the show's concept was immediate inspiration to attend: "I went along as I like anything Hitchcocky and it also seemed a good way to indulge my creepy habit of looking out of the window and spying on passers by on a more sophisticated level."[50] Robin McKie of *The Observer* online could not help but compare the experience to "Hitchcock's film *Rear Window*, in which a helpless James Stewart glimpses odd bits of action in the next apartment block and eventually concludes murder has been committed," concluding happily that *Contains Violence* "is a perfect mix of paranoia and voyeurism."[51]

The cartoonish onstage murder in *Contains Violence* was, however, a dummy, a red herring; the theatrical production did indeed contain violence, just not of the kind or in the place the audience expected. Through his formalist remediation of theater via surveillance, Rosenberg shifted the site of theatrical violence from the actors to the audience. McKie's statement makes clear that, in spite of his active involvement as a spy, he also felt helpless as an audience member, just as James Stewart with his broken leg did. Voyeurism—the practice, some would say compulsion, of taking visual pleasure in a scene from a careful distance—clearly adds to the mechanics of suspense, as the voyeuristic spectator cannot or does not intervene in the scene itself.[52] At the same time, the helplessness of the voyeur, and the paranoia that can accompany such helplessness, lays bare a foundational problem of spectatorship that, when reframed as surveillance, can offer a serious challenge to the habits of theatergoers.

The tension that emerged from balancing their new role as active surveillance agents and their habitual role as passive audience members struck some of the theatergoers as not only exciting but somewhat disturbing: "Gradually, it becomes apparent that what you are watching is a thriller during which a woman will batter her victim to death, every sickening thud relayed through our ears, *while we do nothing, as if the events unfolding in front of our eyes are nothing more than a play.*"[53] On one level, of course, the events were "nothing more than a play." Audience members had purchased tickets, the actors would be paid, the event had a set start and finish time, and no one was actually harmed in the staged violence. Further, "doing nothing" seemed to be the only option given the habitually passive behavior of theatrical audiences and the large distance between the spectators and the unfolding action. And yet audience members were torn because they held in their hands surveillance equipment that symbolized the active duty to stop crime, enforce laws, and bring offenders to justice. As the audience was given the chance to "play at watching" within the medium of surveillance, the seemingly simple question of what it means to "watch a play" became suddenly troubling.

The comment "as if these events were nothing more than a play" serves as an especially telling clue regarding the actual violence that the production contained. The production masqueraded as "nothing more than a play" and the surveillance equipment as "nothing more than props" in order to perform a more subtle kind of violence. The tawdry stage violence and overwrought, underwritten plot that prompted complaints from critics were blanks fired to distract attention in order to enact a dislocation of identity and perspective produced by blurred boundaries between the theatrical and the everyday, the symbolic and the material. Utilizing the tactic of formalist remediation, Rosenberg strategically layered two traditions of spectatorship on one another. He rearranged the formal elements of traditional theater, making small but impactful changes in traditional theater practices with the help of some familiar symbols and practices of surveillance. He placed audience members and actors adjacent to, rather than inside, a traditional theater space, separating them by a gulf that they could see but not "act" across. He outfitted his audience members with individually issued tools of surveillance, which not only allowed them to see and hear the distant action but also served as emblems of their limited roles within the dramatic action. Finally, once they were seated on the rooftop of the theater, clutching the props they had been given to enact their roles, Rosenberg relied on the surveillance equipment to disorient and reframe their sensory encounters within the theater performance.

These three main aspects of remediation at work in *Contains Violence* merit closer examination. First of all, the spatial arrangement of *Contains Violence* placed audience members, quite literally, on the edge of a traditional theater space, peering over the rail of the Lyric's rooftop terrace. By spacing the audience and actors across the gulf of a real-life busy street, Rosenberg pitted the fictional frame of theater against the real world of the everyday and created a visible space that simultaneously demanded and limited the participation of the audience. The fiction of the murder that the audience watched for entertainment was framed and encroached on by the bustling reality of the busy Hammersmith commercial district. As Clap observed, "Beneath the imaginary acts of violence, as in a dreamlike backdrop, buses pass by silently, pedestrians bustle, and ambulances speed to real emergencies."[54] The blurring of the two registers produced a unique and interwoven theater of surveillance as the "imaginary" staged violence slipped between and around "real emergencies." From their rooftop vantage point audience members could freely move between real and staged events, a perspective that some were not quick to leave. As one review noted, "[T]he audience stayed in their seats, scanning the area with their binoculars for several minutes after the play was over."[55] In effect, the spatial frames between reality and fiction were made visible and permeable as the surveillance technologies punctured the borders of theatrical spectatorship.

Second, the surveillance technologies placed in the hands of audience members functioned as "scriptive things," to recall Robin Bernstein's term, which I discussed in the "Introduction."[56] On one hand, these were tools that cast spectators in their roles as rooftop spies, cuing behavior according to received cultural "scripts" of surveillance; on the other hand, as props, they were invested with the slippery, make-believe, symbolic value characteristic of objects and bodies within theatrical representation. Andrew Sofer, who has written about the complex relationships between stage objects and audience members, argues that theatrical props can serve as particularly radical tools with which to challenge theatrical convention.[57] Sofer ascribes this to an important dual capacity of stage props, arguing that they function as "visual emblems" or "symbolic agents," as well as "vital participants in the stage action."[58] In other words, theatrical props function as symbols that reference cultural systems of meaning outside the frame of the play while simultaneously facilitating particular, material interactions within the play world itself. Sofer suggested that props contain

> two temporal processes that move in opposite directions simultaneously within a given performance. On the one hand, props are unidirectional: they are propelled through stage space and real time before historically specific audiences at a given performance event. At the same time, props are retrospective: . . . they are "ghosted" by their previous incarnations, and hence by a theatrical past they both embody and critique.[59]

The surveillance technologies staged in *Contains Violence* can likewise be read according to these dual temporalities. In the first and more immediate temporality, they function materially within the frame of the play as tools that actively mediate processes of watching and being watched. Audience members had to interface with the surveillant media (binoculars and earphones) in order to access and follow the dramatic action of the play. In the second, retrospective temporality articulated by Sofer, the surveillance technologies invoked the "ghosts" of their sociopolitical roles and the contemporary cultural representations of reality TV and crime dramas. Here Bernstein's definition of *scriptive things* is illuminating: "The method of reading material things as scripts aims to discover . . . what a thing invited its users to do. The act of scripting, this issuing of a culturally specific invitation, is itself a historical event— one that can be recovered and then analyzed as a fresh source of evidence."[60] For the audiences of *Contains Violence* the "ghosts" or "scripts" that attended the things they held in their hands conjured familiar specters: police on a sting operation or of the pose that Jimmy Stewart struck while playing at vigilante sleuthing. Such associations attracted audience members to the theater production in the first place and, once there, implicitly instructed them to behave in certain culturally scripted ways, albeit ones that ran counter to their habits as theatergoers. Rosenberg thus effectively drew on the historical scriptedness of surveillance technologies to remediate his audiences' behavior; he counted on their willingness to play along with familiar tools of surveillance in a savvy way yet also to treat these tools lightly, like props in a play, in order to open up their perceptual senses—and their senses of themselves as spectators.

Rosenberg furthered his sly attack on the habits of theater spectatorship through a sensorially disorienting contrast between physical distance and mediated proximity. The significant distance between the audience and the performers—across a large, busy street in Hammersmith's commercial district—contrasted with the visual close-ups and aural amplification provided by the binoculars and earpieces. While the audience members were several hundred yards from the actors, a distance much greater than most contemporary theater spaces allow, the surveillance equipment permitted them to see and hear the action up close. Visually empowered with the binoculars, they could get up close and personal with the characters in a way that the medium of theater does not typically allow. "You make up your own long-shots and close-ups, using their binoculars to zoom in and out at will," described one observer.[61] Another extrapolated, "[T]he experience of being free to follow and zoom in on what interests you can give you a feeling of being closer to the action."[62]

In contrast, the aural experiences of many audience members were unfamiliar and disorienting. "You are, weirdly, much further away from the actors than usual but aurally much closer up," wrote one observer.[63] Another noted, "[T]he sound is extraordinarily disconcerting, as if someone else has taken up residence inside your head."[64] According to a press interview, Rosenberg hoped that the use of headphones would do just that—"transport the audience into the rooms and into the heads of the protagonists"—as the audience hears not only what is audible to the characters but also "what is happening in their bodies: [such as] an accelerated heartbeat."[65] In another interview, Rosenberg shared that he was inspired to use this aggressive form of audio recording by a traumatic experience from his childhood in which his father, a neurologist, had him listen to a binaural recording of savage dogs howling.[66] The childhood memory seems to have inspired Rosenberg to create his uniquely violent theatrical container, as the intrusion of the soundscape into the very skulls of the audience was, by several accounts, the most physically palpable mode of sensorial violence.

While Rosenberg's use of theater conventions to represent the violence in his murder mystery may have been nothing particularly new, his use of conventional surveillance technologies performed a far more radical act of violence to theatrical conventions of reception. Rosenberg forcibly cast his audience members against type, outfitting them with props that cast them as active agents within the frame of the play, rather than observers both literally and figuratively outside of its bounds. However, as I have continued to sift through the layers of actual and conceptual violence contained within the theater piece, I cannot help thinking that Rosenberg could have used the surveillance technologies to enact an even more radical formalist remediation. Positioning his audience members within a frame of theatrical performance while simultaneously placing them precariously at its edge, he constructed the production and his audiences to overstep the boundaries of traditional spectatorship. And yet, by and large, audience members continued to behave according to traditions of obedient social citizenship. Rosenberg's strategies of remediation, while effective, fell short of what could have been a more cutting lesson in the stakes of voyeurism.

This shortcoming of the production is shown most clearly in an interview with an audience member from the world of professional surveillance. As fortune and good press would have it, a private investigator by the name of Michael Colacicco attended *Contains Violence* during its run at the Lyric. In an online interview with the *Guardian*, Colacicco offered his perspective on the accuracy and effects of the representation, reception, and embodied experience of surveillance in the *Contains Violence* setup, as well as some interesting ideas for future remediating dialogues between practitioners of surveillance and theater. While some critics of the show were bored by the complicated, somewhat slow-moving murder mystery plot, private investigator Colacicco had quite a different response: "I wish my current surveillance jobs were half as much fun as this play. More happened in 70 minutes than I would normally see in weeks. . . . In the 15 years I spent working for the police's anti-terrorism branch, I saw perhaps three or four acts of violence."[67]

With this perspective in mind, Rosenberg could have pushed his emulation of surveillance practices much further and challenged theatergoers at a deeper level. He could have staged something more mundane than a murder, or even staged nothing at all, allowing the everyday world outside to be reframed as material for both theatrical performance and surveillance. These alternatives would have put another, even less visible set of habits under scrutiny, interrogating instead the cultural limits and conditions placed on what a proper citizen, like a proper audience member, *should* see. The potential for this critique of surveillance in everyday life was in place: several of the audience comments shared above noted that the binoculars gave them the freedom to watch things that interested them, regardless of whether those things were inside the frame of the theatrical narrative or not, while others stayed in their seats after the conclusion of the play, scanning the street and other buildings for everyday dramas. What would have been the effect on their spectatorial identities and positions as voyeurs if the production had urged its audiences to watch the everyday in the same way they watch a piece of theater? How much more or less or differently would they have watched? Would they have felt more or less responsible to what they were witnessing?

A particularly class-focused comment from one *Guardian* critic sticks out as a fruitful place to apply this line of questioning. Describing the interplay of "real" and "theatrical" action, Clap wrote, "Occasionally, a non-actor—a cleaner or late worker—gets snarled up accidentally in the action."[68] Her dismissiveness of such "accidental" border crossing suggests that these figures are not worth watching, perhaps for reasons that go beyond their nonactor status. Rosenberg would have done well to use the permeable borders of *Contains Violence* to interrogate the invisible scripts of such cultural assumptions. He could have used the liminal position of his production, balanced as it was between the everyday and the theatrical, to ask his audience members to examine the contours of their own subjective vision. By employing a theatrical frame to interrupt—and, in interrupting, hold up for inspection—his audiences' habitual judgments and blind spots, Rosenberg could have enacted a deeper form of violence, one that aimed at habits of *overlooking* in the everyday world of sociopolitical surveillance.

Nevertheless, *Contains Violence* demonstrates a simple but powerful model of formalist remediation available to surveillance theater practitioners. Rosenberg employed popular representations of surveillance to defamilarize habitual processes of theater spectatorship; at the same time, he used a theatrical context to provide a conceptual frame through which audience members could begin to critically consider applications of surveillance techniques to contemporary everyday life.

Bearing Witness, Troubling Evidence

Contains Violence, Point Blank, An Octoroon, and *The Files* illustrate the potential of surveillance theater to challenge habits of seeing, knowing, and history making. Surveillance theater productions such as these challenge paradigmatic constructions of theater and surveillance precisely because they fail to provide fixed points of representation and reception that align neatly or remain secure. Failures and misalignments between traditional processes of watching and being watched and of recording history in both theater and surveillance can do productive violence to normalized habits of discipline in both cultural paradigms. They can make way for alternative experiences of truth and interconnectedness, and create temporary yet invaluable spaces in which interactions with surveillance can be rehearsed, negotiated, and critically reflected on.

Recalling the discussion of Butler in the "Introduction," surveillance theater capitalizes on the performativity of surveillance—that is, the capacity of "ordinary practitioners" of surveillance to "repeat with a difference" the habitual script of disciplinary supervision. Live, copresent, theatrical practices, especially those that feature some aspect of interactivity on the part of audience members, can re-present surveillance technologies in such a way as to offer audiences valuable opportunities to critically and creatively reconsider their relationships and interactions with everyday disciplinary interfaces in theatrical and surveillant contexts. Done well, surveillance theater productions fail to return their audience members to the habitual subject positions in which they entered the theater. Instead, they leave us queasy and keenly aware of being interconnected and mutually constituted, and of living within a mutable, contingent place from which we can all begin again tomorrow.

CHAPTER 2

Streets

———— ꝏ ————

Dear Observer,

Make me a diary and keep it safe. Take care it is mine.
Hold this photograph of my face. Keep all our entries in order.
Put the letters in your desk file and the images in your evidence
locker.
You can edit everyone else out.
I will fill in the gaps, the parts of my diary you are missing.
Since you can't follow me inside, I will record the inside for you.
I will mark the time carefully so you will never lose me.
Don't worry about finding me. I will help you. I will tell you what
I was wearing, where I was, the time of day . . . If there was anything
distinguishing about my look that day, I will make sure you know.
Hold onto my diary for at least seven years.
I am enclosing a cheque. Use it for whatever expenses you have.

Sincerely,
JSM

This love letter-cum-artistic directive opened Jill Magid's durational performance project *Evidence Locker: One Cycle of Memory in the City of L.*[1] In
2004 Magid spent a month in the city of Liverpool, deliberately putting
herself under the surveillant gaze of the city's new state-of-the-art surveillance system. As her opening letter established, Magid brokered a
deal with the police department and surveillance officers of Liverpool to

64

record footage of her via the city's CCTV cameras for "one cycle of memory," that is, thirty-one days, the length of time that CCTV surveillance footage remains on record in the Liverpool Police Department before being erased. She arranged for the footage to be stored in an "evidence locker," the department's name for files of surveillance footage being held "for at least seven years" in case of further investigation.[2]

Magid's request was out of the ordinary, as evidence lockers are typically reserved for footage concerning criminal activity that may lead to an investigation or prosecution. That a young woman's daily perambulations and innocuous habits of sitting in coffee shops, smoking on street corners, and writing letters were to be held alongside footage of perpetrators and victims was not routine procedure. In order to ensure that each day's footage would be stored on file, and to gain access to this footage, Magid was required to fill out daily "Subject Access Request Forms." Magid chose to fill out the formal requests in the language of love letters, addressing them to her "Dear Observer," her term of endearment for the sprawling network of CCTV cameras and surveillance officers that watched her. In the letters she described her comings and goings in "the city of L" and provided detailed accounts of people she met and what she was wearing to make it easier to find her amidst the hours of footage. The letters also filled in the gaps that the surveillance cameras missed—the loneliness and longing she felt, her sensual impressions of being watched by Liverpool's surveillance cameras, and details of interiors she visited that the publicly installed cameras could not capture. Together with a reenactment of a scene from a Godard film and a blind trust walk performed via a live CCTV feed, the "Dear Observer" letters and surveillance footage formed Magid's unique narrative record of her time under surveillance in Liverpool.[3]

At its most foundational, the project staged a provocation to normalized modes of participation in surveillance society. Magid creatively investigated what new forms of participation might be available to both the watchers and the watched across Liverpool's CCTV system. Her unusual contract with the Liverpool police explored the possibilities for surveillance cameras to function not simply as technologies of one-way discipline, as they are typically understood, but instead as media of two-way communication and aesthetic representation. Many other facets of Magid's project bear analysis as well, in particular her savvy exploration of the resonances between the male gaze of visual culture and disciplinary gaze of surveillance. As I analyze at more length later in the chapter, Magid mimicked cinematic models of representation and Hollywood-

Fig. 6. Jill Magid's *Evidence Locker*, 2004, video still

inspired notions of femininity important to feminist theorists and performance makers to structure her durational CCTV performance.

Magid was not the only one to have seen the potential for creative representation via the city's expansive CCTV system. The Liverpool *Echo*, a local newspaper, had run an article several years earlier that presented the story of an "ordinary citizen" told through footage garnered from the city's CCTV cameras.[4] The paper presented the comprehensive surveillance system as a mechanism that would turn the lives of Liverpool residents into a movie, not unlike the 1998 Hollywood film *The Truman Show*. The surveillers were figured as harmless, protective audience members viewing the lives of "ordinary citizens" such as the article's featured protagonist, Iain Bundred; at the same time, the paper assured readers that the watchful eyes would keep pickpockets, muggers, drunk drivers, and other lawbreakers in line.[5]

Surveillance scholar Roy Coleman smartly criticized the *Echo*'s framing of the Liverpool CCTV system, pointing out that the press was merely reproducing dominant and problematic ideologies of surveillance. As the familiar rhetoric goes, CCTV is protective and even empowering for "ordinary citizens" that have "nothing to hide" and therefore "nothing to fear." However, surveillance policies are routinely exclusionary and discriminatory toward people who are outside the norm of "ordinary" citizenship or socially/economically desirable behaviors. Coleman argued that civic CCTV systems such as Liverpool's "hide the consequences of neoliberalisation in creating a particular ambience and exclusivity regarding 'public' spaces."[6] In addition to their role as crime-stopping agents, CCTV systems tend to be used as mechanisms for supporting and maintaining capitalist models of consumption, social normativity, and political cooperation among "ordinary citizens."[7] Behaviors and individuals that do not fit within these hegemonic goals are criminalized (made hypervisible) and/or removed or disenfranchised (made invisible).

Evidence Locker does not escape Coleman's accusation that representations of civic CCTV systems tend to be represented as "sponsor[s] of the freedoms that the citizen-worker-socialite enjoys."[8] As a young, white woman with sufficient economic security to support her artistic pursuits, Magid capitalized on these freedoms to broker her partnership with Liverpool's surveillance authorities and perform her social-aesthetic experiment. Nevertheless, her project illustrated a valuable experimental approach to what it means to participate in surveillance society, albeit from a position of privilege. Whereas most middle-class white women, like Magid, would simply pass by (and passively accept or ignore) the CCTV cameras that line the streets and thoroughfares of urban centers such as Liverpool, Magid fundamentally reimagined the types of interactions that might be available through these increasingly ubiquitous technologies of vision. Her actions sought to change the habits of her observers as well: she invited the participation, collaboration, and understanding of her observers as they mutually produced an aesthetic record of her time in Liverpool. While her status as a nonthreatening, "ordinary citizen" no doubt facilitated the willingness of the police to participate, the project evidenced a capacity for change within the structures of disciplinary surveillance. The artistic partnership Magid forged with "the Man" enacted the possibility of collaboration, empathy, and even love within the supposedly clinical and unemotional "real-world" theater of street surveillance.

"If You See Something . . .": Surveillance Art in Public Space

Evidence Locker, to which we will return later in the chapter, is illustrative of surveillance art and performance works that critique and reimagine models of participation and communication via surveillance technologies in public space. It also evidences the importance of demographic markers, such as gender, race, age, and economic class, that determine the types of participation made available to different individuals. Over the past several decades, as surveillance in public spaces has expanded and intensified, performers, artists, and activist performance groups have staged performances that defamiliarize and reconstruct modes of interacting with dominant systems of surveillance, from CCTV cameras on street corners to corporate surveillance of globalized industry. From the staging of Samuel Beckett's *Waiting for Godot* for publicly installed CCTV cameras by the Surveillance Camera Players (SCP) to Hannah Price's photographs of men who catcalled her on the street, surveillance artworks staged in public thoroughfares make visible and open for revision normalized blind spots and models of participation in surveillance society. These artists employ a range of tactics—from theatrical devices of role-play and reenactment to remediation of surveillance through classic cinema—in order to enact alternative models of usership and prompt audiences and participants to engage with technologies of surveillance in critical and creative ways. They defamiliarize and make newly visible aspects of surveillance that tend to be downplayed or covered over, such as the gendered and gendering gaze of surveillance, ethical pitfalls of state and corporate surveillance techniques, and the capacity for ordinary practitioners to critically look back at—and even talk back to—CCTV cameras in public space.

A challenge these artists face is that discrimination has been normalized within the disciplinary logic of public surveillance. "Ordinary citizens" have been trained to view everyday situations according to certain ideological sightlines. This was memorably propagated in the United States through the post-9/11 campaign "If you see something, say something." This campaign asked citizens to actively participate in policing permissible activity in public space, suggesting that all normal, patriotic citizens are (or should be) on the side of the police in their efforts to report any suspicious persons, packages, or activities. Posters plastered in urban centers asked commuters and passersby to act as surveillance cameras, urging them to become just as consonant with dominant ideologies of security and discipline in their vigilance. The goal of the campaign has merit—to enlist help in preventing more terrorist attacks like the September 11, 2001, World Trade Center attacks in New York City, the London subway bombings in July 2005, and the Boston Marathon bombing in April 2013: nobody wants more lives to be lost in acts of terrorist violence in public space. However, public campaigns of hypervigilance secret within them-selves social and political prejudices and neoliberal projects that embrace certain kinds of difference and mobility while disavowing or criminalizing others. Participants in "If you see something" are not necessarily supposed to see and report every kind of problem that occurs in public space. It is implicit in the campaign that one should not report a police action but rather abnormal actions requiring police attention. To *say something* is to say it to the police so that the offending person or action—that which should not have appeared, that which does not fit established codes of normality—can be addressed within a police-dominated logic of vision: "nothing to see here." That is, rendered invisible again.

To some extent, the "If you see something" directive *has* moved beyond the bounds of police-dominated logic. There have been notable social movements in recent years to use consumer surveillance, mostly through image capture in personal cell phones, to record and report police mis-conduct. In the United States, the widely publicized deaths of Trayvon Martin, Eric Holder, Michael Brown, Freddie Gray, and a tragically grow-ing list of other black men at the hands of police officers have brought attention to systemic racial discrimination and violence within police departments across the country. The national discourses and the "Black Lives Matter" movement that have come to prominence with this string of widely publicized tragedies show that the politics of "seeing something" are still fraught with long histories of racial prejudice and mistrust. Sur-veillance continues to play an important, though yet again ambivalent role in this chapter of racial history. Visual evidence of these many deaths has often been provided through private cell phone video footage of fel-low civilians and circulated broadly through user-generated media such as Facebook and Youtube. Witness documentation has become an ethical imperative to bringing these patterns of racial violence to visibility. Con-versely, one of the only concrete policy proposals from the Obama admin-istration and various local governments has been to require all police officers to wear "body cameras," which would record all their actions and interactions.[9] Ostensibly the increased visibility from both of these sourc-es of surveillance should improve police accountability and protect civil-ians from abuse and deadly violence. However, this arrangement seems thus far to prove that evidence and justice function differently based on the demographic and professional status of the eye of the beholder. Nevertheless, it is my profound hope that watchfulness, care, and "saying something" can change the narratives of racial inequality being staged in cities across America.

Citizen Arrest: Surveillance Art as Public Intervention

Concerns over such injustices and an underlying passive acceptance of surveillance in public and semipublic spaces, have fueled a number of surveillance artworks. To help analyze some of the foundational strategies of surveillance artists working in "the streets," I have identified three main tactics by means of which artists can intervene in and reimagine contemporary surveillance in public space: I call the first tactic "performing citizen arrests."[10] In contrast to the common understanding of the citizen arrest, in which ordinary citizens are permitted to apprehend and detain perpetrators in the event of witnessing a serious crime, the citizen arrests performed by surveillance artists are antidisciplinary. Rather than complying with law enforcement officials and attendant ideologies of either "if you see something" or "nothing to see here," the arrests performed by surveillance artists interpellate everyday subjects of surveillance into alternative ways of seeing in which it becomes clear that there *is* something to see, just not the things that we have been conditioned to look for. As I explore below, works by the SCP and Yes Men serve as particularly good examples of performative citizen arrests. These groups utilize theatrical techniques such as role-play, satire, and Brechtian alienation to arrest the attention of passersby and to defamiliarize scenes of everyday surveillance that have become so familiar that they escape recognition let alone critique. Within the suspended space of theatrical play, in which truth and fiction become productively ambiguous, these artists perform a range of alternative, nonnormative ways to relate to, see, and critique quotidian surveillant interfaces.

Second, the strategy of "remediation" (discussed in chapter 1) is also useful for surveillance artists working in "the streets." Remediation in surveillance performance pieces can be understood on one level as "the representation of one medium in another,"[11] as artists bring other forms of representational media, such as theater, literature, film, and video games, to bear on the medium of surveillance. By placing everyday processes of surveillance within the frame of more recognizable media of representation (such as film, theater, and video games), the representational codes of surveillance that reflect cultural ideologies of power, gender, class, race, and nationality and condition relationships between watchers and watched become visible as strategies of discipline. Remediation, as a kind of cultural re-education, becomes a tactic to help audiences see anew the surveillant interfaces that we have been disciplined to accept and passively participate in. The SCP used familiar dramatic narratives such as *Waiting for Godot* or George Orwell's *1984* to remediate the interfaces between passersby and publicly installed surveillance cameras; members of the Yes Men remediate the hierarchy of surveillance through impersonation, using familiar symbols of power and elitism to insert themselves into positions of authority; Magid uses cinematic realism as a means of exploring both the gender norms and the capacity for creative production within the "documentary realism" of surveillance; and Price uses photographic portraiture as a means of interrupting and reimagining the typically uncomfortable, angry, or silent responses that women have to men who catcall them on the street.

Third, these artists rescript new narratives of participation within the architecture of everyday surveillance. They tell stories that tend not to be heard or imagined within public space. These might be dystopian tales of authoritarian surveillance told in such a way as to urge audiences to ethically reevaluate current models of disciplinary surveillance in state and corporate controlled spaces. Or they might articulate new relationships across surveillant interfaces, imagining the possibility for understanding and collaboration between subject positions that have been traditionally divided between "given to be seen" and "given to see." From a formal point of view, these artists experiment with using surveillance as a storytelling medium, exploring the capacity for surveillance, as a technology of vision, to record and tell personal and collective narratives. Using available technologies and interfaces of surveillance on "the streets," these surveillance artists thus create practical, subversive, and sometimes whimsical alternatives to the more familiar models of discipline that line the streets and keep in line the pedestrians that traverse them.

Surveillance Camera Players: "All the World's a Stage . . ."

Over the course of two decades, the SCP created numerous performances that defamiliarized physical and psychological relationships between social subjects and surveillance cameras. The group began staging performances for publicly installed surveillance cameras out of what it claimed was sympathy for the unseen laborers of surveillance: the security guards and officers paid to watch the streets and inhabitants of New York City on small black-and-white CCTV screens. Their early performances—versions of Alfred Jarry's *Ubu Roi* in 1996 and Orwell's *1984* in 1998—were ostensibly performed for surveillance guards who, the SCP mockingly worried, might be getting bored watching surveillance cameras on which nothing threatening or out of the ordinary ever happened.[12] Tongues partially in cheeks since then, these artists have performed regularly in front of publicly installed surveillance cameras in New York and many other American and European cities, entertaining the odd surveillance guard who catches a performance and, more frequently, the groups of passersby that stop to watch them.

The SCP was one of the first groups to prominently use performance to address the increasingly ubiquitous CCTV surveillance in public urban spaces. As James Harding has chronicled, the SCP became increasingly media savvy in its performance tactics: the group shifted its focus first away from the surveillance guards to passersby, whom it sought to educate about the prevalence of surveillance cameras, and then, increasingly during the 2000s, toward a much broader audience through media coverage and interviews.[13] Nevertheless, Harding has argued that the SCP's critical focus remained somewhat behind the times.

> Rather than actually casting a forward gaze, it tended to look in the opposite direction and captured the last glimmers of a quickly disappearing workforce that was wedded to what is often called first generation video surveillance technology. Contrasting themselves with "law enforcement officers" who watched "video images constantly being displayed" on CCTV screens, the Surveillance Camera Players thus positioned the founding moment of their activism in opposition to a model of surveillance that by 1996 was already on its way out.[14]

Harding's point is not unfounded: the SCP failed to engage the more nefarious aspects of contemporary surveillance, such as covert partnerships between state and private sector surveillance networks and information banks, a failure, he suggests, that ultimately led it to disband. However, I find great value in the clarity and simplicity with which the SCP addressed subjects and purveyors of surveillance. Using deliberately simple tactics of communication and theatricality, it modeled a kind of civic activism that not only critiqued the invasions of privacy and power inequities it perceived in urban CCTV surveillance systems but also, and perhaps more important, suggested that surveillance cameras could be utilized by ordinary citizens as tools of two-way communication, not simply one-way discipline.

To catch the eyes of each of its viewers, SCP performances typically used theatrical devices to highlight processes of watching and being watched, bringing paradigms of theater and surveillance into dialogue. Positioning themselves in front of publicly installed CCTV cameras, members of the SCP would hold up cardboard signs that announced, in bold lettering, the narrative essentials of their dramas. With these hand-drawn posters they referenced famous literary and theatrical texts, such as Beckett's *Waiting for Godot* and Orwell's *1984*. These signs echoed the Brechtian strategy of using textual titles to summarize plot points in advance of their staging as a means of interrupting habitual expectations of spectatorship. Brecht developed the strategy of interrupting the dramatic action of a play with placards, projections, and songs to remind audiences of the political stakes of the narrative they watched.[15] These didactic interruptions prevented audiences from becoming so caught up in the emotional content that they forgot the political and economic factors that created the unjust conditions under which the characters struggled.

Similarly, the SCP's performance strategies interrupted normalized modes of pedestrian participation in public surveillance in daily life. Rather than pass by the increasingly ubiquitous surveillance cameras that line city streets and urban centers as they normally would, pedestrians were moved to step out of their routines and turn, if only for a moment, to reconsider the role of surveillance cameras in daily life. The SCP described its tactics according to a Situationist-inspired approach to defamiliarization known as *detournement,* or the rearrangement of familiar cultural symbols for politically critical purposes.[16] The SCP claimed, "We detourn the pre-existing 'theatre' created by the placement of surveillance cameras in public places to create a theatre of rebellion and trust, rather than a theatre of conformity and fear."[17] By referring to surveillance as "theater," and its members as "players" the group insisted that everyday surveillance technologies such as CCTV cameras are, like proscenium theaters on Broadway, representational apparatuses with codified modes of spectatorship, performance, and production. As in Brecht's insistence that audiences of realist theater needed to be shaken out of habits that kept them subdued with cathartic narratives and passive spectatorship, the SCP performances threw habitual modes of interacting with—or, more likely, not interacting with—surveillance systems into (comic) relief, making these habits newly visible, available for critique, and open for playful revision.[18]

While the spirit of the SCP's performances was intentionally playful, the messages behind them were quite serious. The stories the actors chose

to stage, from canonical scripts to mundane reports of daily life, constituted important cultural referents for passersby, surveillance guards, and
media covering their performances. Through familiar narratives, they
posed questions about the ethics of watching and being watched, and
the politics of putting faith in entities and powers that cannot be seen.
Their performances of *Waiting for Godot*, a play that depicts two men
waiting for a savior who may or may not actually exist, as well as Orwell's
1984, in which every person's mundane action is monitored and controlled by a watchful "Big Brother," asked passersby to consider cultural
beliefs in entities and powers that cannot be seen. In original pieces,
such as *God's Eyes Here on Earth* (2000), the SCP addressed cameras on
the exteriors of churches with printed text such as "I want God to See
Me" and "Who Is Watching?"[19] In *It's OK, Officer* (2000) their placards
announced mundane events: "Just Getting Lunch," "Just Sightseeing,"
and "Going Home Now."[20] In *We Know You Are Watching* (2000) their
tone was a bit more hostile: "We Know You Are Watching" and "Mind
Your Own Business."[21] And, quite poignantly, in *Amnesia* (2002), with
a script adapted from work of the Australian performance artist Denis
Beaubois, a series of signs was held by a solitary performer: "I HAVE
AMNESIA," "YOU ARE WATCHING ME," "YOU HAVE BEEN WATCH-
ING ME ALL DAY," "EVERYWHERE I GO," "MAYBE YOU CAN HELP,"
and "WHO AM I?" WHAT'S MY NAME?"[22] In each case, the signs held by
the players asserted, with distilled clarity, dramatic narratives, personal
experiences, and existential questions within the context of contemporary everyday surveillance.

In interrupting pedestrian traffic with such announcements, the
players not only dramatized individual experiences of life under surveillance, but they engaged foundational (though often overlooked)
debates about the actual effects of CCTV surveillance in public space.
In their important study of surveillance society, *The Maximum Surveillance Society* (1999), Norris and Armstrong argued that publicly
installed CCTV cameras were not necessarily fulfilling their panoptic
promise; they found that statistical analysis did not support the claims
that cameras functioned as a deterrent for crime (which tended to
serve as the primary justification for their adoption).[23] In fact, as was
suggested by Coleman, the main effect of CCTV surveillance in urban
areas has instead been to promote a neoliberal agenda: economically
empowered individuals who adhere to social norms are encouraged to
occupy (and practice economic consumption in) urban spaces, while
nonnormative, potentially disruptive social subjects are scrutinized,

Fig. 7. Surveillance Camera Players, *God's Eyes Here on Earth*, St. Patrick's Cathedral, New York City, 2000

profiled as potential threats to peace, and removed from public space under the (inaccurate) banner of crime prevention.[24]

The logical underpinnings of this agenda can be traced to one of the most common dictums of surveillance society: "If you have nothing to hide, you have nothing to fear." This saying has its roots in state-sponsored efforts to promote the idea that surveillance cameras are focused on the criminal element—those with something to hide—and *not* on the routine, everyday behavior of "ordinary" law-abiding citizens, those with "nothing to hide" (presumably also the people that would be permitted to "say something," as described above). The problem with this is twofold: first, it encourages the mainstream public to turn a blind eye toward the deleterious, exclusionary effects of urban surveillance, which time and again has been shown to profile and persecute individuals of certain racial, ethnic, gendered, and generational groups. Second, secreted within this notion is the fact that while "ordinary" citizens may have "nothing to hide" they have everything to spend. This second valence supports what Guy Debord theorized as the "Society of Spectacle," which equates proper social participation with capitalist models of conspicuous consumption. In a smart reinterpretation of Debord's Society of Spectacle, cultural theorist Jacques Ranciere has described the politics of contemporary public space (and police surveillance within it) as "antispectacle," asserting that social subjects are interpellated into obedient modes of consumption and usership by modes of perception control and habitual blindness. Replacing the Althusserian model of disciplinary interpellation—in which a policeman's "Hey You!" stops a pedestrian in his or her tracks—with another familiar policing phrase, "Move along! There is nothing to see here!" Ranciere wrote, "The police say there is nothing to see, nothing happening, nothing to be done, but to keep moving, circulating; they say that the space of circulation is nothing but the space of circulation."[25]

To counteract the "antispectacle" and "nothing to see" logic of public surveillance cameras, the SCP overlaid the habitual physicality of theater—in which audiences gather to watch a rehearsed set of actions that are explicitly framed as *something* to see—onto the habitual physicality of subjects of contemporary surveillance, characterized by passing by and *not* seeing.[26] In place of relentless cues to consume and maintain the status quo, the SCP performatively insisted that there *is* something to be seen and said: namely, personal experiences and interior thoughts that typically escape recognition in the deindividualizing and dehumanizing disciplinary ideologies of state and corporate surveillance. As Gabriella Giannachi put it, "[B]y feeding art back to the camera, the players literally interrupt the camera's recording of everyday life and thereby sabotage its attempt to transform us from citizens to consumers."[27] In effect the SCP performed a pointed mockery of the "nothing to hide" dictum. The signboards of *It's OK, Officer* and *Amnesia* announced the "nothing" of everyday life and, in doing so, made visible what the players feared they, and all the other subjects of everyday surveillance, would lose: the right to private thoughts, free speech, and even a sense of one's own identity.

The simplicity with which they staged these conceptual interventions is perhaps the most valuable material contribution of the players. To work against the sprawling scale of contemporary surveillance systems, the SCP brought invisible, networked processes of surveillance back to a smaller, more human scale of individual experience. In effect, the SCP not only arrested passersby but also halted the rapid, digitized flow of dehumanized personal data through surveillance networks.[28] Given the trajectory of contemporary surveillance society, it was unlikely that the SCP's performances would lead to a decrease in the number of surveillance cameras in public space, but they succeeded in modeling alternative uses for CCTV surveillance. Beneath the satirical bent of the SCP performances, there lurked a utopian longing for a different kind of surveillance theater, one in which the spectating ranks of security offi-cers and analysts might actually care about the personal dramas of each passing individual, might wonder how his or her day was going and what emotional insecurities or joys he or she was experiencing. The text that the SCP shared with the CCTV networks radically reimagined surveil-lance cameras as conduits to someone who has the capacity to care about them individually. Instead of technologies of control and normalization, they conjured a world in which "watching over" might mean to care or even trust.

Importantly, the admission price to the SCP's reframed theater of surveillance continues to be mercifully low. Anthropologist and activ-ist Faye Ginsberg has cited access to digital technologies as one of the biggest challenges to wider participation in information age activism.[29] The SCP sidestepped the "digital divide" created through unequal access to digital technologies by creating widely available, user-friendly mod-els of performative resistance. In contrast to more sophisticated digital technologies, which tend to be the property of economically empow-ered classes, publicly installed surveillance cameras are encountered by and accessible to nearly "anyone" in the contemporary Panopticon. In keeping with its open-access models of participation, the SCP actively shares its methods and techniques with amateur "surveillance camera players" around the world. The SCP led tours and provided hand-drawn maps that pointed out all the publicly and privately installed surveillance cameras in a given neighborhood, making the cameras visible as tools of both surveillance and activist performance. Visitors to its website are encouraged to download and copy their projects and ideas freely. The group even published an online handbook titled *How to Stage Your Own "Surveillance Camera Theater" In 10 Easy-to-Follow Steps!* The do-it-yourself (DIY) aesthetic and readily available performance spaces utilized by the SCP illustrate to audiences that critical interventions can be made using only cardboard, markers, and existing publicly installed surveillance cameras.

At the same time, while its work has been highly valuable as a model of alternative participation and DIY performative intervention in public space, the SCP tended not to account for the ways in which an individ-ual's gender, race, and economic class might effect his or her relation-ship with surveillance systems and the laborers that "man" them. Nor, as Harding has convincingly argued, did it attend to rapidly increasing

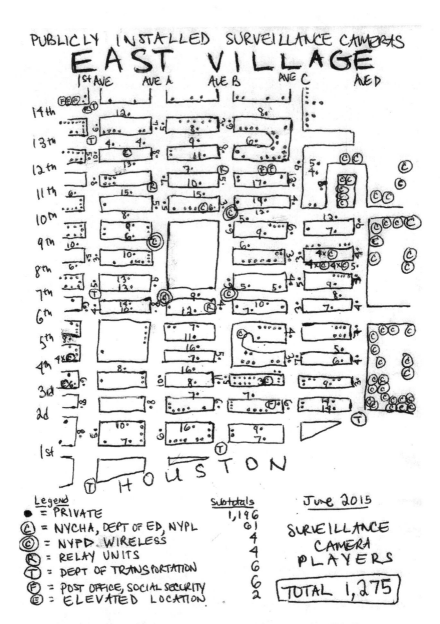

Fig. 8. Surveillance Camera Players, "Map of the Lower East Side," 2015

(and largely invisible) consolidations of power concentrated outside of state-sponsored surveillance, within private industry.[30] As a result, the SCP did not go as far as it might have in critiquing the specific politics of (in)visibility enacted through surveillance in public space. Indeed, it might have done better to stick with its initial focus: the people behind the surveillance cameras themselves. Although the group sought to build a theater of "trust" through its performances, the individual lives, personal prejudices, or ethical responsibilities of the people on the other side of the surveillance cameras remained, by and large, unexplored in its works. Put in terms of another theatrical tactic, the players might have done well to take a page out of Shakespeare's *Hamlet*. In a literary device that is commonly referred to as staging a play within a play, Shakespeare scripted a scene in which Hamlet invites a group of players to pantomime a scene that he hoped would startle his uncle into recognition of the horror and injustice of his actions (his uncle married Hamlet's mother after having murdered his father to become the king). As Hamlet put it in Act II, Scene ii, "the play's the thing / Wherein I'll catch the conscience of the King." With their performances the members of the SCP sought to catch the consciences of passersby and the surveillance guards who, through their participation or passive acceptance, condone the routine surveillance of the streets. However, the "kings"—the ruling elites that employ the guards (who are, often, minimum-wage workers) or the civic law enforcement departments that implement policies about who and what is permissible in public space—tend to go unchallenged.

YES MEN: *Identity Corrections for the Global Elite*

Members of the "culture-jamming" Yes Men have made a business of staging performative interventions that more directly target the "kings" in order to challenge global business practices that exacerbate economic and political inequities. Like the SCP, the Yes Men use theatrical devices of satire and role-play, capitalizing on the slippery relationship between reality and representation that characterizes theatrical performance to destabilize the authority of those that shape surveillance practices from the top down. The techie-activist-performance artists of the Yes Men are known for performing what they call "identity corrections," "impersonating big-time criminals in order to publicly humiliate them."[31] To perform these "corrections," members of the group take on fake roles as experts from established industries, such as the World Trade Organization (WTO), McDonald's, and Dow Chemical, speaking on behalf of these organizations at conferences, trade meetings, and educational institutions. While many of their stunts include outlandish propositions (such as a McDonald's proposal to eradicate Third World starvation with recycled hamburgers created from the excrement of First World patrons), most mimic and exaggerate existing political and economic systems. On their fake WTO website, www.gatt.org (GATT stands for General Agreement on Tariffs and Trade, the forerunner of the WTO), the group offers "corrected" summaries of the WTO's policies. Although they purposefully use terminology that the WTO does not—such as their introduction of a formal slavery model that they call "an initiative for full private stewardry of labor" in Africa—their representations are not entirely false. They are simply more overt about the WTO's support of corporate profit margins over basic human rights around the world.[32]

After they created www.gatt.org, Yes Men founders Jacques Servin and Igor Vamos (aka Andy Bichlbaum and Mike Bonnano, among other pseudonyms) began receiving invitations for speaking engagements and even on-air news interviews as representatives of the WTO. They decided to accept the invitations and present their own version of the WTO's global business philosophy. At a 2001 Textiles of the Future conference in Tampere, Finland, Servin and Vamos impersonated WTO officials invited to speak about textile production in sweatshops around the world. During his presentation, Servin announced that the WTO had designed a wearable solution to two of the largest problems facing corporate managers in multinational corporations: (1) over-seeing a remote work force and (2) maintaining personal leisure. Servin then dramatically stripped off his business suit to reveal the prototype of an "Employee Visualization Appendage," a shiny gold unitard garnished with an inflatable three-foot-long golden phallus with a surveillance monitor on the end of it.[33] As the accompanying animated video explained, managers could comfortably go about their daily leisure activities (on the treadmill, at the pool, reclining on their sofas) while easily watching workers on their monitors, which extended upward from their groins. The actors described the product in their classic tongue-in-cheek manner: "The premise was that managers will be able to see workers in sweatshops and manage them more efficiently. . . . [I]t was a new technology the WTO was introducing."[34]

The suit, designed of course by the Yes Men and not the WTO, was aimed at shocking the corporate audience into critical reflection about accepted business practices surrounding workplace surveillance and the

Fig. 9. Yes Men, presentation at the conference Textiles of the Future, Tampere, Finland, 2001

uneven (and gendered) distributions of power that support them. While the audience chuckled at the theatrical reveal of the suit itself, it otherwise accepted the piece as an actual proposal by the WTO. Sure that their spoof would be called out during the presentation, Servin and Vamos admitted to feeling disappointed that their joke was lost on these highly educated, powerful business leaders. Their goal had been to make a proposal so extreme that their audience would be pushed to recognize the ethical problems of sweatshops, a practice Servin's lecture had satirically argued was even more economically savvy than slavery. Ultimately, the payoff came later, when several internationally distributed news sources, such as *Forbes* and the *New York Times*, ran stories about the hoax, printing glossy photos of Servin touting the golden phallus as the new solution for global industry superpowers.

While surveillance is not the main focus of many of its projects, the Yes Men's work is fundamentally engaged with the politics of watching and being watched, passing and calling out. In a later iteration of their WTO personas, Servin and Vamos traveled to Australia where they announced to a meeting of agricultural business leaders and journalists that the WTO had decided to disband and reconstitute itself with a new, more ethical, humanitarian mission. This falsehood was taken seriously both in and beyond the meeting in Australia, as media reports around the world circulated the breaking news. Several business leaders at the meeting expressed surprise at the announcement but roundly praised the WTO for admitting that it had been going down the wrong path. Circulating, at least for a time, as "real" news, the Yes Men's hoaxes packed lasting punches that were at least somewhat damaging to the ethos of the real corporations and organizations in question. As in Attia's NYPD drone posters, discussed in the "Introduction," and Edit Kaldor's *Point Blank*, discussed in chapter 1, the Yes Men's infiltrations teeter on the edge between real and fake, absurd and normal, thereby throwing seemingly stable ethics and business practices into productive confusion. As I described in the "Introduction," CAE's theory of "recombinant theatre" promotes this kind of playful creation and circulation of *bad copies*, or false informational data. In essence *bad copies* "use elements from the emerging theatre of information and its attendant technologies" to build resistant models of alternative information flow and participation.[35] The ensemble advocates the circulation of bad copies in order to disrupt the stability and truth value of corporate and semiprivatized channels of information.[36] It terms these disruptive practices "virtual theatre" or the "theatre of information," drawing on the tension between real and fake that has characterized debates over theatricality for centuries (see my discussion of this in chapter 1).

Racial, gendered, and economic norms frequently emerge as fodder for the Yes Men's satirical scrutiny. Intervening in normative, commercialized performances of gender was in fact what brought Yes Men founders Servin and Vamos together in the first place. As they describe in their first documentary about their work together, *Yes Men* (2003), Servin had been a video game designer notorious for his programming intervention in SimCity in which a group of male avatars suddenly stripped to their underwear and started making out. Vamos, a professor of media arts at Rensselaer Polytechnic Institute, had recently made headlines with a guerrilla gender-bending action in which he switched the voice boxes in hundreds of GI Joe and Barbie dolls and put them back on store shelves. At Christmas, he recorded children playing (delightedly, I must add) with GI Joes that expressed a love of shopping and hatred of math and Barbies that barked out military commands and her intentions to kill her enemies.[37]

In their escapades impersonating corporate elites, Servin and Vamos utilize their own male gender, bolstered with crisp business suits, buzz cuts, and glasses, to pass as powerful men in charge of running the world. They overtly push their demographic advantage as a means of showing up industry biases and unjust business practices. For example, in their McDonald's recycled burger hoax, which they presented to a class of business school students at the State University of New York, Plattsburg, they unapologetically argued that poor people in the Third World would be thankful to eat burgers made from the human waste of First World McDonald's customers. After members of the class began pushing back against the racist, classist assumptions that the straight-faced Yes Men espoused, the students gradually caught on to the satire; this opened into a frank discussion about unethical business practices and the embedded racism in global development. In this and other of their appearances, the Yes Men make visible the euphemized or hidden assumptions of superiority within male, white, rich, and western-dominated corporate culture.

Like the SCP, Servin and Vamos are invested in helping others perform similar interventions. The Yes Men have created an online forum through which to disseminate their subversive actions and train others to follow suit. In addition to press kits and information about the three feature-length documentaries they have made about the Yes Men's performance work, they have developed the Action Switchboard, an online platform through which interested activists can "propose an idea for an action, receive "Yes Lab" feedback, and solicit help (and funding) from others."[38] They also offer longer-form training sessions for educational institutions, nongovernmental organizations, and other activist groups through their Yes Lab, extending the opportunity for "anyone" to become an active participant.

Magid, Mimicry, and the True Real of Gender under Surveillance

As entertaining and effective as the Yes Men's activist performances have been, even its name evidences the gender bias that continues to operate in the world of activism.[39] As I noted in the "Introduction," within the neoliberal policing of public space, the politics of gender under surveillance has tended to receive scant attention.[40] Magid's *Evidence Locker* and Hannah Price's photography project *The City of Brotherly Love* serve as productive examples of women-led surveillance art that explores the gaze of surveillance as gendered and gendering. These projects interrogate the notion of a desirous gaze of surveillance that twins the disciplinary structures of seeing and being seen. Through embodied performance in public space, they trouble habitual representations of femininity with female bodies that are "given to see" as well as "given to be seen."

Jill Magid's durational performance piece *Evidence Locker: One Cycle of Memory in the City of L*, introduced at the beginning of this chapter, replicated gender norms in order to highlight the often overlooked role of gender within dominant ideologies of surveillance. As in other of her works, discussed in chapter 4, Magid metaphorically combined the "male gaze" of visual culture with the "disciplinary gaze" of state and corporate surveillance. To make this evident, Magid *remediated* the medium of surveillance through the representational forms of cinema and love letters. She layered these more familiar mediums of representation, each with codified modes of expressing (typically heteronormative) desire, onto the supposedly neutral viewpoint of civic surveillance. This tactic makes visible gendered roles and narratives of heteronormative desire that undergird systems of surveillance, security, and discipline in the public space of "the street."

As I have been arguing throughout this book, surveillance is a representational medium that tells certain stories about gender. In her article "Video Surveillance, Gender, and the Safety of Public Urban Space: 'Peeping Tom' Goes High Tech?" surveillance and feminist theorist Hille Koskela argues that surveillance technologies function in the cultural imaginary as devices that at once protect women against sexual assault and promote sexual fetishization of women's bodies through the gaze of a hidden camera.[41] The narrative has been replayed obsessively on big and small screens: a lovely and passive damsel in distress, her innocence threatened by a predatory male figure with nefarious desires, will be rescued by a vigilant, male hero, a "Big Brother" who has been watching all along. Magid's tryst with the Liverpool surveillance system replayed many of these tropes: her letters frequently mentioned feeling safe and desired within the watchful gaze of her "dear observers." At the same time, the cinematic and epistolary media she employed provided Magid with tools she could use to construct her own self-representation of her experience as a woman under surveillance. Her performance and the recorded traces that it left played both with and against normative models of gender, sexuality, and desire, at once revealing and unsettling the gendered power dynamics of surveillance in public space.

A key to unpacking Magid's performative critique comes in one of

her "Dear Observer" letters, in which Magid proposed a piece of cinematic realism as a guide for how her observer should watch her through
the surveillance cameras: "I still need to show you Godard's *Le Mépris*
since you have not seen it. I have selected parts of the film for you. Then
you will know how to follow me like the camera follows her."[42] Jean-Luc
Godard's style has been characterized as a kind of "documentary realism," the goal of which was a "non-fabricated, spontaneous reality."[43] By
simulating spontaneity and naturalistic settings, Godard's films attempted to appear as artifacts of reality, blends of documentary and fiction.[44]
Magid suggested that surveillance cameras could produce a similar form
of "documentary realism" and asked her "Dear Observer" to watch her
according to those conventions.

In so doing, Magid activated a mode of representation that has often
been critiqued by feminist theorists, particularly those associated with
the "second wave" of feminism. Several feminist film and performance
theorists, such as Laura Mulvey, Teresa de Lauretis, Jill Dolan, and Elin
Diamond, argued that part of the repressive function of dominant cinema and theater stemmed from its embrace of the representational techniques of realism. They asserted that realism, while laboring to appear
"real" and natural, is in fact a construction that uses signification, codes,
and conventions to conceal its constructedness.[45] In "Visual Pleasure"
Laura Mulvey argued that in mainstream cinema "the unconscious of
patriarchal society has structured film form."[46] That is, Mulvey argued,
dominant cinema had institutionalized a visual semiotics that posited
the cinematic spectator as male, reflecting and producing the patriarchal notion that women serve as a spectacle of sexual difference to satisfy
and maintain the power position of masculinity; at the same time, those
visual semiotics had the effect of disciplining female spectators into
reductive, surface representations of femininity that could never actually be inhabited. The problem with realism in cinema and theater was
that the spectator is led to believe that the representations therein are
consonant with "reality" rather than distinguishing between, as Teresa
de Lauretis put it, *Woman* (a monolithic fictional construct of idealized
femininity) and *women* (as material, contingent historical subjects).[47]

Feminist theorists and practitioners developed a range of strategies
to identify and resist these processes of naturalizing and identifying with
the male gaze in dominant cinema and theater. In her 1982 essay "Film
and the Masquerade: Theorizing the Female Spectator" Mary Ann Doane
argued that the problem for the female spectator lay in the failure to
maintain a critical distance between the woman audience member and

the Woman portrayed as an image onscreen. Doane posited a solution through an alternative mode of identification in which the female spectator can read and identify with the onscreen "Woman as image" as a masquerade of femininity.[48] Jill Dolan and Elin Diamond articulated similar strategies, recommending Brechtian techniques that highlight and physicalize the usually hidden construction of realist theater and its concomitant patriarchal ideology as as means of building a materialist feminist practice of theater.[49] Drawing a parallel to the Brechtian tactic of "gestus," Diamond argued that a performer can critique realism's claim to truth by making the layers of representation in realism *more* visible rather than less. This mode of layered representation "provides ways to expose illusionism, to pry actor/signifier from character/signified," presenting feminist artists with tactical tools with which to reveal cultural fetishes of femininity *as fetishes*.[50] Diamond distinguishes between *mimesis*, or the replication of normalized signs of gender, and *mimicry*, a critically excessive mode of representation that both shows and disrupts the system of signification: "[T]he sign-referent model of mimesis can become excessive to itself, spilling into a mimicry that undermines the referent's authority."[51] She argued that a feminist form of *mimicry* can expose what she calls "realism's hysteria," as the signs of truth (of normalized gendered behavior, for example) can be themselves exposed as symptoms that have accrued seeming stability and truth value through sheer repetition.

Knowingly mimicking poses and prose from classic Hollywood love stories, Magid made visible the cultural construction of her own body as defined by the male coded gaze of visual culture. Her letters were filled with references to the ways in which she produced her appearance for her observer, always with his watchful gaze in mind: "At home before the mirror, I pinned my hair back and applied concealer around my eyes. I like wearing makeup when I know you will see me . . . . I smoked a cigarette. It was for you and it calmed me down."[52] When she was not "made up" for her observer, she did not wish to be seen: "I didn't want you watching me this morning. . . . I wore no makeup, my hair was a mess, my bag was heavy and pulling me down. I snuck behind your back and ducked into Lewis's Department Store."[53] When Magid and her observer reenacted a scene from Godard's *Le Mépris*, she asked him to direct her in such a way as to capture the alluring elegance of Brigitte Bardot's descent down a long flight of stairs. At another point, Magid described her partnership with her observer as "making love" to the surveillance system, referencing the famous instruction given to fashion models posing for a camera. Preparing for her appearances before the CCTV cameras as if she was performing for a cinematic camera, Magid linked cultural expectations of femininity and desire that lurk beneath the narratives of both cinema and surveillance.

And yet, though Magid seemed to perform a mimicry of classic Hollywood femininity, it would be a mistake to read her work as a confrontational project of entrapment that aimed to catch and shame the male gaze in the act of objectifying her. On one level, she did perform a mimicry of the notion that her identity as a female subject was defined by the gaze of her (male) Observers: "[Y]ou watch me from above. I am your subject; I relate myself to the city by the way you frame me in it."[54] This passage from one of her early "Dear Observer" letters read from a critical feminist perspective sounds like a satirical mimicry of a desperate, lovesick woman who lives to be seen by men. However, Magid's project was also a sincere experiment in relating herself to Liverpool in terms of the way its CCTV system framed her. Her exaggerated gender roles and the overblown romance with her observer was counterbalanced with a desire to use the city's surveillance system to share her own experiences of surveillance, to gain an understanding of the experiences of the surveillers, and, with them, to produce something lasting and beautiful.

Perched precariously between *mimesis* and *mimicry*, Magid's brand of feminism is somewhat ambiguous in its criticism. While she acknowledged the pressures to perform a culturally legible femininity, she did not condemn the disciplinary male gaze of surveillance as objectifying or oppressive. Instead, her words made visible the physical and psychological labor of performing exaggerated representations of femininity. After appearing one day in a blond wig and miniskirt inspired by Bardot's appearance in the Godard film, Magid expressed mixed feelings about appearing in these classic fetishes of feminine sexuality: "[T]here is something about blond hair that makes me feel like a whore. Maybe its because my eyebrows are dark, or the boots. Or the combination."[55] The next day she wrote, "I dressed conservatively to get your respect back."[56] Her strategy was similar to a form of feminist cinema termed "women's cinema" by theorists such as Claire Johnston and Annette Kuhn. Women's cinema used Hollywood's reliance on iconography and traditional portrayals of femininity to make visible the sexist ideology behind the cinematic construction of women.[57] This strategy did not eschew dominant cinematic semiotics but instead used them to display that which was traditionally hidden within mainstream cinema. Spectators were placed in a different relationship with the onscreen images of femininity; rather than being interpellated into the position of the camera, a viewer could

Fig. 10. Jill Magid's *Evidence Locker*, 2004, video still

occupy a position from which she could see the camera's gaze as constructed by patriarchal ideology, thus reading cinematic images and narratives as patriarchal constructions.

Magid's letters supplied such a viewpoint. They served as a means of showing the distance between Woman and woman as they narrated Magid's interior experiences of trying to perform a masquerade of ideal femininity for the CCTV cameras. Her self-representational critique echoed the well-known *Untitled Film Stills* of feminist photographer Cindy Sherman. For *Film Stills*, Sherman photographed her own body in various culturally normative poses, gesturing to familiar narratives of feminine desire, desirability, and victimhood. Feminist film theorist Kaja Silverman posited that the critical power of Sherman's self-framed poses lies in showing the gap between the cultural *ideal* for which the poses reach and the lived *reality* of the bodily conditions that the camera captures.[58] In Silverman's reading, Sherman's camera effectively captured the gap between the *ideal* or *fetish* for which she showed herself reaching and the *real* experience of her failure to attain it. Sherman's failure, however, is productive: Sherman performed a subject inhabiting her own, historically contingent body, while at the same time showing the effort to structure her body according to the expectations of an external cultural gaze. By framing the fraught subject position of a feminist, aware of simultaneous seeing and being seen, Sherman urged the viewer to identify not with the impossible vision of a cultural ideal but rather with the active, vibrant, and problematic attempts of a historically contingent woman to meet that ideal. Similarly, Magid's letters framed the *gap*, drawing the attention of her "Dear Observer" and her broader audience to the distance between her body, which strikes a pose, and the cultural ideal or fetish that the pose quotes. Her letters evidenced the seemingly sincere longing for ideal femininity that Silverman saw in Sherman's photographs. In the letters, Magid made explicit her own desire for Hollywood-inspired models of femininity, mimicking the influence they had on her performance of womanhood. These intimacies stood in stark contrast to the typical disciplinary narratives of a victimized female subject under surveillance or the all-surface representations of femininity in classic Hollywood cinema.

We can gain further insight into the methods of the feminist/feminine criticism Magid employed by looking to an earlier creator of gender focused surveillance art and one of Magid's artistic inspirations. With *Evidence Locker*, Magid followed deliberately in the footsteps of the French visual and performance artist Sophie Calle. Following her abiding fascination with watching and being watched by strangers, Calle created *The Detective* (also sometimes called *The Shadow*) "in order to gain photographic proof of [her] existence."[59] Using her mother as an intermediary, Calle hired a private detective to follow her for a full day, taking surreptitious pictures of her and recording notes about her movements and behavior. Throughout the period of her surveillance Calle recorded her own thoughts, memories, and emotions, producing a detailed, deeply personal account of the places and events she shared with the detective that shadowed her. Her notes emphasized the male gender of her observer and highlighted the libidinal dynamic between watcher and watched: "I want to show 'him' the streets, the places I love. I want 'him' to be with me as I go through the Luxembourg [gardens], where I played as a child and where I received my first kiss in the spring of 1968."[60] In contrast, the detective's notes were brief and clinical. Displayed next to Calle's descriptive entries in the installation and book version of *The Detective*, his notes reduced Calle's day to a series of objective, mundane events. The detective wrote, for example, "At 12:08 the subject leaves the salon and crosses the Jardin du Luxembourg and appears to wait outside Odeon metro station."[61] The notable differences in tone and level of detail between the two accounts clearly highlight differences between information gained through visual surveillance and lived experiences shared through personal writing. Like Magid's *Evidence Locker*, Calle's written accounts made a gentle mimicry of the detective's methods of recording her behavior, as Calle wove together confession, emotional memory, and personal fantasies that contrasted the visual record and factual notes produced by the male private eye. In *The Detective*, as in much of her other work, Calle tenderly pointed out the insufficiency of the gaze of surveillance, which, for all its claims to knowledge and power is unable to truly *see* the subject of its gaze.[62]

As with Magid, Calle's brand of feminist performance is challenging to define. In fact, although her exploration of gender, authorship, evidence, and embodiment resonates with the work of feminist theorists such as Hélène Cixous, Luce Irigaray, Silverman, and Doane, Calle refused to align herself entirely with the feminist theoretical perspectives they expressed. Even while she is often grouped with overtly feminist artists, Calle has denied that she is a feminist in multiple interviews.[63] Calle's work explicitly engages the "male gaze" and the patriarchal ideology of surveillance, psychoanalysis, and Hollywood film, and yet she does so in a way that is qualitatively different from the performance, photography, and film work produced and discussed by most feminist artists and theorists of the 1970s and 1980s. Whereas feminist artists such as Carolee Schneemann, Linda Montano, and Karen Finley aggressively staged their own bodies as art objects in order to reveal the implicit sexual norms that structure visual culture and the observing (male) gaze, Calle embodied seemingly more passive and traditionally feminine roles; appearing as lover, spy, undercover chambermaid, jilted partner, and lonely woman, she performed distinctly feminine identities that both reflect and exceed classic Hollywood representations of femininity. In *The Detective*, despite her position as mastermind of the project, Calle wrote as if from a submissive position, "I keep my eyes lowered. I am afraid to see 'him.'"[64] From this perspective, Calle obsessively studied herself—her body and her thoughts and feelings—under the gaze of classic patriarchal figures such as Sigmund Freud, a male private detective, and various male lovers.

Nevertheless, Calle's work resonates significantly with certain feminist strategies of self-representation and cultural critique. In particular, she performs a tactic of feminist representation known as "voiced writing" or "feminist speech acts," as theorized by Silverman and the linguistic theorist Shoshona Felman.[65] The linguistic strategy of voiced writing, or "writing out loud," is a term coined by the linguistic theorist Roland Barthes to describe forms of writing that reassert the author's body into a text such as a personal diary or journal.[66] Feminists such as Silverman and Felman saw great potential in voiced writing as a means of describing the way the female voice in literature could become a vessel to express and transmit previously dismissed expressions of desire across bodies (both bodies of literature and corporeal bodies).[67] From this Felman developed the idea of a "feminist speech act."[68] Drawing on J. L. Austin's concept of *performative speech acts*—"expressions whose function is not to inform or to describe, but to carry out a 'performance,' to accomplish an *act* through the very process of their enunciation"[69]—Felman examined the female speaking body as a corporeal site of thought and desire, an entity that can both *speak of* and *act on* itself and its desires. Constituting what Felman calls a "scandal," a feminist speech act "is not so much what is *said* or could be said but what is happening, taking effect, producing acts, what is being *done* or could be done between speaking bodies, between languages, between knowledge and pleasure."[70] Felman uses Austin's concept to investigate the radical potential of a feminist speech act, which, as a performative, has "the capacity to *miss its goal* and to *fail to be achieved*, to remain *unconsummated*."[71] This capacity for failure or misfiring in performative speech undermines the philosophical investment in an absolute distinction between the truth or falsity of language—or of surveillance.

Calle's voiced writings, like Magid's "Dear Observer" letters, are characterized by the juxtaposition of documentary photographs and personal narratives shot through with desire. As in Felman's theory of feminist speech acts, they have the effect of destabilizing distinctions between truth and falsity. The black-and-white photographs she displays in *The Detective*, as in other works such as *Appointment with Sigmund Freud* and *The Hotel*, appear to be solidly documentary. However, their authority is slowly corrupted as her stories, laced with fantasies and desires that seem unlikely to have happened and yet cannot be proven *true* or *false*, take hold in the imagination of the viewer.[72] In *The Hotel*, for example, Calle took on the guise of a chambermaid in order to photograph and record the traces that hotel guests left behind in their rooms. Based on the objects they left behind, she imagined what the strangers could have been thinking or feeling or preparing to do.[73] Calle's personal notes, presented as objects collected as part of her socioartistic experiments, are filled with her own fantasies, guesswork, predictions, and desires, as well as those she ascribed to the people she observed. Calle thus situates her audiences as detective-voyeurs, who, like herself, sift through a range of artifacts that cannot be clearly divided according to truth and falsity, self and other, memory and fantasy.

In *The Detective*, the failure of facticity and objectivity is especially significant. In her own description of *The Detective*, Calle stated that she depended on the male gaze of surveillance to provide "photographic proof of her existence."[74] And yet, as Petra Gördüren wrote in *Ctrl [space]*, Calle's true target is "the failure of the 'myth of information.' . . . [H]er investigative pursuits, be they real or invented . . . bear witness to the failure of art to penetrate a stranger's life, to understand and grasp it through observation."[75] Though I would substitute "surveillance" for "art" in Gördüren's statement, she has hit upon the success that Calle has found in failure. Calle's written entries do not function as obedient counterparts to the photographic proofs and clinical notations in the detective's dossier but instead masquerade as deliberately hysteric confessions, feminist speech acts that refuse to be aligned with the causal logic of dominant narratives of surveillance. For Calle there are no innocent clients to be saved by tracking down a perpetrator; her own detective work pursues instead the trails of longing and desire, possibility and memory, and the multiplicity of "truths" stretched between contradictory perspectives.

Calle's investments in the slippery space between truth and falsity, evidence and imagination, shed light on Magid's work, and on her brand of feminism. The pleasure and power of Magid's project lies in the blurred lines between fantasy and fact—one can't be sure which actions, emotions, or thoughts are "real." The important thing is that they all, CCTV footage and voiced writing alike, were, according to her directive, entombed as evidence in the "evidence lockers" of Liverpool's police department. The self-authored portions of Magid's narrative mimicked and exceeded the visual representations of her femininity that were captured by the surveillance cameras of Liverpool, at once doubling and troubling their status as stable evidence of her experiences. Like Calle's voiced writings, Magid's love letters acknowledged her observer's shortcomings with curiosity and tenderness. Even as Magid made it clear that the visual record produced by the CCTV footage could never fully capture or represent her actual experience, her letters demonstrated that she would continue trying to forge connections across that gap.

With all this in mind, Magid's position (and perhaps Calle's as well) can be best located in the murkier territory of third-wave feminism.

While she drew on representational strategies developed by second-wave feminists, Magid, like many contemporary feminists, defied the more stringent lines drawn in that era between dichotomies such as male/female and oppressive/resistant. This position, sometimes (problematically) called "postfeminism," has been notoriously difficult to thematize, in part because of a notable resistance among this generation of feminists to claim a unifying agenda. As R. Claire Snyder put it, "In response to the divisiveness of the sex wars, third-wave feminism emphasizes an inclusive and nonjudgmental approach that refuses to police the boundaries of the feminist political." To do so, third-wave feminism "replaces attempts at unity with a dynamic and welcoming politics of coalition."[76]

The inclusive, multivocal, and also somewhat ambiguous politics of third-wave feminism is well illustrated in another example of street surveillance art by Hannah Price. Price garnered media attention in 2013 with a series of photographs she took of men who catcalled her on the street. She called the project *City of Brotherly Love*, referencing the nickname for Philadelphia where the series was shot. Despite the irony that this title might seem to express, Price meant it as a sincere contrast to the title "My Harassers," which some media outlets, such as the *Morning News*, had assigned to her work.[77] Price saw the project as a means of forging communication and understanding between female subjects and male perpetrators of catcalling. She wanted to use the medium of photography not simply to catch her catcallers in the act but instead as a means of interrupting habitual actions and reactions to catcalling. As she put it, the project "was another way for me to just deal with it on another level besides avoiding it. Sometimes it's easier to just respond and confront people. And then just talking to people, you find out more about them than your initial [impression]."[78] Price did not see her act of "shooting back" with the camera's gaze as a way to stop catcalling; rather, it was a way to make something generative out of an ordinary occurrence that most women either ignore, avoid, or get angry about: "Well, I mean the first initial response is avoiding [it], you don't want to. It's just an everyday thing to men and women, and it was just—yeah—one moment, I just started talking to people and I just realized that I could make their portraits and make something of it."[79]

In many cases, Price said, the men she photographed were not only willing subjects, they were intrigued by her unusual response. While some of her subjects refused her request for a photo, "most of them, the majority of them, respond[ed] quite well just 'cause I'm responding.

Because usually it's expected of me to avoid them so I'm responding. They want a response, so usually they're pretty happy about it—about me talking to them."[80] For herself Price found that the act of taking a photo gave her something active to do in a situation in which many women find themselves trying to ignore or become invisible to the male catcaller(s). Like many women, she found that being catcalled made her uncomfortable, but she did not necessarily wish to make the men who catcalled her feel the same way: "I mean, it's uncomfortable, the act of catcalling. . . . I mean, I think it's kind of dehumanizing. I wasn't trying to dehumanize anyone, it was just a response [to] an experience, . . . I was just trying to . . . point out that we're all human and all confused."[81] When Price would ask the catcaller if she could take his photo, the moment tended to shift from a situation of perpetrator and victim to a conversation between two humans. She felt that the photos allowed her to transform the moment into something positive for both her and the man who had catcalled her: "I ended up making a relationship; I ended up taking time to spend time with people who threw me off guard and ended up making something beautiful out of it." At the same time, she acknowledged that there was also some power in turning a camera on a man who had just catcalled her: "Just turning the photograph on them kind of gives them a feel of what it's like to be in a vulnerable position."[82]

The approach of Price, Magid, and Calle can be elucidated through a later theoretical model developed by Laura Mulvey. Nearly two decades after "Visual Pleasure," Mulvey went on to nuance her former analyses of the Hollywood film industry as a system of patriarchal ideology. In *Fetishism and Curiosity* (1996), she offered an in-depth study of the function of the fetish in relation to the "male gaze" of cinema and visual culture, pairing her critique of habits of patriarchal vision with a novel reading of *curiosity* as a feminist strategy of revision. Mulvey described feminist curiosity as "an active, investigative look, but one . . . associated with the feminine, suggest[ing] a way out of the rather too neat binary opposition between the spectator's gaze, constructed as active and voyeuristic, implicitly coded as masculine and the female image on the screen, passive and exhibitionist."[83] Curiosity, both for the woman represented onscreen and for the female spectator, could thus constitute a way out of the rigid, gendered binary that Mulvey originally saw in the Hollywood apparatus, in which the masculine form was "given to see" and the feminine was "given to be seen." Using the mythical figure of Pandora and her infamous "box" to explore the powerful effects of feminist curiosity, Mulvey constructed the notion of a transgressive feminist gaze: "While

Pandora's surface image, fabricated and fascinating, is highly fetishistic, the inside of the box contains everything that fetishism disavows."[84] In other words, like Pandora, a curious woman can explore both her desirable exterior and her rich, perhaps contradictory interior. As Mulvey put it, "Pandora's gesture of looking into the forbidden space, the literal figuration of curiosity as looking in, becomes a figure for the desire to know. . . . If the box represents the 'unspeakable' of femininity, her curiosity appears as a desire to uncover the secret of the very figuration she represents."[85]

Armed with a Pandorian "aesthetics of curiosity," Magid, Calle, and Price looked inside the conditions of the male-coded gaze of surveillance, both official (CCTV or private detective) and unofficial (catcalling). But rather than unleash a string of misfortunes on the male subjects of the world, they invited the "male gazes" of their "observers" to look with them, enacting what Snyder described as a "dynamic and welcoming politics of coalition" characteristic of third-wave feminism. Price described the aims of her photography in collaborative terms: to start conversations, build relationships, make something beautiful. Similarly, Magid's letters were fueled by an earnest desire not only to be seen but also to understand surveillance as a visual medium through which she and her observers could connect and collaborate as fellow artists. The relationship that Magid brokered with her "Dear Observer" became a collaborative partnership when Magid asked her observer to use the surveillance cameras to direct and film her in a reenactment of a scene from Godard's *Le Mépris*. The scene was a long shot in which Bardot walks down a set of broad stairs on the island of Capri, looking sultry and elegant as the film's femme fatale. Rather than concentrating on mimicking the sultry elegance of Bardot, however, Magid focused more on the collaborative effort between herself and her observer/film crew. In her "Dear Observer" letter of Thursday, February 19, 2004, day 22, she wrote:

> We planned something beautiful. We looked at the steps of the Cathedral through your window, and pulled the window closed. . . . I planned to walk directly up the steps, but you preferred me diagonally, from one corner of the window to the other. We compromised: my way the way up and your way the way down. . . .
> I ran to the house and dropped off my stuff. I wanted to be on the steps with only my handbag. I left my coat open so you could see it move in the wind.

We did the shot 5 times; I walked up and down the stairs for you. Thank you for being patient. I know you like when I go slower. I am sorry I always rush ahead before you are ready. I saw you spinning in circles to find me! It was nice when all the other people went away and it was just the stairs and us. Your directions were really good. The diagonal walk was nice. You did not seem too thrilled on the phone. You think I walk too fast. But I am sure it will be good. We will look tomorrow. Don't worry; it'll be good.[86]

The cinematic reenactment became a mutually produced endeavor that revealed the growing trust between Magid and her observers. Instead of merely mimicking femininity through the view of a cinematic camera, Magid began to use the surveillance system as a means of coproducing a new form of artistic representation.

On another day, Magid had her observer guide her through the busy streets of Liverpool with her eyes closed, using surveillance cameras and an in-ear cell phone to communicate. Magid's description of the experience expressed feelings of interconnectedness with her observer.

I called you. You called me back. I tucked the phone in my pocket and secured the earpiece in place. We were connected, and it was invisible. I told you: I will close my eyes now, and you will walk me there like this. . . .
You told me I looked good, that I looked peaceful, *You look good Jill. You look peaceful,* and asked me how I was.
I like when you use my name.
I said It's easier when you talk to me. Please just keep talking to me. And you did.[87]

At the end of the walk, Magid and her observer lingered in the intimacy of the moment.

I stayed still and kept my eyes closed. I had no desire to open them, no desire to end. I imagined myself as you saw me and let my hands drop to my sides. I felt your approach. You stopped speaking. I could feel when my face filled your window. And you said, *Oh, that's a nice shot.*
And we rested like that, for maybe a minute.
I said, I want to look at you.
You said, *Ok, turn a little to your right. A little more. Yes. Now open your eyes.*[88]

Magid's project imagined for her surveillers a new way to experience watching as well. Her written account of the trust walk described a transformation in attention from the perspective of her surveillant.

> You said, *It's much different, to watch it like this. Things jump out.* You explain: Usually . . . you are also busy with other tasks; you are watching the other windows; you are picking up the phone; you are watching the other yous. But this time, you were responsible. This time, you concentrated. You said, *It's really sensual. You said, Don't take this the wrong way, but it felt a little bit like . . . well . . .*[89]

Filling in the innuendo in another letter, Magid described the growing connection with her observer forged through these collaborative endeavors as "making love" to the surveillance system. However, in contrast to the fraught dictum "make love to the camera," often used as a direction given to fashion models, Magid meant it as a means of caring for and allaying the fears of her observers.

> You are nervous, scared for those above you.
> This city is unique and you want it protected . . .
> And I tell you, hurting the city's reputation is not my intention.
> Neither is it to judge what you do. Let the others do that. I tell you: I did not critique your system;
> I made love to it.
> You blushed.[90]

Magid addressed the emotional life of her observer, attending sympathetically to the anxiety and insecurity that perpetrators of surveillance might feel. She reassured her "Dear Observer" of her devotion to and respect for him, the city of L, and the surveillance system itself.

Set within the frame of her "lovemaking," the CCTV video clips of Magid functioned less as evidentiary verification of her personal narratives and more as mutually produced representations of the deepening partnership between Magid and her observer. Reenacting the scene from *Le Mépris* and doing the trust walk via CCTV were meaningful for Magid and her observer not for their visual elegance or cinematic beauty—in fact, they both acknowledge that the resulting footage was awkward, jolting, and far from the visual pleasures produced by Hollywood—but instead for the intimate, palpable partnership they created between watcher and watched. Using the motif of love letters, Magid reimagined the CCTV cameras lining the streets of Liverpool as the eyes of an attentive creative partner. The typically anonymous and disciplinary relationship between surveillant and surveilled had become an intimate, one-on-one relationship that revealed the viewer and the viewed to one another.

Despite these successes, the project left unexamined some critical issues of sexual normativity, as well as what T. Maureen has called the "invisibility/hypervisibility" of whiteness that conditions the experiences of different individuals under the gaze of surveillance.[91] Magid did not overtly account for certain aspects of her identity that made her endeavor possible: that Magid is white, middle class, and heterosexual placed her within a normative social category that likely smoothed her engagement with the CCTV system.[92] Casting herself to type, she merged her appearance as an "ordinary citizen" with mediatized/cinematized representations of ideal femininity. Her unalarming appearance enabled her to approach it with tenderness, love, and trust because she had, as the dictum goes, "nothing to hide." That said, although this position did not challenge the problems of profiling and discrimination in Liverpool articulated by Coleman, it allowed Magid to explore the potential for surveillance to be generative of something other than totalizing discipline. Ending the project with a distinctly utopian finale, Magid closed her love affair with her "Dear Observer" with a classic fairy tale ending, riding through the streets on the back of her surveillance guard's motorcycle.

Spinning less of a fairy tale, Price used her race and gender more consciously as a means of bridging the gap between watcher and watched. In her National Public Radio interview, Price said that her mixed race identity helped her begin conversations about catcalling: "[B]ecause I'm a black person or a minority, it's easier for me to talk about this subject or make those photographs. And I understand how other people may respond to it." Price elaborated that her race and gender made her familiar with certain kinds of visibility and the complicated ways in which those visible identities influenced social interactions in the streets and other public spaces. As most of the men pictured in her exhibit were also black, Price's camera work not only provided an unexpected response to catcalling, but it also offered a refreshing frame through which black inner city men could be pictured. As numerous recent statistics have shown, racial minorities—and black men in particular—are placed under greater visual scrutiny in urban centers.[93] Price's portraits did not demonize or attempt to discipline the men that catcalled her, but instead sought to represent the relationship in individual human terms.

Like Calle and Magid, Price maintained a productive ambiguity, never fully revealing her stance on the politics of looking and being looked at on the streets of Philadelphia. Vacillating between combative critique and friendly, artistic response to the mild sexual harassment she routinely experienced on the street, Price's photos captured moments of disoriented social relations. The men in her photographs have clearly been caught off guard, their expressions undecided as they wrestle with curiosity, defensiveness, amusement, attraction, or some difficult to describe blend of emotions in reaction to the unexpected reversal that has just occurred before their eyes. While we never get to "see" Magid's observers, her letters give a sense that they, too, were being led down unfamiliar, curiosity-inspiring roads. Viewers of each of these projects are likewise left in the balance, unsure whether the street scenes they have witnessed were the product of mimesis or mimicry, sincerity or satire, reality or imagined utopia.

Conclusion: Postprivate Performances of Sight

The surveillance theorist David Lyon has argued that a foundational problem with contemporary surveillance systems is that they lack a human touch or face. Such individualizing aspects are essential for an ethical, moral society, Lyon asserts, as the face of another human "calls data users to establish trust."[94] Putting a human face on the watchers and watched of urban surveillance systems enacts what Lyon calls a "postprivate strategy," which can counteract the dehumanizing, mechanized, and seemingly anonymous networks of state and corporate surveillance. Coleman concurs, writing, "It is the 'the face' that needs to be brought 'back' into the equation, for it is the face that forms the basis for ethically and morally regulating and humanizing the surveillance society." At the same time, he argues that "it will take more than the presence of the faces and bodies of the oppressed to transform unequal social relations. . . . Rendering visible the faces of those behind the camera lens must also be a priority."[95]

The works discussed in this chapter have aimed to disrupt systems of surveillance and reassert ethical imperatives within them by seeking to humanize faces, experiences, and desires across the typically anonymous surveillant interfaces. Strategies of representation from the SCP's signboards to Price's catcaller photographs show that "arresting" citizens on both sides of the camera can facilitate the potential for human interaction within typically deindividuated social and political surveillance practices. While the interactions described in this chapter were all fairly utopian in their outcomes (none of the performers was arrested or forced to leave), they demonstrated that such strategies can prompt actual interpersonal dialogue across ingrained and divisive social practices. Ultimately, although these performative "citizen's arrests" may not halt the sprawling, larger-than-life systems of surveillance at work in urban centers, such work is valuable precisely because of the small, human scale on which it operates. Seemingly totalizing and connected surveillance systems are, after all, made up of a series of particular instances of surveillance: discrete times and places in which humans interact using tools of vision and communication.

In each case, the performers could have gone further in making visible and accessible the faces behind the cameras that line city streets—faces not only of the "Dear Observers" employed by local police departments but also of corporate elites such as those the Yes Men impersonates. Indeed, future work in this area should make this a priority. Going forward, surveillance artists working in the streets will need to further emphasize the need for human recognition and critically explore the risks of surveillance in public space. This is particularly pressing in biometric surveillance practices such as mechanized facial recognition, as I discuss in chapter 5. Such surveillance systems will only increase their ability to automatically identify and sort individuals according to race, gender, class, and ethnicity, dividing people more decisively between "ordinary" participants who enjoy substantive rewards for their participation and "undesirable" participants who are criminalized, marginalized, and harassed. As city streets become more laden with mechanized surveillance technologies, it will only become more essential to creatively arrest such processes and take the time and space to reimagine ways in which watchers and watched might better communicate and possibly even create "something beautiful" together.

CHAPTER 3

Screens

⎯⎯⎯∾⎯⎯⎯

Thick patches of heavy yellow paint drip from the walls, the floor, the bed, the desk, a small plastic shield guarding a computer. A paintball gun swivels on its mount as it searches for its target: a dark-haired man with a beard and glasses, hunched over the computer. The trigger spasms to life, firing repeatedly at the bidding of an unseen hand. The man flinches slightly but continues typing, one eye on the gun as it swerves in his direction. He is online chatting with the very people who are shooting at him: Internet users from around the world who have taken up his invitation to, in his words, "shoot an Iraqi." The prospect has been disturbingly popular. No paintballs fire but only because the gun's supply has run out. Hackers wrote a code that would turn the remotely controlled gun into a machine gun that would fire without stop, burning through a breathtaking number of paintballs in a matter of minutes. Even without the paintballs flying, the air is tense with the desire for violence, made visible through the restlessly jerking trigger in the paint-drenched room.

This was day 17 of Wafaa Bilal's *Domestic Tension*, a durational performance piece staged in real and virtual space during the spring of 2007.[1] Bilal, an Iraqi born artist living and working in the United States, lived for a full month in a small room in Chicago's FlatFile gallery that year. The room was outfitted with a bed, desk, computer with live internet connection, and a large paintball gun. An online interface invited participants from anywhere in the world to log on, view, and shoot paintballs at Bilal in real time, and to discuss the project directly with Bilal

Fig. 11. Detail from Wafaa Bilal's performance piece *Domestic Tension*, 2007.
(©Wafaa Bilal, courtesy of the Driscoll Babcock Galleries.)

through the project's chat room. In a simulation of the constant surveillance and remote-controlled drone strikes that have characterized the US-led war in Iraq in recent years, the online screenal interface that Bilal and his team built framed Bilal as an enemy target, visible and vulnerable through the sights of the paintball gun at any time, day or night. Utilizing the strategy of "remediation" I introduced in chapter 1, Bilal drew on the familiar rhetoric of multiuser "first person shooter" games to build his performance-based intervention: Bilal staged the hypervisiblity and vulnerability of Iraqis living and dying in the ongoing US-led war, and juxtaposed it against the remote, invisible hands of American soldiers that fired lethal shots, linking that military strategy to casual internet sport of western gamers. Dodging paintballs day and night in the confined space, Bilal sought to physicalize something of the violence and trauma that his family and friends were experiencing in Iraq and, through the chatroom, to share his experience with his attackers. Over the thirty days, the material walls of the gallery became increasingly saturated with yellow paint and the virtual walls of the online chatroom became interactive archives of the fears, anxieties, and concerns of participants from around the world.

There are many layers of political critique and interactive discourse in Bilal's piece that call for in-depth analysis, such as the relationship between simulated and real violence, online gaming and remote-controlled warfare, and the capacity of interactive technologies to facilitate ethical discourse and action among a dispersed set of user-spectators. I discuss these at length later in the chapter. For the time being, the piece serves as an evocative example of surveillance art activism rendered visible through a screenal interface. While the piece could be viewed in person in the FlatFile galleries by those able to make the trip, the interactive screenal interface of *Domestic Tension* was particularly crucial to bringing the multiple registers of violence to visibility. By the end of the month, 65,000 shots had been fired from 136 countries and the website had received over 80 million hits.[2]

A number of artist-activists have similarly utilized screenal interfaces as a means of building new, often transgressive forms of surveillance, mobility, storytelling, and political protest. These include Ricardo Dominguez's reengineered cell phones designed to aid illegal immigrants crossing the border, Steve Mann's wearable technologies of "sousveillance," Coco Fusco's reenactment of a *maquiladora* worker's interrogation, Hasan Elahi's meticulous self-surveillance blog *Tracking Transcience*, the in(ter)ventions the Institute for Applied Autonomy (IAA) has designed for street protesters, and Blast Theory's *Rider Spoke*, an interactively produced site-specific performance. Like artists working in "the streets," discussed in the previous chapter, these artists and activists critically re-vision—that is, they at once bring to visibility and reimagine habitual uses of and interactions with—surveillance technologies in everyday life. They tackle aspects of surveillance that have been hidden or made invisible in order to maintain and protect dominant state and corporate interests; these areas include the emotional and physical hardships of immigrants and migrant workers in the US-Mexico borderlands, the power structures of state and corporate surveillance, racial profiling in the name of national security, and shadow partnerships among state, corporate, and social software systems of surveillance.

I have termed their spaces of performance "the screen" because these artists tend to utilize technologies that are mediated through some kind of a screenal interface, be it an Internet browser window, a video game interface, or a cell phone screen. Moreover, the concept of "screening" points to strategies of both invisibility and hypervisibility, as the verb *to screen* can indicate the intention to either display or hide. The panoptic principle, developed by Bentham and famously theorized by Foucault, is expressed through this dual meaning of the term *screen*: the architecture of the Panopticon depended on strategically displaying or hiding disciplinary operations through distinctly visible or invisible bodies and spaces.[3] In a contemporary context, the screens of surveillance similarly engage the two seemingly contradictory meanings of the term: they display and visibly cue or, to use Robin Bernstein's notion of "scriptive things," they "script" proper usership, even as they hide disciplinary mechanisms that condition and track user engagement.

That screens instruct and accustom users and audience members to desired modes of spectatorship and behavior is certainly not new. As Walter Benjamin and other early-twentieth-century thinkers argued, the advent of cinema served to acclimatize the viewer's senses to the conditions of modern life, training the industrial worker to negotiate the onslaught of stimuli that characterized both factory and city life.[4] Today, Internet screens similarly prepare contemporary viewers for the participatory labor of surveillance society. Digital interfaces that we routinely use for commerce, communication, entertainment, and travel encourage (or more often require) our participation and reward us for it with a sense of personal ownership and connectivity. And yet, while the software interfaces of digital technologies seem to promise the ability to follow one's own desires and interests, they subtly limit a user's behavior, choices, and outcomes, all the while tracking personal information and providing a perpetually accruing data pool for state and corporate surveillance. Thinking along these lines, the techno-cultural theorist Wendy Chun has insightfully analogized digital software interfaces to ideology, noting that "software and ideology fit each other perfectly because both try to map the material effects of the immaterial and to posit the immaterial through visible cues."[5] That is, the software interfaces of personal computers, tablets, smart phones, automated teller machines (ATMs), and numerous other screens we encounter on a daily basis provide material markers through which users are cued to interact with and understand the (typically invisible) operations of digital technologies. Recalling Jacques Ranciere's theory of the "antispectacle" of public space discussed in chapter 2, user-friendly software interfaces tend to reference and reinforce corporate built environments and hypervisible advertisements that move pedestrians on predetermined routes through commercial public space.[6] Shopping malls and social software interfaces alike are visually streamlined to ensure that there is nothing to slow one's constant circulation as a consumer; at the same time, these interfaces are designed to deny users the time or space to stop and consider alternative, potentially subversive uses for the technologies.

The prevalent ideology of participation through user-friendly software in contemporary digital culture has been accelerated by (even as it has helped to accelerate) recent shifts in state and corporate surveillance strategies. Centralized architectural systems of panoptic discipline have given way to more dispersed, fluid, (in)dividualized, virtual, and algorithmic modes of control. These offer benefits of increased efficiency in communication, commerce, and geographic mobility that tend to cover over the risks of networked, dynamic surveillance.[7] Contemporary surveillance theorists have argued that the lack of transparency in the processes by which surveillance data are gathered, shared, and acted has become the most insidious aspect of contemporary surveillance systems. This aspect of dataveillance, sometimes called "panoptic sorting," is so dangerous because individuals may not even be aware of the effects on their daily lives.[8] As Wood and Graham put it, "these techniques of prioritization and inhibition are often so invisible and automated that neither the losers nor the beneficiaries are even aware that they are in operation within the complex socio-technologies that increasingly constitute the ordinary and taken-for-granted environments of contemporary societies."[9] While it is not difficult to observe the ease with which first-class or Global Entry–approved travelers move through check-in or customs lines, the means by which other passengers are deemed to be low or high risks remains a mystery.[10] The cloak of invisibility falls even more densely on virtual environments, such as online call centers, as individuals will likely not realize that their Internet or phone wait time is a result of the prioritization they have received based on real-time, corporate judgments of their potential profitability. Such systems result in what is known as "differential mobility," a social order that threatens to subtly yet decisively divide contemporary societies into classes of high-speed, high-mobility "kinetic elites" and disconnected citizens further disadvantaged by barriers to mobility and limited economic opportunities.[11] The relative invisibility of surveillance networks that enable processes of social sorting makes the discriminatory effects all the more alarming. Assessments of personal data, performed in virtual obscurity by various interconnected state and corporate entities, come back to bear on the material lives of social subjects in the form of open doors or impermeable barriers to mobility, opportunity, political visibility, and legal recourse.[12]

The works analyzed in this chapter stage (via the screen) the sometimes subtle, sometimes glaring differences in mobility, access, and connectivity that various social subjects experience within and across surveillant interfaces. I have organized the works of surveillance artists-activists working across a range of screens into three main categories based on their strategies of representation and audience engagement. The first category is characterized by artists who appropriate and physically rebuild familiar screenal interfaces in order to redirect surveillant capabilities and usership toward politically subversive ends. I refer to these as "user-*un*friendly in(ter)ventions" because, while the reengineered technologies are in fact quite easy to use—they tend to employ technologies with which a large percentage of people are familiar such as online video games, social media platforms, surveillance cameras, cell phones, and GPS mapping—artists-engineers such as Ricardo Dominguez, Steve Mann, and members of the IAA create user interfaces that are pointedly *un*friendly toward dominant systems of commercial surveillance, information exchange, and state-sponsored violence. They bring to visibility the military involvement in the development and manufacturing of civilian digital technologies, challenge hierarchies of state and corporate surveillance that require everyday consumers and citizens to sacrifice their privacy, and intervene in the high-risk act of illegal border crossing by providing immigrants with tools that support their arduous journeys. As I discuss at more length below, "user-unfriendly" artists tend to borrow from practical and theoretical models developed by participants in the avant-garde situationist movement, such as *detournement* and *derive*, as well as other tactics shaped by contemporary "hacker ethics" and "open source culture," to build alternatives to familiar surveillance technologies in the everyday world.[13]

In the second category, which I call "re-visioning rights," artists-activists create online performances that counteract strategies of invisibility within dominant processes of surveillance and discipline. Works in this category, including Bilal's *Domestic Tension*, take to task the ethical and technological failures of systems of surveillance to accurately remember or make visible the lived experiences of marginalized or maligned people. I examine works by Bilal, Hasan Elahi, and Coco Fusco, each of whom uses performance models of reenactment, online gaming, and participatory surveillance (often in the form of social media) to bring to visibility perspectives that have been covered over by political and economic elites invested in protecting their own interests. From the significant military involvement in designing and producing civilian-consumer surveillance technologies to the discriminatory and often violent effects of state and corporate surveillance systems on particular racial, gendered, and economic groups, their works counter strategies of political oversight and "percepticide."[14] These artists labor to create their own methods of making personal memory visible, thereby undermining the often obscured and unjust methods and effects of surveillance used by state and corporate entities.

The third strategy, "new dramaturgies of the screen," describes the work of artists that use screenal interfaces to create new models of storytelling. Works in this final category utilize formal properties of surveillance technologies to create alternative narratives and structures of representation and re-vision. *I Love Alaska* (2009), an unconventional online film created by Lernert Engelberts and Sander Plug, takes as its source material a notorious data leak in 2006 in which three month's worth of search queries by over 650,000 AOL users were accidentally made available online; the British theater group Blast Theory's *Rider Spoke*, which debuted in the Barbican district of London in 2007, weaves geotagged narratives recorded by users through mainstream surveillance screens. Though quite different in their ethical and aesthetic approaches to their source material, both pieces frame state and corporate surveillance technologies as media of representation that, while not necessarily revelatory of radically "new" content, offer uniquely contemporary forms of narrative structure, character development, and audience reception.

User Unfriendly: Surveillant In(ter)ventions

THE IAA, AND THE MODERN DAY TROJAN WAR

The IAA, a collective of artists-activists-engineers who have worked together since 1998, has made a political practice of appropriating and redesigning military robotic systems and surveillance interfaces in order to combat state and corporate control of privatized space. A self-described "technological research and development organization dedicated to the cause of individual and collective self-determination," its mission has been "to study the forces and structures which affect self-determination and to provide technologies which extend the autonomy of human activists."[15] By reengineering existing surveillance technologies and interfaces, the IAA transforms familiar digital technologies into "user-unfriendly" tools with which to ambush and disrupt the smooth flow of capitalist systems of commerce and surveillance. The IAA has consequently termed its products "Trojan horses," applying the term from the Bronze Age story described by Virgil in his epic poem *The Aeneid* more broadly to mean any trick that causes a target to invite a foe into a securely protected area.[16]

The name "Trojan horse," while somewhat playfully applied, prompts the IAA's audiences to look again at contemporary society, what we might think of as a digital-age Troy. Cast as unwitting Trojans asleep in our beds, we trust that the gifts showered on us by advances in digital technologies—gifts of credit cards, online banking, EZ-passes, and cell phones—are boons to our social, political, and economic lives. Yet the benefits we gain from these user-friendly personal gadgets and software systems have led most of us to forget that these digital gifts to civilian life and leisure are, quite literally, the fruits and spoils of war. Nearly all the digital technologies that we enjoy are the products of particularly rapid advances in surveillance technologies and techniques developed for military purposes.[17] While this in and of itself is not condemnable (after all, Silly Putty and the Internet have transcended their initial development for military use), connections between consumer and military markets have been largely obscured as surveillance technologies have been redesigned and marketed as tools of communication, commerce, and entertainment. Such practices shroud ethical questions regarding military involvement in civilian life in the shadowy balance between commercial benefits and martial costs.

As ethically engaged engineers, members of the IAA are thus committed to making visible the military background of civilian surveillance technologies. In some cases this commitment involves airing covert partnerships between military agencies and private contractors. In its project *Terminal Air*, the group sought to uncover interconnections between government agencies and private contractors involved with the extraordinary rendition program of the US Central Intelligence Agency (CIA), through which suspected terrorists have been captured and held in secret locations where they are tortured and interrogated. The IAA described the background of the project as follows.

> A thoroughly modern enterprise, the extraordinary rendition program is largely carried out using leased equipment and private contractors. These private charter planes often use civilian airports for refueling, making their movements subject to public record and visible to anyone who knows which tail numbers to look for. . . . With

only the knowledge of what these planes have been used for in the past, human rights activists are left to view their movements as a vast "black box" and can only speculate whether any specific plane is currently carrying human cargo en-route to being tortured in a so-called CIA "dark prison."[18]

The project, created in collaboration with artist-activist Trevor Paglin, featured both an online interface and a gallery installation. The installation envisioned the CIA's extraordinary rendition program as a sinister travel agency based in Langley, Virginia. Two large wall displays show the flight information of some thirty corporate planes that have been identified as CIA partners. The website allows users to pull up a similar map and data feed, which includes more up-to-date information on the movements of these planes.

In other projects, the IAA reasserts military tactical language into civilian operations, performing what it calls "militarized appropriation of consumer technology by civilian actors."[19] Robotic in(ter)ventions such as LittleBrother and GraffitiWriter borrowed military combat tools and strategies and applied them in civilian political protest situations. Their robotic invention LittleBrother—which rhetorically miniaturized the Orwellian propaganda machine of Big Brother—is a redesigned copy of a military robot designed to go where soldiers cannot. The IAA took this military idea and redeployed the design to infiltrate areas of "denied access" within public space, such as malls, public parks, and squares. The robot was designed to go where it is not safe for protesters and activists to go; once inside, it functions as a propaganda machine, capitalizing on its "robotic cuteness" to distribute subversive pamphlets.[20] Graffiti, like subversive pamphlets, can involve a risky process of infiltrating spaces that have become increasingly privatized and surveilled. The IAA robot GraffitiWriter is a reimagined Mars Pathfinder mounted with five orange spray paint cans and a 16K brain; it can tag surfaces on the street, in a park, or even on indoor carpet. In a 2002 interview with Erich W. Schienke, one of the IAA members described the logic of GraffitiWriter: "Due to surveillance a person can't really go in and tag a bank or a shopping mall, so we intended to make a disposable robot that an activist could use instead."[21] With these street-ready inventions the IAA pointedly redeployed military surveillance technologies to actively support the strategies of political protesters. Rather than fully demilitarizing the surveillance technologies (as corporate entities have done with RFID tags, cell phones, and consumer GPS technologies), the IAA carried over the combative strategies and military tactics associated with them in order to provide aid in civilian activist scenarios.

In its article "Defensive Surveillance: Lessons from the Republican National Convention," the IAA described its projects as specifically designed to support civilian activist strategies: "Activists counter police tactics with increasingly sophisticated tools and strategies. . . . These tactics rely on intelligence gathering and information sharing to coordinate actions and react quickly to changing conditions."[22] For example, the group developed TXTmob, a cell phone software application designed to assist protesters during the 2004 Republican National Convention in New York City to more efficiently and safely perform the protest tactic "swarming." Swarming is a tactical model described by military theorists as "the dispersion of command among many small, autonomous units that are able to collectively attack an enemy from all directions."[23] TXTmob facilitated a more decentralized approach for the protesters, helping them to revise their tactics in response to changes in those of riot police. Activists using TXTmob at the convention utilized "command and control" techniques that were similar to DARPA's vision of small, highly mobile groups of soldiers that can use communications technologies to "identify and engage moving targets at moments of heightened vulnerability."[24] The IAA described the success of TXTmob in the political protest scenario as follows.

> Significant [TXTmob] traffic was dedicated to identifying undercover officers, reporting on police activity, and monitoring delegate movements. This enabled activists to coordinate a variety of actions across the city. Warned of police blockades and impending mass arrests, spontaneous demonstrations dispersed at a moment's notice, only to regroup minutes later several blocks away. Responding to reports of police violence, independent journalists were dispatched to videotape arrests all over the city, providing documentary evidence of police misconduct. Text message reports of delegates sitting down to brunch in quiet East Side restaurants resulted in groups of more than fifty demonstrators waiting to greet them by the time the check arrived.[25]

Other products are more symbolic than combative. Following the Situationist tactic of the *derive*, which was predicated on a deliberately undisciplined walk through urban space,[26] the IAA's iSEE smart phone application gives users the opportunity to navigate urban centers according to an antidisciplinary pathway. For iSEE the IAA used real-time GPS mapping technologies (originally developed by the military for use in combat situations) to provide civilian users with a software interface that can interactively map "the path of least surveillance" through urban centers around the world.[27] This software system can be downloaded for free onto any wireless tablet or smart phone, allowing mobile users to avoid as many publicly installed surveillance cameras as possible.

In its discursive publications, the IAA critiques mainstream portrayals of civilian surveillance systems as unbiased, logical, and ethically neutral. To correct these assumptions, it urges users and engineers alike to ask what ideological viewpoints are programmed into the software systems that govern surveillance practices. Who or what entities are responsible for the discriminatory and disciplinary effects of surveillance? In *Engaging Ambivalence: Interventions in Engineering Culture,* the IAA confronted the "service industry" mentality of engineers who develop products regardless of the political aims of their employers. The article critiqued assumptions that technology is "value neutral" and technological development is "an ethically indifferent activity."[28] To help this message reach software engineers, the IAA routinely circulates its subversive products in academic and engineering trade journals and conferences, aiming to start conversations with professional engineers on the ground about the ethical ambivalence that surrounds the engineering and marketing of surveillance technologies.

In all its efforts, the IAA embraces the ability of humor to engage audiences that might otherwise remain stuck in their habitual approaches to social and political issues surrounding surveillance technologies. Infusing its products with a touch of the absurd allows the group to more easily engage industry engineers in discussions about the ethics of product development and cultural applications. In an interview about its conversations with engineers, members of the IAA said:

> It's always been that we need to have a very pointed conversation, but at the same time we're not going to let you know exactly where it's coming from. We want people to ask, is this "real" or is it not? We try to get that experience to vibrate between those two poles. The content is real, the message is sincere, the robots—they're real, the stuff we say we do we do. But at the same time people see no apparent rational explanation or profit motive, so they just don't understand . . . (*laughing*).[29]

The commercial "irrationality" of its products makes the IAA unthreatening as a market competitor; at the same time, these sophisticated, functional products gain the group entry into legitimate engineering circles. By modeling politically subversive uses of surveillance technologies, the group makes visible normative ideologies that are embedded in more mainstream surveillance interfaces. While profit motives will no doubt continue to fuel DARPA-funded engineering projects in civilian markets, the IAA provides a valuable, alternative model for ethically engaged design and usership of surveillance technologies.

STEVE MANN: RECUPERATION, REFLECTIONISM, AND SOUSVEILLANCE

Dr. Steve Mann, a professor in the Department of Electrical and Computer Engineering at the University of Toronto, is similarly committed to designing and circulating alternative models of surveillance. He has spent the last three decades developing a range of wearable surveillance devices that reverse the gaze of dominant, disciplinary surveillance. In his discursive and engineering projects Mann has argued for the abolition of hierarchy in surveillance culture, stating his ideal as a society in which everyone would watch everyone else through instruments of surveillance that would be distributed at all levels of society. To describe this social architecture Mann coined the term *sousveillance,* substituting the French *sous* (below) for *sur* (above).[30] Mann has integrated this challenge to sociopolitical hierarchy into his own life: he requires identification scans of police officers in order to access his own personal information (his ID wallet will literally not open unless another ID is scanned).[31] In his ongoing Glogging project, the name he has given his cyborg log, he lives with an "eye-tap" device secured to one of his eyes, which broadcasts everything he sees on a website.[32]

In order to disseminate his theory of sousveillance, Mann has developed a line of functional dome-style surveillance cameras, which he calls "wearcams," or "SixthSense" technologies, that can be easily worn by users in everyday life. He has affixed these sousveillance cameras to backpacks, pendants, shirts, and even a bra (see chapter 4 for an analysis of the gender politics of the "wearcam bra"). In this ongoing project, which he has titled *Shooting Back,* he encourages participants to wear these hypervisible, mobile surveillance cameras to school, work, and in semi-public spaces such as shopping malls.

By transforming surveillance interfaces into personal accessories, Mann's wearable cameras aim to start difficult conversations with peo-

Fig. 12. Steve Mann's
Synthetic Synesthesia of
the Sixth Sense, 1998

ple who may be unconsciously replicating the disciplinary norms of
surveillance society. If the motives of a wearcam user are questioned,
Mann instructs the user to explain that they are wearing the sousveillance cameras in accordance with the orders of their supervisor from the
local Safety Management Organization (SMO). With this logic, Mann
attempts to pit two hierarchical structures of vision and power against
each other in order to show that the the disciplinary power structures of
the shopping mall (and other privatized public spaces and institutions)
are as combative and arbitrary as his own. He explains:

> [I]f an INDIVIDUAL complains about video surveillance systems in
> use by a CLERK, then the CLERK will simply refer the INDIVIDUAL

to management, and management will likely be available only during certain limited hours and only after extensive delay. . . . However, if the INDIVIDUAL takes out his or her own personal handheld camera and photographs the CLERK, indicating that the SMO requires it, . . . quite often the MANAGER will immediately become available.[33]

Mann calls this tactic "empowerment through self-demotion," writing, "[I]n the same way that clerks facilitate empowerment of large organizations, I was able to facilitate personal empowerment by being a clerk. My self-demotion provided a deliberate self-inflicted dehumanization of the individual that forced clerks to become human."[34] His reimagined hierarchy of power—in which an imaginary supervisor requires him to wear the sousveillance camera around his neck when shopping—is clearly invented, and yet Mann uses it to performatively challenge the equally abstract and dehumanizing hierarchy of surveillance in corporate public space.[35]

As entertaining and provocative as these tactics may be, Mann's sousveillance theories and practices have prompted spirited criticism by surveillance theorists. His in(ter)ventions have provoked questions about the efficacy of his strategies of appropriation and reversal. Despite the implied ideological opposition to dominant systems of surveillance, sousveillance has been critiqued as a reproduction, and even an expansion, of the disciplinary aims of state-sponsored surveillance. Theorists such as Gary T. Marx have argued that countersurveillance tactics such as Mann's merely expand a panoptic system (the few watching the many) into a synoptic system (the many watching the many), a process, he asserts, that does not in fact alter the foundational disciplinary operations of surveillance. Rather, Marx argued, a synoptic—or, for Mann, sousveillant—system only expands the panoptic principle and its disciplinary operations, re-creating and multiplying the problem in dispersed, miniature structures.[36]

The controversy over Mann's sousveillance—and countersurveillance techniques in general—echoes the quandary posed by the feminist scholar-activist Audre Lorde in her 1979 essay "Can the Master's Tools Dismantle the Master's House?" Lorde, writing from the perspective of a black, lesbian feminist, answered her own question with the statement "[T]he master's tools will never dismantle the master's house," arguing that language and its disciplinary operations have been constructed by means of patriarchal logic and social hierarchy to such a great degree that they cannot be redeployed to attack white, male, heterosexual systems of power and knowledge production.[37] Mann's theoretical model of sousveillance attempted instead to answer Lorde's question in the affirmative: he took tools of surveillance and reconfigured them in order to critique and restructure the unbalanced power structures in contemporary surveillance society. However, as the visual studies scholar Kirsty Robertson has argued, the efficacy of Mann's strategy of sousveillance depends on and reinforces a patriarchal, privileged subject position that may in fact replicate rather than counter dominant power structures.

> Echoing feminist debates from the 1970s over the one-way power of a gendered gaze and scopophilial pleasure, many responses to surveillance follow an often invisibly gendered virtualization of the omniscient male gaze through increasingly intangible systems of power. It would seem that the work of Steve Mann, Bill Brown, and the Surveillance Camera Players, Denis Beaubois, and others is involved in recapturing the gaze and, as often as not, of resituating it in a series of prosthetic eyes—cameras, glasses, and lenses that attempt to return the gaze to a re-empowered viewer. Given the relative privilege of those able to engage in projects that take on surveillance I wonder at the focus on the gaze—do such projects contest the power of surveillance or simply replicate it?[38]

I take up Robertson's feminist critique at more length in chapter 4 with regard to Mann's *HeartCam* a set of dome-style surveillance cameras, which, when worn, function as a pair of prosthetic breasts "enhanced" with the power of sousveillance. Applied to his strategies more broadly, Robertson's critique suggests that Mann's work is at risk of reproducing dominant cultural ideologies and structures, even as he, in the words of feminist scholar Judith Butler, attempts to perform "a different sort of repeating" through the practice of sousveillance.[39]

The Situationists, after whom Mann has modeled his approach to intervening in corporate- and state-controlled public space, encountered similar criticisms. The Situationist International group used the term *recuperation* to critique an insidious capitalist strategy of cultural reproduction and control by means of which dominant capitalist entities take up subversive ideas or images and repackage them to be marketed on a mass consumer level.[40] In the process of recuperation, a politically subversive idea or image is turned into a corporate brand or commodity that can be purchased rather than enacted, thus becoming depoliticized.[41] The commercial recuperation of revolutionary ideas or images literally transposes subversive products into storefronts, presenting them in highly visible corporately controlled spaces and in forms that can be purchased by consumers. The result increases the financial power and political security of the corporation that displays them. The situationists found this process particularly threatening to their own political aims in that dominant bourgeois culture could recuperate revolutionary aims and tactics of the situationist movement itself and use them in procapitalist projects.[42]

Mann's logic of sousveillance is similarly risky, as it mirrors the justifications used for state-sponsored surveillance even as it attempts to critique them. In a move that echoes the well-known state-sponsored "If you see something, say something" campaign, Mann has argued that sousveillance is a potential antidote to current threats of terrorism, claiming that the more people watching the better.[43] His definition of *sousveillance* employs what could be read as politically conservative language, as he describes the tactic as "watchful vigilance from underneath."[44] Similar language is often used in politically conservative nationalist movements in the United States. In a controversial example of conservative "vigilance from beneath," a service called blueservo.net gave users access to a series of surveillance cameras along the Rio Grande. Created by the Texas Border Sheriff's Coalition, the service partnered with the private company BlueServoSM to crowd-source a virtual border patrol. Users can log on to become "Virtual Texas DeputiesSM" and participate in guarding the US-Mexico border.[45]

Mann has defended his position by claiming that sousveillance is a form of "reflectionism," referring to a combative use of technology to mirror and confront bureaucracies and authoritative organizations such as police agencies. He wrote, "Reflectionism seeks to increase the equality between surveiller and the person being surveilled (surveillee), including enabling the surveillee to surveil the surveiller."[46] With his redoubled use of *surveil*, Mann argued that reflecting tools of authoritative organizations in a deliberately disorienting manner is an effective way to critique and undermine dominant systems of surveillance. However, his thickly refracted language reveals the unwieldiness and precariousness of his tactical approach. Sitting somewhere between the politically transgressive *detournement* and corporate recuperation, sousveillance may be a flashy technological distraction that does little to actually change the normative systems of discipline and corporately controlled usership. If, as critics claim, sousveillance is a doomed strategy of ever-increasing surveillance, then the most effective aspect of Mann's critique of contemporary surveillance society may be his spectacular performance of its absurdity. Fueled by the hope that exaggerated versions of surveillance can be used for serious interventions—or, to borrow Lorde's language, that the master's tools *can* have some use beyond supporting the master's ideological fortress—Mann has built a structure of funhouse mirrors through which disorienting, ridiculous, and slightly terrifying images of contemporary surveillance society peer back. Intentionally or not, his sousveillance technologies perform the absurdity of surveillance society. It is doubtful that sousveillance will bring an end to surveillance, but it serves as a convincing sign that the monster has begun to eat its own tail.

DR. RICARDO DOMINGUEZ:
ON CALL AT THE US-MEXICO BORDER

Like Mann, Professor Ricardo Dominguez of the University of California, San Diego, has retooled existing consumer technologies, but he does so with a more directed political agenda. A member of CAE since the 1980s and a founding member of EDT, Dominguez is dedicated to creating a range of activist events and tools, which he (and the CAE in a publication with this title) calls "electronic civil disobedience" (ECD). Building on the more familiar activist concept of "civil disobedience," the ECD

> is a nonviolent activity by its very nature, since the oppositional forces never physically confront one another. As in CD [civil disobedience], the primary tactics in ECD are trespass and blockage. Exits, entrances, conduits, and other key spaces must be occupied by the contestational force in order to bring pressure on legitimized institutions engaged in unethical or criminal actions."[47]

Dominguez and the EDT have organized numerous acts of ECD and "hacktivism," ranging from a series of virtual reality sit-ins to reengineered tools of political dissent.

Of these, Dominguez is best known for his *Transborder Immigrant Tool* (TBT), a project that gained national attention in 2009–10 when it became the subject of a Federal Bureau of Investigation (FBI) investigation. With the TBT, Dominguez reimagined the user interface and purpose of GPS technologies in one of the most ubiquitous consumer technologies: the mobile phone. To create the TBT, Dominguez and his b.a.n.g. lab at USCD gathered cheap cell phones and redesigned them as mobile GPS devices that helped Mexican immigrants cross the US-Mexico border. In a 2009 interview with *Vice* magazine, Dominguez described the TBT.

> We looked at the Motorola i455 cell phone, which is under $30, available even cheaper on eBay, and includes a free GPS applet. We were able to crack it and create a simple compasslike navigation system. We were also able to add other information, like where to find water left by the Border Angels, where to find Quaker help centers that will wrap your feet, how far you are from the highway—things to make the application really benefit individuals who are crossing the border.[48]

The inclusion of GPS was intended by cell phone manufacturers to help users navigate urban and commercial centers, find friends and favorite businesses, or, in criminal cases, enable state and federal agencies to track and monitor cell phone users. In contrast, Dominguez reformulated the ideological construction of widely accessible GPS-enabled cell phones, turning them into tools to make high-risk border crossing a safer, technologically supported endeavor.

As evidence of its political power, TBT soon caught the attention of the FBI. Beginning early in 2010, Dominguez and the b.a.n.g lab, already under investigation by UCSD for several virtual reality sit-ins, were investigated by the FBI's Office of Cybercrimes.[49] The series of institutional investigations prompted debates across a range of national media regarding academic funding for political art projects and "irresponsible" uses of technology by artists.[50] Although the broader consequences of the federal and university-led investigations of Dominguez's activities are certainly cause for concern over civil liberties, the conversations and media attention they provoked had the benefit of bringing his arts-activist tactics more fully into (inter)national media headlines and political discourse.

The most threatening and powerful aspect of the TBT was the way in which it reframed the ideological stakes of illegal border crossing. Instead of focusing on the (il)legality of border crossing, Dominguez sought to make visible (but not too visible) the multidimensional humanity of immigrants crossing the border, and to address the devastating risks that such a journey poses to the bodies and minds of Latino immigrants. Once activated, the cell phone would emit a single ping to a GPS satellite (more than one ping would enable officials to track the location of the user) and then load an up-to-date map of water locations and potential

Fig. 13. Electronic Disturbance Theatre/b.a.n.g. lab, Transborder Immigrant Tool, 2007

help stations. Slyly reinterpreting "GPS" to mean the "global poetics system,"[51] the cell phones were also outfitted with audio tracks that shared practical survival tips for the desert journey and poems about fortitude and endurance. From an ideological perspective, the poetics loaded into the screenal interface were as important as the phone's geolocative capabilities, as both supported the often marginalized or overlooked needs of immigrants in the borderlands. While Dominguez and EDT acknowledged that the TBT is "incapable of resolving the long histories of fear, prejudice and misunderstanding on both sides of the Mexico-US border,"[52] the retooled phone provides a practical and symbolic model for activism in public space through artistry and engineering.

This project, as well as the virtual reality sit-ins EDT has organized, resonates with the theories of cultural theorist and activist Jacques Ranciere. Arguing for political actions that counter the police-dominated logic of public space, Ranciere wrote, "Politics consists of reconfiguring that space, what there is to do there, what there is to see or name there. It is a dispute about the division of what is perceptible to the senses."[53] Ranciere suggested that this kind of political action be achieved through strategies that consist of "making visible that which has no reason to be seen . . . of lodg[ing] one world into another."[54] In contrast to Mann's efforts to turn the "master's house" against itself, Dominguez's design asserts a wholly alternative structure within otherwise inhospitable terrain. The screenal interfaces of the repurposed phones serve as spaces of refuge and guidance that operate according to a radically different logic than the virtual border patrols set up by Texas Border Sheriff's Coalition. The EDT/b.a.n.g. lab website describes the ideological shifts embodied in the TBT as "a multi-valenced code switch, a queer technology.'"[55] By "queering" the intended uses of a mainstream user-friendly technology like a Motorola cell phone, Dominguez produced the means for politically subversive usership and a transgressive form of techno-humanitarianism.

Re-visioning Rights

Within the borderlands of state and corporate surveillance there lurk systemic injustices that are strategically hidden or buried by deeply enculturated blindness. Despite the nearly constant presence of surveillance technologies, ruling elites in state and corporate institutions exercise their power to not only record but also to erase from the record or suppress the public memory of events that might damage their reputations or provide evidence of illegal actions. For individuals that are in high-risk categories due to their citizenship, race, gender, and/or economic status, risks such as deportation, detainment, or abuse threaten to accompany any infraction, act of protest, pursuit of justice, or heightened state of visibility. Even lower-risk individuals are dissuaded from looking too closely at the injustices wrought by politically and economically powerful entities. As the 2013 Snowden-NSA scandal revealed, even those who have "nothing to hide" have reason to fear that their private information is being routinely surveilled and potentially (mis)interpreted by state and corporate entities. Performance theorist Diana Taylor coined the term *percepticide* to describe "the self-blinding of the general population." In this kind of political (in)visibility, people *do* see things, often horribly unjust things, but they act, under political, social, or physical duress, as if they do not.[56] These systematized blind spots in the field of public vision serve to protect the interests of powerful political and economic entities.

The second category of screenal surveillance artists confront various forms of percepticide.[57] Their works utilize screenal interfaces as a means of restoring visibility toward injustices that have been otherwise lost or obscured within official records. Coco Fusco's *Dolores: From 10 to 10* (2001), Wafaa Bilal's *Domestic Tension* (2007), and Hasan Elahi's *Tracking Transience: The Orwell Project* (2008–present) restage bodies and spaces that have been disempowered through state-supported practices of erasure, invisibility, or mis-sight. These "re-visionary" artists utilize performance forms of reenactment, online gaming, and participatory surveillance in order to correct the official record and bring their own stories and experiences to greater visibility.

DOLORES: FROM 10 TO 10

In 2001 performance artist Coco Fusco performed a live webcast that reenacted the confinement, interrogation, abuse, and isolation of Dolores, a Mexican *maquiledora* worker who was accused of union organizing.[58] The roots of the story reached into the decade before to a woman named Delfina Rodriguez, whom Fusco met on a research trip to Tijuana, Mexico, in 1993. After Rodriguez's employer accused her of attempting to organize a labor union, Rodriguez was locked in a room without food, water, a bathroom, or a phone for twelve hours. These coercive measures eventually succeeded in forcing Rodriguez, under duress, to sign a letter of resignation. When she attempted to sue her former boss for these violations of her human rights, her boss insisted that her story was a lie, an "insane" fantasy that Rodriguez had no way to prove. With no surveillance tapes to serve as evidence, and coworkers who were too afraid to testify on her behalf, Rodriguez was forced to drop her case.

In order to bring attention to the injustice suffered by Rodriguez and the abuses of power by the factory management, Fusco took several actions. The first was a radio piece in which Fusco shared her extensive research into the systematic violations of human rights that had become common both among *maquiladoras* and at other sites of globalized economic development in Latin American countries. Fusco's research revealed that factories and assembly plants on the US-Mexico border tend to employ a work force that is predominantly female. The women who work in the factories are at the mercy of their nearly all male management force; along with poor living conditions and the frequent need to move as factories close and relocate according to new tax breaks, these immigrant factory workers live in precariously invisible spaces, as their vulnerable economic, gendered, social, and political positions battle the ethical quicksand of the borderlands.[59]

Fusco decided to then further amplify these systemic injustices through a live performance broadcast that staged a real-time enactment of Rodriguez's detainment. Fusco reasoned that there must have been surveillance cameras present, their footage deliberately lost or destroyed when Rodriguez attempted to litigate; her performance sought to retroactively provide the visual evidence that Rodriguez was unable to furnish in her own defense. Her performance, in which Ricardo Dominguez played the interrogator, represented Fusco's interpretation of what may have happened during Rodriguez's internment. Fusco fictionalized Rodriguez's story, calling the protagonist Dolores instead in order to dramatize the personal suffering of Rodriguez and others like her. The surveillance video of Fusco as Dolores was broadcast live online from the Kiasama Museum of Contemporary Art in Helsinki, Finland; it was screened at that time at art festivals in Los Angeles and Ljubiana and has since become a museum installation piece.

Whereas Rodriguez's coworkers had been victims of percepticide, as the threat of similar punishment forced them to pretend they had seen nothing of her abuse, Fusco's performance called on a dispersed international audience to bear witness to the injustice that Rodriguez suffered. By broadcasting her performance via a live online webcam, Fusco worked directly against the strategies of invisibility, isolation, and silence employed by the US and Mexican governments and countless multinational corporations to quell unionization efforts and hide harsh interrogation techniques. The online webcast of *Dolores* mimicked the visual rhetoric of CCTV surveillance, thereby casting its audiences as reviewers of the surveillance footage, the jury that should have been assembled to review such evidence on behalf of Rodriguez's complaints. Though necessarily fictionalized, *Dolores* built on the evidentiary status of CCTV footage to perform the means to justice that had, in reality, been denied Rodriguez. Although the circulation of Fusco's reenactment has been limited by the economics and proprietary structures of the art institutions that sponsored it (the piece is no longer publicly viewable as a video online), the piece serves as a good model for using theatrical reenactment and screenal technologies as a means of combating systemic injustice and percepticide. The work well illustrates that the visual rhetoric of CCTV surveillance can be used by artists-activists to performatively critique and bring to international visibility local injustices caused by abuses of economic and social power.[60]

ELAHI ONLINE: *TRACKING TRANSIENCE*—
THE ORWELL PROJECT

Hasan Elahi's ongoing *Tracking Transience* uses consumer GPS tracking technologies, smart phone photography and screen captures, and
a personal blog to record and make publicly visible his movements in
physical and virtual space.[61] Anyone with an Internet connection can
log on to Elahi's perpetually "live" website trackingtranscience.net and
view Elahi's exact location at that moment, as well as a backlog of his
movements and photos he has taken during each waking hour of the
last several years. While it may sound like the Facebook page of any teen-
ager, Elahi's choice to make his movements constantly visible to a virtual
public was not motivated by an exhibitionist drive or a desire to live a
reality TV experiment. In the summer of 2002, Elahi was detained by
immigration agents as he reentered his native United States at Detroit's
international airport following a trip to the Netherlands. Six months of
questioning, including nine lie detector tests, followed; it seemed that
Elahi was suspected of involvement with the September 11 attacks led by
al-Qaeda in 2001. He was told by the FBI had evidence that suggested he
was keeping explosives in his storage unit in Tampa, Florida (in fact this
unit contained winter clothes, extra furniture, and the like).

Despite his innocence, Elahi decided against bringing in a lawyer
or resisting the FBI's interrogation. As he put it, "It was clear who had
the power in this situation. And when you're face to face with someone with so much power . . . you dare not take any action." Later, however, Elahi did take action, deciding to "cooperate with a vengeance."[62]
In the months following his intense interrogation period, Elahi began
e-mailing the FBI with detailed records of his whereabouts and interactions. On every flight he took, he photographed the meal he ate, as well
as each knife he was provided with. In 2003 he decided to make his
personal records even more accessible; he created an interface for his
phone, which turned it into a tracking device that would automatically
update his location on a detailed world map at every hour of every day.
As he described his thinking, "You want to watch me? Fine. But I can
watch myself better than you can, and I can get a level of detail that you
will never have."[63]

Whereas Fusco's online reenactment was motivated by the lack of visibility and access to self-representation of her protagonist, Elahi's arts
activism project capitalized on the hypervisibility and broad band of

Fig. 14. Hasan Elahi's *Tracking Transience*, 2005–

access provided by the participatory, public nature of online social software systems. His project suggests that, in a digital age that threatens to undo the distinction between public and private, online visibility and the public eye of the Internet may provide the best means of protection. Elahi sought to performatively critiqued the FBI's covert surveillance techniques by rendering them redundant through the screenal interfaces of social surveillance.

Elahi acknowledges that social practices have changed since he started his project; he has been joined by many who are, intentionally or not, making their personal lives similarly hypervisible.

> When I first started talking about my project in 2003, people thought I was insane. Why would anyone tell everyone what he was doing at all times? Now eight years later, more than 800 million people do the same thing I've been doing each time they update their status or post an image on Facebook. What I'm doing is no longer just an art project; creating our own archives has become so commonplace that

Fig. 15. Hasan Elahi's *Tracking Transience*, 2005–

we're all—or at least hundreds of millions of us—doing it all the time. Whether we know it or not.[64]

Moreover, as the 2013 Snowden revelations made evident, our personal archives of digital communications and transactions are treasure troves of personal data, whether or not we post them online or e-mail them directly to the feds. Elahi has commented on the overlapping industries of self-representation and state and corporate surveillance with a degree of fatalism, suggesting that "In an era in which everything is archived and tracked, the best way to maintain privacy may be to give it up."[65]

However, Elahi's project is not simply a matter of choosing Facebook over the FBI. The volume of data that Elahi has amassed in over a decade of performing his own hypervisibility has sprawled, strategically, into an unwieldy tapestry of personal information. In contrast to the user-friendly visual interfaces of software systems like Facebook, Elahi makes his material record deliberately user-*un*friendly: "A lot of work is required to thread together the thousands of available points of information. By putting everything about me out there, I am simultaneously telling everything and nothing about my life."[66] As a viewer, it is quite difficult to navigate the website if one is trying to find a certain date and time; the site does not display a chronology of movement, even if every day, meal, and transit is represented. Using his website as a form of camouflage, Elahi has created a body of evidence that, overwhelming in its sheer size and cacophony of visual imagery, can at once stand in for and protect his (misread) physical body.

In the end, the unwieldiness of Elahi's interface is his most effective critique of contemporary digital culture and the trend of participatory social surveillance. The participatory arrangement of contemporary digital culture has turned the daily communications and transactions of Internet users into ever-expanding historical archives of individual lives.[67] Albeit with a trace of irony, Elahi's project foregrounds the evidentiary power and political import of the expansive, fragmented digital self, especially when the corporeal self comes under fire. It is doubtful that Elahi's project has upset the FBI's practices of surveillance; in fact, his overt use of social media as a means of providing forensic evidence may have even served as a model for state-mandated mass surveillance of consumer data and communication. However, as he put it, his project "may be more symbolic than not, but if 300 million people started sending private information to federal agents, the government would need to hire as many as another 300 million people, possibly more, to keep up with the information and we'd have to redesign our entire intelligence system."[68] Elahi has, in essence, re-visioned digital visibility: the project is seemingly all about making his personal life transparent, and yet the organization of his personal data is deliberately opaque. As such, his project provides an alternative, resistant model to corporate social software systems such as Facebook, a defensive form of electronic civil disobedience in the face of an overwhelming trend towards digital self-exposure.

DOMESTIC TENSION: MAKING THE PERSONAL VIRTUAL

The Iraqi American artist Wafaa Bilal has employed similar strategies of hypervisibility, self-disclosure, and radical interactivity to create his critiques of virtual warfare and the disastrous effects of US military attacks on Iraqi citizens. As described in the opening to this chapter, Bilal lived in a warehouse studio filled with live webcams and a paintball gun for a full month in the spring of 2007.[69] According to Bilal's retrospective writing on the work, the piece initially emerged out of his desire to personally reckon with the conflicted feelings he had about living so far away from his family and friends in Iraq. Several had been injured, and his father and one of his brothers had recently been killed in the wartime violence. As in others of his works, Bilal channeled his feelings of anger and mourning into a public-facing artwork.[70] As his plans for the work developed, Bilal sought to make visible incongruities in "domestic" daily lives between his native Iraq and his adopted US home. As he saw it, the majority of Americans were going about their daily lives without much thought about their decades-long involvement in consecutive wars in Iraq, even as the ongoing (and at that time escalating) conflicts continued to bring daily terror and suffering to the people of Iraq. In order to capture these incongruities, which were typically not made visible in US media, he created a frame of "play" that could link leisure-based online gaming culture to the dire situation of his people in Iraq.[71]

In performance, *Domestic Tension* quickly became more intense than even Bilal had imagined. Midway through the project, after being featured in the *Chicago Tribune*, Bilal's site was promoted by Digg.com, a website that tracks and advertises the websites with the most hits on a given day.[72] With the heightened visibility came an intensification of online visits, vitriol, and violence. On day 17, described in the opening of this chapter, Bilal was barraged with more than machine-gun-style paintball attacks; he also received messages in the online chat room that accompanied the user interface such as "Come out and get shot little man," "Fuckin' Iraqis," "Did you enjoy it when the bombs fell on Baghdad? I had an erection and was eating a cheeseburger. Shoot that fucker," and "Those are cum shots on the glass . . . fuck and kill."[73] The comments, full of hatred and anger and intended to hurt Bilal more than the paintballs could, shocked and troubled him. Although he had sought to catch the attention of a broad swath of the American public, he didn't anticipate "how brutal the anonymous internet culture could be."[74] For the remaining fortnight, the paintball gun hardly rested and the chat room filled with wide-ranging comments that quickly proved wrong an early criticism of the project that Bilal would only be "preaching to the choir." Although the results were far from comfortable, Bilal had successfully jumped the boundaries of the stereotypically liberal, pacifist art world.

No doubt Bilal's provocative invitation to "shoot an Iraqi" would have caused a media splash on its own, but without Bilal's commitment to chatting with his participants it may have succeeded only in replicating normalized video-game-style violence. Wisely, Bilal paired the online "game" with a forum through which users could communicate with Bilal live. Whether or not they chose to fire the gun, online visitors could use the website's chat room as a forum in which to share their own responses to the project, ask questions of Bilal, and engage each other in discussions about resonances with the ongoing war in Iraq. Although in some cases users took the invitation to engage in violence to such an extreme that Bilal could do little more than take cover from the physical and verbal attacks (in fact, he was left with symptoms of post-traumatic stress disorder), the screenal interface more often facilitated communication and interconnection with an impressively wide swath of people from around the world. By the end of his thirty-day residency in the gallery, more than sixty thousand users had logged on to fire at and/or chat with Bilal.

More than any of the examples discussed so far, Bilal's screenal interface succeeded in representing injustice and political tension while at the same time facilitating active discourse and open debate with and between his audience members. Although the piece, viewed by most from a distance and through a computer screen, could not communicate the phenomenological experience of living under the constant threat of violence and visibility, it nevertheless facilitated ethical reckoning with issues of remotely controlled, anonymous violence and warfare. The chat room became a platform through which Bilal could share details of his experience as an Iraqi American, stories about his family and friends living (and dying) under real gunfire and missile attacks in Iraq, and his concerns about American citizens' apathy toward or ignorance of the war. Through his conversations with particpants Bilal often succeeded in grounding the virtual, anonymous "game" of online target practice in far more personal, human terms.[75] As Clio Unger has argued, the live, interactive interface of *Domestic Tension* succeeded in transforming a community of spectators into a community of action: a group of actors that, through a structurally open system, have the possibility to bring about change. This was most evident in the formation of a group that called themselves the "Virtual Human Shield." In this "community of action," anonymous individuals who had not met prior to the performance organized online to protect Bilal from taking direct hits by the paintballs. The group maintained a schedule such that at least one of their members would be present to click the curser on the website and

Fig. 16. Detail from Wafaa Bilal's performance piece _Domestic Tension_. (©Wafaa Bilal, courtesy of the Driscoll Babcock Galleries.)

aim the gun away from Bilal so that other users who wished to shoot at him could not.[76]

At its conclusion, bringing the project to a close was not only a necessary act but also a symbolic one for Bilal. As he disconnected the gun and prepared to leave his gallery home, he shared his hopes that this, too, could be a virtual simulation of real world actions: "We silenced one gun today and I hope we will silence all guns in the future."[77]

New Dramaturgies of the Surveillance Screen

The final category of screenal surveillance art focuses on the work of artists that utilize formal properties of surveillance technologies to create alternative narrative structures of representation. Projects such as _I Love Alaska_ and _Rider Spoke_, which I discuss below, along with Manu Luksch's film _Faceless_, discussed in chapter 5, experiment with telling stories _with_ surveillance systems rather than *about* them. In so doing they reframe state and corporate surveillance technologies as media of representation that, while not necessarily revelatory of radically "new" content, offer uniquely contemporary forms of narrative structure, character development, and audience reception. They also pose prescient questions about the theatrical potential of contemporary surveillance systems, new subjectivities, and affective connections forged through the anonymized personal data they collect and the attendant acts (and failures) of privacy legislation that serve as script, mise-en-scène, and publicity agent.

RIDER SPOKE: ANONYMOUS VOICES

AND ASYNCHRONOUS COMMUNITY

Blast Theory, a British theater company known for creating interactive, site-specific performance scenarios, debuted *Rider Spoke* in the Barbican district of London in 2007. Each evening, roughly thirty-five participants were provided with a bicycle and a GPS-enabled recording device (a Nokia mobile phone enhanced with an earpiece and microphone) and sent out individually into the neighborhood surrounding the theater complex. Through their earpieces, participants were each guided by the recorded voice of Ju Row Farr, cofounder of Blast Theory, to find a location they liked and record information about themselves. At the first stop, they were asked to give themselves a name and describe themselves; at later points they were prompted to describe a dream they had had or a fear they continued to hold. In each case, the answers they recorded were geotagged (linked to a geographic coordinate triangulated with mobile phone towers and/or Wi-Fi access points); as the number of geotagged recordings grew, participants could listen the messages of their fellow participants by riding to the locations at which the stories were originally recorded. The performance expanded over time as participants populated the landscape with these voiced meditations.

On its website, Blast Theory described *Rider Spoke* as a game of hide-and-seek that explored larger cultural concepts of participation, documentation, and digital information exchange through mobile technologies: "You search for a hiding place and record a short message there. And then you search for the hiding places of others."[78] These directives playfully defamiliarized the processes of self-disclosure, documentation, and observation that have come to structure contemporary digital communication practices. Social media sites such as Facebook and Twitter, as

Fig. 17. Blast Theory's *Rider Spoke*, 2007

well as digital communication and entertainment platforms more broadly, depend on the willingness of users to participate in an asynchronously and remotely connected community through practices of self-disclosure and mutual surveillance. Media theorist Mark Andrejevic traces this willingness to the tacit promise of democratization and distributed power that undergirds the logic of digital culture.

> Many of the celebrants of the digital revolution . . . argue that interactive technology will enable "meaningful" participation not only in the sense of enhanced opportunities for gaining relevant information and participating actively in public deliberation, but also in the sense that citizens will gain power over the political and economic systems that help shape the society in which we live. . . . The assumption is that to the extent that interactivity facilitates the process of redistribution it is inherently subversive and democratizing.[79]

He cautions, however, that empowerment through participation, at least in the digital age of data tracking and sorting, is always a double-edged sword: "The genius of the 'selling of the Internet' is that the latter is equated with the former: the participation of consumers in the rationalization of their own consumption is sold as empowerment."[80] This rather dark outlook posits that the promise of democratized participation through the Internet has essentially become a facade for a systematized form of surveillance in which users facilitate their own consumption as corporate data. To this is added the common concern that mobile, digital interfaces have the effect of further alienating people from one another, as remote, screenal engagement is commonly favored over face-to-face or even voice-to-voice, real-time conversations. With these concerns in mind, the architecture of *Rider Spoke* seems to be a reinforcement of insidious structures of surveillance and fractured social communities.

What, then, was radical about the experience of exchanging stories with a crowd of strangers through mobile interfaces in an industrial neighborhood of London? Media and performance theorist Jason Farman has argued that *Rider Spoke* added to the familiar processes of documentation and remote communication an experiential layer that elucidated valuable new forms of community and intersubjectivity.[81] The piece modeled what Farman called "asynchronous engagement," a process "in which users engage each other without regard to the demands of real-time performance" and "intersubjective embodiment." This constitutes "simultaneously a sensory experience through the body and also a process of decoding and encoding the various cultural inscriptions that inform every interaction."[82] That is to say, *Rider Spoke* experimented with transforming remote, anonymous, virtual communication into a sensory, embodied experience that, temporarily yet intensely, grounded participants in the geographic locales they inhabited and made them accountable to the other players, who were likewise engaged in sharing personal stories and desires.

Thought about in this way, *Rider Spoke* illustrates what has been theorized as "neogeography," showing that commercially available mobile technologies can function as tools that enable new spatial practices and alternative politics of mobility. Neogeography has been defined as the use of interactive online mapping technologies by nonexperts in which there is "a blurring of the distinctions between producer, communicator and consumer of geographic information."[83] In contrast to the traditional profession of geography, neogeography studies amateur uses of digital mapping technologies in which cartography functions as a means of recording and representing an individual's experiences, interactions, and travels. While much of the commercial rhetoric surrounding neogeography focuses on the leisure-based pursuits of amateur smart phone users, neogeographic technologies such as Google Maps can also serve as important platforms for social and political resistance, self-representation, and circulation of marginalized experiences. Recalling my discussion of de Certeau and resistant spatial practices in the "Introduction," neogeography is a spatial practice that can operate in opposition to "strategies" of hegemonic geography and also function as a key site of political formation. As Sarah Elwood and Katharyne Mitchell argue in "Another Politics Is Possible: Neogeographies, Visual Spatial Tactics, and Political Formation," neogeographic technologies open up important "tactical" practices that empower marginalized users to share knowledge and organize socially and politically.[84]

In turning the practice of social surveillance and anonymous, remote communication into a neogeographic pursuit, *Rider Spoke* defamiliarized the common experience of asynchronous mobile communication, in which material space holds as little weight as synchronous time. Participants were prompted to not only produce and consume personal stories and observations but to experience these messages as indelibly linked to physical, geographic spaces. To emphasize this, several instructions asked participants to record stories or desires inspired by their surroundings. For example, one prompt asked participants to "seek out a house or a flat with a window that could be looked through, one that they would like to enter, and to record a message explaining why."[85] Although the participants did not occupy the same physical spaces at the same time, they encountered each other through vocal traces accessed through screenal interfaces. As Farman highlights in his analysis of the work, the voiced element of the recordings "establish[ed] embodied connections and a sense of presence between interlocutors."[86] Anchored to physical locations, the voices of their coparticipants became sensorial stand-ins for face-to-face encounters and copresent community. The voice functioned as the surrogate of the person who had been there just before the listener, indexing that person's absence while at the same time filling the space with a new form of presence that was at once more mysterious and revealing than a physically present stranger.

In addition to dramaturgically orchestrating a sense of connectedness to physical locales, *Rider Spoke* challenged participants to reinvest in an intersubjective experience of urban, digital life through their personal screens. Rowan Wilken, writing about narrative structures and interactivity in Blast Theory's locative games, argued that the process of creating and listening to voiced stories with strangers counteracts habits of what Erving Goffman called "civil inattention" within the conditions of "alienation and proximity" in densely populated yet isolated urban life.[87]

Listening to another's voice, even though it was the voice of a stranger, created a heightened sense of accountability within the performance. Although the exchanges were anonymized and disembodied, the voiced messages built a sense of intersubjective community with an imperative toward reciprocity. As Wilken put it, the creators of *Rider Spoke* built a narrative structure that required the "swapping of confidences with strangers," creating a dramaturgical expectation of give and take that fostered deepening levels of intimacy and self-exposure over time: "As a participant listener-recorder, one cannot expect to give or listen to a secret told in confidence and then provide something rigidly formal straight after."[88] Despite the asynchronous physicality of the piece, in which participants were never in the same space at the same time, participants confirmed this, describing the experience as "a disconnected intimacy with a total stranger."[89]

Within this evolving structure of intimate and anonymous exchange, new stories populated the landscape traversed by *Rider Spoke* participants each night. The piece itself was not a story but rather a dramaturgical structure that was mobilized through screenal technologies of communication. In effect, the elements of the game functioned as stage directions "around which the larger narrative threads of the game are woven by players."[90] Reinforced by a heightened awareness of physical location and the embodied sensation of speaking their own stories, the voices of their coparticipants functioned less as mirrors of daily communication practices through Short Message Service (SMS) text or Twitter or Facebook and more as physical markers of a time and a place-bound communal process of creation. To emphasize the difference between the participant experiences of *Rider Spoke* and more typical user experiences of social media, Blast Theory artists performatively rebranded the corporate terminology "user generated content," offering the description "publicly created contributions" in its place.[91]

Importantly, these publicly created contributions remained anonymous, even as users traversed the same street corners and alleyways. As in Bilal's chat room, the anonymity of the digital interface, coupled with the playful, performance-based frame, encouraged participants of *Rider Spoke* to share their fantasies and desires, intimate details that would likely not have flowed quite so easily if they had been face-to-face with their listeners. The frame of play and the assumption of mutual self-disclosure built a horizontal structure in which alienation could still foster engagement. Echoing Jill Magid's *Evidence Locker*, discussed in chapter 2, *Rider Spoke* successfully expanded the capacity for intersubjective intimacy, communication, and storytelling through quotidian systems of social surveillance.

I LOVE ALASKA: A "HEARTBREAKING" SEARCH FOR MEANING

Whereas *Rider Spoke* modeled a neogeographic scenario of interconnectedness and intimacy through anonymous, surveillant interfaces, the online film *I Love Alaska* painted a far less utopian picture. Based instead on a case of accidental, involuntary, and far more widespread data exchange between strangers, the ethos and method of storytelling within *I Love Alaska* is quite different, though it is no less illuminating with regard to the narrative potential of digital screenal interfaces. The film, made by Danish artists Lernert Engelberts and Sander Plug, took as its source material personal data gleaned through a massive data leak in 2006. In the data leak, one of the largest to date, three months' worth of search queries of over 650,000 AOL users were made available online. While the leak was not wholly accidental—AOL explained the move as "an innocent enough attempt to reach out to the academic community with new research tools [that] was obviously not appropriately vetted"—it was roundly and apologetically deemed "a screw up."[92] Company spokespeople offered assurances that the leaked data contained no details that would reveal the identities of individual users, as the approximately 658,000 affected users were identified only by randomized numbers. However, the data leak, which was one of the first cases of a massively open online leak of user information, brought dicey questions of ownership, access, and authorship to bear on the mountains of personal data amassing in virtual space.

The entertainment value of the search data surfaced nearly as quickly as the criticism of AOL's privacy gaff: programmers established websites that facilitated searches of the leaked database, and bloggers began compiling posts of especially amusing or shocking searches. Playing amateur detective, curious onlookers quickly found ways to compile and trace the some three months' worth of anonymized searches to individuals using "ego-based searches," which included the user's name, as well as location based searches that indicated his or her geographic location. It proved hard to resist participating in the virtual sleuthing; even the *New York Times* ran an article about following the data trail of User Number 4417749, which led a reporter to the doorstep of a sixty-two-year-old widow in Lilburn, Georgia.[93]

Artists Engelberts and Plug decided to use the leaked personal data as source material for a short film project. The resulting film, *I Love Alaska*, available for free online, sought to tell the story of one of the AOL users through the text of her search queries.[94] While its protagonist remained unnamed, the film's thirteen "episodes" (each of three to four minutes in length) revealed in candid detail the mental and emotional meanderings of AOL User Number 711391. Viewers can readily deduce through contextual clues in her searches that she is a middle-aged woman from Houston, Texas. In the film, an (unnamed) female performer with a slight Texas accent dispassionately voices the queries, which are organized simply by the dates on which the search queries were entered. Inspired by several searches by User 711391 on the subject of Alaska— such as "Alaska is so awesome"—the voiced search queries in each episode are set against a video backdrop of vast Alaskan landscapes, slow-moving long shots nearly vacant of life.

Within the context of cinematic storytelling, the dramaturgy of *I Love Alaska* is notably unconventional, as it requires the viewer to piece together a narrative based on the fragmented, disparate search queries. Indeed, a cohesive narrative seems, especially at first, nearly impossible to find: over the course of one day (March 9), the searches of User 711391 migrate from "crystal wand sex toy" to "red spots on my leg that look like ingrown hair but they aren't" to "farting preacher" to "how to deal with shy men." On another day, the query "why does my dog always have to go to the bathroom?" is followed immediately by "masturbation with a turkey baster." The remote vistas and evenly paced voice-overs give a detached, leisurely feel to the diverse, often amusing searches of User 711391. Viewers are privy to a host of sometimes moving but still disconnected concerns that plague her, such as "why can't I sleep since I had a hysterectomy" and "how do you know if you are an alcoholic," as well as pieces of advice, seemingly gleaned from her own mistakes, such as "Don't cut your hair before a big event." Through the first several episodes, the point of the film seems to be to foreground the random and idiosyncratic patterns of Internet searches and feed the voyeuristic engine of social surveillance.

While the dramaturgical labor required of the spectator of *I Love Alaska* might frustrate someone expecting a Hollywood blockbuster, the setup is in keeping with analytical practices of surveillance, or at least the public imaginary of these practices, in which a detective must piece together fragments of data to solve a crime. Eventually, this kind of careful attention pays off, as the lines of thought that the searches trace begin to coalesce around particular desires and life circumstances that give depth to the character of User 711391. Tracing causal relations between searches, such as "online friendships can be very special," "nervous about meeting an online friend," and a search for hotels in the San Antonio area, yields fruit, as these are soon followed by the entry "people are not always what they seem over the internet." At this point, the desire to assemble a dramatic narrative becomes difficult to resist. That User 711391 has chosen to seek fulfillment outside her marriage is further affirmed when, not long after, the term "online friend" is replaced with "cyber lover," followed by a climactic confession in episode 11: "I'm afraid the affair I had will cause me to lose my job and marriage" and "I thought I could handle an affair but I couldn't."

The dramaturgical structure that the filmmakers set up mirrors what visual studies scholar Thomas Stubblefield called the "labor intensive nature of digital culture," an outcome of the required self-disclosures and participatory surveillance that is "the cost of admission to the otherwise 'free' space of the internet."[95] Taking a similar position to that of Andrejevic, discussed above, Stubblefield argued that films such as *I Love Alaska* "ask the viewer to reproduce the forms of surveillance labor which circumscribe their protagonists" by placing the burden of narrative labor on the spectator.[96] In so doing, "the possibility of narrative coherence is contingent on the viewer's participation and mastery of relations of surveillance, his or her ability not only to successfully monitor and analyze an absent subject, but to mine this human-machine interaction for data."[97] Comparing this mode of spectatorship to that of traditional cinematic narratives, Stubblefield notes that the spectator of *I Love Alaska* is called on to construct not only the plot but the setting, the stakes, the protagonist, and the larger message that the piece might have: "[T]he viewer is not only prompted to ask what exactly has transpired between these searches, but to produce a kind of structuring absence to accommodate these events, to interrupt and redistribute the temporality of the film across plot points so that a fully formed narrative emerges."[98]

For spectators to perform this labor and arrive at a recognizable narrative arc is clearly the goal of the filmmakers. On the Minimovies website, which hosts the episodes, Engelberts and Plug introduced the film as "the heartbreaking search history of AOL user #711391," setting up from the outset a narrative of hope, betrayal, and loss. They present the user, in narrative summary, as "a somewhat obese middle-aged lady in her menopause, who is looking for a way to rejuvenate her sex life. In the end, when she cheats on her husband with a man she met online, her life seems to crumble around her. She regrets her deceit, admits to her Internet addiction and dreams of a new life in Alaska."[99] These prompts provided by the filmmakers frame the fragments of personal data that make up the ensuing episodes as a data set that, if carefully analyzed and interpreted, will yield a satisfyingly melodramatic picture of a stranger's life.

Without dismissing the important parallels between participatory surveillance and spectatorship that Stubblefield points out, or the entertainment value of the film Engelberts and Plug created, I find that, in the case of *I Love Alaska*, the push toward constructing a "fully formed narrative" risks overlooking a far more interesting dramaturgical structure within the film's material. To begin with, the description of the film's narrative and protagonist presented by Engelberts and Plug forces a melodramatic, somewhat misogynistic framework that limits a viewer's understanding of the film. Their marketing of the protagonist as "a somewhat obese middle-aged lady in her menopause, who is looking for a way to rejuvenate her sex life" smacks of the tawdry advertising campaigns of reality TV shows; they seem to be aiming for something like "the real housewives of AOL." This description, while not necessarily inaccurate, reduces User 711391 to the lowest hanging fruit of her self as expressed through her search data. Most tragically of all, it misses the more interesting story that the search data tells.

Given a more open dramaturgical framework, a viewer might see, for example, that User 711391 used the AOL search engine to perform an unusual mode of address, one that would be better understood through the feminist self-representational strategy of *écriture feminine* rather than a traditional patriarchal cinematic narrative. Feminist linguistic theorists such as Hélène Cixous and Luce Irigaray argued that female social subjects have long been trapped within a linguistic system that is defined according to a male viewpoint of the world. [100] As a potential solution to what Irigaray described as a prison of "phallogocentric language," Cixous coined the term *écriture feminine*, literally "women's writing," arguing that, as there was no room for women's self-expression within patriarchal language, "Woman must write her self: must write about women and bring women to writing, from which they have been driven away as violently as from their bodies."[101] By privileging nonlinear, cyclical structures of writing, *écriture feminine* was thought to better express female experiences and desires.

While the search query set of any user would likely be nonlinear and somewhat cyclical, User 711391's search patterns reveal a particularly unusual and surprisingly moving method of expressing her personal concerns and desires. Rather than using the Internet search engine simply as a means of retrieving information, User 711391 had an idio-syncratic habit of inputting declamatory statements and personal ques-tions that followed on her queries. "Jake Gillenhal is hot" was followed by "Brokeback should have won an Oscar"; "Famous actresses that are short" prompted the conclusion "men love petite women." At other points, she shared seemingly unprompted advice with the world at large: "If a stranger asks you to stop your car do not stop." On another occa-sion she asked, "Did anyone ever tell you how proud of you they are?" Then, as if to answer herself, she submitted the phrase "I am so proud of you." While this may have been due to some naïveté on the part of the user (many of her full-sentence searches would impede rather than assist even the AOL search engine), her search style enacts a reflexive, circular mode of address that expresses not only longing, alienation, and loneliness but also resourcefulness, comfort, and agency. Her searches seem not always to have been for factual information; instead they tran-scend the intended bounds of Internet searches and function as per-sonal expressions of her desire and experience.

This layer of analysis moves the project beyond the "heartbreaking" portrait of a lonely, desperate woman put forward by Engelberts and Plug and places it instead in the company of projects by feminist artists such as Janet Cardiff, Sophie Calle, and Jill Magid. These artists, whose work I discuss in chapters 2 (Magid and Calle) and 4 (Cardiff), skillfully produce representations of their own affective experiences of surveil-lance that contradict or complicate the authoritative, patriarchal nar-ratives that surveillance technologies otherwise construct about them. Through the feminist strategy of *écriture feminine,* as well as that of "voice-off," utilized in particular by Cardiff, their works implicitly critique domi-nant (patriarchal) habits of representing and interpreting female desire in visual culture.

Without necessarily doing so consciously, Engelberts and Plug cre-ated a platform for these feminist techniques. Their choice to have a female narrator voice the search terms of User 711391 embodies the strategy of "voice-off." As I discuss at more length in chapter 4, "voice-offs" establish an alternative space from which a woman might speak without being visually objectified or layered over (as in a voice-over). As Britta Sjogren theorized the term, the voice-off is a means by which the female voice can *speak for itself,* as it occupies an alternative space alongside (and therefore in relation to) but elsewhere (distinguished from) the image on the screen.[102] Both the narrator of *I Love Alaska* and the protagonist remain invisible; the only visuals presented on screen are of remote Alaskan landscapes, which represent User 711391's desire to escape her life in Texas, even if only for a vacation. Whereas Engelberts and Plug took her invisibility as license to impose their own (rather predictable) narrative on her search queries, and Stubblefield saw the "structuring absence" of a protagonist as being filled by the spectator, I would suggest that her visual absence could be read instead as a model of feminist performance within surveillance culture (overlooking for the moment the fact that the performance came out of a disastrous, involuntary circulation of personal information). Rather than prompting the spectator to work as a forensic detective or dramaturg/director working toward a cohesive "heartbreaking" narrative or a "revealing character study," a feminist interpretation of User 711391's series of search queries would position the spectator quite differently. To begin with, this reading constructs an alternative structure of communication and storytelling, one in which observation and character construction are not a one-way street. The call-and-response pattern of User 711391's search queries seems, already, to conjure the audiences that would one day—through the AOL data leak and the efforts of Engelberts and Plug—hear her words. While I am certainly not arguing that User 711391 dreamed that her search queries would one day be part of a mass data leak or hoped that they would one day be made public through something like the Minimovies.org platform, her methods of using the AOL search engine seemed already to conjure an imagined interlocutor, one that, through the fluke of a mass data leak, turned out to take the form of the spectator of the film *I Love Alaska*.

Where *Rider Spoke* worked at constructing a kind of "neogeography," we might think of the dramaturgy of User 711391's search queries as a kind of "neotemporality," which is likewise heralded by contemporary structures of digital technologies. Nate Anderson, writing on the project for *Ars Technica* online, begins to theorize the outcomes of such an understanding of the film. In his analysis, viewing the film invites viewers to do more than reality-TV-type gawking or amateur forensic detective work; the film "lead[s] us all to reflect again on just how much of our lives are now catalogued by computers around the world, and how search engines are becoming the new confessional."[103] In this construction, User 711391 is not stripped of agency, despite the loss of privacy she suffered through the AOL data leak. As in feminist strategies of voiced writing, her neotemporality is circular and intersubjective, at once open for and in excess of interpretation.

Like User 711391, like Hasan Elahi, we are all active participants in surveillance society through the screens we use. Our keystrokes, blog posts, search queries, geotagged photos, travel histories, and border crossings locate us on a range of maps and for a variety of audiences, some intended and others unintended. Though these may feel like tiny pings sent into a vast Alaskan wilderness, we must remember that our individual screened lives are acts of creation and performance. And our usership, like time, like theater, is mutable, intersubjective, and full of loops and leaps.

CHAPTER 4

Sex

———— ᴡᴧ ————

A critical feminist reading of . . . all the texts of culture . . . changes the
representations into a performance which exceeds the text. For women
to enact the contradictions is to demonstrate the non-coincidence of
Woman and women. To perform the terms of the production of woman
as text, as image, is to resist identification with that image. It is to have
stepped through the looking glass.[1]

Sousveillance practitioner Steve Mann, whose work as a self-proclaimed
cyborg and countersurveillance activist was featured in chapter 3, has
developed his wearable mobile surveillance technologies, or "wearcams,"
into a device specifically designed "for Her." Featuring prosthetic breasts
implanted with surveillance cameras instead of silicone, Mann's *Heart-
Cam* paired the most iconic—and perhaps most fetishized—markers of
femininity with the resistant gaze of sousveillance. Retailing for nearly
fifteen hundred dollars, the *HeartCam* runs on a 12-volt battery, with an
infrared surveillance camera in one breast cup and a color surveillance
camera in the other.[2] Each sousveillance product in Mann's wearcam
line was built to be worn on the body: the dome-style surveillance cameras are affixed to backpacks, t-shirts, and pendants in order to arm
participants with the technological means to reverse the gaze of surveillance and, as Mann describes it, surveil the surveillers. However, only
the *HeartCam* features a surveillance camera that doubles as an explicitly gendered body part. Sousveillance: strong enough for a man, now
designed specially for a woman.

Fig. 18. Steve Mann's HeartCam, 2001

Setting aside for the moment the implication that all of his other sousveillance technologies were designed for men (the default gender), Mann clearly intended the *HeartCam* to merge his strategy of sousveillance with a feminist challenge to the male gaze. As he put it, the *HeartCam* not only reverses the disciplinary gaze of surveillance, but "*HeartCam* turn[s] the tables on the 'male gaze' by allowing the female wearer of the apparatus to capture images."[3] By ostentatiously displaying markers of sexual difference, the *HeartCam* made hypervisible the traditional construction of female bodies as "given to be seen" by a male gaze that is "given to see."[4] The pairing of sousveillance and feminist critique seems promising, at least on the surface. Mann's design attempted to challenge the gendered binary by endowing the prosthetic breasts with the power to actively look back with the gaze of sousveillance. When Mann unveiled the *HeartCam* as part of his wearcam line in 2004, a blogger wrote this enthusiastic response: "Just wait until someone decides they don't want to be on camera and tries to cover those up!"[5] This comment suggests that the conflation of gender and surveillance in the wearcam bra raised the stakes beyond Mann's already combative campaign against surveillance society. Any attempt to "cover up" the breast-mounted sousveillance cameras, the blogger implied, would not only confront the ubiquity of surveillance cameras in public space, which Mann's sousveillance projects critique; it would also raise the ire of generations of feminists hell-bent on defending a woman's right to "look back at" patriarchal culture.

For all its promise, Mann's foray into the territory of explicitly gendered visual representation raises a host of knotty problems. Mimicking silicone breast implants motivated by the desire-based gaze of social surveillance, Mann's device falls back into many of the traps of fetishism, objectification, and normative gender roles that it seems to critique. From the way in which Mann cropped the promotional image of the HeartCam—the female model is beheaded and unarmed, signified by her breasts alone (see fig. 18)—to the rhetoric of victimization that he used to explain the *HeartCam*'s programming, discussed below, Mann risks replicating many of the fetishizing effects of the male gaze that feminists have long critiqued. Sousveillance, as it turns out, is just as vulnerable to replicating repressive gender norms as surveillance culture is.

This chapter is concerned with the importance—and difficulty—of addressing the sexual politics of surveillance. For all its problematic aspects, which I analyze in greater depth later in the chapter, Mann's breast cameras importantly foreground what so many discourses of surveillance fail to see: that surveillance as a theory and practice is far from gender neutral and that dominant ideologies of both disciplinary surveillance and countersurveillance replicate normative representations of gender that feminists have critiqued for decades. The wearcam bra makes evident significant and useful parallels between the disciplinary gaze of surveillance and the male-coded gaze of visual culture: the practical and semiotic construction of Mann's device combines the politically combative aims of sousveillance with a rich history of feminist challenges to an objectifying male gaze. That Mann's device literally turns the female body into a wearable device also raises important questions about the status of the gendered body as an object in both surveillant and sousveillant ideologies. Reading Mann's project alongside other works, such as Giles Walker's *Peepshow*, Jill Magid's *Monitoring Desire,* and Mona Hatoum's *Deep Throat,* I begin to unpack notable parallels among dominant ideologies of sexual desire, institutional knowledge, gender identity, and surveillance.

The title of this chapter, "Sex," is deliberately broad and suggestive. Not a spatial category per se, as the previous chapter titles have been, I use the banner of sex to refer to the complex interplay of gender identity; normative and transgressive sexual desires; visual, aural, and embodied eroticism; and the anxiety over controlling these as they are manifested in bodies of and under surveillance. There are several significant parallels and partnerships among cultural constructions of sex, gender, and surveillance: as normative cultural concepts, gender, sexual desire, and surveillance all govern and produce socially permissible behaviors.[6] They are structured through practices of observation and discipline and historically assign power and agency to the watcher and passivity/docility to the watched. Recalling Butler's definition of gender as constituted through performative acts, as well as Bernstein's concept of "scriptive things," both discussed in the "Introduction," the scripts of both gender and surveillance are at once individual and collective; they are enacted by and inscribed on the body, and they gain credence through "stylized repetition."[7] While sex, gender, and desire do not directly reference physical spaces in the same way the stage, street, and screen do, they are acts staged on the body. As Butler put it, "Just as a script may be enacted in various ways, and just as the play requires both text and interpretation, so the gendered body acts its part in a culturally restricted corporeal space and enacts interpretations within the confines of already existing directives."[8]

Attention to parallels between surveillance and sex reveals that gender serves as a foundational concept within cultural constructions of surveillance. Normative gender roles and heterosexual desire have long been produced through surveillance—the gendered body has always already been under surveillance as a means of protecting, maintaining, and justifying social, political, and economic structures that support patriarchal power and knowledge. At the same time, signs of sex and gender are also used to produce surveillance—surveillance depends on signs of heteronormative gender to express itself and maintain its cultural status as an arbiter of legality, evidence, and knowledge. Or, put in simpler terms, inspired again by Butler, surveillance depends significantly on the ways in which we "do" gender in order to "do" surveillance.

Our cultural imaginary has long produced the disciplinary gaze of surveillance as gendered and gendering. Gendered terms such as "the Man" and "Big Brother" commonly describe powerful, centralized systems that watch and discipline social subjects in a range of institutions and public and private spaces. In her article "Video Surveillance, Gender, and the Safety of Public Urban Space: 'Peeping Tom' Goes High Tech?" Hille Koskela discussed ways in which dominant narratives of gender difference play out within urban surveillance systems. As her title suggests, she employed cultural models of the desirous voyeur, "Peeping Tom," and the protective disciplinarian, "Big Brother," to argue that surveillance technologies function in the cultural imaginary as devices that both protect women against sexual assault and promote the sexual fetishization of women's bodies through the male-coded gaze of the hidden camera.[9] From these familiar gendered roles, there seem "naturally" to emerge equally familiar patterns of discipline, desire, fetishism, control, and (dis)empowerment that shape the cultural operations of surveillance. Together the gendered language and normative gender roles within these familiar cultural tropes indicate that surveillance systems function as what the feminist film theorist Teresa de Lauretis called a "technology of gender."

In order to theorize the work of surveillance artists exploring the gendered and gendering forces of surveillance, I draw on feminist theories that critique imbalances of power maintained through modes of looking and being looked at in film, theater, and other representational media. Over the last half century many feminist practitioners and scholars, particularly those in the so-called second-wave of feminism, have specialized in defining and critiquing gendered habits of representation and reception. Feminists have used psychoanalytic theories of sexual difference and fetishization and Marxist theories of commodity fetishism to analyze representations of women in visual media and culture. These critiques are prominent in many gender-focused surveillance works and provide a useful language with which to analyze their goals and strategies.

As in Mann's *HeartCam*, the well-known concept of the male gaze shows up in most gender-focused surveillance artworks. Laura Mulvey, one of the early champions of this concept, located the engine of the male gaze in mainstream Hollywood cinema, arguing that "cinematic codes create a gaze, a world, and an object, thereby producing an illusion cut to the measure of desire."[10] Mulvey famously described the portrayal of women in classical Hollywood cinema as productive of a visual economy of consumption in which women are meant to be seen but not to see: "In their traditional exhibitionist role women are simultaneously looked at and displayed, with their appearance coded for strong visual and erotic impact so that they can be said to connote to-be-looked-at-ness."[11] Jill Dolan argued that such an arrangement likewise governed habits of representation and reception in realist theater, writing that it "creates an ideal spectator carved in the likeness of the dominant culture whose ideology he represents." As in cinema, that spectator "has been assumed to be white, middle-class, heterosexual, and male."[12] As John Berger summarized in *Ways of Seeing*, this visual logic has been normalized to the extent that both men and women internalize and reproduce it: "*[M]en act* and *women appear*. Men look at women. Women watch themselves being looked at. This determines not only most relations between men and women but also the relation of women to themselves. The surveyor of woman in herself is male: the surveyed female. Thus she turns herself into an object—and most particularly an object of vision: a sight."[13] Foucault's theory of panoptic discipline parallels this logic, extending it to all subjects of surveillance, as the surveilled subjects become so aware of their visibility that they discipline themselves.[14] That is, like women watching common representations of femininity, subjects of surveillance internalize their own hypervisibility.

While not all the artists in this chapter self-identify as feminist, they each mobilize a range of feminist strategies to make visible their critiques of surveillance society. To varying degrees, they also explore surveillance technologies as tools that actively construct and are constructed by norms of gender and sexuality. Like Mann, surveillance artists Jill Magid, Mona Hatoum, Giles Walker, and Janet Cardiff explore the impacts of a gendered gaze on bodies of/under surveillance and work to make visible (or audible in the case of Cardiff) the ways in which surveillance systems function as technologies of gender. To do so, they employ established feminist strategies of re-vision and re-presentation to defamiliarize and challenge the sexual politics and gender ideologies embedded in cultural configurations of surveillance. Many of the artists in this chapter explore Marxist and Freudian constructions of fetishism that have been significant to feminist media and performance theorists, applying them to the visual culture of surveillance. They represent surveillance both as a *fetishizing* technology that, like classic cinema, produces overdetermined images of sexual difference and as a *fetishized* commodity that stands in for—and in standing in for covers over—patriarchal power and control.[15] They show that surveillance technologies not only depend on fetishes of sexual difference to express disciplinary power but also that surveillance systems function *as fetishes*—glittering spectacles of high technology and fabled security—which distract from underlying anxieties about state security and heteronormative control.

As I analyze these works, I also point out the challenges that arise when using representations of the gendered body to critique surveillance; the pitfalls these artists encounter are as instructive as their successes. Pairing fetishized representations of gendered bodies and the "sexiness" of surveillance technologies does not always give rise to critical feminist readings of surveillance culture. In fact some, like Mann's *Heart-Cam* or Walker's *Peepshow*, largely fail as feminist interventions but are nevertheless valuable for their explorations of the erotics of surveillance and what we might think of as a cultural desire for discipline. As part of my analysis, I propose ways in which such pieces could be reconceived to make a more effective feminist critique of dominant representations of surveillance and sexuality.

Looking Back through (Wo)Mann's Gaze

Like many second-wave feminist theorists, Mann conceived of sousveillance as a strategy he could use to critique the objectifying, disciplinary gaze of surveillance and the power imbalance it fosters between watcher and watched. In *The Explicit Body in Performance*, Rebecca Schneider argued that a feminist performer can challenge such imbalances within the visual field by deliberately "looking back" at the gaze for which she poses.[16] By *looking back* across the dyad of seeing/being seen, a feminist performer attacks the related binary structures of active/passive and masculine/feminine within visual performance, waging what Schneider termed "binary terror."[17] A widely theorized example, whom I discussed in chapter 2, is the well-known feminist photographer Cindy Sherman. In her self-portrait photographs, Sherman "looks back" at her viewing audience through the classic poses of femininity she strikes. Sherman's strategy of simultaneously posing for the observing gaze and looking back at it implicates the viewer as a participant in the process of objectification and "terrorizes" the damning binary to which female bodies have been culturally relegated.[18] As both subject and author of her photographs, Sherman is both "given to be looked at" *and* "given to see"; she is in control of the viewing apparatus even as she is the knowing subject of its gaze.

Mann's technologies of sousveillance supply everyday subjects with the means of critically "looking back" at their surveillers. With the *Heart-Cam* in particular, Mann effectively loaded the guns, so to speak, with the feminist strategy of looking back: he reassigned the power of a disciplinary gaze to female subjects who are already doubly surveilled by virtue of their cultural production as "given to be looked at." However, despite these promising intentions, Mann ultimately misfired the feminist weaponry he constructed. If we look more closely at the narrative in which he places the wearer of the *HeartCam*, we will see that the device was not actually designed to release the wearer from the culturally constructed prison of her body or her social role of object of desire and/or victim of violence. For all its transgressive potential, Mann's *Heart-Cam* does not escape the trap of the familiar damsel in distress story that has long shaped narratives of surveillance. In fact Mann builds this narrative into the sousveillance hardware itself. In an article introducing the device, Mann explained that the *HeartCam* is so called for the way in which the embedded cameras are triggered to capture images: "[*HeartCam*] used heart rate as a natural index to frame rate (i.e., frame rate was proportional to the wearer's degree of arousal)."[19] Because the device is not voluntarily controlled by the wearer—as heart rate is not consciously controlled—Mann argued that the *HeartCam* measures the degree of threat an external incident or person poses to the wearer: "Thus, a potential perpetrator . . . would cause her heart to beat faster, which would cause her to take more pictures of him."[20]

That the wearcam bra was made and marketed not only *for Her* but *for Her protection*, suggests that women are only able to participate in sousveillance if they accept the role scripted for them in so much of Hollywood cinema: the little lady in need of defense. The female wearer of the *Heartcam*, it is implied, would still have to wait to be rescued by a patriarchal system of protection or legal evidence that would read her distress through the device on her chest. The final sentence in his analysis is particularly troubling, as it reduces the female wearer to a mechanism of capture: "Since this feedback loop [heart rate as index of frame rate] was beyond her control, it could be said that the assailant was taking pictures of himself by agitating her."[21] Even though Mann is aware of the powerful conflation between sousveillance and feminist critiques of the male gaze and, no doubt, did not intend the device to be sexist, there is little room in his explanation of the *HeartCam* for a critique of the cultural trope of woman as victim. As a defensive device programmed to record any assault or threat from a male perpetrator, Mann's device misses its mark as a tool of feminist empowerment, instead replicating dominant narratives that negate women's agency and instead position them as victims that can fulfill the heroic desires of men.

It is important to take a moment to unpack where Mann went wrong and imagine how the *HeartCam* might be recuperated as a tool of feminist activism. A large part of Mann's difficulty can be traced to his essentialist approach to the female body. In his design, the breast cameras remain too tightly bound to that which they first seemed to be: fetishes of sexual difference. They were designed to function according to the wearer's bio-logical response to being looked at: increased heart rate due to fear or arousal. Trapped within the essentialist narratives of sexual difference, in which women's identities are made visible through biological indicators of sex, Mann's *HeartCam* replicates the equation in which women's experiences are legible only through their bodies. In dubbing his sousveillance bra the *HeartCam*, he emphasized cultural associations of Woman's emotionality (as opposed to criticality of logic), substituting her "heart" for more physically explicit terms that might foreground the fetishization of her body. Even though it seems to arm the wearer through her breasts, the *HeartCam* instead relegates a woman to the sign of her breasts and the fear in her heart, limiting her ability to critically look back at the determining gaze of surveillance by hobbling the (anti)disciplinary, liberatory gaze of sousveillance to a desirous (and threatening) male gaze.

Admittedly, I have set up the *HeartCam* as a straw-Mann through which to illustrate the risks of replicating markers of gender to critique patriarchal surveillance culture. However, Mann is not alone in these struggles. Problems of proximity and distance between sign and referent, object and subject within representations of female bodies have been part of long running challenges within feminist performance art. Mann's conflation of surveillance cameras with breasts is, as the feminist performance theorist Elin Diamond would put it, too mimetic, identifying the performance and reality of femininity as one and the same.[22] Mary Ann Doane described this as a problem of conceptual distance, or lack thereof, between the image and reality of femininity. Comparing images of Woman (iconographic performances of femininity) to hiero-glyphic writing, Doane explained, "Too close to herself, entangled in her own enigma, [Woman] could not step back, could not achieve the necessary distance of a second look. . . . For the female spectator there is a certain over-presence of the image—she *is* the image."[23] Critical feminist spectators, a term introduced and well theorized by Jill Dolan and discussed in my "Introduction," need instead to create mechanisms to provide a critical distance between themselves and the iconographic rep-resentations of Woman with which they are asked to identify.

Surveillance and Masquerade, or Putting Big Brother in Drag

Out of these debates over the distance, or lack thereof, between image and reality have come strategies to hold representations of femininity

at a distance, from the position of both the performer and the spectator. Doane theorized the concept of the "masquerade" of femininity as
a method of creating critical distance between women spectators and
Woman as image. "The masquerade," Doane wrote, "in flaunting femininity, holds it at a distance. Womanliness is a mask which can be worn
or removed."[24] Doane argued that iconic representations of Woman in
classic Hollywood cinema should be viewed as exaggerated versions of
femininity—masks that are donned in instances where such a performance might be desired but that should not be identified with as fully
realized, inhabitable subject positions. As a strategy of critical spectatorship, Doane argued that the idea of masquerade could help female
spectators to remain aware of the disjunction between representations
of ideal femininity and their own, far more complex and rich internal
experiences as women. Sue-Ellen Case took up this theory in her essay
"Towards a Butch-Femme Aesthetic" (1989), arguing that lesbian roles
of butch and femme translate the idea of masquerade into an active strategy of embodied performance and desire.[25] As a mode of camp, lesbian
performances can ironize the symbolic power of the phallus as well as
the compensatory role of womanliness. For Case, lesbian performances
of gender are important for feminist theory more broadly in that they
mimic but do not replicate the heteronormative matrix of desire. They
repeat the signs of gender and desire, but with a critical difference. They
are enacted across a broader range of gender identities and performed
within a matrix of desire outside the heterosexual male gaze.

System Azure, a project by the surveillance artist Jill Magid, intentionally applied the strategies of "masquerade" and "drag" to surveillance
cameras in public space. Working for her own, invented company, System Azure Security Ornamentation, Magid gained permission from the
Amsterdam Headquarters of Police to hand-glue rhinestones to some
two hundred newly installed security cameras around the city's red light
district.[26] By bedazzling the security cameras in Amsterdam's red light
district with rhinestones, Magid performatively "dragged" the masculine
gaze of surveillance and reframed it as part of the libidinal economy of
the city's sex industry. In doing so, she showed the malleability of the
gendered sign system of surveillance and brought attention to surveillance systems as fetishized commodities that, like the highly visible bodies of sex workers in that district, are staged to appeal to the anxieties
and desires of passersby.

As a borderland of abject desires, transgressive sexual practices, and
libidinal commerce, Amsterdam's red light district stands as an especial-

ly potent ground on which to stage a critique of the disciplinary gaze of surveillance and the heteronormative desires it mandates. Amsterdam's red light district had long hosted the watchful eyes of security guards and cameras with the aim of providing a safe commercial space for both patrons of and workers in legalized prostitution houses and sex shows. The addition of two hundred surveillance cameras was popularly interpreted as an effort to standardize the policing of that district and, by extension, to neutralize its unique character. Magid's bedazzling project responded to the increase in cameras by making the devices hypervisible, and thus more available for critical discourse.

These visual modifications suggested that if surveillance cameras were going to change the character of the red light district, the red light district would in turn change the character (and gender/sexual orientation) of the surveillance cameras. As Magid put it, the "performativity of surveillance systems" allowed her to experiment with "how the body is reconfigured, how representation is altered and effected, [and] how architecture is activated and warped."[27] For Magid bending gender served as a means of destabilizing the (straight, male) authority of surveillance cameras. She symbolically troubled their status as *given to look* with eye-catching ornamentation that staged them as also *given to be looked at.* To illustrate this move, she advertised the project with silk-screened posters that read "Big Brother in Drag" and "Why be a silent witness when you can be a glamorous ornament?"[28] The posters inferred that, previous to her bedazzling efforts, the surveillance cameras embodied "straight" heterosexual masculinity. However, with the help of some rhinestones, the desire-based economy of the red light district might instead "warp" the architecture of disciplinary surveillance and its normalizing force on behaviors in public space. Further, by targeting the surveillant newcomers, Magid teasingly suggested that, like tourists seeking out the transgressive freedoms of the red light district, the cameras might also long to throw off the repressive ideologies of surveillance as they entered the district. Panoptic discipline, which trades on the ability of a visible but unverifiable gaze to interpellate subjects of that gaze into self-disciplining bodies, would instead throw off proper social behavior for the unruly desires of the body.

Magid's project thus made visible the multiple, often conflicting layers of discipline, desire, and fetishization embedded in surveillance cameras installed in public space. The rhinestones drew attention to the already fetishized status of CCTV cameras, which have been widely mythologized as stopgaps for crime and improper behavior. Like drag queens who both

Fig. 19. Jill Magid's System Azure Security Ornamentation, 2002

Fig. 20. Jill Magid's
System Azure Security
Ornamentation, 2002

celebrate and destabilize the iconicity of feminine glamour, Magid's cameras ironically overcelebrated the cultural power of CCTV cameras and made visible a cultural worship of total security and safety. The glittering rhinestone jackets performatively dragged surveillance from a lofty position of power, knowledge, and security into the libidinal economy of prostitution. This move not only highlighted the CCTV cameras as fetishes of security, but it also framed the cameras as workers, laborers that, not unlike the sex workers they watched over, were marketing their services.[29]

Returning briefly to Mann's *HeartCam*, we might apply the strategy of masquerade to reimagine a means of more successfully "queering" sousveillance. Consider the performative possibilities of the *HeartCam* if we reinterpreted Mann's gender mimesis instead as feminist masquerade and drag. Viewed as a gendered mask that can be donned and shed by *any body*, regardless of that body's socially constructed gender, Mann's sousveillance bra could function as a wearable prosthetic that could exhibit the fluidity of gender as a representational act of identity. As such, the *HeartCam* could assist in dislocating (rather than reifying) cultural gender norms from their naturalized attachments to the biologically sexed body. Said another way, the *HeartCam* has the potential to perform what we might think of as a kind of *surveillance drag*. As described above, drag performance, undergirded by a "camp" style of delivery has the effect of showing the iconicity and cultural thrall of popular imagery of gender while at the same time unsettling the truth and authority that these images have accrued through sheer repetition.[30] By providing the means with which to performatively "drag" surveillance, the *Heartcam* would empower the wearer to repeat signs of gender and surveillance with a critical difference and a critical attitude. The breast cameras would circulate as consciously femmed-up versions of classic Womanliness, turning any body into a hypervisible fetish of femininity. Even for the femme female wearer that Mann had in mind, the *HeartCam* could thus be read as doubly gendering the body, adding an additional layer of gender masquerade. Performed ironically and knowingly, the wearer of the *HeartCam* could utilize the tool of sousveillance with a critical feminist edge, not only "looking back" but also demanding a second look.

Peepshow: *"Ruining Strippers and Surveillance Simultaneously"*

Giles Walker's *Peepshow* (2007), which garnered international attention in 2008–9 when it was exhibited in the United Kingdom, Spain, and Australia, featured robots that blended two potent cultural symbols: pole dancers in a strip club and municipal CCTV camera surveillance. Though not without pitfalls, the project utilized mimicry and masquerade to create a defamiliarized scene of surveillance and sexuality. Walker constructed the pole-dancing robots to appear unmistakably feminine, with hard white plastic bikinis connected to long metallic limbs. Leaning backward to display their molded breastplates, the fem-bots gyrated their hips against the pole in a mechanical simulation of erotic dance. In place of their heads, large industrial surveillance cameras scanned the crowd. A third robot, equipped with a loudspeaker for a head, played disc jockey; coded masculine by its lack of sexual display and position on the periphery of the stage, the robot pumped out bump n' grind beats from behind a turntable. As part of Walker's ongoing *Suspectart* series, in

Fig. 21. Giles Walker's
Peepshow, 2007

which he builds interactive, kinetic sculptures out of industrial detritus and found objects, the bodies of all the robots were built from scrap auto parts, while windshield wiper motors, wired through a wizard board into a personal computer, controlled their movements.

Walker designed the installation to critique the rapidly increasing CCTV surveillance in London, where he lives and works.

> At the time of building *Peepshow* there was a lot of news coverage encouraging the British public to readily accept the huge increase in surveillance cameras. They were everywhere. I wanted to build a piece as a reaction against these mechanical "Peeping Toms" that were appearing on every street corner. . . . I chose pole dancers as a subject and gave them CCTV cameras as heads—playing with the concepts of voyeurism and its relationship with power. I also was interested in the challenge of whether I could make a pile of old scrap, sitting in the middle of my workshop, into something sexy![31]

Using the pole-dancing robots, provocative symbols of sexuality and desire, to draw attention to the rapid increases in CCTV surveillance in London. Walker also suggested that there was something illicit, tawdry, and objectifying about municipal surveillance programs that targeted the British public. As he wrote on his website, he wanted the installation to suggest that "we are all living in a peepshow now."[32]

Walker's strategy of grafting the head of state surveillance—that which is most *given to see* in contemporary society—onto the familiar trope of the female figure, *given to be seen*, proved to be a savvy, though not unproblematic, means of critiquing contemporary surveillance society. The familiar scene of hypervisible feminine sexuality Walker staged effectively connoted the objectification that he felt he and his fellow Londoners were suffering under the increased municipal CCTV cameras. By choosing the scene of a peepshow to express this critique, Walker followed a history of feminist performance art that has knowingly performed feminine sexuality as a means of destabilizing the objectifying power of the male gaze. In his 1985 essay "Posing," feminist theorist Craig Owens compared the panoptic principle with the arrangement of the traditional peepshow, suggesting that "the peep show is an inversion of the Panopticon: in the former, the voyeurs occupy the peripheral booths, the spectacle, the central stage; whereas in the latter, the (over)seer occupies the central tower, the prisoners the peripheral cells."[33] Owens applied the system of visual power of the Panopticon to the peepshow, arguing that the given to be seen female form at center stage in the classic peepshow commands a kind of power through the intentional act of striking a pose. Owens read the consciously posing female body as resisting the powerful gaze of the male spectator because, in the act of posing, the subject of the gaze participates in, or seems to choose, her own visual capture.[34] As in Schneider's concept of binary terrorism described earlier, the act of posing radically undoes traditional binary oppositions of subject/object and passive/active, creating a form of agency that Owens has described as the "middle" voice.

> *To pose* is, in fact, neither entirely active nor entirely passive; it corresponds rather to what in grammar is identified as the *middle* voice. . . . Both the active and the passive voices indicate activity or passivity vis-à-vis an external object or agent; the middle voice, on the contrary, indicates the *interiority* of the subject to the action of which it is also the agent.[35]

While it is difficult to assign what we might think of as "interiority" or "agency" to the robots themselves, Walker's robots nevertheless waged a form of binary terrorism with the poses they struck, troubling institutions of surveillance and strip clubs simultaneously. Like the *Heart-Cam* or Cindy Sherman's photographs, Walker's robots signified female bodies empowered to look back through their pose of being looked at. The bodies of the fem-bots mimicked female strippers, imbued with the intention to attract the attention of a classic male, heterosexual gaze, while their surveillance camera heads threatened to police that gaze, implicitly labeling it as incriminating. At the same time, the robotic dancers unsettled the ontological divide between artificial intelligence and human sexuality and desire. The exhibit reframed surveillance technologies as overtly sexual and female strippers as distinctly mechanical, resulting in an uncomfortable performance of eroticism, which, as culture critic Adam Frucci blogged, "ruin[ed] both robots and strippers simultaneously."[36]

Indeed, many responses to *Peepshow* expressed a mixture of excitement, confusion, and anxiety over the destabilizing gyrations of Walker's robots. While Frucci's blog post disparaged it ("I mean, I know that people have a lot of insane, indefensible fetishes, but robot strippers with CCTV cameras and bullhorns for heads? Total bonerkillers. No thank you"), Adario Strange of *DVICE* wrote that Walker's "Pole Dancing Robots Make CCTV Surveillance Sexy." Strange praised Walker for having "perfectly meshed the UK's new national symbol (the CCTV) with robotics in a way that almost makes their Orwellian future sexy."[37] Another blogger, identified by the name Geekologie, remained defensive and misogynistic in his interpretation of the project: "As a vehement hater of all things robotic, these stripper-bots have me in quite the quandary. I f***ing hate robots, *but my god I love some strippers*. So, what's the deal—should I hate them? Should I love them? Should I still tip? Haha—like I ever tipped in the first place!"[38]

Although several of these comments indicate that Walker's cultural critique may have, for some viewers, been subsumed by an overwhelming culture of misogyny, the robots' purported power to "ruin" sexuality and surveillance at the same time and to "almost" but not quite make CCTV sexy speaks to binary terrorism that threatened not only institutions of surveillance but also institutionalized performances of sexuality and seduction. In her analysis of Sherman's *Untitled Film Stills*, Kaja Silverman argued that the critical power of Sherman's self-framed poses lay in showing the gap between the cultural ideal for which her poses reached—familiar narratives of feminine desire, desirability, and victimhood—and the embodied reality of her failure to attain it.[39] That is, Sherman's self-portraits show the "pose" as a means by which a photographed subject seeks to enter a culturally seductive narrative and thereby escape the reality of his or her life. As Silverman puts it, Sherman's photographs make visible the means by which "the subject gives him or herself to be 'photographed' in a generally self-idealizing way by the camera/gaze, and the conditions under which this solicitation generally meets with failure."[40] In Silverman's reading, Sherman's failure is productive and essential to her visual critique of normative femininity. Sherman performs a subject who inhabits her own, historically contingent body even as she shows the effort to structure it according to the expectations of an external cultural gaze. By framing the fraught subject position of a feminist, aware of simultaneously seeing and being seen, Sherman's photographs urge the viewer to identify not with the impossible vision of a cultural ideal but rather with the active, vibrant attempts of an individual woman to meet that ideal.

Similarly, the feminist critique mobilized by Walker's robots lies in their "failure" to close the gap between robot and human, surveillance and seduction. Although Walker was attempting to "make something sexy!" out of the detritus in his workshop, the robots did not succeed in passing as agents of surveillance or sex. Instead they were seen as "almost sexy" versions of surveillance that "ruined stripping" with their mechanized performances of seduction. As part of his theory of posing, Owens wrote of the potential for, or expectation of, a feminine mimicry of sexual pleasure, an act of fakery that "entails a certain *splitting* of the subject, [as] the entire body detaches itself from itself, becomes a picture, a semblance."[41] Here, the "mask" that covers over the "gap" between reality and fiction in feminine erotic performance is the pose of *faked* pleasure. While there are a host of problems with cultural imperatives requiring that women exhibit signs of pleasure regardless of whether or not they feel it, the capacity to fake orgasm can also be read as a threat to the stability of visual evidence within representations of female sexuality. If the "show" or visual performance of sexual pleasure does not necessarily correspond to the interiority of a woman's experience, then the signs of feminine sexuality must be seen as separate from the reality of lived experience (even as they indicate the cultural pressures to perform those signs, as in Sherman's photographs).

With this layer of feminist critique in mind, the overdetermined poses of feminine seduction that Walker's CCTV robots struck suggest that both surveillance and sexuality are built on a slippery relationship between truth and fiction. That the installation conflated signs of surveillance with the "show" of feminine sexuality serves to "show the show" of surveillance.[42] Remapping the performative "untrustworthiness" of female bodies across the supposed truth-telling bodies of the surveillance cameras suggests that surveillance technologies possess the same proclivity for mimicry and fakery that women are purported to enjoy. The femmed-up robots reveal that CCTV cameras might, like the fetish of the feminine body exhibiting pleasure for a male gaze, be all surface. Their surveillance camera heads would thus be revealed as fetishes of truth that cover over deep anxieties at the heart of surveillance society about the stability of knowledge and power.

Sadly, this feminist interpretation of Walker's robots has been undermined by the uses to which the robots have been put since their retirement (or, rather, purchase) from the art museum circuit. Walker's robots, now assigned the human names Lexy and Tess, began resurfacing in 2012 at electronics trade shows. Now owned by Tobit, a software company, the robots underwent breast augmentation and are now controlled through a downloadable smart phone application. At the Tobit Software booth at the 2014 CeBit trade show in Germany, viewers were encouraged to download an app that would enable them to send commands to the robots to perform certain erotic dance moves.[43] These redesigns folded the robots more firmly into masculinist fantasies of a future in which humanoid robots function as programmable sex workers and, as a result, stabilized the robots as obedient signs of masculine control and heteronormative desire. Any disruptive agency that the robots may have possessed as binary terrorists was transferred back into the hands and imaginations of the (male-coded) spectators.

Nevertheless, Walker's robots serve as a model on which future feminist surveillance artists can build. The robots illustrate that fetishes of surveillance and femininity can be most productive when they are shown up as failures, imperfect copies that show the impossibility (and irrationality) of attaining normative ideals. The fetish that *fails* as a perfect fetish can thereby succeed as a marker of cultural anxiety over practices like sexuality or surveillance that purport to be more stable than in fact they are.

Explicit Bodies and Critical Feminist Spectators

The examples thus far in this chapter have focused on the bodies of
surveillance technologies themselves, using surveillance cameras as
prosthetics or stand-ins for corporeal gendered bodies. The next two
examples turn attention instead to the female corporeal body and experiment with how feminist surveillance artists might self-represent through
a strategy Schneider termed "explicit body performance." Schneider
described the strategy of explicit body performance as follows: "Manipu-
lating the body itself as *mise en scene,* [explicit body] artists make *their own
bodies* explicit as the stage, canvas, or screen across which social agendas
of privilege and disprivilege have been manipulated."[44] In their respective performance pieces *Monitoring Desire* and *Deep Throat,* Magid and
Hatoum stage their own bodies as sites of investigation and performance.
In doing so, they make visible the historical uses of women's bodies for
the production of male-dominated sexual and medical knowledge. At
the same time, using their own bodies as both canvas and subject, form
and content, they enact distinctly feminist forms of investigation, as they
claim representational agency over their bodies and create alternative,
resistant economies of looking/knowing.

To create *Monitoring Desire* (2000), Magid attached a mobile surveillance camera to a strappy black sandal and aimed it up her short skirt;
as she walked around in the stiletto heels, the camera captured images
of her legs and glimpses of her underwear.[45] Magid first performed
Monitoring Desire (later titled *Surveillance Shoe*) in the lobby and on the
second floor of the Harvard Science Center as part of her master's thesis project at MIT. As she walked throughout the space she displayed
the images from her surveillance shoe via institutional surveillance
monitors installed in the building. Another female performer stood
by the bank of monitors, watching the projected images from Magid's
shoe camera. After a time, Magid approached the other woman and
the two performed an exchange of the surveillance shoe, unbuckling
the multiple leather straps that bound the camera to Magid's leg and
restrapping it to her partner's leg. The camera continued to transmit
the images of the two women wrapping and unwrapping the cords,
straps, and camera around each other's legs. The walking and watching process was then repeated, with Magid watching the images of the
camera shooting up her partner's skirt. The two women eventually left
the building together.

Magid invoked a number of cultural clichés through the visual rhetoric of her piece. She positioned the camera as a "Peeping Tom," connoting an illicit gaze driven by sexual voyeurism to use surveillance not for its security function but instead to peer up the skirts of young women. The surveillance camera she chose was a consumer model commonly referred to as a lipstick or bullet camera, so named for its small, sleek shape. With a name reminiscent of the genre of film noir, well known for its glamorous fetishization of femme fatales wrapped in shades of black and white, the petite camera functioned as a technology at once fetishizing and fetishized. The black straps Magid used to attach the camera-laden stiletto heel to her leg further invoked fetishistic imagery of sado-masochistic bondage and shoe fetishism. Combining the camera with the stiletto heel, Magid suggested that surveillance cameras and female bodies function in parallel manners when it comes to fetishism: they both are overdetermined focal points that cover over and soothe cultural anxieties about in/stability, in/security, and (loss of) power.

In so doing, Magid invoked decades of feminist theory that has used psychoanalytic tropes of fetishization to critique visual representations of gender. The female form in classic Hollywood cinema was read by psychoanalytic theorists as a fetish, a fragmented, surface-oriented representation of femininity that at once served as an overdetermined stand-in for the social power of the male phallus and disempowered women as active, whole entities (instead women were signified by what they lacked).[46] Following psychoanalytic film theory, the figure of the surveillance camera appended to Magid's leg functioned, not unlike the figure of the femme fatale in classic Hollywood cinema. As stand-in for masculine power, the fetish promises to guard against fluid and deorganized bodies, spaces, laws, and social structures. As the female form has been constructed against the supposed latent fear of castration, so, too, do surveillance cameras function to staunch a range of anxieties, blind spots, hidden labors, and markers of difference. As I argued earlier in relation to Magid's *System Azure*, CCTV cameras on city streets and in commercial spaces function as signs of a desire for security and anxiety over the loss of it; they appear as totems that are believed to prevent crime, terrorism, and a range of socially aberrant behaviors.

Deliberately bringing these visual and theoretical tropes into play, Magid attempted to then subvert the traditional role-play in which the male gaze consumes the female image. Rather than *looking back* at the male gaze, she looked *through it*, focusing instead on the exchange of looks between herself, her performance partner, and the images of their

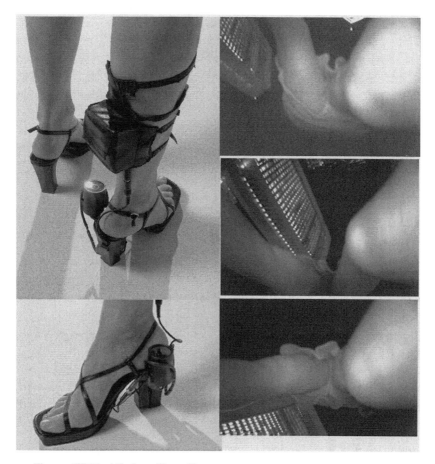

Fig. 22. Jill Magid's *Surveillance Shoe,* **2000**

bodies on the screens. Magid's inclusion of a second woman performer/
observer sought to interrupt the familiar narrative of a woman displayed
for the male gaze by building an alternative economy of looks exchanged
between two women and their own/each other's bodies. As Magid wrote
in her master's thesis, which accompanied the performance:

> This performance is structured around two women who are enjoying
> watching one another. This model of pleasure does not fit the domi-
> nant heterosexual construction of looking and viewing. The reading
> of the performance as being potentially for two women, between two
> women, or designed by two women problematizes the spectator's pos-
> sibly conventional notions of gender relations.[47]

Informed by feminist theories of the male gaze, Magid wanted to create a means by which two women could at once control and consume the visual representation of their own bodies. In contrast to Walker's robots, which were relegated to being commanded and consumed by a masculine-coded gaze, Magid complicated the architecture of the peepshow by staging an economy of looks between two women. Her performance foregrounded the women watching each other and appreciating the new, alienated representations of their own bodies that the surveillance shoe produced.

In doing so, Magid negotiated a challenge that Schneider has identified within explicit body performance.

> Sitting before an "object" of study, the question becomes one of how to apprehend—with the double connotation that word bears of both "know" and "fear"—that object a second time, that is after/in/aware of the history of objectification, which is always already a history of bodies in social practice. . . . [H]ow can we see otherwise, without replicating the dynamics of indifferent visuality as if for the first time . . . ? How do we see for a second time?[48]

As a solution to this challenge, Schneider suggested that the oxymoron "showing the show," or seeing sight itself through a kind of second sight, may indeed "fit the scene of 'woman' with some precision" because "as 'woman' she is preceded by her own markings, standing in relation to her body in history as if beside herself."[49] Through the screens and her female performance partner, Magid physicalized Schneider's image of a woman standing beside herself to observe her own representation and the historical burden it carries. By standing beside herself— in the form of both her screenal image and her female performance partner— Magid urged her audience to join her in "see[ing] for a second time" her own body as at once objectified by an external gaze and empowered to observe itself.

Her emphasis on the exchanged gazes of two women seems to suggest that she was connecting also to lesbian feminist theory and performance practice. However, Magid took pains to note in her thesis that she was not staging a lesbian encounter. As she put it in her thesis, she was interested in "instigating a process that entails a movement between zones of alienation and eroticism." Instead, we might understand Magid's tactics of visual alienation and intimacy as what Diamond described as an activated feminist gaze, a "looking at being-looked-at-ness."[50] Magid intended not only to distort familiar representations of femininity produced by and for a dominant male gaze but also to provide heterosexual women with new models of representation through which they might understand and enjoy their own and each other's bodies.

As my earlier critiques have made evident, efforts to stage the female body as *given to be seen* in order to critique her cultural production as such are balanced always on a razor's edge. Despite Magid's intent to use visual distortion as a means of interrupting the replication of the male gaze and fetishism, the extent to which this strategy subverted the male gaze is questionable. Although they may have provided Magid with a new view of her own body, the distortions that the camera produced were, in effect, indistinguishable from "up the skirt" videos on YouTube created for virtual Peeping Toms. Moreover, as a graduate student performing as part of the completion of her degree, her performance inevitably brought into question the fetishizing gazes at play in the art institution, in which she, a young female student, was seeking the approval of her thesis committee. Positioning her audience of academic advisers and art critics as Peeping Toms, Magid was under double scrutiny. The architecture for a critique of these layered power dynamics was in place: through the surveillance shoe, Magid sutured the surveillance camera and the elite educational institution—fetishized markers of a socially positive desire for security and status—to the fetishism of a voyeuristic sexual gaze. Had she chosen to emphasize this aspect of the scenario, her performance could have performed a comparative critique of the power structures of surveillance, education, and artistic performance. Of course, to acknowledge these power dynamics would have brought into question the limits of Magid's own empowerment and perhaps gone against her own (reasonable) desire to gain approval and recognition from the institutions of higher education and art for which she performed.

Interestingly, the professional installation that has toured internationally under the name *Surveillance Shoe* has sidestepped some of these challenges (and also some of the successes) I have identified by removing live performing bodies from the scene. In the installation, Magid chose not to include live performance by herself, her partner, or any other woman. Instead, the exhibit featured the surveillance shoe itself and a screen showing prerecorded footage from the shoe camera of Magid's legs as she walked around the public thoroughfares of Boston and New York. Without the more complicated matrix of gazes between women, this iteration loses much of the critical impact that I detailed above. However, Magid reclaimed some of the agency supplied by her

live presence by accompanying the prerecorded footage with a statement: "It is as if the city is a scroll, and with the kick of my free leg, I can unroll it."[51] This language of mobility and agency contradicts common tropes of objectification and passivity and instead tells a story of feminine empowerment. It also effectively expresses the double bind she and other feminist performers continue to occupy. While one leg remains bound to the objectifying gaze of the oversexed stiletto surveillance camera (and all the cultural and institutional weight it carries), her other leg kicks out into the night, unencumbered, moving her forward into a world that opens responsively to her presence.

A Seat at the Table: The Critical Feminist Spectator in Surveillance Art

So far the strategies we have seen have all had to do with making both gender and surveillance more visible, as fetishes, masquerades, and mechanisms of (dis)empowerment. The challenges that feminist performers have faced using this strategy—namely, that the sexualized feminist body always risks being reobjectified—plague these surveillance art pieces as well. While the combinations of sex and surveillance offered thus far make evident that the signs of gender are performative, social constructs that can be mimicked by robots or donned as costume pieces, this alone does not constitute a resistant or liberatory form of feminist subjectivity. As Schneider reflected, "After all, to discover the degree to which gender codings are performative rather than 'natural' does not in and of itself alter the show. To be 'just acting' doesn't necessarily mean anything to Desdemona if the climax continues to result in her death."[52] For feminists to use representational media such as film, theater, photography, or surveillance to critique representations of gender, they therefore must negotiate the risks of redeploying the same tropes of fetishization they seek to critique. In practice, then, the challenge becomes how to deploy female sexuality and surveillance *as fetishes* while at the same time pointing to the *real problem*—the cultural anxiety, habit, trauma, or blind spot—that lurks underneath?

Mona Hatoum's *Deep Throat* offers a version of an explicit body performance that both exhibits and escapes the politics of knowing and being known within male-dominated institutions of sexual and medical surveillance. As in several of her other works, *Deep Throat* stages the interior of Hatoum's own body through the at once alienating and highly intimate lens of medical surveillance. To create the video used in *Deep Throat* Hatoum had a doctor insert an endoscopic camera through her mouth and record the interior of her own body with the tiny camera. The procedure produced footage of her esophagus and internal organs as she performed mundane human activities such as swallowing, speaking, and digesting.[53] Displayed as a solitary set piece in a large white gallery room, *Deep Throat* features this video footage of Hatoum's esophagus projected onto a clean white dinner plate on a dinner table set for one. In the exhibit, the table and projection stand starkly alone, devoid of any recognizable body save an absent one suggested by the empty chair. This arrangement invites the viewer to take the empty seat and partake in the visual consumption of her image projected onto the empty dinner plate.

The multiple layers of Hatoum's installation and the feminist strategies of representation she employed merit careful unpacking, as I find *Deep Throat* to be one of the more successful feminist explorations of sexualized bodies under/of surveillance. Hatoum's work employed several strategies of "explicit body art," described above. She used her own body as a stage on which to make visible the processes of surveillance and knowledge production while at the same time escaping the visual objectification they historically have produced.[54] To do so, Hatoum first invoked several "ghosts" of culturally familiar models of looking/being looked at. The endoscopic camera stood for the institutionalized system of medical knowledge whose authority depends largely on the presentation of a docile body. Another ghost appeared in her title's reference to the 1972 soft-porn cult film *Deep Throat*, in which fetishism, pleasure, and the authority of medical surveillance intertwine. As we will explore in more depth below, the choice of these institutions of knowledge were significant in that pornography and medical research both historically located power and authority in a masculine gaze and passivity and desirability in the female body. Hatoum invited these ghosts, represented by the endoscopic camera and reference to pornographic filmography, along with her viewing audience, into the deeply intimate and alienating territory of her own interior. The resulting "binary terrorism" provocatively penetrated the high art of a gallery exhibition and the high-tech science of medical imaging with the low art of pornography. Importantly, throughout these representational strategies, Hatoum maintained authorship of the gazes that probed her: "The video was shot with the help of a doctor using an endoscopic camera. It didn't hurt at all. I was given a drug that seemed to dull the pain, but I remained completely conscious, and as my insides were being filmed—I was directing the video at the same time."[55] As Schneider put it, this strategy of explicit body performance challenges "the presumed passivity and ignorance of the given to be seen: She is 'doing it to herself'—so she must 'know.'"[56]

Second, Hatoum used the visual field of medical surveillance to defamiliarize her own body, making it strange, foreign, alien to her viewers. Drawing on her personal experience as a foreigner living in exile for most of her adult life, Hatoum constructed a scenario in which traces of her presence were visible but her total self escaped recognition. Finally, despite the defamiliarized, radically unappetizing image of her body, Hatoum invited her viewers to confront their own habits of visual consumption. By absenting herself as a recognizable body, she not only defied the histories of objectification but also left a deliberately open space, signified by the chair, in which a critical (feminist) spectatorship could to take up (fugitive) residence.

While several of the artists I have examined so far have similarly sought to author and make visible their own experiences of being looked at, Hatoum's self-directed medical examination skillfully negotiated the tautological challenge of using representations of the female body to critique representations of the female body.[57] Hatoum strategically "showed the show" of objectification by making visible the historical conditions of female representation within histories of medical and sexual surveillance. She did not to banish the ghosts of fetishization, fragmentation, and distortion within these institutions but worked to "make them appear as players."[58] Unlike Magid, Walker, and Mann, however, whose works more or less stopped with making visible the ghosts of fetishization, Hatoum negotiated an additional challenge facing explicit body performance. As Schneider argued, "The trick is that in . . . explicitly showing the show, the performer would simultaneously have to *escape the very signification her body speaks*—the performer would have to comment on that hysteria at the same time that she exhibits it."[59] In order to perform this "trick" of at once exhibiting and escaping the entrapment of historical constructions of femininity, Hatoum summoned a cacophony of historically significant methods of being looked at, then slipped between the cracks of competing male gazes. She gestured to the fetishization of the female body under medical surveillance and pornography, exhibiting and yet at the same time absenting herself from the dominating effects of these gazes.

Hatoum's strategic references to medical and pornographic surveillance are central to her project's successes and bear careful unpacking. Like most pornographic movies, *Deep Throat* (the film) relied heavily on familiar representational strategies in which women's bodies are displayed explicitly for the male gaze. In this film in particular, the inside of the female throat—the odd and fictional location of Linda's clitoris—was the site of sexual satisfaction and desire for both Linda and her male sexual partners. Clearly farcical, with tongue-in-cheek dialogue, a humorous soundtrack, and fireworks and bells going off at orgasm, the film has been both lauded and critiqued as an ironic representation of the ultimate male fantasy—that blowjobs are the most longed for sexual act by both parties. As satirical as the film was, both versions of *Deep Throat*—the pornographic film and Hatoum's installation—invoked somber histories of femininity, fetishism, and surveillance. In Jean-Martin Charcot's infamous "theatre of hysterics," staged as part of weekly lectures that were attended by eager young men studying medical psychology (among them Sigmund Freud), female patients suffering from symptoms of hysteria were probed and stimulated into dramatically frenzied spasms that mirrored sexual pleasure even as they indexed psychoneurological pain. Charcot conducted these medical orgies as his male pupils watched, transfixed by pedagogical and scopophilic drives that, as Elin Diamond wrote in *Unmaking Mimesis*, permitted them to "identify both with 'the great Charcot' and with a hero who can maintain the arousal of a screaming heaving woman, aided by a few carefully chosen props."[60] In addition to destabilizing cultural assumptions of the dispassionate gaze of medical research, Diamond's analysis points out the historical production of medical knowledge through sexualized scientific exploration of women's bodies at the hands of male researchers. Drawing on Foucault's theories of sex as a cultural and medical figuration of truth and fiction, Diamond argued that the figure of the hysterical woman, signified by her overexpressive, uncontrolled sexuality, becomes the explicitly gendered site/sight in which truth can emerge from falsity: "[T]he fallen woman . . . by allowing [male] figures of cultural authority to strip her of falsehood, creates a theater of knowledge, [and] makes possible the production of truth."[61] The upshot of this arrangement, as Diamond and numerous other feminist theorists have pointed out, is that the burden of exhibiting sexuality in all its untamed messiness has historically fallen on the woman's body, whereas truth, knowledge, and bodily and moral order belong to the gaze and gesture of the intrepid male doctor.[62]

Hatoum's *Deep Throat* invoked such a female "hysterical subject" of sexualized medicine (or medicalized sex) while at the same providing critical distance from her own production. Hatoum's *Deep Throat* replaced familiar fetishes of the female body in porn with alienating medical representations of her throat. The endoscopic camera, which extended the gaze of medical surveillance into Hatoum's interior, stood in for the male penis that gives Linda Lovelace pleasure when she is giving a blowjob. While the *site* was the same (Linda's sexual pleasure and Hatoum's medical surveillance are both located in the throat), the *sight* was, importantly, very different: in Hatoum's version the porn star's throat was replaced with a frontier of visual representation that was at once more alienating and more intimate. With the substitution of an endoscopic camera for a cinematic camera, Hatoum gestured to the semblance of female pleasure in pornography while at the same time citing the viewpoint of the medical eye that might interpret its signs. That is, Hatoum paired the purported "truth" of medical surveillance with the theatricality of porn, wherein women's bodies routinely fake pleasure in order to please the male gaze. While a culture of "faking it," alive and well in the porn industry, points to deeply problematic understandings of female pleasure, the possibility of faking it also constitutes a potentially productive form of theatrical mimicry in which the female body defies the male gaze that seeks to interpret it. Even as the female form has served to secure medical and sexual knowledge, it has also produced anxious doubts about visual falsehood or truth, a problem that the gaze of the male doctor (or endoscopic camera) might attempt to solve through scientific objectivity. In performing this kind of mimicry, the woman becomes both performer and critic of her own performance. Within her version of *Deep Throat*, Hatoum thus unfolded oppositional models of knowledge and power, art and porn, real and fake, foreign and familiar, science and seduction in order to, knowingly, lay them on a table and invite her viewers to dine.

Importantly, the table she spread never produced a recognizable version of herself. In contrast to the work of other explicit body performers (Carolee Schneeman and Annie Sprinkle, for example), who have likewise reclaimed pornography and/or self-directed embodied performance as a means of feminist self-representation, Hatoum chose not to appear as a recognizable female body. She juxtaposed the "known" bodies of female porn stars and medical patients with the visually disorienting territory of her own interior. Describing *Corps Étranger* (1994), an earlier work, also created using an endoscopic camera as a tool of representation, art critic James Parry wrote that Hatoum "presented the internal human form as a sort of science fiction creation, transforming it into something unworldly and confrontationally abstract."[63] Hatoum's fragmented, alienated interior thus sidestepped more familiar, consumable representations of femininity by turning them, quite literally, inside out.

In *Deep Throat*, Hatoum's palpable absence, further emphasized by the empty chair at the table, demanded that the audience take up the role of critical witness of her own body under surveillance.[64] Sitting in Hatoum's chair, viewers are left to consider the relationship between cultural processes of fetishism and personal trauma. The trauma that came to my mind, as I sat fascinated and horrified by the images of Hatoum's esophagus and digestive tract, was the trauma of medical disorders such as anorexia and bulimia—costs of an impossibly thin ideal of femininity. The images she projected onto the dinner plate of her own body chewing and swallowing conjured disturbing dieting tactics recommended to girls and women trying to lose weight. I recalled from my own teenage years an article in a mainstream magazine that advised readers to sit naked in front of a mirror while eating in order to disgust themselves with the appearance of their own bodies. Hatoum's alienated body called my body, as a stand-in for Hatoum's, into a productive queasiness, a visceral critique of the visual ideals of femininity that so many women painfully attempt to attain.

For Hatoum, her own personal history and experience of trauma is also significant in the way in which she has constructed her own body both for and against visual consumption. A Lebanese-born Palestinian, Hatoum's young adulthood was impacted by political exile and displacement (a brief trip to London in 1975 coincided with the beginning of a civil war in Lebanon, forcing her to stay in England in exile).[65] Drawing on her own cultural ambivalence and dislocated identity, Hatoum asks her viewers to consider their ambiguous relationship with institutional surveillance, medical knowledge, sexual desire, and experiences of power and powerlessness. As she put it, she wants her work to push viewers toward "a kind of self-examination and an examination of the power structures that control us: Am I the jailed or the jailer? The oppressed or the oppressor? Or both. I want the work to complicate these positions and offer an ambiguity and ambivalence rather than concrete and sure answers."[66] The result of her work is productively uncomfortable: the complicated, ambiguous blend of cultural citation and visual distortion in Hatoum's *Deep Throat* succeeds in staging a representation of femininity that at once indexes and escapes its historical territorialization. The partial, defamiliarized image of herself that she offered to her spectators is fascinating and yet radically unconsumable. In its place yawns an insistent and open space for critical feminist spectatorship.

Sound (E)scapes: Janet Cardiff and Eyes of Laura

In this final section, I examine a strategy of feminist performance that invests in aural representation as a means of circumventing some of the problems of visual fetishization of the body. Janet Cardiff's *Eyes of Laura* makes reference to the Hollywood cinematic thriller *Eyes of Laura Mars*, which is part and parcel of the traditions of visual fetishism critiqued above, while at the same time escaping its visual traps by "appearing" to her audience only through her voice. Cardiff references yet replaces a gendered body image with what feminist film theorists have termed the "voice-off," creating a reorienting aural field in which her audiences can likewise shed some of their habituation to the visual. Moving beyond the tyranny of visual representation, *Eyes of Laura*, along with other sound works of Cardiff's, asks what the female *voice* can evidence in surveillance society that the visible body cannot.

Cardiff is a rare example of a conceptual feminist artist who is more frequently heard than seen. Best known for her "sound walks" and sound-based installations, Cardiff embarked on an exploration of virtual identity and surveillance with her 2004 *Eyes of Laura*. Resembling a personal blog, *Eyes of Laura* featured a fictional character and a factual webcam set atop the Vancouver Art Gallery in Vancouver, British Columbia, where it was exhibited online for several years at www.eyesoflaura.org. In fifty-eight narrated blog entries, the fictional blogger, a security guard named Laura, shared her observations of the happenings of Robson Square in downtown Vancouver via a surveillance camera situated on the gallery's rooftop.[67] Visitors to the site were given the following conspiratorial introduction to Laura's project: "Hello, I am Laura, a security guard at the Vancouver Art Gallery. Through work, I have access to a lot of security cameras. I hacked a way to put one of these online on my blog so you can see it and control it."[68] In order to make the project interactive, as well as to give the project the illusion of reality and immediacy, a live webcam transmitted real-time images of Robson Square and its vicinity to the website, showing panoramic views of the area. Users could click on another box to control the view of the webcam, watching the live feed on the right half of the screen.[69] The project was periodically restarted over the course of several years, resetting to day 1 on completion in order to appear "live" for online viewers.[70]

Importantly, Cardiff as "Laura" remained unseen throughout the process, acting as the invisible yet palpably present protagonist of the serial blog. On day 1, Laura speaks to her visitors in a husky, conspiratorial voice: "My name is Laura. I am tall with reddish-blonde hair. I've lived in Vancouver for ten years working as a security guard. I'm waiting for something to happen in my life."[71] Laura's physical self-description is the only peek her visitors get of her. Other than learning that she bears a resemblance to Nancy Drew, girl detective, visitors never get to *see* Laura; her facial expressions, habitual gestures, and the color of her all-seeing eyes remain a mystery. By leaving her visitors "in the dark," Laura's voice, soundscape, interior thoughts, feelings, and desires are brought into sharper relief. In clipped phrases, Cardiff voices the boredom, desire, restlessness, and curiosity that shapes the fictional Laura's days as a security guard. In the early days of her blog, Laura obsessively watches a cute, unrepentant thief she calls Rabbit: "I just saw Rabbit steal a woman's walkman! He's always stealing, I think, but I don't usually catch him at it. I don't know what to do. I should report him but I've gotten to like him too much. I'll think about it."[72] In Cardiff's characteristically unperturbed voice, Laura also spends time pondering the physical and metaphysical boundaries of contemporary life under surveillance: "There are more surveillance cameras around here than even I would ever have imagined. . . . I wonder how far those cameras could film a person walking through the city before there would be a blank spot that no camera reached. It's almost as if we all live privately only in the gaps." Through these visceral yet disembodied descriptions, Laura gives her audience access to her inner life and sensory experiences: when she is not examining the odd things she sees people do, she makes audio recordings of herself walking in stiletto heels, drinking water, reciting the alphabet; she posts photographs of her favorite pair of glasses (though not of herself wearing them); and she passes the time by letting visitors take control of the security cameras where she works. With her voice in their ears, visitors can peer at the monotonous scene of urban banality surrounding the Vancouver Art Museum. They see what she sees from her surveillance post and can get a sense of what it feels like to sit where she sits.

By transferring representational power from vision to voice, Cardiff employed the feminist representational strategies of *écriture féminine* and voiced writing. Just as Theresa de Lauretis and Laura Mulvey theorized the female body as trapped within a "given-to-be-looked-at-ness" under the male gaze of visual culture, feminist linguistic theorists such as Hélène Cixous, Luce Irigaray, and Kaja Silverman argued that female social subjects have long been trapped within a linguistic system that is defined according to a male view of the world.[73] Silverman argued that in classic Hollywood films "women's words are shown to be even less her

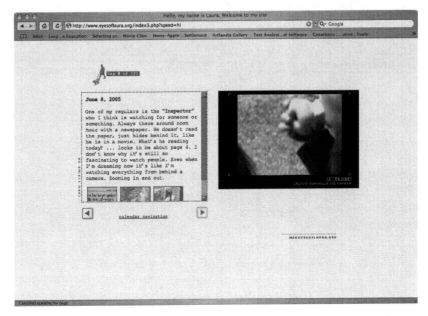

Fig. 23. Janet Cardiff's *Eyes of Laura*, 2004, website still

own than are her 'looks.' . . . [Her words] are scripted for her, extracted
from her by an external agency, or uttered by her in a trancelike state."[74]
As a means of creating feminist literature, Cixous coined the term *écriture
feminine*, literally "women's writing," arguing that, as there is no room
for women's self-expression within patriarchal language, "Woman must
write her self: must write about women and bring women to writing,
from which they have been driven away as violently as from their bodies."[75] Fueled by the belief that "Hollywood requires the female voice
to assume similar responsibilities to those it confers upon the female
body . . . filling in for and covering over what is unspeakable within male
subjectivity,"[76] Silverman and others, such as Mary Ann Doane, concluded that in feminist cinema the *disembodied* female voice is the key to
resisting patriarchal psychology, as a disembodied voice is "freed from its
claustral confinement within the female body."[77] More recently, feminist
film theorist Britta Sjogren finessed the theory of a distanced, disembodied voice-over privileged by Silverman and Doane. Sjogren argued
that voice-overs risked leaving the female speaker dangerously stranded
without recourse to a body from which she can be recognized as a speaking subject.[78] Sjogren's term *voice-off* described instead a separate but

equal space from which a woman might speak. In her construction, the voice in cinema can, in essence, *speak for itself,* as the voice-off occupies an alternative space *alongside* (and therefore in relation to) but *elsewhere* (distinguished from) the bodily image onscreen.[79]

In *Eyes of Laura,* as in her famous audio walks, which I analyze later, Cardiff used strategies of *écriture feminine* and voice-off as a means of avoiding the visual fetishism and narratives of victimization that shape Hollywood cinema, as well as several of the performance works discussed thus far in this chapter. Cardiff's investment in voiced narration is most clearly juxtaposed with Irvin Kirshner's 1978 Hollywood thriller *Eyes of Laura Mars,* from which Cardiff took her title. In the film, Faye Dunaway portrayed Laura Mars, a fashion photographer whose commercial success and cutting edge reputation had come from her graphic representations of stylized violence. At the height of her critical success, Mars began see visions of real murders—themselves eerie restagings of her published photographs. Despite her uncanny connections to the murders, the police refused to accept her visions as serious evidence. In twist after twist, the plot eventually concludes with Mars shooting through a series of mirrors to kill the only person who believed her story, the handsome young detective, played by Tommy Lee Jones, who turned out to be a schizophrenic killer obsessed with her violent artistic vision. In keeping with countless other Hollywood thrillers, the plot of *Eyes of Laura Mars* illustrates criticisms raised by feminist film theorists such as Linda Williams, who have argued that the woman who "looks," or, even worse, makes a profession of looking, as in Mars's photography, is often punished for doing so.[80]

Whereas *Eyes of Laura Mars* repeatedly features close-ups of Dunaway's eyes stretched wide in blind terror as her sixth sense/third eye shows her yet another horrific murder being committed, Cardiff chose instead to foreground Laura's own voyeuristic drive and the pleasure she found in watching others. Instead of showing Laura's *eyes,* Cardiff showed her spectators Laura's *viewpoint,* placing them, as it were, *behind* Laura's own eyes. Even when Laura's curiosity led her into danger—she eventually finds herself the subject of surveillance—she continued to voice the pleasure she found in surveillance, narrating her own surveillant imaginary: "[I]t's still so fascinating to watch people. Even when I'm dreaming now, it's like I'm watching everything from behind a camera. Zooming in and out."[81]

Cardiff's choice to screen Laura from view was, it seems, a protective tactic undertaken to shield Laura from the visual commodification, idealization, and fetishization that characterize feminine experiences within the visual field of film and surveillance. However, the script of her gender as a surveillance guard still exerted its cultural pull. As in *Eyes of Laura Mars*, Cardiff's Laura was disturbed, and possibly put in danger, by her own exceptional power of sight. A woman playing too fast and loose with the patriarchal gaze of surveillance, Cardiff's Laura found herself caught between the reality of her life as a surveillance guard, in which she is given to see, and her experience as a woman, in which she is not only given to be seen but also given to be punished for seeing. Increasingly fascinated by her power of sight, Laura began to take ethical and physical risks on the job, crossing boundaries of anonymity and professional distance and becoming personally involved in the lives of those she watches. When Rabbit dropped his wallet on the ground, Laura picked it up in order to stalk him. She found that she had no desire to turn Rabbit in and instead used his library card, found in his wallet, to go in search of the text of "Blow Up," Julio Cortázar's short story about a crime solved by the enlargement of a photograph. (Here Cardiff expanded her list of filmic references, as Cortázar's short story is the basis for Michelangelo Antonioni's 1966 *Blow Up*, a film centered around surveillance, sexuality, and the male gaze.) Laura was aware of the risks she was taking; in fact, she seemed proud of abusing her position as a surveillance guard to entertain her viewers: "[R]emember this is all illicit and voyeuristic and illegal. Remember, I am putting my job on the line so you can see this stuff."[82]

A month into the blog, Cardiff's story seems set to mirror that of classic thrillers critiqued by Williams. Like Laura Mars, Cardiff's Laura mysteriously becomes the victim of her own professional sight; she reports, "[T]oday when I was almost home there was a photo lying on my sidewalk. It was a picture of me walking along the street."[83] The phone rings, interrupting her. On the supposedly "live" surveillance viewfinder, one of the people she routinely observes turns and looks directly up at the camera. A few days later chalked on the sidewalk are the words "why are you watching?" Like Mars, Cardiff's Laura seems poised to be victimized for her ability to see crimes that others cannot. In the end, however, Cardiff's *écriture féminine* swirls past this fate. Sinister as they were, the mysterious events never culminated in anything happening to Laura; at the end of the fifty-eight days, Laura is still working as a bored guard. By letting Laura off the hook, as it were, and back into her dull but safe job as a surveillance guard, Cardiff broke the pattern of the classic Hollywood thriller in which the "woman who looks" winds up dead.

Instead, Cardiff's script has Laura getting away with assuming the classic male gaze of surveillance and living out her own fantasies of watching and being watched. Viewers, now only able to lazily spin the live camera that Laura "manned," are left to wonder if Laura created the entire story merely to entertain herself.

Eyes of Laura raises valuable questions about the relationship between truth and fiction in surveillance and visual culture. Within the narrative frame of the project there is an unresolved ambiguity as to whether or not the bored Laura invented the whole murder mystery plot as a source of personal entertainment. The questions of truth and fiction extended beyond the diegetic frame as well: Cardiff's choice to design *Eyes of Laura* to appear as a real blog (and Laura as an actual surveillance guard) caused some amount of controversy. The web-based project was, at least initially, carefully disassociated from Cardiff's name. Despite the fact that her name is registered as the site's domain name and her voice is palpably familiar to anyone who has gone on one of her "sound walks," her anonymity did last for a few months. When it came out that "Laura" was not an actual surveillance guard posting rogue blog entries, the discovery, interestingly, came to some as a disappointment rather than a pat on the back for Cardiff. As Sarah Boxer of the *New York Times* wrote of the project, "What a disappointment to learn that Laura is not a real surveillance guard. . . . Despite all the trouble Ms. Cardiff has taken to camouflage herself, in this case the Laura fiction does not hold. The illusion breaks and it breaks completely."[84] Although Cardiff's identity is apparent in other fictional works she has presented, such as *Her Long Black Hair* (2004), an audio walk in New York's Central Park,[85] *Eyes of Laura* upset cultural expectations regarding surveillance and borders between truth and fiction, fame and anonymity to a surprising degree. After it was discovered to be a piece of fiction created by Cardiff, the piece suffered dismissals, such as "the Web is a hotbed of hoaxes, false identities and illusions, and this is just one more. Who cares if this fiction happens to be the work of a master sound artist?"[86] This review concluded with a comment that the only redeeming aspect of the work was the real surveillance camera that viewers could log onto as "Laura" and control in real time: "All of this just goes to show that there is only one thing better than a really compelling illusion, and that is the plain old truth."[87]

While *Eyes of Laura* received more positive notices in surveillance art and web art circles, the piece has been largely overlooked in catalogs and references to Cardiff's body of work. The oversight is unfortunate because the piece is thematically consonant with Cardiff's more widely lauded artistic projects and it offers valuable insights into her overarching investments in surveillance, embodiment, and communication. While Cardiff's famous "sound walks" are not explicitly about techniques and technologies of surveillance, they are deeply concerned with the relationship between narration and sensation, seeing and not seeing. To create her sound walks, Cardiff uses binaural recording techniques (like Rosenberg in *Contains Violence*, discussed in chapter 1) in order to surround her listener from all sides with her voice and direct her audience's gaze and movements through a given space.[88] At the same time, her authority as a spatial guide is continually unsettled by temporally chaotic observations: the listener's ears may be flooded with a honking horn or street musician's serenade that Cardiff encountered when she recorded the walk, while his or her eyes see only an empty sidewalk and a car quietly parked at the curb. Cardiff's voice urges her listeners to witness things they cannot see, filling their perceptual field with sounds that correlate with often long absent objects and events.

Read in this way, Cardiff's audio walks should be considered surveillance art pieces in which auditory stimuli powerfully counteract normative understandings of looking and being looked at. Like Magid's *Evidence Locker* or much of Sophie Calle's work (both discussed in chapter 2), Cardiff's sound walks and *Eyes of Laura* privilege affective experiences of surveillance that escape and/or complicate the visual record. As a form of voice-off or embodied writing, Cardiff adds her voice to the visual register of surveillance in order to represent spaces and experiences that cannot be seen. Her investments in interior experience over external representation function as a critique of the large volume of knowledge that surveillance, as a visual, ordered medium, misses. Like Magid and Calle, Cardiff implicitly critiques the limits of visual surveillance and suggest that such images can never tell the whole story of desire.

In her sound walks, as in *Eyes of Laura*, Cardiff plays provocatively with normative constructions of linear temporality (another characteristic of *écriture feminine*). In her walks, Cardiff speaks descriptively of events and people that are no longer present in a given space, challenging ordered, chronological time with time soaked in loops of memory. Visual art theorist Kirsty Robertson has described Cardiff's sound walks as "surveillance turned inside out," as Cardiff's voice guides her listeners to observe people, places, and sounds that may no longer be present before them. Robertson explains, "[T]he voyeuristic moment is thus simultaneously created and consumed. . . . In an uncanny flip, the directions given by Cardiff give the feeling that she might be there herself, watching."[89] Instead of thinking of Cardiff's audio walks as *inverse* surveillance, as Robertson suggests, I argue that the walks use a feminist form of temporality in which associative memories or desires bring the past and future into the present, breaking with linear, patriarchal temporality.[90] Cardiff's time is ordered by a *surveillance drag*, different than the kind ascribed earlier. Her colorful descriptions of past spaces and movements exert their gravitational pull, folding time back across the body and space of her audience members.[91] In effect, Cardiff pits her own surveillant time against the surveillant time of her audience, forcibly restaging (or resounding) her own past time within the listener's present imaginary. Near the beginning of a walk Cardiff will say to her listener, "Try to walk with the sound of my footsteps so that we can stay together" or "I am standing with you, facing the window. Place your fingers against the glass. It feels cold to me."[92] Cardiff's voice asks her listeners to mimic her now absent body, telling them what they would see and feel if only they had been in the same time and body as her. The effect is notoriously disorienting to her walkers' senses. As one reviewer put it, the process demands that the walker give up control over any normative orientation in time and space: "[I]n the end, you are not quite sure how to orient yourself and become almost entirely dependent on the recording to lead the way. The listener, thus, temporarily hands over control to Cardiff by putting on headphones and is lulled into the rhythm she establishes."[93]

The effects of Cardiff's surveillance drag, different but no less effective than the potential for "drag" in Mann's *HeartCam* or Magid's *System Azure*, move listeners beyond the realm of visual and chronological order into a feminist reconception of time that we can think of as a *hysteric temporality*. Once understood as a pathological display of an uncontrolled "wandering womb," feminist theorists such as Irigaray, Diamond, and Juliet Flower MacCannell have reclaimed the theory of hysteria as a strategy of feminist mimesis in which women tactically exhibit symptoms of the patriarchal reality they are expected to inhabit.[94] Cardiff's brand of hysteria teeters on the edge of impossibility, as she asks her audience members to attempt a merger between recorded past and living present, self and other, sound and sight. By aurally merging her own palpable yet absent body with that of her listener, Cardiff asks her audiences to experience the symptoms of her own lived experience. Guided by her authorial voice, participants become hysteric subjects of surveillance, mimicking her motions and emotions from the past as they flinch at sounds made by long gone cars and smile at a passerby who left the vicinity days ago.

Cardiff's hysteric temporalities and aural representations are importantly separate from—and often more intimate than—visual representations. By refusing to appear as temporally ordered, visual representation, Cardiff avoids the tendency to cohere to iconicity in critiques of fetishization of the female form. Whereas the feminine bodies represented by Walker's robots, Magid's surveillance shoe, and Mann's *HeartCam* largely conform to cultural expectations of feminine sexuality—with gyrating hips, molded domes as breasts, stiletto heels, and short skirts—Cardiff under surveillance, like Hatoum, is nowhere to be seen. She speaks instead from outside of visually ordered time and space, voicing her authority as the creator of worlds that have either long since passed or are yet to come.

Conclusions: Looking Ahead

My analyses in this chapter have drawn primarily on feminist media theory and performance practices from the so-called second wave of feminism. This was intentional, as I see much to be gained from mining a period of feminism that was, in many ways, far more visible and vocal in articulating tactics and critiques of visual culture than today. At the same time, it is necessary that feminist surveillance artists also take cues from more recent feminist theories and practices. The challenges faced by the feminist surveillance artists that I described in this chapter—such as using visual fetishism to critique visual fetishism, the razor's edge of feminist self-representation—are only augmented by the increasing availability of social media platforms that rely on self-representation as a means of communication. In light of this, feminist theorists have more recently voiced concerns about cultural imperatives to perform desirability as a means of securing approval, status, and security. For example, in her essay "Terror and the Female Grotesque," in the collection *Feminist Surveillance Studies,* Rachel Hall argues that increasingly routine and mandatory surveillance practices, such as body scans at airport security checkpoints, promote "feminine heterosexual acquiescence to the new surveillance technologies." She points to cultural trends that subtly encourage women to respond to the post-9/11 politics of fear by turning potential invasions of privacy into romantic encounters with "knights in shining armor" in the form of TSA body scans. As she puts it, "[P]erforming voluntary transparency is coded as 'hip' in the postfeminist spirit of agency and empowerment via preparation of the body in anticipation of the male gaze."[95]

Exposing similar trends in performing for a male gaze, Dubrofsky and Wood, also in *Feminist Surveillance Studies*, argue that in the "postfeminist" digital age social software systems such as Facebook and Twitter make the recipient of the gaze an active participant in her own objectification, as women actively fashion their bodies for visual consumption through everything from diets and exercise to carefully cropped selfies.[96] In their study on self-surveillance and public critique on Twitter, Dubrofsky and Wood looked at over a thousand articles in celebrity news blogs, tabloid websites, and celebrity gossip magazine websites that discussed the Twitter activities of celebrities. Their first finding was that an overwhelming number of the discussions focused on female celebrities (as opposed to males) who chose to share pictures of themselves via Twitter. Overall, they concluded, "Discussion of the Twitter activity of celebrities in tabloid articles enables the framing of women as agentic, empowered, and authentic in their sexualized bodily displays: they control the means of objectification and willingly self-objectfiy." However, they caution, "This dangerously elides the misogynist context that hails them to perform in particular ways."[97]

That is to say, although Mulvey's theory of the production of the male gaze has become outdated in light of more interactive, agential social media, contemporary feminist theorists such as these maintain that that gaze retains its power as an imagined arbiter of desirability and self-worth.[98] Indeed, as I explore at length in chapter 5, newer surveillance technologies that focus on capturing and interpreting personal data (from e-mails to DNA) are only intensifying these concerns. Within digital networks of social and political surveillance, the production of "digital bodies," or "the ways we write ourselves into being online," continues to be a site of gendered expectations and heteronormative desires.[99] Interestingly, although the recent trend toward biometric and digital surveillance techniques is troubling in many ways, it has served some feminist concerns well. More than the seemingly mundane CCTV cameras in urban space, the rise of biometric surveillance has brought issues of race, gender, sexuality, age, and economic class to greater amplification within discourses of privacy, privatization, differential mobility, and sociopolitical discrimination.[100]

Before turning to a deeper discussion of technological developments in biometrics and artistic responses to them in the following chapter, I conclude this one with a challenge to feminist practitioners, theorists, and subjects today. Situating themselves within a "postfeminist" discourse, the more recent feminist theorists I have just discussed find the demands of self-representation in social and political surveillance today a cause for concern, anxiously posing questions such as "What does it mean that these women are presented as the subjects and objects of their own desiring: 'owning' the gaze and explicitly aiding in reproducing it?"[101] Without diminishing the import of their alarm, as I agree that there is plenty of uncritical reproduction of patriarchal structures of power and knowledge within contemporary social media, I would suggest that rather than framing self-representation as a risk we instead should emphasize performance-based strategies that promote and support the formation of active, conscious feminist practitioners within the context of everyday surveillance. From histories of feminist performance art and theory come invaluable guidelines for contemporary feminist surveillance artists and critics. Along with those discussed in this chapter, Hannah Price's and Jill Magid's projects, discussed in chapter 2, and those of Erica Scourti and Stephanie Young in chapter 5 are also particularly good examples of surveillance artworks that employ feminist strategies to distinctly contemporary conditions of self-representation under surveillance. These artists have taken the first steps in what must be a greater commitment within surveillance art and society to interrogate and critically utilize surveillance as a technology of gender.

CHAPTER 5

Skin

———— ❧ ————

The British sci-fi series *Black Mirror*, first broadcast in 2011 and released in the United States on Netflix in 2014, cannily imagines what our relationships with evolving digital technologies and virtual communication might look and feel like in the near future. The title of the series refers to the appearance of a computer or smart phone screen when they are powered down: dark surfaces that reflect our faces, expectations, desires, hopes, and anxieties. Each episode is a stand-alone story that focuses on new technologies of communication, record keeping, entertainment, and commerce as they intersect with familiar human struggles with memory, jealousy, regret, anger, death, and mourning. The first episode of the second season ("Be Right Back," originally aired in February 2013) tells a particularly prescient story about the virtual and material connections between our corporeal human selves and the digital records of our lives.[1] A man and woman in their early thirties drive to their new home—the man's childhood home in the British countryside, which they inherited after his parents died. In the requisite bickering of an established couple, Martha chastises Ash for overusing his cell phone in the car, on the couch, while eating. Like many smart phone addicts, Ash is constantly fueling his online persona with tweets, instant messages, selfies, and wry observations.

The story quickly takes a tragic turn when Ash is killed in a crash as he returns the moving van after their move. At the funeral, another young widow friend of Martha's recommends a new online service that helped her during her mourning period. Still in beta testing, the service collects and mines a deceased person's online profiles and communications (from Twitter, Facebook, etc.) to build a virtual replica with which a bereaved partner can communicate. If Martha chooses to pay for the next level, the service can gain access to all of Ash's personal e-mail correspondence, which will enhance its ability to build an ever more accurate model of his conversation style, thought process, and sense of humor. Although Martha is at first resistant, she finds herself logging on to the service to sooth her bereavement; soon she is obsessively texting and then talking to the digital reanimation of Ash, a being that sounds and thinks uncannily like her late partner. Not unlike the virtual love interest in Spike Jonze's 2013 film *Her*, the digital Ash possesses machine intelligence with which it rapidly assimilates the additional details Martha provides about their inside jokes and researches conversational topics instantaneously online.

Black Mirror takes the virtual relationship a step further when the online bereavement service offers Martha a more extreme (and expensive) option: giving a physical body to the digitally reincarnated Ash. Using the biometric data garnered from every image that Ash's online profiles can provide of him, the system creates a fleshly doppelganger, delivered to her door in a large wooden box. Ash, in the flesh and seemingly alive again, can resume his role as embodied companion and lover. Martha remarks at one point that the reincarnated Ash looks remarkably good, the best version of his living self; he responds by crediting his source material: "Well, the photos we keep tend to be flattering." Despite the seemingly utopian promise of a digital afterlife, the plot soon turns nightmarish and uncomfortable. Over time the bereavement system's attempts to reincarnate a satisfying version of Ash prove shallow, ending up in the uncanny (and unsatisfactory) valley between living human and virtual record. For Martha, living with the digital double of Ash soon becomes more frustrating than comforting: he doesn't sleep or eat; he acquiesces too quickly, asserting his opinion or desires only when prompted by her; and he lacks the close-up, real-life details of her late beloved, having been built without pores or fingerprints, as the digital photographs did not provide the system with that level of detail. In keeping with all episodes of *Black Mirror*, this one concludes with a queasy ethical choice for the protagonist. In the closing scene, now several years later, we find that Martha has relegated the digitally reincarnated Ash to the attic. Their young daughter (not long after Ash's death Martha found out she had become pregnant right before he died) goes up to the attic to share her birthday cake with this simulation of her father, even though he cannot eat it.

While the episode is a work of speculative fiction, it poses important questions about personal, corporate, and state investments in the formation and maintenance of digital re-presentations of individuals. How are we re-membered (or mis-membered) through the digital interfaces we use? How and to what end do these bodies of data, created through virtual interactions, become material? How and when do our data selves stand in and even speak for our corporeal selves? What are our ethical, political, and personal responsibilities in managing and caring for these digital selves created through digital and biometric surveillance technologies? And how do we reconcile the likelihood that these "digital doubles" will outlive our corporeal selves? Although the techno-social situations dreamed up by *Black Mirror* creator Charlie Brooker are several sleek steps beyond the smart phones, facial recognition software, and touch screens we currently have, the prospect of using personal data to re-create a posthumous likeness of a loved one is on a continuum with our reality. Indeed, it is not difficult to find evidence of the value placed on what have become commonly known as our "digital doppelgangers" or "digital doubles."[2] Social and commercial applications of digital doubles have ballooned in recent years as biometric surveillance and predictive analytics have become increasingly sophisticated, automated, and, as of yet, relatively unregulated. Online communications, transit records, medical databases, bank cards, browsing histories, and CCTV cameras with facial recognition software automatically produce records of users' intimate habits, preferences, movements, influences, genetic predispositions, and social networks. These digital doubles are valued for both their predictive and archival capacities; from this source material insurance companies and law enforcement agencies attempt to manage risk, corporations build personalized advertising campaigns, and individuals curate online personas. As in *Black Mirror*, the impacts of these digital doppelgangers extend beyond the virtual realm into material reality. Lisa Nakumura has argued that digital surveillance technologies "such as body scanners, ultrasounds, networked genomics, and other increasingly compulsory forms of biometric monitoring" not only define and regulate populations, but they "create new gendered, racialized, and abled or disabled bodies through digital means."[3] Assessments of personal and biometric data, performed in virtual obscurity by various interconnected state and corporate entities, come back to bear on the material lives of social subjects in the form of permeable or impermeable barriers to mobility, opportunity, political visibility, and legal recourse.[4] As a result, contemporary digital surveillance "does more than simply watch or observe bodies. It *remakes* the body as a social actor, classifying some bodies as normative and legal, and some as illegal and out of bounds."[5]

This chapter looks at the ways in which individuals are represented and, in some cases, reembodied through their corporeal and informational data. I build on the previous two chapters, which focused on screenal representations of individual identity and experience; surveillance screens as tools of subversive action and storytelling; and on sexualized, gendered bodies under surveillance, in order to look more closely at the ways in which surveillance technologies interpret and reproduce our bodies through categories of race, ethnicity, age, gender, sexual orientation, and other culturally and biologically recognized markers of identity. The title of this chapter is meant metonymically: *skin* functions as a material and conceptual term with which to frame this chapter's focus on the tripart relationship between the body as exterior image, interior lived experience, and source of biological data. *Skin* functions in several, somewhat contradictory ways: as a protective and exposing layer of our corporeal identities, a supposedly stable indicator of biological identity, and malleable surface with which to express one's self. Within critical discourses of biometric surveillance, skin is understood as a porous boundary, a contested space that is both private and public through which social subjects "continually leak biometric information into public space."[6] As Shoshana Amielle Magnet has argued, "[B]iometric data thus produces individual bodies as publicly available human inventory," a shift that has "dramatic ramifications for how we understand privacy and personal information."[7]

A number of performance artists and activists have utilized skin as a stage on which to explore issues of identity, privacy, prediction, and profiling in surveillance society. Works by Zach Blas, Adam Harvey, Manu Luksch, Erica Scourti, and Wafaa Bilal, among others, investigate the relationship between the corporeal body and its digital double, often by figuring digital traces as tangible entities that amass political, social, and economic weight. They explore and expose incongruencies between the digital and lived self and challenge the often uneven and unjust effects of biometric surveillance on the corporeal, lived experiences of certain individuals and groups.

As in previous chapters, I have organized my analysis of these artists' works according to their strategies of representation and critique. I have termed these "masking," "mirroring," and "mapping." The strategy of masking is well illustrated by recent works by Zach Blas, Adam Harvey, and Leo Selvaggio. Each of these artists-activists has variously experimented with transforming body data into "masks" that can be worn by individuals as protection from identification by facial recognition algorithms. Works by Erica Scourti and Manu Luksch, as well as the episode of *Black Mirror*, illustrate the second strategy, "mirroring." These works investigate the processes by which biometric or informational data are translated into a copy of an individual, however inaccurate that copy may be. These works by and large protest "official" copies of an individual made by state and corporate analyses of personal/corporeal data. Finally, "mapping" is a strategy of representation that occurs, quite literally, at the level of the skin. Several projects by Wafaa Bilal illustrate this method of representation: in *3rdi*, Bilal had a camera surgically implanted on the back of his head, and in *and Counting . . .* he tattooed his body with a map of Iraqi and American casualties in Iraq.

The New Naturalism: The Theatricality of Biometric Surveillance

While theatrical performance may seem an odd practice to invoke in so mathematical and supposedly objective a method of surveillance, theater history—and the style known as naturalism, in particular—can provide an illuminating precedent for the ideological underpinnings of biometric surveillance. To make these resonances clear, I draw on theatrical history from the late nineteenth to the mid-twentieth century to identify parallels between the practices and philosophies of naturalism and biometric surveillance. Theatrical movements such as surrealism, absurdism, Brechtian materialist performance, and Artaud's "theater of cruelty," which developed in opposition to naturalism, offer useful analogs to the representational tactics and goals of artists and activists who have critiqued philosophies and practices of biometric surveillance. More than a transhistorical thought project, I invoke these comparisons to help contextualize and theorize the strategies of artists and activists who have responded to the racist, sexist, classist, ageist, and homophobic effects of predictive analytics and biometric surveillance.

As I argued at length in chapter 1, there are significant parallels between the conceptual and material operations of theater and surveillance: both depend on the strategic display of certain objects and bodies (actors, sets, and props for theater; surveillance cameras or guard booths for surveillance), while certain other elements of production remain strategically hidden (lights, dressing rooms, and the backstage area or the "verifiable" gaze of a real-time surveiller). At the same time, surveillance, understood as a means of securing stable evidence, has been constructed in opposition to "theatrical" representation, which has been commonly thought of as contrived, posed, and faked. Surveillance has historically been aligned with photography, especially candid or surreptitious photography, as a means of capturing "authentic" reality.[8] I traced these assumptions back to the advent of photography in the late nineteenth and early twentieth centuries in chapter 1, and it remains true today. In their study of female celebrities posting on Twitter, Dubrofsky and Wood observed that a celebrity's "authenticity" was directly linked to her seeming candidness and unguardedness in image or speech. They concluded that

> the more one is seen as disclosing via surveillance technologies like Twitter, the more one is constructed as being "real." . . . For instance, when a tweeting celebrity gets "in trouble" because of what she tweets, she is seen as more authentic because, despite the context of surveillance, she was completely herself and behaved as if she were not under surveillance.[9]

Within theater history, the naturalist movement was likewise opposed to the ostentatious theatricality of melodrama (highly popular in the mid-nineteenth century), aligning instead with the thrall to authenticity offered by photographic technologies. Champions of naturalism, which gained popularity in theatrical practice in the late nineteenth and early twentieth centuries, sought to utilize theater as a laboratory for the objective representation and scientific study of real life.[10] In his preface to the stage adaptation of his novel *Thérèse Raquin* (1873), Émile Zola argued that naturalism was superior to previous forms of theatrical representation (most recently melodrama) because it reflected the scientific and technological advances of the day, which included Charles Darwin's theories of evolution and animal behavior and photography, among others. Aiming for photographic representation of daily life, naturalist theater aimed to faithfully represent human characters as products of their social milieux, determined by "the inevitable laws of heredity and environment."[11] To this end, Zola wrote of the importance of portraying a character's environment in complete, realistic detail in a theatrical setting. In contrast to models of theatrical representation during much of the seventeenth and eighteenth centuries, which used stock sets and symbolic characters to tell their stories, Zola argued that enlightened nineteenth-century theater makers and audiences had become aware of the impact that nature and one's environment had on behavior, character, and life conditions. These principles should thus be applied to theatrical sets, costumes, props, and narratives; as Zola wrote in his famous treatise "Naturalism in the Theatre" (1881), "[T]he environment should determine the character."[12]

The logic of naturalism also governs biometric science. Under biometric surveillance and predictive analytics, individuals are understood to be predictable based on their genetics, social and ecological environments, education, and economic class. The massive amounts of physical data that can be collected and statistically analyzed in order to identify a given individual include facial geometry and expressions, fingerprints, retinas and irises, DNA, vocal patterns and qualities, bodily smells, and behavioral traits such as one's gait while walking, or travel patterns between physical locations. Using these markers, predictive analytics examine an individual in relation to his or her biological heredity, behavioral history, and socioeconomic environment in order to predict risk, profit, behavior, and what we might think of in theatrical terms as character. Such methods of reading the body are perceived to be more reliable—though not necessarily more ethical—than other methods of human surveillance or self-reporting because they purport to remove the bias of a human observer or avoid the complicated process of defining one's own identity or character.[13]

In an extension of this notion that machines have the capacity to see us better than ourselves, leading facial detection software developers compete over how close their systems come to matching and even exceeding the accuracy rating of human facial recognition. In 2014 Facebook purchased and further developed a facial detection program called DeepFace, which, at over 97 percent accuracy, boasted the highest accuracy rating for facial detection on the market.[14] This level of accuracy was marketed as a means by which users can more easily tag their own photos, seeming to place the sophisticated machine vision within the service of everyday users. However, Facebook later announced plans to use DeepFace even on untagged photos, meaning that it will be applying facial recognition outside users' choice to identify themselves or their friends.[15] As Facebook holds the largest collection of personal photographs in the world, the capabilities of DeepFace have caught the attention of governments, marketing analysts, other tech entrepreneurs, and privacy advocates, particularly as the program has the potential to be unhinged from a user's prerogative.[16]

Technological advances such as this have not surprisingly raised a good deal of concern, as the ethics of identifying and assessing individuals without their permission, knowledge, or ability to defend or explain themselves are questionable at best. The mounds of metadata that individuals routinely produce can be stitched together by state and corporate entities alike (sometimes in collaboration with each other) to form a comprehensive, though not necessarily correct, record of a person's behavior, movements, spending patterns, social networks, health, and preferences. Individuals often retain little control over the appearance of their digital doubles, let alone the interpretation of their aggregate data by legal, medical, or commercial authorities. As Kathryn Conrad put it, "Faith is placed in the anatomical body as a repository for correct information about the subject, bypassing the mediating filter of human language, memory, desire, need, and so forth—that is, the complex and fallible human subject her- or himself."[17] This, as Magnet sees it, is the primary failure of biometric surveillance: "[T]he assertion by biometric scientists and biometric industry officials that binary maps of bodies produce bodily truths is a form of corporeal fetishism by which bodies are transformed into reified 'things,' objects imagined to exist outside of culture."[18] In *When Biometrics Fail*, Magnet critiques the assertion within the biometric industry "that identities are no more than their binary code," calling this "a 'philosophical-cognitive' error mistaking a mapping or troping narrative for a 'concrete entit[y].'"[19] This "error," of course, supports the economic and political interests of state and corporate entities that have raced to employ biometric science as a means of increasing security and avoiding risk. Beneath these attractive narratives, biometric surveillance practices "spin the bodies of prisoners, welfare recipients, and travelers into valuable data,"[20] turning them into fetishized "proofs" of identity that privilege the corporeal body as a data source over the agency or rights of the individual, a being capable of self-determination and change.

This odd and troubling imbalance, in which individuals are authors of but lack any editorial control over their digital doubles, is intensified for socially, economically, ethnically, and politically marginalized and disempowered groups or individuals. In law enforcement in particular, there has been a race to use predictive analytics in lower income, urban districts with high rates of criminal activity.[21] In 2014, for example, the

Chicago Police Department (CPD) was the top recipient among a number of police departments funded by millions of dollars of grant money from the National Institute of Justice (NIJ).[22] With these funds the CPD launched a pilot program called the Violence Reduction Strategy (VRS), which entailed the collection and analysis of personal and environmental data to detect "individuals within certain groups [that] are identified as having the increased likelihood of victimization or engagement in criminal activity."[23] The VRS team employed the term *custom notification* to describe this predictive profiling.

> Custom Notification is a process that identifies potential criminal actors and victims associated with the continuum of violence. The Custom Notification is predicated upon national research that concluded certain actions and associations within an individual's environment are a precursor to certain outcomes should the individual decide to or continue to engage in criminal behavior.[24]

Couched in the language of statistics and predictive diagnoses long used in the medical profession, Custom Notification was presented as an objective, scientific practice that "evaluate[s] the risk of violence in an unbiased, quantitative way," thereby supposedly transcending the subjective decisions of both police officers and targeted individuals. In order to assure the public of its validity and objectivity, Miles Wernick, a professor of medical imaging, who led the team that developed the analytics software for VRS, likened the law enforcement project to using mammography to identify anomalies that might point to developing breast cancer. Like a medical scan presented to a trained doctor, "the recommendations of the mapping system . . . highlight potential concerns so that police officers can take them into account."[25] Although the CPD and its experts, like Wernick, have denied that they use racial or economic markers when assessing their data, critics of programs such as the CPD's rightly question the assumption of objectivity in the program's predictive criteria. The term *custom notification* at the center of the CPD's initiative has been read by critics as justification for police to invade an innocent person's home at any time. The concept of a "heat list" has drawn its own heat as a euphemism for racial profiling (indeed, the CDP's "heat list" has been overwhelmingly comprised of African American males).[26]

Accusations of racism embedded within biometric surveillance practices are widespread, even as state and corporate entities invest in biometric technologies at greater rates each year. Many cultural theorists, such as Simone Browne and Magnet, argue that biometric techniques must be viewed as distinctly racializing (and, I would add, gendering, sexing, and aging) processes. Drawing on Paul Gilroy's theory of "epidermal thinking" and Frantz Fanon's concept of "epidermalization," Browne developed the term *digital epidermalization* to theorize the ways in which biometric surveillance techniques racialize bodies, as well as the ways in which "the body materializes with and against biometric technologies."[27]

> Digital epidermalization is the exercise of power cast by the disembodied gaze of certain surveillance technologies (for example, identity card and e-passport verification machines) that can be employed to do the work of alienating the subject by producing a "truth" about the body and one's identity (or identities) despite the subject's claims.[28]

The critical emphasis here is again on the ways in which the seemingly disembodied and objective gaze of biometric surveillance privileges the biologically legible body over an individual's own claims about him- or herself. The problems of digital epidermalization stem from the reliance of biometric surveillance systems on statistical norms as a means of producing categories that can be sorted and assessed by computerized algorithms. This often results in systematized discrimination that is both produced by and productive of racial and gender normativity, what Lewis Gordon termed "white prototypicality."[29] This pattern can be seen most clearly in what biometric research and development experts call an individual's "failure to enroll" (FTE), which in fact means a biometric surveillance system's failure to recognize the characteristics of an "abnormal" individual. Though FTE tends to be framed as an individualized problem, FTE rates increase significantly in relation to certain demographic and biological factors. According to several recent studies, FTE occurs more frequently with certain individuals whose fingerprints are more difficult to measure due to age, race, occupation, or gender: "Elderly users often have very faint fingerprints and may have poorer circulation than younger users. Construction workers and artisans are more likely to have highly worn fingerprints, to the point where ridges are nearly nonexistent. Users of Pacific Rim/Asian descent may have faint fingerprint ridges—especially female users."[30] Facial and iris scanning technologies have also had more difficulty reading features of "very dark-skinned users" because the technologies have been calibrated to detect the physical attributes of lighter skinned users.[31] These results indicate that biometric systems are far from neutral, even in their baseline assessments. They have been designed in such a way as to reinscribe whiteness, masculinity, youth, and high economic class as the "normal" center, while blackness, femaleness, old age, and lower or working class identities are pushed to the margins, or worse, off the map altogether. Citing such technical failures and the systemic discriminations they facilitate, Magnet argued that the adoption of biometrics in the surveillance of welfare recipients in the 1990s and in national security and border control in the post–9/11 era have served as a means by which "state institutions deploy biometrics to enact institutionalized forms of state power upon vulnerable populations."[32]

As in the example of Chicago's VRS, the most problematic aspect of biometrics in state, corporate, and medical industries is the underlying claim that biometrics can replace human subjectivity (and fallibility, prejudice, etc.) with scientific, mechanical objectivity. As Magnet put it, "The industry claims that biometrics are able to transfer subjective decision making processes to objective machines, rendering human assumptions invisible."[33] However, biometric surveillance is far from neutral, as biometric technologies routinely exclude certain FTE populations and overprofile others, such as members of Arab and Muslim communities in the post-9/11 climate of counterterrorism policies. Investigating the material processes secreted behind such claims, James Harding has offered a pointed analysis of the links between performative dimensions of biometric surveillance and the ways in which cultural biases regarding race, ethnicity, gender, and age are programmed into predictive analytic systems. In examining the ADABTS report, he discovered that, after they were initially programmed, advanced behavior recognition cameras had to undergo a period of "retraining" in which the machines had to be taught that the appearance of certain racial features alone (such as dark skin) did not necessarily constitute an "abnormal" threat. This retraining was accomplished through simulated performances of behaviors that employ "[staged] training situations with deliberate variety in characteristics."[34] Harding surmised that such efforts indicate that, without the role-play retraining sessions, the biometric systems would reveal with mathematical clarity the racial bias of their programmers.

The working assumption is that the only way that the surveillance industry can compensate for the basic "abnormalcy" and threat of ethnic and racial diversity is by orchestrating and performing fictional scenarios in front of advanced behavior recognition cameras. Otherwise, the automated data processing systems would identify race and ethnicity as indicators of potential threats or as indicators of abnormal or antisocial behavior. The point of departure is programed discrimination.[35]

Harding, only somewhat ironically, called the role-play scenarios that "train" the smart cameras "the surveillance industry's own version of the Surveillance Camera Players," referencing the group of surveillance activists that in the late 1990s and early 2000s performed for publicly installed surveillance cameras in New York City (see chapter 2). He pointed out that there is, of course, a crucial difference in the corporate performers, for "these player-trainers support rather than challenge advanced forms of CCTV."[36] Moreover, rather than catching the eye of the public, as the SCP has sought to do with their performances, the performances used to retrain biometric software systems are hidden within the vaults of corporate trade secrets.

All of this is to say that even though biometric surveillance, like naturalist theater, has attempted to better analyze the conditions of lower economic and socially marginalized groups, its processes of supposedly objective analysis risk stigmatizing individuals and superseding their humanity and agency by focusing only on physical and environmental factors of their identities. Biometric science, which has bloomed under the justification of risk management, has rationalized a philosophy that views social subjects as specimens rather than individuals caught within socioeconomic and political systems that could be changed. Indeed, naturalism was accused of falling into similar traps. Plays such as Maxim Gorky's *The Lower Depths*, Gerhart Hauptmann's *The Weavers*, Zola's *Thérèse Raquin*, and August Strindberg's *Miss Julie* were marked by a shift in focus from wealthy, mythic, and/or stock characters to an examination of the conditions and effects of poverty. These works were lauded for their unflinching look at the lower classes, and the inescapable effects that poverty and vice had on even the most kindhearted, heroic characters. However, just as facial recognition software and other forms of biometric surveillance have met with criticism for representing (or misrepresenting) the gaze of machine surveillance as objective and universal, many theater makers and theorists censured naturalism for its rigid efforts to "hold up the looking glass to nature." Bertolt Brecht criticized naturalist and realist theater for a tendency to so closely align an individual with his or her environment and genetics that these appeared as predetermined, closed systems that could not be changed. In "A Short Organum for the Theatre," Brecht described practitioners of natural- ist theater as "children of the scientific era" who created out of audi- ences "a cowed, credulous, hypnotized mass." He argued that naturalism succeeded in bringing the "field of human relationships . . . within our view, but not within our grasp," largely because naturalist theater "shows the structure of society (represented on the stage) as incapable of being influenced by society (in the auditorium)."[37] In response, Brecht argued for a revolution in theatrical representation, one that "not only releases the feelings, insights and impulses possible within the particular histori- cal field of human relations in which the action takes place, but employs and encourages those thoughts and feelings which help transform the field itself."[38] His well-known methods for achieving this included epic or dialectic theater, presentational acting and design styles that would pro- duce an alienating effect (or V-effeckt), and stage pictures that captured historically contingent social conditions (gestus).

In his first surrealist manifesto (1924), André Breton took a similarly vehement stance against naturalism: "[T]he realistic attitude, inspired by positivism . . . clearly seems to me to be hostile to any intellectual or moral advancement. I loathe it, for it is made up of mediocrity, hate, and dull conceit . . . and stultifies both science and art."[39] He mocked the positivist obsession in literature and drama with describing in over- wrought detail the characteristics of a given person or organism: "If in a cluster of grapes there are no two alike, why do you want me to describe this grape by the other, by all the others, why do you want me to make a palatable grape? Our brains are dulled by the incurable mania of want- ing to make the unknown known, classifiable."[40] Breton proposed that surrealism, which he defined as "psychic automatism," was the aesthetic and practical antidote to the tyranny of classification, logic, morals, and other social-scientific conventions imposed upon the human body and psyche through naturalism and realism. The surrealist practice of "auto- matic writing," performed in a dream state between waking and sleep- ing, would instead provide the means of accessing and exploring subcon- scious truths unfettered by social convention and artificial logic.[41] Along with automatic writing, surrealist artists experimented with finding or creating masks that could free and represent internal psychic states; these masks often employed physical distortion as a technique of rep- resentation and simulated African and Asian tribal masks as a means of critiquing oppressive aspects of western culture.[42] (Here it must be noted that, although the surrealist fascination with "primitive" art objects and masks was meant to be a means of rejecting western bourgeois ideals, the habit of many surrealist writers, painters, and performance makers to collect and display these artifacts carried an undeniable colonialist privilege. I discuss this further below.)

As I will demonstrate in the following analyses, many of the strategies (and some of the pitfalls as well) of the political and aesthetic critiques of naturalism throughout the twentieth century have been employed by contemporary surveillance artists and activists. In their efforts to critique and resist biometric surveillance, many surveillance artists have employed surrealist masks, automatic writing, and Brechtian techniques of alienation, along with representational strategies that echo other movements, such as absurdism and theater of cruelty, which similarly countered ideologies of naturalist theater. These tactical precedents from the avant-garde theater have helped surveillance artists challenge assumptions of objectivity in biometric surveillance and make visible its discriminatory and dehumanizing effects. Rather than biological material or products of the environment to be interpreted, surveillance artists have figured the individual and his or her cultural environment as mutable and subjectively determined. Some strive to undermine notions of scientific objectivity and rational politics, showing them to be absurd and senseless; others utilize distorted masks and prosthetics to show the violent effects of biometric surveillance on the individuals it targets; and still others confront the tendency for biometric surveillance practices to privilege the evidentiary status of the body over the enunciative agency of the individual by providing performative actions which individuals might take against the dehumanizing effects of biometric surveillance.

Realist Algorithms and Surrealist Masks: The Politics of Facial Recognition

Masking is a common strategy that has emerged in response to developments in facial recognition software, one of the most widely adopted forms of biometric surveillance. Recent projects by Zach Blas, Adam Harvey, Stephanie Young, and Leo Selvaggio have utilized masking as a means of distorting the readable features and proportions of an individual's face. These surveillance artists-activists have designed masks, makeup, hairstyles, and facial accessories that at once represent the distorting effects of biometric surveillance and make wearers unrecognizable to systems of facial detection. Their strategies resonate with surrealist art and performance, which frequently used distorted representations of the body and warped facial masks as a means of rejecting enforced social identities, reimagining social ritual, and expressing the inner experience of an individual. By the same token, just as the surrealist use of masks and primitivism in visual representation must be read as retaining something of a western colonialist perspective, so, too, do some of these artists struggle with embedded racial and gendered biases in the design and context of their antisurveillance masks.

BLAS(TING) STRUCTURAL VIOLENCE
IN FACIAL DETECTION SOFTWARE

Zach Blas's *Face Cages* (2013–15) are wearable devices that feature a series of metal bars set at the data points used by standard facial recognition software.[43] Taking inspiration from Magnet's description of biometric surveillance as producing a "cage of information," Blas wanted to create a device that expressed the structural violence of biometrics. He based his design on the visual motif that has come to be associated with facial detection scans—the colorful geometric lines connecting the data detection points on a face. As he described them, "These diagrams are a kind of abstraction gone bad, a visualization of the reduction of the human to a standardized, normalized, ideological diagram. When these diagrams are extracted from the humans they cover over, they appear as harsh and sharp incongruous structures; they are, in fact, digital portraits of dehumanization."[44] Citing the failure to recognize nonnormative, minority persons such as those described above with regard to FTE rates and "white prototypicality," Blas's *Face Cages* make material the process by which an individual is reduced to a narrow, normative band of identification. They dramatize the abstract and structured violence of facial detection by invoking disciplinary devices such as muzzles, prison bars, handcuffs, and even torture devices. The masks, which are reportedly painful to wear, "exaggerate and perform the irreconcilability of the standardized, neoliberal biometric diagram with the materiality of the human face itself—and the violence that occurs when the two are forced to coincide."[45]

Surrealism and its close cousin, dadaism, both of which emerged in the late 1910s and grew in popularity through the 1920s, used masking as a technique of aesthetic distortion. Although the surrealists were staunchly anticolonialist, there was a trend among artists in the move-

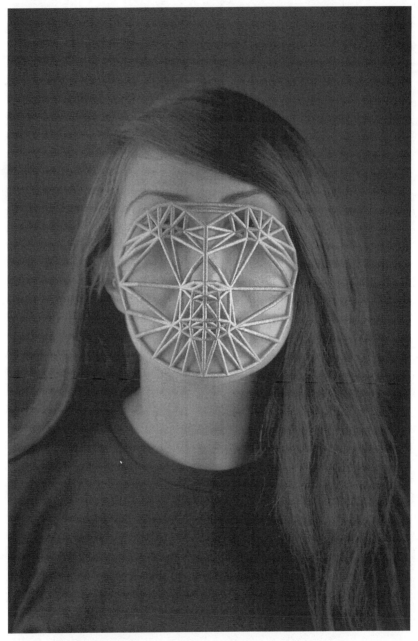

Fig. 24. Zach Blas's *Face Cage* #2, endurance performance with Elle Mehrmand, 2014. (Photo by Christopher O'Leary.)

ment to collect, display, photograph, and wear tribal masks from various parts of Africa and Asia.[46] These masks were seen to retain some of the spiritual mysticism they were invested with in their native cultures, a subject of fascination for the surrealists more broadly. Masks were also used to highlight or downplay sexuality, building a kind of androgyny that was particularly interesting to many surrealist artists and/or to reject oppressive aspects of western culture ranging from warfare to bourgeois ideals. As noted above, the surrealist embrace of primitivism as a means of rejecting bourgeois western culture was seen on one hand as a progressive attitude toward nonwestern cultures and on the other as an objectifying cultural appropriation that implicitly replicated the colonialist attitudes they sought to critique.[47]

Aware of the risk of further essentializing "otherness" through his masks, Blas has taken pains to contextualize his projects within complex dynamics of racism and sexism in contemporary culture. He is careful to explain the design and intention behind his masks, providing well-researched and clearly argued textual justification, which he publishes online and shares with his workshop participants. Presented against a backdrop of research on the prevalence of racism, sexism, and homophobia within facial detection software and visual culture more broadly, his better known *Facial Weaponization Suite* draws on the methods of abstraction and distortion used in surrealist masks in order to make an aesthetic critique of the identity politics of facial recognition software. Instead of simply obscuring the face of the individual wearer, as in *Face Cages*, Blas's *Facial Weaponization* series features masks formed of aggregate data taken from multiple faces of individuals with a given demographic background (black, female, homosexual, etc.). Taking the form of brightly colored, amorphous plastic shapes, the masks are collective distortions that at once symbolize and protect against the targeted discrimination and profiling experienced by particular groups of people.

> *Facial Weaponization Suite* protests against biometric facial recognition—and the inequalities these technologies propagate—by making "collective masks" in community-based workshops that are modeled from the aggregated facial data of participants, resulting in amorphous masks that cannot be detected by biometric facial recognition technologies.[48]

These masks reference the racial profiling of black men through human and mechanized systems of surveillance, as well as "biometric

Fig. 25. Zach Blas's *Facial Weaponization Suite: Fag Face Mask*, October 20, 2012, Los Angeles. (Photo by Christopher O'Leary)

racism (the inability of biometric technologies to detect dark skin), the favoring of black in militant aesthetics, and black as that which informatically obfuscates."[49] Another series takes on the recent veil legislation in France, which made full facial coverings worn by some Muslim women illegal. These blue masks were formed from aggregate images of veiled women's faces and have been worn to protest such legislation as an effort that "turns visibility into an oppressive logic of control."[50] The mask that has gained the most media attention is known as the "fag face mask," which is generated from the biometric facial data of a number of queer men's faces.[51] Fag face masks, made of shiny pink plastic, are deliberately hypervisible even as they seek to distort beyond recognition the faces of gay men who might be profiled for their sexual orientation. The masks also challenge maxims of contemporary surveillance such as "If you have nothing to hide, you have nothing to fear," which are distinctly male and heteronormative. Fear and hiding loom large in the histories of sexually marginalized groups; for women and LGBTQ individuals and communities, the hidden is often equated with shame, criminalization, or violence.[52]

Blas has hosted mask-making workshops and distributed the masks to be worn at various conferences, galleries, and public protests, including recently along the US-Mexico border, as biometrics have been increasingly deployed as border security technology. By mobilizing aggregate data, his* masks form communal identities that refuse to be ignored or identified. The masks make wearers illegible to recognition algorithms while at the same time, by virtue of their unusual appearance, creating "autonomous visibilities for collective protest." As Blas put it, the masks form a "fog of a queerness that refuses to be recognized. . . . Becoming non-existent turns your face into a fog, and fog makes revolt possible."[53]

DIY DAZZLE: HAIR, MAKEUP, AND FEMINIST POLITICS

Adam Harvey's *CV Dazzle* (2014) received a good deal of media attention as an inexpensive DIY means of thwarting facial detection software. A fashion designer and privacy advocate, Harvey experimented with fashion (makeup, hairstyles, accessories) as a means of camouflaging the face of a wearer. He discovered that asymmetrical hairstyles that hide parts of the face and geometric patterns applied as face paint render the wearer's face unrecognizable to facial recognition software. Named after

Fig. 26. Zach Blas's *Facial Weaponization Suite: Procession of Biometric Sorrows*, June 5, 2014, The Museo Universitario Arte Contemporáneo (MUAC), Mexico City. (Photo by Orestes Montero Cruz.)

one of the most widely used facial detection programs, OpenCV Face Detection, *CV Dazzle* consists of an online portfolio and user's manual that illustrate a range of hair and makeup styles that can thwart facial recognition technologies.[54] Harvey's project aims to educate as well as dazzle. His website provides detailed explanations and diagrams of how computer vision programs such as OpenCV Face Detection detect a face and then extrapolate and analyze data that can identify the age, race, gender, and emotional state of a given individual.[55]

Although Harvey's designs are eye-catching and clever in their simplicity, they lack the political context that Blas provides. Harvey tends instead to present his designs within the framework of the fashion art world. Though this strategy succeeds in making antisurveillance fashion hip, the photographs that Harvey has published of *CV Dazzle* feature tall, thin female models in high-fashion couture poses, reifying rather than challenging cultural pressures to conform to standards of beauty placed on (particularly women's) bodies. As in my critique of Harvey's antidrone "hijabs," discussed in chapter 6, his designs do not address the ways in which facial detection, and body surveillance more broadly, might come to bear differently on individuals based on their race, gender, nationality, or other physical markers. Indeed, his rather carefree couture appropriation of tribal face paint designs is reminiscent of accusations of sexism lodged against the surrealists for the frequent depiction of women (even fellow artists in the movement) as objects of male sexual fantasy and desire.[56]

Despite its reputation as a male-dominated, misogynistic movement, surrealism was a form taken up by numerous women and even feminist artists, Stephanie Young, an Oakland-based poet, has recuperated Harvey's *CV Dazzle* designs and created with them a savvy feminist critique of gendered norms in social and political surveillance. In 2014 Young planned and hosted the first *Anti-surveillance Feminist Poet Hair & Makeup Party*, an event that has since been replicated by other antisurveillance feminists across the country.[57] Although it focuses primarily on thwarting the ability of facial recognition software to identify one's face using Harvey's designs, the "A-SFPH&MP" responds to the reality that women experience particularly intense visual scrutiny in public and private spaces. As Young described the party on her blog and in a pamphlet she published to accompany the event, the aim of the A-SFPH&MP is to teach other women to use asymmetrical makeup and hair designs so as to "scramble the gaze." For Young the gaze includes the widely theorized "male gaze" of social and media culture, the "machine gaze" of facial-recognition-enhanced surveillance cameras, and the critical evaluations that women apply to themselves and each other.[58]

Young's pamphlet, available online for others who might want to throw their own parties, opens with the acknowledgment that surveillance is a complicated topic for women, one that does not have an easy, catchall answer.

> A-SFPH&MP techniques won't help at all with the undercover cop who wants to fuck you, gets you pregnant and disappears, nor the informant who introduces himself after the talk and says he's interested, wants to turn his life around, stop doing drugs, says he believes Islam can provide a purpose in life.

> TODAY'S TOPIC IS HOW TO HIDE FROM CAMERAS. SO IT'S NOTHING LIKE SMOKEY EYES OR BLUSH BASICS TODAY, RIGHT NOW WE'RE GOING TO BE DISCUSSING DIFFERENT TECHNIQUES WHICH WILL LET YOU WALK AROUND THE CITY UNDETECTED BY CAMERAS.[59]

Fig. 27. Stephanie Young's Anti-surveillance Feminist Hair & Makeup Party. (Top photo by Emily Raw, bottom photos by Stephanie Young.)

While the notion of "antisurveillance" pushes back against the "given-to-be-looked-at-ness" ascribed to the female body, the focus on "hair and makeup" connotes traditional beautification regimes to which women have long been enculturated.[60] Young walks the line between these seemingly oppositional stances, slipping her critique between familiar beauty magazine fashion tips: "IF YOU FOLLOW THESE EASY STEPS, YOU'LL BE UNDETECTED BY CAMERAS AND YOU WILL LOOK GREAT."[61]

The complicated terrain of femininity and visibility that Young traverses is illustrative of the emergent agenda of contemporary third-wave feminism. As I discussed in relation to works by Jill Magid and Hannah

Price in chapter 2, although third-wave feminism is difficult to define, it has tended to follow three main strategies: to foreground personal narratives as a means of forging a multiperspectival vision of feminism; to choose action over theoretical justification; and to attempt to view other women from an inclusive, nonjudgmental standpoint rather than policing the boundaries of what makes a woman feminist.[62] Young's inspiration for the party came after a mediatized event that prompted critical and judgmental reactions among the feminist poet community over the self-representation of several feminist writers. In 2013 the *New York Daily News* published a controversial photo spread of contemporary female poets in New York City.[63] Even as the article celebrated the gains of these women in a traditionally older-male-dominated field, several of the accompanying photos featured the women writers in pinup model outfits and poses (reclining on a blowup plastic couch, leaning up against a fence in a bustier and short skirt). The photographs prompted interfeminist debates in the poetry community about the sexual politics of the visual choices made by the photographer and the poets.

With the A-SFPH&M pamphlet Young responded to the harsh criticisms and polarized perspectives regarding feminist self-representation, as well as the hypervisibility that women experience in public and private life. Amid facts about biometric surveillance systems and the operations of facial recognition technologies in the party pamphlet, she shares ironic and pseudoscientific factoids about the many ways in which women are scrutinized visually such as "The internet says science says Women's Facial Features Can Determine Length of Relationship," and "a woman's face is said to be most attractive when the space between her pupils is just under half the width of her face from ear to ear."[64] In the spirit of a Riot Grrrl Zine, Young also maps questions and contradictions about the politics of gender and surveillance onto a deeply personal framework. Toward the end of the pamphlet, she recounts late-night debates with herself over self-image and her simultaneous rejection and embrace of her feminine appearance.

> What's my problem? This body's mostly symmetrical, marked by some primary traits around which structural privilege gets organized and others for which I receive less pay while doing the same amount of work but all in all: comfortable. Most days I wear the assigned gender without thinking about it too much, mobility within a passing range of characteristics that comprise the hateful standards of beauty I'm ruled by. Still, at the end of the day when I take it off and get ready for

bed, when I see myself I often feel stupid and ugly in a low-grade fever sort of way that comes and goes, stupid I can't identify more successfully with a body pleasingly non-threateningly attractive to employers and advertisements for banking and yogurt alike.[65]

This passage, which stands out as the most personal of the statements in the pamphlet, illustrates the mashup of visual identities and expectations that magnify and complicate women's experiences of surveillance. Looking good for one's boss and mirroring the shiny, happy woman in a yogurt advert are benefits that double as burdens.

Ultimately, Young refuses to offer any easy solutions to the complicated position of being a feminist in today's media-saturated surveillance society. Deeply suspicious of the countless surface remedies supplied by the commercial fashion industry, she does not pretend that an edgy new hair or makeup style will necessarily liberate her from inner and outer scrutiny. Her pamphlet concludes:

> Anything you do with your (young, attractive) female body to evade or critique its commodity status will be recuperated as fashion.
> No matter what. . . .
> You can have your body back when they're done with it. By then you'll probably hate it as much as they do.[66]

The heart of Young's message is fatalistic, but this helps it ring true. She and many young feminists like her may feel angry, confused, and fed-up. Though not an antidote to gendered scrutiny, the communal event of the party can at least offer an active, material focus, a chance to gather and discuss; to rant, laugh, and rehearse transformation; and, perhaps most important, to take things into their own hands.

URME: HACKING WHITE MALE PRIVILEGE

The Chicago-based artist Leonardo Selvaggio offers a rather different approach to critiquing facial recognition software and the replication of white, male prototypicality therein. Instead of protecting an individual's identity through cruel metal accessories or surrealistic makeup and masks, Selvaggio decided to go for realism, albeit with a touch of absurdism. His URME mask series features exact replicas of his own white, male face, which he lends to others so they can temporarily assume his

Fig. 28. An individual wearing Leo Selvaggio's URME Surveillance Identity Prosthetic, 2014

identity in public space. Although he took inspiration from Blas, Harvey, and Young, Selvaggio felt that dramatic obfuscations of the face are not an effective solution for individuals who might not want to stand out in public space (none of the previous projects claimed to be subtle). Building on the concept of open source software, Selvaggio decided to experiment with open sourcing his identity: "[R]ather than hide a face, substitute it."[67] He designed a high-quality resin likeness of his face, testing it to ensure that sophisticated facial recognition software, such as Facebook's DeepFace and the CPD's Virtual Shield surveillance cameras system would positively identify the mask as the actual Leo Selvaggio. Once he gained success with the camera vision, he distributed the masks to others and has made them available for purchase online.[68] Regardless of their own identities and demographic profiles, wearers will be recognized by cameras equipped with facial recognition software not as themselves but as Leo Selvaggio.

A fair-skinned white man with an amiable baby face, Selvaggio is aware that the project risks promoting white male privilege as a panacea for the racism and sexism that others may experience based on their appearance. He maintains that this is part of the project's political critique.

> The URME Surveillance Prosthetic, if undetected, allows for an individual to temporarily experience and consequently perform white male privilege in public space, while at the same time drawing attention to the very nature of privilege as a component of a patriarchal power structure that excludes the majority of Americans. . . .
> URME Surveillance asserts the utopian ideal that everyone could and should benefit from the same privilege that white men do, which is to simply be themselves and valued for it despite their behavior, even when its criminal.[69]

Furthermore, Selvaggio does not see distributing his likeness as a one-way street. He considers the masks to be a cyborgian experiment through which the race, age, gender, and other biological markers of identity of wearers might exert mutual pressure on his own identity. If a black woman wears a mask of his face, does she become a white man or does he become a black woman, he asks? Or is there something else created altogether? With this line of thinking, Selvaggio aims to push the notion of identity to its limits and, in the process, challenge the authority of disciplinary surveillance systems.

> [I]f multiple users were to wear my face and each become a "Leo" in different areas of the same city at the same time, facial recognition systems would have conflicting locative information: the identity "Leo Selvaggio" would be inhabiting more than one space at a time. Consequently, as the bodies of each individual wearer are different, there may also be inconsistent data gathered about my height, weight, and gender. If one wearer is tall, athletic and female, while another wearer is short, rotund, and male, then the collected data would reflect that "Leo Selvaggio" is tall, short, athletic, rotund, female and male.[70]

For all his dedication to replicating the "real" visage of himself so that facial recognition software will positively identify the wearer as Leo Selvaggio, there is a touch of the absurd in URME. Selvaggio coordinated several performances in which a group of people, all wearing masks of Selvaggio's face, walked throughout areas of Chicago. The effect was something akin to the dream sequence of the Charlie Kaufman/Spike Jonze film *Being John Malkovich* (1999), in which Malkovich (inhabited by an "everyman" named Craig played by John Cusack) is surrounded by people who look exactly like him and can only speak his name. (In fact the theatrical release poster of *Being John Malkovich* could be an advertisement for Selvaggio's project: it shows a large crowd of people all covering their own faces with masks of Malcovich's face.) Like that film, Selvaggio's project is an absurdist take on the solidity and proprietary nature of identity.

The original meaning of the word *absurd* came from a musical context, in which it meant "out of harmony."[71] As theater historian Martin Esslin observed, this connotation carries over to what he called the Theatre of the Absurd, in which absurdity was used to connote a lack of purpose, a senselessness, and a deliberate disharmony with regard to the supposedly rational operations of a society.[72] If we take a moment to recall one of the best-known examples of an absurdist play, we will see that Selvaggio's approach to identity mirrors many of the imaginative experiments with logic and social propriety found in both Eugène Ionesco's *The Bald Soprano* and Theatre of the Absurd as a genre. The inspiration for this play, Ionesco's first, came from his experience learning English. In the lessons he studied, two characters, Mr. and Mrs. Smith, informed each other of basic facts about their lives (e.g., Mrs. Smith informs Mr. Smith that they have had several children together). As Ionesco later explained, his diligent study of Mrs. Smith's methodical articulation of these basic truths (such as "the ceiling is up" and "the floor is down") began to take on a significance of their own.

> [T]he text began imperceptibly to change before my eyes. The very simple, luminously clear statements I had copied so diligently into my notebook, left to themselves, fermented after a while, lost their original identity, expanded and overflowed. The clichés and truisms of the conversation primer . . . disintegrated into wild caricature and parody, and in the end language disintegrated into disjointed fragments of words.[73]

In the resulting play, Ionesco has his character Mrs. Smith tell her husband Mr. Smith of such facts of their daily life, informing him of what they had for dinner and the number of children they have (Mr. Smith had been present for these occasions, we imagine). The plot whirls from there into a farcical evening in which language obfuscates rather than clarifies and intimate relationships seem to be stilted, formal social constructions.

Selvaggio's entry point to URME was not dissimilar. He began experimenting with distributing his own face via facial recognition software interfaces when he took a virtual walking tour of a neighborhood in downtown Chicago where he was to create a work art in a of storefront. The day he was visiting the gallery it was raining too hard to take the walk in person, so Selvaggio logged on to the Google Street view feature and toured the neighborhood that way. As he took his virtual "walk" he was struck by the frequent sight of digitally blurred faces of passersby, a policy implemented by Google in 2008 after concerns over the privacy of those photographed by its camera trucks. The images stuck in Selvaggio's mind long after the virtual walk and became the inspiration for his work *IMU: Google Street Portraits*, in which he pasted his own face over the blurred, anonymized faces.[74]

For Selvaggio, the effect of replicating and distributing his identity on a massive scale, as he has done in several consequent projects, jars disharmoniously with the rigid logic and technical efficacy of facial recognition technologies. As he put it, "[T]he massive generation of contradictory data, as it relates to my identity in facial recognition databases, by users of URME Surveillance challenges and subverts facial recognition technology by questioning its ability to identify a body in space accurately."[75] At the same time, Selvaggio does not position himself as an enemy of facial recognition technologies in quite the same way that Blas, Harvey, and Young have done. Similarly, Ionesco did not see himself as an enemy of realism (although he has been painted as such). Instead, Ionesco claimed that he believed "communication was possible through language"; as Esslin put it, "Ionesco's own attack against fossilized forms of language . . . appears to him to be as deeply concerned with objective reality as any social realism."[76] Selvaggio's project is likewise deeply concerned with the highly accurate and increasingly pervasive facial recognition technologies in social, virtual, and physical spaces of everyday life. To follow the (il)logic of absurdism, his performative masks create multiple Leo Selvaggios at once (either through coordinated outings or simply by creating the conditions under which this could happen). This strategy suggests that the notion of individual identity as stable and unique may in fact be merely convention, a cultural obsessions that is, in the end, rather ridiculous, something akin to creating a world without risk or chaos. While the only identity he is willing to put at risk at this point is his own, he dreams of a future in which more people open source their digital identities, making identity as flexible and multiplicitous as putting on a different mask: "I look forward to a day when we are all trying on each others' faces and identities."[77]

Dark Mirrors and Uncanny Echoes: Data Doubles and the A-Effect

The rather eerie strategy of erasing and replacing faces has proved inspirational to several other surveillance artists as well. Filmmaker Manu Luksch cannily employed Brechtian aesthetics of dialectical materialism in her 2007 film *Faceless* in order to defamiliarize and critique the conditions of urban life under perpetual surveillance. The film was created according to her "Manifesto for CCTV Filmmaking" (2006), that is, made entirely using footage from publicly installed CCTV cameras. Luksch's manifesto reinterpreted the United Kingdom's 1998 Data Protection Act (DPA) as a handbook for making films using CCTV footage produced through routine government surveillance.[78] Luksch used the formal constraints of CCTV surveillance footage and the DPA to produce an engaging yet alienated portrait of the personal and social risks of life under surveillance. From the black circles superimposed on the faces of the "actors" caught on CCTV cameras to the time stamps and grainy video characteristic of such footage, the narrative and aesthetics of *Faceless* utilize the Brechtian alienation effect, gestus, and the structure of epic theater to tell a cautionary tale about the loss and recovery of personal identity within a surveillance state.

According to the DPA, individuals have the right to request a copy of any information that has been gathered about them as a matter of routine (as opposed to criminal) surveillance, including publicly recorded CCTV footage in which they themselves appear. However, identifying markers (such facial features) of any other persons appearing in this footage must be removed as a matter of protecting individual privacy.[79] Luksch's manifesto reimagined these lawful rights as a method that can be used to produce films through publicly available cameras, a process she calls "CCTV filmmaking."[80] In accordance with her manifesto, she planned and meticulously documented her appearances in front of CCTV cameras around London, noting the precise times and locations of her performances. She sent her requests for this footage to the London data protection commissioner, along with a small fee. After receiving what footage she was able to gain access to through the DPA (still

Fig. 29. Manu Luksch's "Manifesto for CCTV Filmmakers," London, 2008.
(Photo by Mukul Patel.)

only a fraction of that which she requested), Luksch retrospectively constructed the footage for her film.

The "facelessness" of all the people surrounding her in the CCTV footage she received served as her inspiration for the dystopic narrative of *Faceless*, in which all people have forgotten their previous identities and lives. As the film's narrator, Tilda Swinton, informs viewers, the fictionalized society has been shaped by an entity called the "new machine." Following an era of distraction, regret, and longing in which "the present was continuously in short supply," the "new machine" was developed as a means of creating internal and external peace by abolishing personal attachments to the past and present. "Real time" is the new state of being for inhabitants of this world: with no memories of the past or anticipation of the future, regret and anxiety have been eradicated and replaced with a perpetual state of being in the present. Faceless people go about their daily lives without memories or anticipations. As in George Orwell's *1984,* the inhabitants of this world are monitored carefully for any signs of dissatisfaction or memory and disciplinary overseers are dispatched to deal with any suspicious outliers. A woman, portrayed by Luksch, works at a data-monitoring facility; her job is to "inspect data traces . . . mined by the new machine."[81] Although she is faceless like all the others, she begins to be disturbed by recurring dreams. Sometimes

Fig. 30. Manu Luksch's *Faceless*, 2007, film still

she sees a child, also faceless, which she can sense has a special significance for her. At other times she has visions of large-scale dances performed in an open foyer by crowds of faceless people moving in synchro-
nized lines and circles. One day, on her way to work, the opaque oval
that covers her head begins to fade away; she catches a glimpse of her
face in a pane of glass. A mysterious letter sits on her work desk, informing her of her previous life, which included a lover, a child, and artistic
expression. The plot accelerates from there into a thriller in which the
woman attempts to reunite with her lover, the author of the letter and a
leader in the resistance movement against the new machine. Together
they plan for the woman to rescue their child from the "sanctum" of the
new machine, a place where children are sent to be disciplined into living in the regime of facelessness. In so doing, she not only recovers her
past but also destroys the oppressive forces that have robbed society of
individuality and personal expression.

Though relatively engaging as a story and well voiced by Swinton,
the narrative itself is not the most significant contribution of the film.
Instead, it is the ways in which Luksch mobilized Brechtian material-

ist aesthetics to critique contemporary surveillance culture. Luksch employed several strategies to create what Brecht described as "epic" theater, using the "alienation effect" (*Verfremdungseffekt* in German, or the "V-effekt").[82] Epic theater (or "dialectic theater," as Brecht called it in "A Short Organum for the Theater") had the effect of always reminding audiences that they were watching a representation of reality, not reality itself. Brecht argued that temporal displacement of the action is necessary to achieve critical distance from which audiences can observe, contemplate, and judge the conditions portrayed: "[I]f we play works dealing with our own time as though they were historical, then perhaps the circumstances under which [the spectator] acts will strike him as equally odd; and this is where the critical attitude begins."[83] With a sense of familiarity, but not of total identification, the viewer "cannot simply feel: that's how I would act, but at most can say: if I had lived under those circumstances."[84]

While Brecht tended to use the distant past as a means of achieving a critical detachment for the spectator, the futuristic framing of *Faceless* achieves a similar effect. Although viewers of *Faceless* could, quite literally, have been among the faceless passersby in the film, had they been in London in the spring of 2005 when most of the footage was recorded, the dystopic science fiction framework sets the story at a temporal remove from the viewers' own lives. Indeed, the representation of time within the film is a central part of the V-effekt produced by Luksch. Just as Brecht recommended the insertion of songs or placards, Luksch inserted screen shots of CCTV nonlinear time codes, jumping rapidly in temporal chaos. The voice-over and extradiegetic, electronic music soundtrack, both of which function to create some amount of narrative continuity across the disparate, grainy images, are frequently interrupted by these shots of CCTV time codes. These breaks in the action foreclose the tendency toward identification and immersion when watching realist narrative cinema, while simultaneously reminding the audience of the film's unique means of production and source material.

Brecht also advised the use of "gestus" in creating stage pictures; he imagined gestus to be a physical symbol that expressed the social relations in place at a given time.[85] The most obvious gestus in Luksch's film is the symbol of "facelessness" itself. The opaque circles that cover the faces of all persons within the frame illustrate the loss of personal identity and individual expression under the regime of constant visibility—a condition that has clear referents to contemporary surveillance society. While the "actors" featured in *Faceless* do not "stand beside themselves" in as conscious a way as actors in a Brechtian stage production might, the viewer is always aware that the film's "characters" are produced through a strategic layering of reality and representation. It is impossible to forget that the onscreen characters were (and presumably still are) real people living in London. Other manifestations of gestus appear as well; large communal dances reminiscent of flash mob videos on YouTube serve as emblems of creative freedom and community in contrast to the discipline and anonymity that characterize life in the "perpetual present." When the protagonist brings down the "sanctum" of the new machine the screen fills with a technological gestus: screen shots of "camera failure" text and icons, as well as the blank blue screen familiar to anyone who has experienced computer difficulties while trying to project. These symbols, also taken from found footage, signify that the system of the new machine has broken down, ending the mass surveillance of the populace and returning memory and hope to all.

Remaining conscious of the means of production—a tenet of Marxist materialist theory from which Brecht drew much of his inspiration—keeps the audience from being absorbed into the film's narrative. Even as it maintains its fictional frame, the film is continually filled with visible reminders of the "real world" labor that Luksch performed in order to create the footage, labor that the audience must also perform as a means of piecing together the disparate shots. In *Faceless*, the time codes depart completely from the linear progression of the film's narrative, making it evident that the videos are neither spatially contiguous nor temporally linear. While many films are comprised of scenes shot out of sequence, postproduction editing typically removes the traces of such temporal disorder. In contrast, Luksch retained and emphasized the discrepancies between "real" (CCTV) and "representative" (cinematic) labor shown through the jumbled time codes, purposefully displaying them as part of the film's aesthetics. This aesthetic choice makes the film's audiences aware of their own real world labor in producing similar CCTV footage and requires them to take on the active labor of piecing together the narrative through disparate clips of surveillance footage.[86] Here the goal of the film's protagonist—to reclaim artistic expression and autonomy within a totalitarian state—echoes Luksch's goals in her manifesto, in which she coaches others to use Britain's CCTV systems and associated privacy legislation to create films using their own recovered footage.

The conscious display of markers of the source material and labor of production have gained Luksch's films and manifesto the moniker "readymade cinema."[87] An aesthetic/political strategy made famous by Marcel Duchamp in the 1910s and 1920s, "readymade art" featured manufactured items from daily life, reframed as objects of high art.[88] In transforming a given object from "useful" to artistic in its function, the artist would change the meaning of the readymade object itself—Duchamp's titles for his works aimed to give the object "new thought," or new meaning.[89] For Luksch, the readymade object is the CCTV footage, recorded and stored by British security agencies, and repurposed by her as an object with which to make art. The title of *Faceless* similarly aims to make new meaning of routine surveillance in urban settings and the now familiar practice of blurring faces to protect the identities of passersby. Luksch's title reframes these practices as antithetical to autonomous identity, personal memory, and artistic freedom.

SCOURTI'S LIFE IN ADWORDS

While Luksch's project targeted the cameras and policies of state surveillance, surveillance theorists and activists have become increasing concerned with a trend toward privatization in surveillance society. As surveillance techniques of military, state, and private commercial entities become increasingly integrated, they have formed what Simone Browne has called a global "identity-industrial complex," which "work[s] the body wholesale" as individuals are "profil[ed] through patterns" and reduced to their bodily information.[90] In many cases, private sector surveillance occurs below the threshold of visibility (and regulation), as data services and companies buy and sell caches of personal data online without the knowledge of the individuals to which the data pertain. Despite the ethically dubious processes involved, the practice of personal data trading has become normalized through increasingly common practices of personalized advertising and customized product development. Services such as Google AdWords mine the e-mails and search queries of individual users for information that can aid businesses in sending out advertisements that target given individuals. Wearable devices, from the Apple Watch and FitBit to "brainwear" devices such as the Emotiv headsets (commercially available electroencephalogram [EEG] sensors) claim to read a user's vital signs and brainwaves to produce personalized data about fitness, sleep, cognitive function, and emotional state.[91] Websites such as My Virtual Model present users with the opportunity to input measurements and body type to create a virtual likeness of themselves that they can use to try on clothes, accessories, and hairstyles as they shop online.[92] As Conrad argued, these devices and services illustrate "the extent to which the drive toward information gathering is driven as much by consumer capitalism as by criminal justice. There is a parallel drive between the 'actuarial justice' that surveillance has enabled and the 'predictive marketing' enabled by new information technologies, particularly those operating on the Internet via 'data mining'—both part of the larger trend of 'dataveillance.'"[93]

Over the course of a year (2012–13), British artist Erica Scourti experimented with getting to know her corporately produced data double through a performance project she called *Life in AdWords*. Presented as a series of videos available on her personal website, Scourti created a surrealist portrait of her online self as it was reflected back to her through the fast-growing arena of digital surveillance: personalized advertising. To create the project, Scourti input her daily diary into her Gmail account, e-mailing the text to herself. Based on these emails, Google AdWords automatically created a list of suggested keywords that would identify Scourti's interests, habits, and character to participating advertisers.[94] Scourti then read this list of words aloud into her webcam each evening, recording the efforts of Google's advertising algorithms to interpret her personal life into a marketable data set. As she described the project, "Started in March 2012, and running until 20th January 2013 following a change in Gmail ad settings, the video charts personal experience channeled through Google algorithms to create a long-list of objects, brands, emotional states, desires and anything else identified as potentially sale-able from my daily journal."[95]

The obvious villain in Scourti's serial performance is Google. Although Google cloaks its use of dataveillance in objective language such as "automated processing" of personal correspondence, the corporate motives behind the company's processes of keyword mining are rather sinister.[96] In many digital culture forums, Google (along with other giants such as Microsoft and Amazon) has become a focal point for criticism of changes in Internet culture, which has threatened to become a platform for state and corporate surveillance rather than the democratic freedoms it once promised. Techno-cultural theorist Lisa Nakamura has described what may have felt to many like a bait and switch in the ethos of Internet usage: "Early Internet utopians claimed the Internet would give everyone the power to surveil, to see and not be seen, to become a bodiless and thus unseeable user. Instead, we have become more visible and trackable than ever."[97]

Fig. 31. Erica Scourti's "Life in AdWords," composite, 2012–13

Scourti's performance makes evident her critique of this invasion of privacy for commercial gain, and yet it does more than simply protest her own commodification. She approached the process of personal-data-driven surveillance with investigative curiosity, exploring what the automated processes of data analysis might reveal about her personality and the desires and frustrations she expresses in her diary. In the resulting performance, Scourti employed a range of strategies, from surrealist automatism to Brechtian alienation. Read in relation to surrealist practices of automatic writing, the project offers an unusual yet insightful method of engaging with one's commercially produced digital double. As Breton wrote in his "Surrealist Manifesto," "psychic automatism" was a means of capturing "the actual functioning of thought."[98] The thought being captured in AdWords was that of the algorithmic processes by which commercial entities might make Scourti into a customer. The AdWords catalogued by Scourti were, in effect, a kind of "stream-of-machine-consciousness," a glimpse at her own subconscious through computerized algorithms designed to maximize profit. As Breton admitted, the product of automatic writing was often at first glance absurd, but "the quality of this absurdity, upon closer scrutiny, begins to give way to everything admissible, everything legitimate in the world: the disclosure of a certain number of properties and of facts no less objective, in the final analysis, than the others."[99] In *Life in AdWords*, the stream of words supplied by the automatic algorithmic mining of Scourti's diaries was likewise often absurd in its associations. "Heart problems. Match single. Video funny. Makeup look," Scourti read one evening, sitting in front of her computer in a robe and what appeared to be a partially dry, greenish facial mask, a corner of her cluttered bedroom visible in the background.[100] On another day, slumped in bed, she intoned, "Love relationship. Love relationships. Love and romance. Severe sore throat. Lyrics lyrics. Anxiety and depression. Anxiety and stress. Depression and anxiety."[101] These strings of verbal associations might not illuminate anything profound about the engineering design that shapes the "thought" of computerized surveillance systems, but Scourti's attention to them puts their significance in a new light. More than a barrage of advertising aimed at her pocket, the AdWords were presented as a new form of writing, mutually produced by Scourti and Google's computer algorithms. Her engagement with these coauthored data streams suggests that something other than consumption can come of the "soft biopolitics" of algorithmic identity production, something "no less objective" and almost certainly more interesting.[102]

Scourti's duet with her own digital double was sharpened by a Brechtian style of alienated acting. As was mentioned in my analysis of *Faceless*, the type of acting style recommended by Brecht was for the actor to "stand beside" the characters portrayed, taking the position of an accidental eyewitness describing a situation he or she happened to see. With a deadpan face and voice, Scourti stood (or more often sat) beside the version of herself that the commercially oriented algorithms returned to her, observing the objective and objectifying interpretations of her personal life. She dryly ventriloquized the range of unseen actors that mined her data: Google; the advertisers and lists with which Google shares its user data; and, lurking in the shadows, the Government Communications Headquarters (GCHQ), Britain's counterpart to the NSA. Her detached demeanor showed the distance between her lived self and the data self produced through commercial dataveillance, suggesting a relationship between a medical examiner and a cadaver being dissected.[103] This is not to say that her performance was without resistance. Her dispassionate, sometimes bordering on hostile tone made it clear that she will not happily be thus commodified. Rather than enlivening a consumer, these predictive algorithms were sucking the life out of her.

When Scourti had to conclude the project unexpectedly when Google changed its advertising preferences in response to revised "cookie" laws,[104] she staged a final, communal event. Gathered in her studio with a group of friends and colleagues, Scourti read aloud the comments she had received on Facebook in response to the daily AdWords that she had published as status updates over the past year.[105] In the video of the performance, a stream of AdWords scrolled across a screen while Scourti read aloud the comments and conversations that had unfolded in response to them on Facebook. As in the recorded performances of her AdWords project, Scourti's reading defamiliarized the online communication style of her Facebook friends. In a flat, measured tone she read the typed expression of laughter: "ha . . . ha . . . ha . . . ha . . . ha." Toward the end of the performance, a series of AdWords read, "A Kiss/ Drunk/ Humor/ Sleep." It had solicited the comment from a Facebook friend "TMI." "TMI?" Scourti queried in reply. "Too much information," came the explanation. "Sounds good," she wrote.[106] The assembled audience laughed as she recounted the exchange.

Scourti's quippy response to her friend's lighthearted criticism points to the more pressing questions that undergird her project: how might the TMI that we all produce be used to critique and challenge structures of state and corporate surveillance? Might TMI be utilized as a creative/critical shield that might protect rather than expose individuals? To use Brecht's terminology, it has become increasingly difficult for ordinary citizens to appear "strange" to the systems that so readily identify and track us. However, as Scourti's project suggests, "becoming more strange" may in fact be our best defense.

Mapping: Third Eyes and Second Skins

Some of the more literal illustrations of surveillance art staged on the "skin" come from the prolific visual and performance artist Wafaa Bilal. As in his 2007 work *Domestic Tension*, discussed in chapter 3, Bilal's body of performances creatively and often violently represents his personal and political experiences as a means of foregrounding larger cultural issues of racism, prejudice, and fear. As an Iraqi-born Shia Arab living in the United States since 1991, Bilal has frequently experienced racial hypervisibility. His durational performances and interactive installations powerfully trouble divisions between personal memory and the political record, discrimination and self-surveillance, and make visible ideologies of "othering" that put certain bodies under heightened scrutiny in public and private spaces.

Bilal's works have been written about extensively in popular and academic media, as well as by the artist himself.[107] My analysis here focuses on the ways in which several of his works, in particular his project *3rdi*, have embodied physical and conceptual strategies of Artaud's "theater of cruelty" as a means of critiquing the dehumanizing and painful physical effects of contemporary surveillance and remote control warfare. In his theatrical theory and practice Artaud espoused that the concrete reality of the body was the sole means by which the metaphysical might be experienced and expressed. Originally part of the surrealist movement, Artaud rejected the realist theater of the day, arguing that it was too narrow in its focus on the psychological struggles of individuals. Instead, he argued that a "theater of cruelty" was necessary to wake up the public and engage its "nerves and heart."[108] It is important to keep in mind that Artaud did not use the term *cruelty* according to its common usage, instead thinking of it as a visceral, embodied means of awakening the senses of an audience and expressing the true, violent nature of life: "Imbued with the idea that the public thinks first of all with its senses and that to address oneself first to its understanding as the ordinary psychological theater does is absurd, the Theater of Cruelty proposes to resort to a mass spectacle."[109]

While he has not garnered the same violent and psychologically unstable reputation as Artaud, Bilal stands out among contemporary surveillance artists for the extreme physical conditions in which he places his own body. As Artaud worked to do in his own theater and theory, Bilal has created "mass spectacles" of his own suffering in works such as *Domestic Tension*, that involved large numbers of online audience-participants.[110] Though he is decidedly a pacifist, Bilal, like Artaud, is not opposed to the possibility that "a little real blood will be needed" in his politics and art.[111] Just as Artaud famously rejected the notion that art is an imitation of life, insisting that "I cannot conceive of a work of art as distinct from life,"[112] Bilal relentlessly blends his life and artworks. In 2008, after he learned of his brother's death in a missile attack on a checkpoint in Iraq, Bilal created a video game called *Virtual Jihadi* in which he appeared via avatar as a suicide bomber to track and assassinate then president George W. Bush. Bilal created the controversial piece to critique negative stereotypes of Arabs in western media and entertainment, modeling the work after popular video games such as *Quest for Saddam*. As in most "first-person shooter" games, the player of *Virtual Jihadi* takes on Bilal's character via his avatar, playing out a narrative in which Bilal is recruited to fight for al-Qaeda after his brother was killed in a US missile strike.

While *Virtual Jihadi* involved a virtual stand-in for Bilal, most of his performance works feature his own corporeal body as a stage on which to represent the brutal effects of remote control warfare and racial violence. In *and Counting . . .* (2010), Bilal quite literally used his own skin as a canvas: he had his back tattooed with a map of Iraq on which a dot was placed for each American and Iraqi death in the war so far. Performed over a twenty-four-hour period in a gallery that was open to the public, Bilal received the tattoos while audience members read aloud the names of the dead. The politics of visibility loomed large in this piece: the deaths of Americans were tattooed in permanently visible red ink, whereas the Iraqi deaths were marked with a green ink that was invisible unless viewed under a black light. The painful experience of receiving such an intricate and lengthy tattoo was made public, an expression the personal pain that Bilal felt over the wartime deaths of his father and brother.

In his most extreme physical, durational performance to date, Bilal arranged to have a small, live feed camera surgically embedded in the back of his head. Programmed to automatically take a picture every minute of every day, the camera transmitted the images to a publicly viewable website, as well as to screens installed in an exhibit in Doha, Qatar.[113] The camera supplied Bilal and his gallery and online viewers with a constant stream of surveillance images amassed into an "objective" and "automatic" record of Bilal's daily activities for over a year. The work, called *3rdi* (2010–11), embodied the violence of seeing and being seen, as well as Bilal's personal desire to be able to look back and understand his life, disrupted and displaced as it has been by multiple wars and emigrations.

In his own description and analysis of *3rdi*, Bilal writes that he was motivated by a long-felt need for a means of reviewing the many disparate places he has been as a result of his exile and immigration from Iraq to the United States.

> During my journey from Iraq to Saudi Arabia, on to Kuwait and then the U.S., I left many people and places behind. The images I have of this journey are inevitably ephemeral, held as they are in my own memory. Many times while I was in transit and chaos the images failed to fully register, I did not have the time to absorb them. Now, in hindsight, I wish I could have recorded these images so that I could look back on them, to have them serve as a reminder and record of all the places I was forced to leave behind and may never see again.

The project is also, inescapably, about surveillance in public and private life. As Bilal said in an interview, "For me, it is a personal record. But by having the camera on my head, it also makes people aware of how much we are under surveillance."[114] Indeed, this aspect caused some of the greatest controversy, as Bilal planned to wear the camera in his work as a professor at the Tisch School for the Arts, New York University (NYU). (In the end, the university and the artist reached an agreement under which he covered the lens of the camera during his time on campus.)[115]

Although the idea of embedding a camera in one's skull and automatically transmitting its images around the world was beyond the technical and medical capabilities of his time, Artaud would almost certainly have approved of Bilal's method of performance. (Although Artaud eventually broke with the surrealist movement, the ideas of surrealism and the importance of the subconscious remained influential in his own theory and practice.) As in Scourti's AdWords project, Bilal's camera tells his story through a process of automatic and constant image capture, producing a kind of "psychic automatism" promoted by surrealist artists and writers. (Although Artaud eventually broke with the surrealist move-

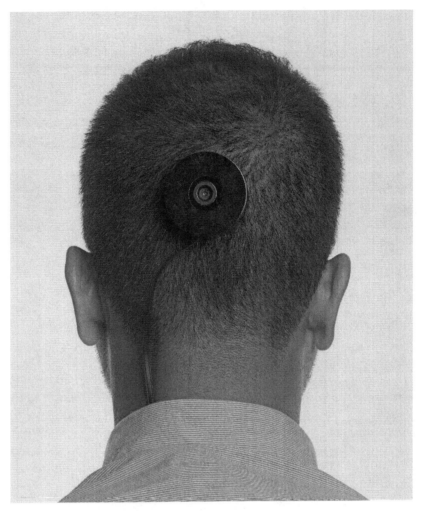

Fig. 32. Wafaa Bilal's *3rdi*, a year-long performance, 2010–11. (©Wafaa Bilal, courtesy of the Driscoll Babcock Galleries and Mathaf: Arab Museum of Modern Art.)

ment, the ideas of surrealism and the importance of the subconscious remained influential in his own theory and practice.) As Bilal described it, "3rdi arises from a need to objectively capture my past as it slips behind me from a non-confrontational point of view." He called the form "anti-photography," as the automated system removed his own curatorial hand and eye from the process. He believed that this would give rise to images that were "denoted" rather than "connoted," citing Roland Barthes on the innocence of the former: "[F]rom an aesthetic point of view the denoted image can appear as a kind of Edenic state of the image; cleared utopianically of its connotations, the image would become radically objective, or, in the last analysis, innocent."[116] Bilal's attraction to the "innocence" of images captured without logical interference recalls Artaud's interpretation of "Oriental theater," the methods of which he saw as "speaking directly to the unconscious."[117] Of course, the idealization of "Oriental" performance and art by Artaud (as well as the surrealists, and Brecht) carries with it problematic undertones of essentialism. The "innocence" and clarity that many avant-garde artists ascribed to eastern art forms has been criticized by critical race theorists as a symptom of a widespread, patronizing view of Asia, in which it was made to stand in opposition to the modernization in the West that these artists sought to critique.[118] That said, Artaud's impulse to use images from eastern art forms as a means of subverting the primacy of text in western theater was nevertheless useful to his theory. In his first manifesto he argued, "[I]t is essential to put an end to the subjugation of the theater to the text, and to recover the notion of a kind of unique language halfway between gesture and thought."[119] Later in the manifesto, he espoused theater that was "a kind of total creation in which man must reassume his place between dream and event."[120] Returning to Bilal's surgically implanted camera, it is hard to imagine a more fitting (albeit uncomfortable) position between gesture and thought, dream and action than in the skin covering one's skull.

Such experiments take a physical toll, however. Although it would be misguided to equate Artaud's eventual psychiatric confinement with Bilal's choice to undergo surgery, both artists suffered physical hardships that extended from their deep commitment to their art practice. Historians often remark on the physical transformation Artaud underwent during his relatively short lifetime. A strikingly handsome young man, he appeared in plays and films such as *The Passion of Joan of Arc* (1928). Not much later, after a period of psychiatric confinement, he appeared, according to Daniel Gerould as "an ancient martyr, his ravaged body gnarled with pain, his gaunt face wrinkled and toothless, his deep-set eyes burning with the inner fire of a visionary."[121] While Bilal has not lost his looks, his artistic choices have certainly exacted a lasting toll on his body. The surgery that he underwent for *3rdi* involved a highly uncomfortable, durational form of violence: at a body-modification clinic in Los Angeles, three titanium plates were inserted under his scalp and three transdermal pins screwed into it to support the custom-built camera mount. As described by Ashley Rawlings in *ArtAsiaPacific*, the surgery took quite a toll on Bilal's body and mind.

When I met him in late December, six weeks after the surgery, the physical toll of the project was already evident. Noticeably thinner, he explained that the trauma of the operation was worse than he had anticipated. In the following days, his body went into shock and he started having severe panic attacks; these have since subsided, but he now carries prescription drugs should another occur. Maintenance of the apparatus is also a demanding commitment. As the skin around the pins cannot fully heal, it is uncomfortable; Bilal has to wash the area three times a day and apply a steroid cream when the skin becomes irritated.[122]

Together, the automatic record keeping and violent hybridity of man and machine in Bilal's project create a high-tech, mobile application of Artaud's vision of a Theater of Cruelty. As Artaud would have had it, the theatrical stage and proscenium arch would be abolished; instead the audience would sit in the center of an open space surrounded by the action, which would unfold as a "mass spectacle."[123] The gallery installation of Bilal's *3rdi* enacts a similar use of space. Visitors to the *Told/Untold/Retold* exhibit in Qatar move from space to space surrounded by projections of images produced by Bilal's body camera. The online version capitalizes on the massive reach of the Internet, distributing the performance internationally through virtual space. As Bilal put it, "The 3rdi makes a technological apparatus part of my body and distributes the recorded content openly within space using the internet."[124] Although it might not surround the viewer in quite the same way, the online version of *3rdi* is widely and constantly distributed, constituting a virtual "mass spectacle" that is at once publicly available and radically personal.

The *3rdi* images are not necessarily any more enlightening than other forms of personal documentation shared via social media. As Rawlings wrote, Bilal's "activity is ultimately little different from anyone taking a photo in a public space and posting it on an open profile on Facebook, MySpace, Flickr or any other website (though he does take care to inform people of the camera when entering private property)."[125] And yet the conceptual and material framework of Bilal's project lends it far more gravity and edginess than these more common "life-logging" practices facilitated through smart phones, photo-sharing sites, and wearable cameras.[126] The difference here can again be summed up by looking to Artaud. Artaud opened his essay "The Theater and Cruelty" with the criticism that most realist theater "transform[s] the public into Peeping Toms." Although Bilal literally sutured the gaze of his audience to that of a roving camera, a "third eye" that peers out at passersby on the street, the effect is quite different than that of *Candid Camera* or an amateur voyeur. The perspective of the viewer of *3rdi* is mapped on to Bilal's body, sutured to his unhealed skin holding the camera in place. This viewpoint is further defamiliarized by virtue of the fact that viewers saw images of what Bilal would see if he chose to glance backward (although, if he did, we would see what was in front of him instead).

At this point, it is difficult to avoid and not altogether inappropriate to make mention of Walter Benjamin's famous passage in his "Theses on the Philosophy of History" regarding Paul Klee's painting *Angelus Novus*.

> A Klee painting named Angelus Novus shows an angel looking as though he is about to move away from something he is fixedly contemplating. His eyes are staring, his mouth is open, his wings are spread. This is how one pictures the angel of history. His face is turned toward the past. Where we perceive a chain of events, he sees one single catastrophe which keeps piling wreckage upon wreckage and hurls it in front of his feet. The angel would like to stay, awaken the dead, and make whole what has been smashed. But a storm is blowing from Paradise; it has got caught in his wings with such violence that the angel can no longer close them. The storm irresistibly propels him into the future to which his back is turned, while the pile of debris before him grows skyward. This storm is what we call progress.[127]

Like this "Angel of History," Bilal's camera looks backward, figuratively straining to see the times and spaces that came before. At the same time, the figure he cuts is futuristic, a harbinger, perhaps, of the cyborgian partnerships between humans and the machines that are already seeking to define who we are and what we can do.

Shadowy Conclusions

Like the Angelus Novus, all the artists discussed in this chapter attempt the difficult task of looking back at the present moment. Using their digital doubles as a means of achieving some critical distance, they examine the body under surveillance in several ways: as cultural concept, marker of personal identity, and source of biological data that can be read toward predictive and archival ends. Locating these claims at the surface of the body, these artists-activists variously represent digital bodies of knowledge and evidence that promise/threaten to stand (in) for the lived experiences of the individual.

In order to theorize work on a topic that is still very much unfolding, I, too, have looked back into history to find models of formally innovative, politically critical works that sought to counter scientific objectification of the human body. Although I have framed the avant-garde movements of surrealism, absurdism, Brechtian materialism, and the Artaudian Theater of Cruelty as reactions to naturalism, they are richer than such a reactionary account would suggest. Nor, necessarily, is naturalism ethically corrupt, as my alignment of this movement with biometric surveillance might suggest; it was an important and experimental artistic response to the modernist innovations of its time.[128] As shown by the resonances between the performance tactics developed by avant-garde artists of the early to middle twentieth century and the work of contemporary surveillance artists, the avant-garde has a still vital afterlife. James Harding persuasively argues in his book *Ghosts of the Avant-Garde(s)* (2013) that the "death of an avant-garde . . . opens up possibilities of unexpected, surprising, and haunting moments of signification." His historiography of the avant-gardes (for, he insists, they were and are multiple, refusing to be reduced to a single historical narrative or movement) invites "the stealing of one historical moment for the purposes of another."[129] It is in this spirit—and the spirit in which Richard Schechner boldly considered the events of 9/11 as an avant-garde performance—that I have drawn parallels between historical practices of the avant-garde(s) and contemporary surveillance art.[130]

Just as the avant-garde(s) of the twentieth century were various, fueled by each other's work even as they engaged in fierce disagreements, the works of these body-focused surveillance artists are diverse and difficult to sum up. While there is not yet enough distance to be able to classify and distinguish their work into the convenient "isms" of the avant-garde, certain trends and differences within and across their projects are already evident. Blas's *Facial Weaponization Suite,* Scourti's *Life in AdWords,* and Luksch's *Faceless* each reject the notion that amalgamations of data can stand in for individuals. Selvaggio's URME and Bilal's *3rdi* experiment with the possibility of living beyond the discomfort and distortions rendered by digital algorithms and perpetual surveillance. Because their numbers are still few, the artists working in this area are, for the most part, welcoming of each other's company and supportive of the work being undertaken. The only overt articulation of a difference in approach that I have yet come across in the writing of these artists came from Leo Selvaggio. He deliberately distinguished his strategy of masking from that of Blas and Harvey: "Though Harvey and Blas' work is well suited for those willing to assert themselves in public space without fear of repercussion, I aimed to produce something others could use without drawing unwanted attention to themselves."[131] As a result, Selvaggio designed masks that were as close to a naturalist response as we might find in this chapter; despite the absurdist elements of the project discussed above, he was concerned with three-dimensional photo realism that would convince not only facial recognition cameras and Facebook but also passersby that they were seeing his own face on another person's body.

Surrealist artists experimented with tapping the unconscious as a means of subverting the dominance of social and scientific logic; similarly, these contemporary surveillance artists delve into the psychological dimensions of a world in which digital doubles are gaining more substance and weight. Recalling the final scene of *Black Mirror*, described in the opening of this chapter, they gesture to the digital doppelgangers that we all have rattling around in our virtual attics, golems that we keep, perhaps, because they are oddly comforting, they make us feel less alone, and, quite frankly, we don't know what else to do with them. Instead of ignoring these shadowy masses, or succumbing to what Harding has called the "new amnesia," a process by which we might choose to forget about data doubles that we cannot see or control, these artists call on us to examine the ties and responsibilities that we have to our digital doubles.[132] What might biometric surveillance and the data it produces be changing about what it means to be, or become, human? What will we, as the human counterparts of our digital doubles, do in response?

CHAPTER 6

Skies

———— ⚭ ————

When one goes up there, he leaves behind the mass that carries off and mixes up in itself any identity of authors or spectators. As Icarus flying above these waters, he can ignore the devices of Deadalus in mobile and endless labyrinths far below. His elevation transfigures him into a voyeur. It puts him at a distance. It transforms the bewitching world by which one was "possessed" into a text that lies before one's eyes. It allows one to read it, to be a solar Eye, looking down like a god. The exaltation of a scopic and gnostic drive: the fiction of knowledge is related to this lust to be a viewpoint and nothing more.

—Michel de Certeau, "Walking in the City"[1]

Lights come up on the figure of a man, naked but for a flesh-colored loincloth, his long black hair swinging loose and wild as he paces across the empty stage as though on a hunt. He spots a small, metallic object hovering at the edge of the pool of light. The man drops immediately to a crouched position, uncertain whether the object is friend or foe, prey or predator. From this defensive posture the man studies the small, glowing device as it begins to skim across the floor toward him. Man and machine circle one another, suspicious and curious in equal parts. Suddenly, lights flashing along its four arms, the device takes to the air, floating straight up and hovering aloft as the man rolls backward in shock. The audience erupts in laughter, now in on the joke: the man has just encountered a drone, the slickest new surveillance technology to hit the skies, and he is just as unsure of what to make of it as we are.[2]

Seraph, the 2010 piece created by the innovative Pilobolus dance theater company, was built in partnership with robotics lab scientists at MIT in order to explore contemporary society's increasing fascination with and reliance on robots, and, in particular the new, flying kind. With its humorous choreography and "primitive man" protagonist, the piece recast the politically laden subject of drones as a mythic, land-before-time scenario, constructing an alternative, largely depoliticized narrative of human-drone relations. Whereas unmanned aerial vehicles (UAVs), commonly called drones, are best known for their use in military surveillance and combat operations, the Pilobolus dance piece imagined instead a more innocent first encounter. The un-tech-savvy nature of the man—emphasized by his scantily clad body rippling with muscles, long black hair loose and wild, and movement vocabulary that kept him close to the ground—was starkly contrasted with the slick, metallic bodies of the drones. As suggested by the title, the piece imagined these flying, seemingly sentient machines to have descended from the order of seraphim, winged creatures in traditional Christian liturgy that belong to the highest order of celestial angels. Outfitted with flashing LED lights, these mechanical "angels" soared throughout the space with ease, entertaining their fellow performers, as well as the audience, with their ability to glide swiftly along the floor and then rise straight up and soar through the expansive fly space of the theater, far above a human's reach. In response to the drones and the artificial intelligence (AI) that seemed to animate them, the man was in turns curious, frightened, playful, combative, submissive, and finally defeated: he eventually ran from the stage, leaving the drones to their aerial pursuits. As the lights dimmed, the drones continued to play, seemingly relieved to engage in their own, infinitely more advanced AI games in peace.

The tone and narrative of *Seraph* were light and humorous, and the piece proved to be an audience favorite throughout Pilobolus's 2011–12 world tour. Yet, for all its playfulness, *Seraph* skirted the edges of a much weightier and more complicated story that has been unfolding in contemporary surveillance society. Since the dawn of the twenty-first century, drones have been employed with increasing regularity to carry out lethal strikes and military reconnaissance in Middle Eastern war zones.[3] The US military, which has led the way in developing drone technologies, has come under much criticism for the civilian casualties that result from drone strikes in official wars in Afghanistan and Iraq, as well as in unofficial acts of state-sponsored violence in Yemen, Pakistan, Syria, Somalia, and beyond. Despite such criticism, the volume and variety of drones have only proliferated. Militaries around the world have scrambled to develop their own drone forces, attracted by the benefits of lower costs, increased efficiency, and decreased risk to their own soldiers.[4] Early in 2012 the Federal Aviation Administration (FAA) in the US and the Civil Aviation Administration (CAA) in the UK revised regulations that had previously prohibited the use of drones in domestic air space. In the years since the revised regulations, domestic law enforcement programs, environmental agencies, and consumer delivery services such as Amazon have raced to launch their own (thus far unarmed) drones.[5] Together these developments in military and civilian drone use have compelled people around the world to grapple with the risks and benefits of drones in everyday life.

While there are undeniably positive applications for drone technologies in nonviolent sectors of life, from wildlife and forest fire surveys to natural disaster aid distribution, the proliferation of drones around the globe has rightfully raised a host of ethical quandaries. How will drones augment the already significant network of state and corporate surveillance, and what new concerns over privacy, discrimination, human rights, and concentrated power will they raise? Do the environmental and security benefits of drones outweigh the potential abuses of power and erosion of privacy that their domestic use would entail? Do drones make it easier for secret special forces in the US military to perform and hide extrajudicial killings outside declared war zones? Do remote controlled UAVs turn the reality of wartime violence into video game scenarios, diminishing the lives of civilians mistakenly killed in drone strikes as "collateral damage"? What are the psychological effects, such as PTSD, on military pilots assigned to fly drones remotely? Will the drastic asymmetries in proposed uses for drones—delivering Domino's pizzas and Amazon home goods domestically and Hellfire missiles abroad— only deepen global rifts? These concerns are only the tip of the iceberg. Less visible problems with remotely fought warfare—such as the psychological strain placed on pilots stationed far from zones of combat—are already demanding increased attention. As more civilian hobbyists take to the skies in consumer-level drones, practices of exploring and documenting quotidian spaces via drone will foster new modes of phenomenological experience, even as they intensify debates over privacy rights. As drones turn the skies into the new "Wild West," the FAA and other regulatory organizations are already struggling to keep pace with the private drone market and the challenges of shared air space between commercial aircraft and UAVs, let alone the risks posed by hackers of military and commercial drones.[6]

Despite lurking allusions to histories of violent colonial encounters between Christian conquistadors and indigenous peoples, the Pilobolus dance piece did not pretend to tackle such ethically complex questions, sidestepping political debates in favor of a more technophilic celebration of the entertainment value of drones. Nonetheless, *Seraph* hit a timely nerve, illuminating some of the bewildering new terrain of drone use. Daniela Rus, director of MIT's Computer Science and Artificial Intelligence Laboratory, led the team of students that built and flew the *Seraph* drones. In an interview, she observed that audiences around the world responded, not unlike the piece's protagonist, with fascination, wonderment, and trepidation to the performing drones. This suggests that the piece's characterization of the human-drone encounter, divested as it was of the violent capabilities of drones, may not be too far from reality, at least for attendees of dance theater in economically and politically stable urban centers. Indeed, many see drones as doing more overall good than harm. Heralded by many as technological angels of a kind, remotely piloted drones facilitate advances in scientific exploration in toxic or difficult to reach areas of the globe. Smaller, consumer-level drones have been flying, so to speak, off the shelves, as these remote control toys have fast become popular gifts for hobbyists and children.[7] At the same time, it is difficult (and problematic) to overlook the very real effects of the lethal military drones: drones are viewed around the world as emblems of military might, prized by some as a way to keep pilots out of direct combat, criticized by others as feeding western arrogance and carelessness in combat. For the many civilians around the world who continue to live with the threat of drone strikes in their own communities, drones are material and symbolic agents of regimes of state-sponsored violence, indiscriminately raining payloads of Hellfire missiles from above.

Like Pilobolus, increasing numbers of artists and activists have begun to make works that explore the complex territory of drone use. There are three main discourses that have, thus far, emerged in artworks featuring drone technologies. The first, most prevalent response is characterized by representations of drones as violent machines that should be met with extreme caution and calls for deproliferation. Like Essam Attia's satirical NYPD drone campaign posters displayed in the streets of midtown Manhattan, discussed in the "Introduction," artists working in this mode emphasize the devastating and unjust effects of military drones around the world. Their works remind their primarily western audiences, which may be swayed by more user-friendly representations of drones, that drones are dangerous technologies of war. Like the aboriginal protagonist in *Seraph*, these artists position themselves in opposition to drone technology, figuring humans as subjects of the drone's gaze and potential victims of the violent, colonizing politics that animate it.

The second approach is similar to that of Rus and her team of MIT drone engineers. Intrigued by new frontiers of mobility and vision, artists, entrepreneurs, and amateur drone hobbyists have been drawn to experiment with the new spatial practices and models of embodiment that drones invite. Consumer-level drones that have hit the market in recent years offer growing numbers of amateurs and hobbyists the opportunity to explore public space from a mobile, aerial vantage point. In an increasingly popular practice among amateur drone pilots, referred to as "first-person view" (FPV), hobbyists experience aerial mobility as if from the viewpoint of their drones. The practice unites the visual perspective of the pilot with that of his or her drone, as FPV users pilot their drones using an immersive view through the drone's aerial camera (rather than from their vantage point on the ground). The amateur practice of FPV drone flight and other demilitarized uses for drones notably shift away from a model in which humans are targets of drones, focusing instead on the possibilities of a symbiotic, cyborgian partnership between drone and human. These experimental roles for drones, which range from dance partners to spiritual guides to taco delivery devices, counterbalance the overwhelming militarization of drones by investing in the new aesthetics and mobilities of drone flight.

A third category of drone art grapples with the ethical and emotional effects of military drone use. George Barber's short film/installation *Freestone Drone* and George Brant's play *Grounded* explore humanitarian and interpersonal aspects of drone technologies in the overlapping territory between everyday civilian life and the military industrial complex. In Barber's short film, the protagonist is a drone that questions the ethics of his job. The "Freestone Drone" is haunted by the humanity of his victims, as well as existential questions about his own death. Brant's play *Grounded* stages the story of an Air Force pilot who, after the birth of her daughter, has been recommissioned to pilot armed drones in Afghanistan from the Nevada desert. These works do not fundamentally question the arrival of drones as a technology of war and surveillance; rather, they dramatize the difficult position of the labor force called on to operate them. Through individual stories, they call attention to the steep psychological costs of drone use for pilots and victims alike.

As public opinion and legal regulations for drone use are still very much in flux, drone art pieces in each category provide valuable fodder for the burgeoning public discourse over drones. Works in all three categories create valuable spaces in which audiences, be they attendees at a formal performance, consumers, or passersby on the street, can reflect on the ethical challenges, practical solutions, and aesthetic opportunities that attend drone use in both peaceful and war-torn skies.

Fight or Flight: Drones and the Politics of Contemporary Surveillance

Most of the works I discuss have been made and performed in the United States and United Kingdom in the years since 2012, after the FAA regulatory revisions. These legal changes brought the subject of drones to greater prominence in mainstream media and public discourse, as civilians in the West were suddenly among the potential subjects of drone surveillance and violence. While the availability and awareness of drones spiked after the 2012 change in regulations, a study of drones in recent history must include attention to the watershed moment that shaped and justified so much of contemporary surveillance society: the terrorist attacks of September 11, 2001. Drones have figured particularly prominently in the ongoing "War on Terror," which began with the US invasion of Afghanistan in response to the terrorist group al-Qaeda's claim of responsibility for the September 11 attacks. In stark contrast to the heavy human load the jets carried, drones fly without even a pilot, instead bearing cameras for surveillance, GPS units for navigation, and, in the case of military UAVs, hefty payloads of missiles. Although this genealogy is by no means direct or uncomplicated, we might think of military drones as the offspring of those two jumbo jets that flew into the World Trade Center. This dark family tree has continued to grow as consumer models have proliferated in the wake of the FAA regulatory revisions in 2012 and the promise of more liberal regulations in coming years assures more branches to come.[8] Artists and activists who are appropriating drones for the purposes of politically critical installations and performances in turn introduce the troublemaking, illegitimate black sheep of the family. This chapter is an attempt to map these artistic black sheep onto the branches of the drone family tree. The picture that emerges is, not surprisingly, as complicated and contradictory as the commercial and political landscape of drone use.

By March 2012, when the FAA in the United States and CAA in the United Kingdom revised their regulations concerning unmanned aerial vehicles, permitting these UAVs to be flown in domestic air space, civilians around the world already had strong associations with drones. They had been appearing for over a decade in headlines and news reports that announced lethal Predator drone strikes during military offensives in Afghanistan, Iraq, Syria, Yemen, and Palestine. Military use of drones in these regions had already been the subject of lengthy ethical debates. Opponents argued that remotely controlled, armed aircraft increased the number of civilian casualties, further dehumanized enemy targets, and threatened to turn the reality of combat zones and wartime violence into casual video game scenarios. Supporters insisted that drones were far more efficient, as they were considerably cheaper to build and operate than fighter jets, could stay in the air far longer, and kept the military personnel who piloted them out of harm's way. With new permissions for domestic UAV use on the table, drones became all the rage—or something to rage against. Although surveillance in the form of CCTV cameras, airport body scans, online data mining, and GPS locative media, to name a few, had long since become a fixture in the daily lives of civilians in the United States, United Kingdom, and around the world, the prospect of drones being used for domestic law enforcement, environmental surveys, or consumer delivery services was met with more controversy and anxiety than any surveillance technology in living memory. Would remotely controlled, camera-equipped drones flying over neighborhoods and backyards and past open windows in the name of public security, corporate advertising, or consumer research finally erode privacy to an unacceptable degree? Would military drones, designed to make lethal precision strikes on enemy targets, be used by federal and domestic law enforcement agencies against civilians perceived to be activists, political dissidents, or criminal suspects in the United States and Europe? Or would the commercial, environmental, and law enforcement benefits of drones drown out these concerns?

Within the first year of the new regulations, the FAA licensed several thousand drones to fly over US soil. By mid-2012 police departments in Florida and sheriffs in Texas were routinely using UAVs in their patrols, and border security operations had begun deploying blimp-style UAVs, as well as military Predator drones, to watch the US-Mexico border for drug traffickers and illegal immigrants.[9] Environmental agencies began employing drones to count sea lions in Alaska, conduct weather and environmental research, and help coordinate the ongoing cleanup of the Fukushima nuclear reactor in Japan.[10] In the United Kingdom, the CAA granted several hundred permits, including drone licenses for municipal law enforcement departments across England, the BBC, National Grid, and a sports entertainment company called Video Golf Marketing.[11] In late 2012, the Internet giant Google gave a sizable grant to the World Wildlife Fund to use drones to police wildlife poaching in parts of Africa and Asia.[12] Interest in drones soon trickled down from large corporations and government-funded agencies to fuel more grassroots experiments with drones. Engineering programs in research universities across the United States and United Kingdom raced to provide students with educational opportunities to design, build, and pilot drones; hobbyists and amateur aerial photographers organized exhibits of videos and photographs taken by drone.[13] Only days after the FAA announced the new drone regulations in March 2012, a San Francisco–based start-up announced plans for a drone food delivery service called the TacoCopter, through which customers could place a taco order from a computer or smart phone, electronically send credit card payment and GPS location, and then wait for a small drone to fly their tacos from the company kitchen to their location.[14] As if to prove that the appeal of drone delivery will indeed be massive, the online retail giant Amazon announced plans in December 2013 for Prime Air, a delivery service that would aim to get packages to customers within thirty minutes via UAV.[15]

Meanwhile, resistance to the new drone legislation flooded newspapers, talk shows, city halls, and blogs. Fears ranged from unconstitutional incursions of privacy to lethal strikes on suspected terrorists or political dissidents. Activists organized local protests, published blogs such as *Drone Wars UK* and *Stop Drones*, and turned to social media platforms such as Twitter, Facebook, and Instagram to document atrocities being waged by military drone strikes in the Middle East.[16] Privacy advocates and civil liberties groups lobbied to pass revisions to existing privacy laws that would include limitations on drone use within private and semiprivate spaces. In February 2013, Charlottesville, Virginia, became the first city in the United States to formally pass antidrone legislation; several other US cities have followed suit, imposing moratoriums on the testing or use of drones in local air space for at least the next two to five years.[17] Experts in privacy law, such as M. Ryan Calo, director of privacy and robotics at the Center for Internet and Society, capitalized on the visibility of drones and the risks to personal privacy that they pose in order to lobby for radical reforms in privacy legislation that other, less visible innovations in digital surveillance had not managed to inspire.[18]

As UAV technology has become more accessible and affordable, examples of rival factions that employ drones for opposing purposes have multiplied. For example, the New York graffiti artist Katsu developed the "spraycopter," the world's first spray-paint-can-wielding quadcopter for street artists, and within months Deutsch Bahn, the German national railway company, began testing an antigraffiti drone that would employ infrared cameras to search for nighttime vandals at work.[19] Law enforcement and criminal groups alike have employed drones to perform search and seizure missions at drug-growing sites and to track wildlife to prevent or enable poaching.[20] Federal and commercial drones patrolling the US-Mexico border share space with *Lowdrone*, an online project that allows participants to conduct remote-controlled border transgression flights with a small drone positioned to fly across the fence that marks the California-Mexico border.[21]

All of this is to show that the discourse and practice of drone use are complicated and still unfolding. Drones are used for both normative and subversive goals, legal and illegal actions, and violent and peaceful purposes. Our positions as users, consumers, and targets of drone surveillance are ethically and practically complex. Artists using drone technologies thus provide valuable forums in which to reflect on the ethical debates, political realities, and public imaginary of drones as they enter our daily lives. Armed with flying prosthetics of sight, their works explore nightmarish scenarios, harsh realities, paranoid predictions, progressive dreams, and imaginative flights of fancy. They mourn, protest, critique, empathize, and dream along the pathways that drones are charting into a wild blue future.

Blood in the Streets: Artistic Warnings of Drone Violence

The most pressing political issue in relation to drone use continues to be the high numbers of civilian deaths in and beyond official war zones in the Middle East. Many of the works of drone art and activism that have emerged in recent years have been motivated by concerns over these unjust deaths and the prospect of more civilian damages from the adoption of armed drones in domestic law enforcement and surveillance programs. In this section I look at drone artworks that strive to make visible the violent realities wrought by military drone operations. Works in this vein challenge the ethics of using drones within missions of state-sponsored violence and caution against inviting drones further into domestic law enforcement and counterterrorism projects. In order to emphasize these arguments, artists in this genre have developed two central tactics thus far. In the first, artists represent the violent effects of drones on the lives of civilians living in Middle Eastern war zones and caution against the use of drones in the West. The second tactic is characterized by the production of practical defensive materials for use in everyday life, such as drone-resistant architecture and clothing designs that would offer civilians protection from armed drones. Both of these tactical approaches remind their (primarily western) audiences that, despite the promising applications they may have in other civilian arenas, drones are, at base, tools of war that bring with them a host of ethical and material risks to daily civilian life.

DUCK AND COVER: THE THREAT FROM ABOVE

Essam Attia, the artist behind the fake NYPD drone campaign signs described in the "Introduction," exemplifies the first tactic. His posters, which featured a man, woman, and child running in fear from an NYPD drone, pointedly (if dystopically) portrayed the risks of using armed drones in domestic law enforcement, as well as the need for transparency in domestic surveillance programs. Operating in a similar spirit, though through more legitimized channels, the London-based artist James Bridle created an exhibit titled *Drone Shadows* in order to bring visibility to the controversial military use of drones in conflicts in the Middle East and to the ramifications of allowing drones to fly over urban centers in the United States and Europe. The piece featured life-sized representations of military Predator drones, outlined in white paint in urban public spaces. In its first incarnation, these drone shadows appeared in a series of London parking lots. The piece, which then moved to the Corcoran Gallery in Washington, DC, forced the specter of the military aircraft into the urban everyday of western capitals. For western audiences, the exhibit built a chilling connection between civilians strolling through relatively peaceful, western centers of power and civilians living in Middle Eastern regions that are under the threat and reality of drone attacks.

The inspiration for *Drone Shadows* came from pictures of shadows of military drones from Afghanistan, Iraq, and Palestine that Bridle and his collaborator, Einar Sneve Martinussen, found on Google Maps. These

Fig. 33. James Bridle's *Drone Shadows*, 2012. (Image courtesy of James Bridle and booktwo.org.)

images represented, albeit from afar, what it looked like to live with drones flying overhead. As Bridle wrote in a blog post on the project, he felt the need to familiarize himself and other western civilians with the physical reality of military drones.

> The thing that bothered us the most then . . . was trying to get a feel for what it would be like to stand next to one. To stand before, or under it . . . , to measure oneself against it. Despite occasional appearances in the day-to-day world (air shows, for example, or museums), most people have never seen one IRL [in real life]; in operation, their very point is invisibility. So we drew one.[22]

After the FAA and CAA regulatory changes in March 2012, Bridle decided to bring outlines of actual Predator drones to visibility in urban centers in London, Istanbul, and Washington DC.

Bridle employed a number of representational tactics that pointedly reframed his western audiences as potential targets of drone warfare, rather than its agents, and reminded viewers of the deadly capabilities of military drones. As in Attia's posters, in which pedestrian viewers were meant to identify with the figures of the man, woman, and child running in terror from the drone that chased them, Bridle cast audience members as subjects of the drone's surveillant and potentially predatory gaze. Rather than representing the Predator drone itself through a lifesized model that audiences could have touched or walked around, Bridle chose to focus on drone shadows, cast as though the drones were flying above his audience. This positioned his viewers as if they were visible to a drone's gaze, subjected to its scrutiny and evaluation in the same way civilian and enemy targets were in war zones half a world away. Bridle's installations also symbolically suggested the need for criminal investigations into drone attacks in the Middle East. Whereas a darkened patch on the earth would signify the actual appearance of a shadow cast by a drone flying overhead, Bridle outlined the shape of the drone in white paint. This representational tactic conjured the visual rhetoric of a crime scene in which the outline of a body remains as an index of the act of a murder even after the corporeal evidence has been removed for autopsy and burial. The choice added a layer of productive ambiguity to the piece. Perhaps Bridle was calling for the death of the drone, or perhaps he was representing a fearful premonition of the future deaths that domestic drone use could bring to London, Washington, DC, or other urban centers around the world.

Social media platforms have become popular tools for disseminating such critiques in virtual space. Josh Begley has been tweeting the location of every reported drone strike in Iraq since 2002 on his Twitter feed @Dronestrike. More recently, Begley has developed a free iPhone app called Metadata+, which catalogs and maps drone strikes by the US military.[23] The app notifies users of the date, location, and victims of each strike, sending push notifications when a new strike occurs. In a similar, though more mobile fashion than Bridle's *Drone Shadows*, Begley's app transposes the violence and anxiety experienced by civilians in countries such as Iraq, Afghanistan, and Syria into the pockets and purses of western users half a world away. In push notifications, which have come to be a familiar (if sometimes obnoxious) feature of many user-friendly applications such as Facebook, Twitter, and Snapchat, Begley saw an opportunity to broaden the spectrum of visibility within social media platforms. "I wanted to play with this idea of push notifications and push button technology—essentially asking a question about what we choose to get notified about in real time," he said in an interview with *Wired* magazine. "I thought reaching into the pockets of U.S. smartphone users and annoying them into drone-consciousness could be an interesting way to surface the conversation a bit more."[24]

Even as Begley mirrored the familiar user-friendly interfaces of other products that utilize Apple's iOS operating system, the content he provided was deliberately unfamiliar—and uncomfortable. In an interview with *The Atlantic*, Begley responded to a question about the incongruity between the violent content of the app and the iOS interface he used to get it distributed by Apple.

> For me, borrowing the visual vernacular of Apple's expertly built interface opens up the potential for a different kind of seeing. If the folks on the other side of our missiles are presented to us in the same places we see pictures of our loved ones (James Bridle's dronestagram) or communicate with our friends (@dronestream), might that nudge me to learn a little more about the contours of covert war?[25]

In fact Begley had to perform some semantic gymnastics to get Apple to support the app. He originally submitted it under the name Drones+ but was repeatedly rejected because he was proposing content that "many audiences would find objectionable."[26] Eventually he resubmitted it under the more ambiguous title Metadata+. Stripped of an overtly political title, the Metadata+ app nevertheless provides users with the opportunity to download real time updates on national security.

Platforms such as Twitter, Facebook, and Instagram get far more daily traffic than any art gallery or theater and, as such, they are savvy choices for artists and activists seeking to reach a broad swath of people with their critiques. At the same time, placing metadata about drone strikes among other, less politically incendiary metadata that smart phone users receive—from photos posted by their friends to news of a sale happening nearby—risks neutralizing such information, as news of drone strikes could be easily subsumed into the fabric of everyday life. However, Begley hopes for the opposite; he believes that translating real time news of drone strikes into an interactive application for smart phones can be both convenient and politically critical, as policing military drone use could become a part of the daily communications and social activity of smart phone users. If users see drone strikes represented through familiar Google Maps location markers and push notification chirps, these violent actions occurring half a world away should, Bagley believes, begin to feel too close for comfort.

ANTI-DRONE DESIGNS

A second performative tactic used in staging cautionary representations of drones is that of producing antidrone designs for everyday living. Bridle's *Drone Shadows* exhibit included a "drone identification kit" modeled after existing kits used to train military and civilians in the Middle East to spot and recognize different types of aircraft. While not yet a necessity for most museum patrons in the United States and United Kingdom, this skill is one in which many other civilians around the world have already become well versed, and, Bridle seemed to warn, we might do well to study up on it as well. Other particularly innovative examples of this tactic can be found in works by Asher J. Kohn and Adam Harvey. By figuring clothing and building designs as defensive systems, Harvey and Kohn assert that the arts of fashion design and architecture can be critical political acts. Their defensive designs provide "ordinary practitioners" with tools they can use to resist and undermine the efficacy of state surveillance and military operations.

In *Shura City*, law student and conceptual artist Asher J. Kohn considered ways that urban architecture could be made resistant to aerial surveillance and drone strikes. With the goal of utilizing architecture as a politically subversive practice, he designed *Shura City* to be an "architectural defense from drones."[27] Describing his logic for the project, Kohn wrote, "Drones are a way to use the city. Architects will have to interact with them and create built environments that will either promote or inhibit their use."[28] His conceptual plan for the city included seven design elements borrowed from a range of historical time periods and cultures. Minarets, inspired by medieval towers and mosques, would prevent drones from flying very low while a net of wires and Plexiglas would cover common areas. Together, the whole network of living spaces in *Shura City* would create a pattern of randomness that would "present drones with an inscrutable puzzle," confounding the ability of state or corporate entities to use drones for surveillant or combative purposes.[29] As Kohn described it, the design was intended as a creative mode of defense.

> The goal is not defense-through-hardening, but defense-through-confusion. By turning the entire community into a closed circuit, drones targeting individuals will not be able to select and detect the individuals they desire once they enter the city . . . This built environment presents drones with an inscrutable puzzle.[30]

Kohn's plan was not designed for a particular locale and is currently only symbolic. However, he clearly intended it to resonate with the everyday needs and political plight of Muslim inhabitants in regions under the routine threat of drone attacks and surveillance. Kohn chose the name *Shura City* because the Arabic word *shura* means "consultation," and refers to a group of assembled elders and respected individuals who take responsibility for the decision making of a community. The title symbolizes an effort to support and empower Muslim leaders and communities that have been the overwhelming targets of drone strikes in recent years, a process in which they are rarely if ever consulted. Applied more broadly, *Shura City* imagines a solution that could protect and strengthen any community that might come under the threat of drone strikes and surveillance.

New York City–based fashion designer Adam Harvey likewise drew on Islamic cultural symbols in his line of antidrone clothing. As airborne surveillance systems began rapidly proliferating in 2012, Harvey felt the need to outfit everyday subjects of surveillance. So he took what the Pentagon calls "countermeasures" into the realm of fashion design.[31] Harvey's Stealth Wear hoodie, hijab, and burqa were designed to block x-ray radiation, preventing the wearer from being detected from overhead by drones with heat- or light-sensing cameras.[32] In addition to referencing the fact that thus far Muslims have constituted the majority of drone strike targets, Harvey drew on Islamic garments in his clothing designs in order to emphasize his oppositional stance toward drones: "The rationale behind the hijab and burqa is that it provides a separation between 'man and God.' Similarly, the rationale behind the 'Anti-Drone' Burqa and Hijab are to provide a separation between 'man and drone.'"[33] These garments, along with Harvey's other personal countersurveillance devices—such as antipaparazzi sunglasses, which emit a photo-ruining flash back when a camera flash is detected, and the Off Pocket, which "zeroes out" a user's cell phone signal and GPS locative media, rendering it invisible to surveillance efforts—constitute practical tools of resistance to state and corporate surveillance in everyday life.[34] As Harvey described the clothing line, "Stealth Wear continues to explore the aesthetics of privacy and the potential for fashion to challenge authoritarian surveillance."[35] Put in de Certeauian terms, Harvey tactically mobilizes tools of everyday life, creating street-ready clothing and accessories that "ordinary practitioners" might use to defend their corporeal privacy and recover some of the terrain "below the threshold where visibility begins."[36]

However, despite the art world and media acclaim he has received for his fashion-forward critique, Harvey's designs leave other thresholds of invisibility unchallenged: in particular, the gender politics of the Islamic garments he chose to emulate and the economic class divisions that his costly products reinforce. More than a separation between "man and God," the head-to-toe covering of the burqa (or the broader, more generic category of the "hijab," which refers to all manners of veiling) symbolizes stringent separations between men and women in Islamic society, not only from each other but also between women and a wide range of social, political, geographic, and economic mobilities. Although Harvey almost certainly meant *man* as a catchall term for human subjects (his product video features both men and women wearing his products), we should not overlook the significant fact that such garments were designed to be worn by women in order to hide their bodies from the gaze of any man outside their own immediate family. Women's bodies in Islam have long been a site on which moral and political ideologies have been displayed and imposed. Under more repressive Islamist regimes such as that of the Taliban, burqas have gone hand in hand with laws that prohibit women from pursuing an education, a career, inheritances, and custody of their children.

Harvey's decision to base his designs on these gendered garments of fundamentalist Islam thus puts the project in complicated political territory. To bring up the politics of hijab garments is to open a host of complicated debates in feminist, cultural, and religious arenas.[37] While arguments in favor of outlawing burqas and other hijabs abound, there are as many defenses of the right to wear them, as many Muslim women actively support the practice for social, political, and religious reasons. Aligning burqas with the Taliban's acts of terrorism would be severely misguided, and yet the symbolic act of wearing a burqa is, at this moment in history, unavoidably connected to deep philosophical and practical oppositions expressed by fundamentalist Islamic factions against dominant western political, social, and economic practices—notably among them the cultural freedoms experienced by women in many western countries. Burqa-clad women and girls are frequently pictured in the visual imagery of fundamentalist Islam, serving as propagandistic figures that young men are called on to protect and defend through jihad. As Persian and women's studies scholar Shahin Gerami put it, women are told that wearing hijabs is a means of honoring the blood of martyrs that fight for their protection: "As official slogans and graffiti everywhere read, 'My sister, your hijab is your martyrdom.'"[38] Framed as an act of martyrdom, or even an expression of religious modesty, donning a hijab has become a loaded political act.

Further, although Harvey utilized the protective aspect of the burqa in order to defend wearers from the surveillant, weaponized gaze of drones, his representations and marketing of the Stealth Wear line place the products within a matrix of elitist art and secular, capitalist consumption that risks alienating rather than inviting the participation of a broader, intercultural audience. The images that Harvey uses to advertise the Stealth Wear line demonstrate a hip, couture vibe. With highly toned midriffs bared under the hijabs and hoodies, Harvey's models (both male and female) make visible the significant cultural disparity between his target audience and the modest Muslim women who typically don burqas.[39] It is not hard to imagine that the countersurveillance burqa, worn by otherwise scantily clad non-Muslim men and women, might alienate rather than unite Islamic and western opponents of drone surveillance. His correlation between drones and God would likely not sit well with many Muslims either. These disparities are compounded by the price of Harvey's designs; selling for four hundred to two thousand dollars a garment, the steep couture prices and westernized style of these hijabs make his products economically and culturally exclusive.[40]

That said, Harvey's idea of combining the protective covering of the burqa with a political critique of drone surveillance has a great deal of potential, particularly as a tool for Islamic feminism. While some Islamic feminists take a firmly secular route and refuse to wear coverings such as the burqa, many others seek to find a middle ground that allows them to embrace the tenets of the Qur'an, including the modest dress of hijabs, while at the same time arguing for social and political rights for women within Muslim societies. Islamic feminist scholar Margot Badran described the small but growing transnational movement within Middle Eastern and international Muslim communities. Coming to greater visibility throughout the 1990s, "Islamic feminism is a feminist discourse expressly articulated within an Islamic paradigm, and behaviours and activisms inspired by it are enacted in Islam's name. [It] also articulated itself within nationalist, humanitarian/human rights, and democratic discourses."[41] If they were marketed with this religious and political context in mind, Harvey's redesigned burqas might appeal to Islamic feminists as practical and symbolic tools of political resistance. Donning burqas made of infrared-blocking material would provide Muslim women with culturally apt tools through which to express criticism of the violence and surveillance that drones have brought to Muslim communities.

In their current iterations, both Harvey's and Kohn's works are more symbolic than practical. Kohn's *Shura City* exists only in theory and sketches, and Harvey's clothing line is priced more for museum collections than individual consumers. They have circulated through western media sources, serving primarily as cautionary symbols of what life would be like (and is like for many in the Middle East) with routine drone operations overhead. As designers, consumers, city planners, and activist groups continue to respond to the increasing numbers of drones being employed around the world, it will be important to shift projects such as these from symbolic designs to the functional, affordable stuff of daily life for actual targets of drone surveillance and violence.

Flying in the City: New Spatial Practices

To focus only on the violent capabilities of drones, however, would not tell the whole story of UAVs in contemporary culture. Whereas the works in the previous section seek to warn and protect viewers against the surveillant gaze and deadly attacks of drones, practitioners in this section approach drones as tools with which to explore the world from a different vantage point. Hobbyists use drones to create "first-person" videography, entrepreneurs dream of delivering food and service items via drones, and theater artists, musicians, and choreographers explore the unique aesthetics and entertainment potential of drones. Such practices are characterized by curiosity and interactivity, as users explore the social, aesthetic, and even spiritual aspects of UAVs. In order to take drones out of a distinctly military context and reframe them as quotidian tools of leisure or sport, users must enjoy a certain level of political freedom, peace, and economic stability. I thus invoke Benjamin's notion of the "flaneur" and Donna Haraway's theorization of cultural cyborgs to both critique and celebrate the sociopolitical privileges that facilitate such experiments with drones, as well as to think through how these experiments constitute alternative, resistant spatial practices.

While the use of drones in live performance is not yet a common practice, so far there have been a number of notable experiments in this area, particularly in the world of dance. In addition to Pilobolus's *Seraph*, described in the opening, Eleven Play, a Japanese dance company, created a piece in 2014 that used several drones to create a futuristic scene of ritual annihilation. For my own part, I collaborated with Jamie Jewett, Jewett's dance company LostWax, and sound and media artist

Luke DuBois to create *Zoologic*, a dance theater piece that dramatized Thalia Field's poetic text on the ethical quandaries of putting animals and humans in captivity and under surveillance.[42] In the piece, drones of various shapes and sizes joined the dancers onstage, in turns surveilling them, protecting them, and becoming fellow living creatures. As anyone who has flown one might imagine, there are a host of challenges in appropriating drones for performance; artists and hobbyists alike have widely reported difficulties in stabilizing drones and directing them in intended paths. As Itamar Kubovy, executive director of Pilobolus, shared in media interviews about *Seraph*, the company quickly learned that using drones in a performance brought with it new physical challenges and a new learning curve: "We crashed them all the time, crashed them constantly [during rehearsal]. . . . We learned what the limits of the technology are and then learned to push those limits."[43] However, as drones become at once more affordable and more sophisticated, we can expect to see many more such "dances with drones."

Other artists have more fundamentally reframed the materiality of the drone itself. As philosophy professor and musician Robin James wrote on her blog, "What if, instead of making art *about* drones, we make art *with* drones? What if we don't jump immediately to the question, 'What are drones used *for*?', but first ask . . . 'What is a drone, as a *medium*? Maybe if we stop overlooking materiality and medium in our enthusiasm to praise or critique drones, we'll be better equipped to think about their effects and consequences?'"[44] James and her partner Christian Ryan, who together form a band called *citation: obsolete*, plan to use consumer-level quadcopter drones outfitted with contact microphones to record a series of pieces called "Music for Drones."[45] Media artist Nadav Assor has likewise designed a "musical" exploration of drone technology. In his installation work *Ophan* (2014), he played with the term *drone* as it also appears in religious music traditions: a customized hexacopter becomes a mechanized, flying cantor, reciting verses from the first chapter of the biblical book of Ezekiel. Assor elaborates on how he merged the two concepts into an aesthetically and conceptually rich work.

> The Yemenite style of Cantorial singing-chanting (cantillation) is monotonous—that is, there is no melody, rather a droning recitation similar to other eastern musical traditions. The cantor who recorded the verses for Ophan tuned his voice to the pitch of the buzzing generated by the hexacopter's rotors, so that they create a harmonized sound when combined.[46]

In a similar exploration of the aesthetic materiality of drones, the Austrian arts and technology group Ars Electronica Futurelab choreographed a piece for forty-nine remotely controlled quadcopter drones. The drones performed as part of a public arts festival held in September 2012; outfitted with lights of changing colors, they flew in various formations in the night sky.[47] The effect was unusual and beautiful; at times the drones resembled flocks of birds and at others they appeared to be nearby stars or floating candles. These artists are primarily motivated to find ways in which drones might be used as tools of aesthetic production. James puts this goal in a broader social framework: "[I]t's very important to us that some of it is legible *as music* to lay audiences. Toy drones are fun: you play with them. How can our performances evoke the pleasures we take in drones? How can we use sound and performance/installation to bring these pleasures to conscious attention and reflection?"[48]

A virtual exhibit titled *Drones of New York*, launched in 2012 through the Museum of the Moving Image in New York, portrayed the most likely widespread commercial applications of drones in coming years. The project asked a group of artists to imagine what the cityscape of New York might look like if drones were to become common features of advertising, leisure activities, and entertainment. The exhibit featured fifteen designer drones, each conceived for a different neighborhood around the city.[49] In digitally rendered videos, the drones appeared to be touring the city. An MSG drone flew down Canal Street in Chinatown, a Central Park drone hovered over joggers and bikers, and a John Lennon drone circled the block where he was shot. Nearly all the drones in *Drones of New York* were, if not overtly peaceful in nature, devoid of any violent or even surveillant purpose. Although each resembled the body of a military Predator drone, the projects embraced the likely outcome that many of the domestic drones of the near future will function as advertising canvases, the next generation of the Goodyear blimp. The *Drones of New York* exhibit also offered an interactive component, which provided viewers the opportunity to create their own drone and choose a geographic site over which to have it fly. Unable to resist, I created a drone that I flew over a virtual image of the Stanford University campus, where I was presenting a paper on drone art at the annual Performance Studies International conference. The effect of watching my drone fly over the courtyard that we had all just walked across to get to the conference panels was both entertaining and unnerving, lending a political edge to the otherwise entertaining *Drones of New York* project.

CYBORGIAN FLANEURS: NEW SPATIAL
PRACTICES IN THE CITY

While not a formal "arts" practice like the projects just described, UAV hobbyists have developed "first-person view" (FPV) videos as a genre through which to fly their drones and share their drone footage. FPV flight features an unmanned aerial vehicle, typically a quadcopter drone, piloted remotely by way of an onboard camera, which is wirelessly linked to video goggles or a monitor worn by a user. The pilot on the ground maneuvers the drone from a "first-person" perspective, using the live feed from the drone's camera to make piloting decisions, as opposed to watching the body of the drone from his or her perspective on the ground. This provides the grounded pilot the same point of view as an onboard pilot, and allows the user to fly the plane well beyond the line of sight from the ground. The most cutting edge systems offer a "fully immersive FPV experience," linking two onboard cameras (for a bicameral, 3D effect) to video goggles enhanced with "head-tracking" capabilities, such as the Oculus VR/Rift system, which cause the drone to move in relation to the pilot's head motions.[50] Primarily practiced in countries that have loosened their regulations on consumer drone use, FPV is currently most popular in Australia (which has the most liberal domestic drone regulations in the world), and in the United States and United Kingdom, where regulations are a bit tighter but often not enforced.[51]

Although FPV is not categorically artistic in its aims, many practitioners post dramatic footage of their FPV flights on social media sites such as YouTube and Vimeo. A closer look at one such video illustrates both the promising and problematic aspects of FPV as a spatial and aesthetic practice. In 2012 a YouTube contributor and FPV drone enthusiast who goes by the handle "Tretch5000" posted aerial footage of abandoned urban areas in Detroit, Michigan.[52] Using a consumer-level quadcopter drone outfitted with a high-level digital video camera, Tretch explored the bankrupt and largely vacated city, documenting the urban blight that has followed the decline of the auto industry and years of municipal corruption. The resulting video was a beautiful yet tragic portrait of the city, providing viewers with vertiginous, high-definition perspectives of churches, factories, and homes that had fallen into ruin. Flying with the drone, viewers swoop down on a lush green park by the water with the skyline of Detroit on the horizon, then move swiftly above a lot filled with old tires, discarded vertebrae of the vanished auto industry that once gave the city—and its unrepresented inhabitants—its grandeur. Tretch paired the FPV footage with music that cued triumphant wonder, seemingly celebrating the new technology of the drone, which allowed him to tour the city from a more aesthetically pleasing angle. His FPV perspective notably avoided any interaction with or representation of the realities of everyday life in a city recovering from bankruptcy. No live human inhabitants could be seen in the dilapidated neighborhoods, only traces of lives that had once been.

Tretch's widely viewed example of FPV drone video illustrates the draw of the unique and visually thrilling viewpoint of FPV. Although the YouTube video is an archival product, one can imagine the thrill of exploring a landscape from such a mobile vantage point in real time. At the same time, the politics of such a viewpoint are ambiguous and cause for some deeper analysis. The video, which has been classified as part of a burgeoning category dubbed "ruin porn" for its blend of disaster tourism and amateur digital videography, highlights the capacity of drones to traverse spaces that attract the human imagination but are unsafe or inaccessible to curious pedestrians. Tretch's drone floated unscathed above industrial hazards that many of the film's viewers would likely not dare to traverse. The ability to explore devastated, violent, or toxic environments without risk to a human pilot is, of course, what makes drones attractive as tools for war, forest fire management, environmental surveys, and disaster management. However, this vantage point simultaneously deepens social, economic, and political divides between those who can afford such a viewpoint and those who cannot be "lifted above" the dangers and risks of such a place. Drones provide certain people—be they economically empowered amateur hobbyists, military personnel, or YouTube audiences—a vantage point from which to explore a world peopled by certain others. In the case of Detroit, this "other" group would be largely comprised of un- or underemployed African Americans. In the case of Tretch's video, privileged viewers not only avoid the physical risk of walking through Detroit's ruined spaces, but they also avoid having to see the plight of the disenfranchised people still living there, as the film features no people at all.

Keeping these criticisms in mind, FPV drone use, as well as the films and videos produced by it, is an emergent spatial practice through which to explore the new politics of embodiment and techno-human subjectivity that come with the arrival of drones in everyday life. Within the leisure-based economy of amateur drone use, FPV users experience a mode of mobility that is practiced within everyday space and yet remains separate from more traditional, organized, and regulated patterns of movement and commerce. In light of this, I suggest that we think of FPV hobbyists as a contemporary incarnation of the "flaneur," famously theorized by Walter Benjamin and Charles Baudelaire as the sauntering man of leisure, a connoisseur of the streets who takes the time to follow his own roving interests as he explores urban space.[53] Baudelaire described the perfect flaneur as a "passionate spectator" who is at home "amid the ebb and flow of movement, in the midst of the fugitive and the infinite." The flaneur moves with the goal "to see the world, to be at the centre of the world, and yet to remain hidden from it."[54] As aerial flaneurs, FPV pilots utilize drone technology for a leisurely pastime that exists in distinct opposition to the working drones of the military, law enforcement, or environmental research. FPV drone flights move in excess of the structures of state control and commercial capitalism, that which Benjamin thought of as the death of the flaneur.[55] The concept of the flaneur also points out that the spatial practice of drone hobbyists is dependent on certain demographic conditions. The flaneur, for Benjamin and Baudelaire, was almost certainly white and male; his invisibility, which comes from belonging wherever he goes, as well as his ability to be detached from and yet an active agent in the world, assumes a white, male privilege. First-person view users tend to replicate the privileged demographic position of the flaneur. They must have a certain abundance of leisure time, sufficient means to purchase the technology, and live in a time and space of leisure and peace.

It is precisely the detached, leisurely viewpoint of the flaneur that makes FPV videos such as Tretch5000's both aesthetically innovative and politically problematic. Producing romantic, nostalgic imagery by flying a drone over the ravaged sites of Detroit risks overlooking the harsh realities of life in the troubled city. In a review of the video, Alexis Madrigal of *The Atlantic* incisively observed that drone films such as this displace the viewer into an impossible vantage point: "We are above the city. We are not subject to the fears of the beings below." He concluded that this "is not a human perspective," noting that FPV films such as Tretch's do not depict "the fear of a failing city or the complex reasons for its decline."[56] Rather than evoking viewpoints familiar to viewers from their own experiences of mobility, the film produced sweeping cinematic shots reminiscent of Hollywood blockbusters. FPV "is not a human perspective" and yet it does provide a contemporary perspective on being human; or, as Donna Haraway famously suggested in her "Cyborg Manifesto," on the ways in which contemporary humans have all, to some degree, become cyborgs. Functioning as prosthetics of sight and flight for amateurs, artists, and a range of other nonstate users, consumer-level drones enact a cyborgian politics that, following Haraway, importantly expands beyond the military-industrial complex that first created them. To describe this important difference within cyborgian ontology, Haraway defined two kinds of cyborgs: the "material cyborg," which is shaped by dominant social and political systems such as the military, pharmaceutical companies, and Hollywood cinema (paired with machismo, advanced weaponry, and a supernormative human body); and the "metaphorical cyborg," which is fictional yet politically subversive for its transgressive, nonnormative status as a hybrid, liminal being impossible to fix or stabilize.[57] Drones, as a broad category, likewise operate in both modes. As instruments of military might, they are like "material cyborgs," carrying out the missions of Air Force pilots stationed at military bases; at the same time, the demilitarized, alternative uses of drones by amateurs and artists that make available new modes of embodiment and experience that resonate with Haraway's construction of the transgressive "metaphorical cyborg."

Thought of in this way, the aerial perspective and leisure-based practice of FPV drone use has the potential to serve an innovative, even resistant spatial practice, an improvisational script through which users can move above and beyond the prescriptive pathways and organized spaces of planned city spaces. The pilots move, via drone, according to their own desires to explore a landscape, performing an aerial version of a situationist *derive* that reterritorializes the panoptic design of the city even as the practice physicalizes the voyeuristic desire to "be a viewpoint and nothing more."[58] In other words, FPV pilots mobilize a hybrid mode of experiencing contemporary life, one that lifts them "out of the city's grasp" through the flight of the drone while simultaneously allowing them to explore it in a meandering mode of "displacement" and "wandering" that de Certeau and the situationists championed as resistant pedestrian practices within everyday life.[59] The largely depoliticized narratives in the marketing and applications of the small, unarmed commercial drones used by hobbyists can seem troubling given the strong associations between military aggression, civilian casualties, and drones. However, there are important and potentially impactful perspectives to be found in the alternative, civilian uses of aerial "cyborgian flaneurs."

As in Haraway's writings on the cyborg, FPV drone use has also brought with it new metaphysical and even spiritual experiences. First-person view videos (though not Tretch's) frequently feature a shot in which the pilot flies the drone back to hover above his or her own body. In this shot, the pilot views him- or herself from an "out-of-body" position. Visual artist Nadav Assor saw in this a spiritual dimension that recalled mystical theories such as astral projection or spiritual visitations. Inspired by this FPV practice, he developed an interactive installation in which an audience member dons an Occulus Rift immersive headset; as the wearer moves his or her head, the viewpoint of a camera-equipped drone positioned above the wearer moves in response, offering different views of the wearer from above. Assor has further explored the spiritual dimensions of FPV drone use in the documentary *Lessons on Leaving Your Body* (2014).[60] The film features Jake Wells, an FPV hobbyist who builds his own drones and uses them as part of his Christian ministry. Much of the footage in this fascinating documentary was shot by Wells, who films himself from the aerial perspective of his custom-made tricopter as a means of building his spiritual awareness and connection to God. While the politics of such projects remain, perhaps deliberately, nebulous, these observations speak to the new hybridities and perspectives offered by consumer-level UAVs. Recasting drones as instruments for largely peaceful, leisure-based, and even sprititual meanderings implicitly resists the martial, panoptic origins of drone technology. Where military, law enforcement, and border patrol drones replicate panoptic, disciplinary strategies and entrepreneurs seek to create new markets for drone delivery, aerial photography, and personal protection, civilian practitioners continue to find applications for drones that, as de Certeau put it, "chart another path."[61]

Importantly, there have also been deliberately politically transgressive uses of FPV drone piloting that more directly counteract disciplinary and violent applications of drones. As was described in the "Introduction," Angel Nevarez and Alex Rivera's *Lowdrone* project gives online users the opportunity to cross the US-Mexico border using a consumer-level drone. Positioning a drone on one of the most surveilled sites in the world, the US- Mexico border between Tijuana and Southern California, Nevarez and Rivera offer users the chance to pilot the drone up and over the border fence and back again. The video of the border crossing is shot from the drone's onboard camera, providing users with an FPV of their aerial transgression. Certain aspects of the online project are playful (the website features flashing text warning users of the transgressive act in which they are about to participate, and the drone itself has a model of a lowrider automobile mounted on top of it), yet its ideological underpinnings remain serious and significant. As Nevarez and Rivera write, "Inverting invasive technologies is a technique of resistance that has a deep history in Latino communities. With our project for Tijuana

Fig. 34. The lowdrone, invented 2005, website still. (Image courtesy of Alex Rivera and Angel Nevarez.)

Calling, we are beginning that kind of inversion/aesthetic warping with the aerial drone."[62] *Lowdrone* provides a symbolic alternative to the disciplinary applications of drones proliferating along the border: in addition to blimp-style UAVs and Predator drones deployed to fly over the US-Mexico border, a conservative vigilante group, American Border Control, uses consumer drones to police the border for illegal immigrants.[63] As Nevarez and Rivera describe it, the project aims to "demonstrate that the skies should not, and do not, belong only to the military/industrial complex," nor to conservative watch-dog groups like American Border Control. With the project they are "making a performative gesture against the concentration of power and wealth that the Border Patrol's drones represent. With LowDrone.com [they] hope to demonstrate that another world is possible—a world where technology serves many communities, and the line between watcher and watched is never absolute."[64] The *Lowdrone* project is a model for Haraway's radical hope for the cyborg, as it uses the drone as a mechanical prosthetic through which users can transgress and, to use a situationist term, *reterritorialize* a border that is, at the same time, being policed by federal and state drones.[65]

Because of its virtual, remote piloting interface, the *Lowdrone* mirrors some of the same advantages—as a well as the pitfalls—of Tretch's ruin porn. The *Lowdrone* interface allows users to perform an action that, through the FPV drone camera, feels something like an embodied form of political transgression and critique. At the same time, the online platform and the distance from which the drone can be piloted remove much of the individual risk. Participants can casually fly across the border, but they are physically far removed from any real consequences. The drone becomes a safe substitute for a body that could be detained, deported, or disciplined in an actual illegal border crossing. As a result, while the symbolism of the project is quite powerful, the stakes of participation for online users are in fact quite low. Using FPV to take a transgressive "step" across the border is intellectually provocative as a new model of civil disobedience, and rather thrilling the first time, but the remote controlled, online interface does not ask users to put any "skin in the game," as it were. This only reifies the distance between online users and the actual bodies of the immigrants who make the high-stakes border crossing themselves. Nevertheless, these experimental uses of drones should not be dismissed as apolitical or merely symbolic; they constitute nascent cyborgian identities that can provide valuable insights into our changing relationships with environment, embodiment, and mobility in contemporary surveillance society.

Flying with a Payload of Empathy

In the final section, I look at two examples of drone artworks that explore the impact of UAVs on the psychological well-being and emotional lives of military drone pilots. George Barber's film *The Freestone Drone* (2013) and George Brant's *Grounded* (2013) both acknowledge the realities of military drone combat and present audiences with insight into the complicated demands placed on the labor force of contemporary warfare. While they do not valorize military use of drones—both pieces leave a distinct aftertaste of pacifism—they aim to show the ethical and psychological complexities involved in using drones in combat.

THE FREESTONE DRONE

In a small gallery, tucked away in the sprawling outskirts of London, visitors stood among lines of laundry that crisscross the space, peering around worn shirts and pants to view a short film with a surprising protagonist: a drone with free will and a conscience. Narrated as a dark children's story and represented through found footage, *The Freestone Drone* told a fragmented tale of a Predator drone that had a mind of its own. In an interview with *Wired*, Barber described his reasons for making the protagonist of his film a drone that was more humane than his human operators.

> There's the idea of workers in edit suites, trained on Playstations, sitting around killing people and then jumping in cars and rushing home to have dinner. It's the sense of a soldier who risks nothing and just fits in with civilians. . . . This image of a high-tech guy raining down what they like to think of as targeted violence on people who are not helpful to America. It caught my mind. So I thought about a drone who could talk, and who could start to feel bad about it, and who disagreed with ground control and decides to go see New York instead.[66]

Like the children's book character Thomas the Tank Engine, from which Barber took inspiration, the Freestone Drone was mischievous, curious about the larger world and his place in it. "Do you remember the Freestone Drone? God, what a drone. He never obeyed orders, but answered back and argued. . . . He flew, thinking and reflecting on the world."[67] Despite the comforting fablelike beginning, the portrait that soon emerged was at once more illuminating and more frightening than any amount of statistics about the payloads of missiles carried by working Predator drones like the Freestone. In a tinny, chipper voice the Freestone Drone shared thoughts that vacillated between poetic musings about emotional attachments between lovers and quips about his power to obliterate human life. "Love, what did it feel like?" The Freestone Drone longed to know, as he cruised through time and space, observing people. But before viewers could get too cozy with his poetic leanings, he chirped, "I just happened to be in the neighborhood and I thought I'd burn you up." Adding to the fragmented personality of the drone, a gruff American voice interrupted the Freestone Drone's reveries several times with a question: "Were you aware that he was killed during an American drone strike?" It seemed distinctly possible that, after too many missions over Afghanistan, the drone was suffering from a mechanical version of PTSD. The rogue and possibly damaged psyche of the Freestone Drone took him off course on several adventures. One day, flying over the Pacific, the Freestone Drone decided to visit New York, the thrall of tourism outweighing his military orders ("I didn't fancy Waziristan today"). The drone described his mentality as a tourist: "New York in summer. I just popped over, you know. Ignored orders to see it all myself. I was lightly armed at the time, relaxed, in a nice place. Underneath I had a couple of small missiles, nothing much. I could take out an apartment or a car, that kind of thing."[68] As if to prove these darker aspects of his identity, the drone veered suddenly away from his tourism narrative to disclose a disquieting obsession with laundry lines. The significance of the laundry hanging in the gallery was revealed, as the Freestone Drone let visitors in on a little military secret: intimately connected to the people who wear it and often hung to dry outside a house, laundry provides military surveillance operatives with details that can help determine what individuals might be residing in a given house. As the Freestone Drone put it, "The laundry tells me things, like who is visiting. . . . A lot can be told by the washing."

This detail of military strategy had clearly caught in Barber's mind. He had expanded the motif of laundry lines beyond the frame of the film and turned the gallery that housed the film into the semblance of a courtyard humbly decorated with crisscrossing laundry lines pinned with well-worn clothing. By physicalizing the domestic scene of hanging laundry, Barber wanted to literally bring home the disturbing asymmetry between lethal drone strikes and the simplicity of everyday civilian life. Barber explained in the interview, "People are often in their domestic situation, going to sleep at night or dreaming, they're very vulnerable. Then this thing just suddenly comes and visits them. We regard that as a kind of bullying, it's not honest combat."[69] While the film depicted laundry lines shot from above (from the drone's point of view), gallery visitors were positioned among and beneath the lines themselves, complicating the already ambiguous relationship between the audience and the film's volatile protagonist: would he treat us to another story or blow us up?

While Barber's main objective was to launch a political critique of the "bullying" strategies he saw in military drone strikes, his film also poignantly touched on the psychological pain of a self-conscious being that

has been involved in contemporary warfare. The Freestone Drone exhibited signs of PTSD, a form of suffering that came, it seemed, from his
humanlike conscience and ability to self-reflect. Although the Freestone
Drone could not necessarily be trusted by either his military command-
ers or the civilians he flew above, his troubled, guilt-ridden soul solicited
empathy. He mournfully reflected on the impact of his lethal missions: "I
will be taking out somebody with a little bit of washing. Just one person
who probably washed the clothes that evening, before they lay down to
sleep." Reflecting on his role in such violent acts, the drone articulated
a deep-seated discomfort with his identity: "I wanted to be something
else. I didn't like being me. Even with just two rockets I make people
feel uneasy. Could I ever be a nice drone? I admit, I give no warning.
I'm a bit creepy." By projecting this moral uneasiness onto the Freestone
Drone, Barber sought to challenge the objective and ethically uneven
rhetoric often used to justify military drone strikes: "That's the problem
with drones, it's promoted as surgery, as not invasive—it's targeted with
precision, but that's not really the case. They don't seem to mind three
people as collateral damage, but if it gets to ten, or a whole bus, that's not
acceptable. There's a strange, wandering principle there."[70]

Although Barber's critiques leave little room for sympathy with military personnel who actually pilot drones, his film's tragic conclusion calls
to mind the disturbingly high rates of suicide among military veterans in
the United States and makes a statement about the tragic and wasteful
costs of warfare on all sides. Throughout the film, the Freestone Drone
had pondered death; in addition to reflecting on the cruel fate of his
unsuspecting victims, he wrestled with the existential question of his own
death, his tinny voice pondering, "What will happen when I die? Will I fly
across the sun, happen on a dry valley and then curve in, getting closer
and closer, like a suicide bomber before I finally meet my target?" In the
end, Barber scripted the Freestone Drone to meet his own death, prophetically tangled in a laundry line.

GROUNDED

Where Barber's short film imagined a drone with more conscience than
its human operators, American playwright George Brant's *Grounded*
investigates the human struggles of a US military drone pilot. Brant's
empathetic dramatization of the human costs of remotely fought
warfare—primary among them the psychological effects of PTSD—

places *Grounded* in the company of other recent plays, such as Christine Evans's *You Are Dead. You Are Here* (2013), Lindsey Ferrentino's *Ugly Lies the Bone* (2015), Paula Vogel's *Don Juan Comes Home from Iraq* (2014), Juggernaut Theatre's *Oh What War* (2008), and Laura Kepley and Deborah Salem Smith's *Boots on the Ground* (2006), that explore the devastating effects of contemporary warfare from the vantage points of military veterans. While Brant offers no easy answers to the debates surrounding military surveillance and the politics of drone use, *Grounded* manages to simultaneously humanize and hold responsible participants on all sides of contemporary warfare and global surveillance, present theater audiences included.

When *Grounded* hit the scene in 2013–14, with productions mounted in Edinburgh, London, San Francisco, and New York within the space of a few months, it fell on fertile soil. The advantages that many military, state, and corporate entities have seen in unmanned aerial vehicles have, at the same time, raised a host of humanitarian concerns. Among these concerns are the high numbers of civilian casualties in drone strikes; the concern that remotely piloted planes turn the reality of wartime violence into video game scenarios for pilots stationed far away; and the psychological costs, such as PTSD, accruing to military personnel engaged in remotely fought warfare. Brant planted the heroine of his solo play firmly in the midst these ethical quandaries. *Grounded*, recipient of the 2012 Smith prize for plays about American politics, does not shy away from any of these difficult questions or the complex politics that undergird them. The answers it stages break down the sedimented positions that characterize the debates over this polarizing technology. By dramatizing the particular demands that his protagonist faces as a woman in the Air Force, *Grounded* also gives voice, though more obliquely, to important and often overlooked experiences based on gender in relation to aviation, the military, combat, and surveillance. Grounded first by her pregnancy (Air Force regulations prohibit pregnant women from flying) and later by military investments in drone warfare, the story of *Grounded* portrays the experience of a woman coping with the competing pressures of civilian motherhood and a military combat career.

The performance I attended was a production of Page 73 Productions staged in the intimate venue of Walkerspace in downtown New York City.[71] The plot line unfolded quickly, delivered in rapid-fire stream-of-consciousness descriptions from Hannah Cabell, the actress playing "the Pilot," the otherwise unnamed protagonist of the solo play. The Pilot's pregnancy, an unanticipated development after "a very good three days" with Eric, a man she met in a bar while home on leave, was the first event that led her to be "grounded" from flight.[72] "The Blue"—her term for the freedom and power she experiences as a fighter pilot in the sky— was replaced with a gray ultrasound image of her little girl. Still, feeling "sorry-happy" with the life change, she returned home to marry and live with Eric, determined to raise a daughter who was not a needy "hair-tosser" but as strong-willed and free as herself.[73] Although her flight suit—a material symbol of the pride and commitment she maintained toward her military identity throughout the play—could no longer contain her pregnant body, her husband insisted on taking a photograph of her in her uniform; despite her protests—"I must look ridiculous / Can't zip up the front / Naked tight belly spilling out"—it took up residence on their living room wall, a visual reminder of the dual identities of mother and pilot she would need to perform.[74]

While, like myself, the majority of my fellow audience members had likely not sat in the Pilot's place or worn a flight suit like hers, the struggles she narrated provided valuable insight into the conditions of a growing number of military personnel, as martial investments in drones increase each year. The insights we gained into the civilian life of the Pilot—her marital ups and downs and efforts to find "extra special time" with her daughter—were easier points of identification, and they granted emotional access into more controversial aspects of her professional role in military combat. The Pilot's challenges also rang true with those more familiar with the lives of military women. After attending a performance of *Grounded* at the San Francisco Playhouse, retired Air Force sergeant Eduardo Ramirez wrote that the creative team of that production had succeeded in portraying the challenges facing military personnel, particularly women, involved in contemporary combat: "War is hell but having to fight it from a trailer stateside is [the] worst, daytime warrior, nighttime wife and mother, a hard life to live."[75]

Even as the Pilot's pride in being "one of the boys" was evident, the personal challenges and institutional surveillance to which she is subjected throughout the narrative of *Grounded* foreground the particular pressures and scrutiny that women still experience in military contexts because of their gender and reproductive decisions. The Pilot's affinity for heavy metal music, shooting pool with her fellow flyboys, and thinking of her husband as her "little woman at home" ("like some 50's movie . . . know who I'm fighting for / All that true corn") contradicted many cultural assumptions about womanhood.[76] Though neither Brant nor director Ken Rus Schmoll made an overt crusade of the Pilot's gender, her struggles with pregnancy, motherhood, and marriage in tension with her profession brought to life the precarious personal battles that women in the military, and particularly in aviation, have long fought.[77] A woman flying in military combat is a relatively recent phenomenon and still a rarity around the world, with most "firsts" in this arena only having occurred in the mid-1990s in many western countries (1993 in the United States and 1994 in the United Kingdom) and much more recently in other European and Asian countries.[78] Media reports on pioneering female pilots in the US Air Force celebrate these gains for women while also revealing a common desire of the pilots, their officers, and peers to overlook the gender issue altogether; efforts tend to be directed toward seeing the women as pilots first and (ideally, it seems) not as women at all.[79]

As the play progressed, the physical changes of motherhood were not the only ones to which the Pilot had to adjust. When she donned her flight suit again, ready to return to the Air Force and her beloved "Blue" after three years at home with her daughter, her commander assigned her to an aerial body of a new kind. To her dismay, the space for her body, pregnant or not, had been removed altogether in this new plane: a Reaper drone. In response to her protests—"A million dollars to train me / You don't spend a million dollars so I can fly a remote control plane"—her commanding officer explained that drones are at the top of the new order of the skies: "They're not making F-16s anymore Major / The F-16s are dinosaurs / Put out to pasture / Used for drone target practice / The drones? / Can't make 'em fast enough / . . . In one year / The drone will be king / And you / Patience / You will be top shit again."[80] And, importantly, the arrangement would allow the Pilot to return safely to her family each night. Although she derisively referred to her new position as the "Chair Force," she was aware of the advantages: "I get to fly again / Sort of / But I will not be eight thousand miles away while I do it / I will see my daughter grow up / I will kiss my husband goodnight every night/ . . . The threat of death has been removed."[81]

Through the dramatic narrative of the Pilot's personal and professional struggles, Brant presented the audience with oft-debated advantages and disadvantages of drone warfare. Sealed off from the sky in windowless trailers far from the battlefields they patrol, pilots worked in grueling twelve-hour shifts to guide Reaper drones that stay in the air for forty hours at a time; at eleven million dollars a plane, drones were far cheaper than fighter jets, carried hefty payloads of missiles, and greatly reduced the risk of physical harm to pilots.[82] At times more alienating

Fig. 35. George Brant's *Grounded*, 2014. (Photograph by Rob Strong.)

than playing a video game—"A video game has color / I stare at grey"—this mode of combat still brought back some of the white-knuckled thrill from her F-16 days, as she hunted for "military age males" through the drone's eye.[83] At the same time, the drone, which would linger after an attack instead of allowing the Pilot to escape into the "Blue," afforded her new glimpses of wartime devastation: "I didn't notice that last time / Flying through the air / Body parts / Those must be body parts."[84]

As in Barber's *The Freestone Drone*, Brant's Pilot acknowledged the imbalance of power in this mode of constant surveillance: "It's not fair / Not really / We should make an announcement: / Attention People of the Grey Desert / Everything is Witnessed / The Moment You Step Outside You are Under Suspicion / That would be fair."[85] Nevertheless, policing a desert that was "12 hours ahead, but only 1.2 seconds away" through the joystick gave the Pilot a feeling of invincibility and omnipotence; she was part of a new mythological order, "the headset gods of the sky," who could track enemy targets for days and nights on end.[86] The darker, less recognized aspects of a drone pilot's life were also brought to the fore: "Driving to war like it's shift work" exacted a toll, as contradictions between the war she fights while at work and the expectations of peace in her civilian life at home created fissures in the Pilot's psychological armor.[87] Lacking the coping mechanisms she had when she was stationed in a war zone, the Pilot succumbed to frustration: "[C]an we pretend that I don't come home every night every single fucking night can we do that can we do that very simple thing can we can we can we all pretend that I'm really in a real fucking war."[88] Exhibiting signs of an escalating stress disorder, the Pilot began to see her life as it would appear through the eye of a drone: her daughter and husband visible in their house as thermal readings; her car commuting through the desert, watched from above; on a trip to the local mall with her daughter, she imagined the CCTV cameras evaluating her own guilt or innocence, just as she did with the "military age males" she searched for in Afghanistan. She began to wear her flight suit obsessively, desperate to maintain an identity she could recognize, even as she attempted to leave the pressures of her job behind by creating a makeshift burial site in the desert to mark casualties she witnesses through her drone screen.

Mediatized debates over the impacts of drone warfare have made many of these troubling issues familiar to audiences of *Grounded*. However, encountering them within the space of a theatrical performance felt categorically different than in newspaper articles, Technology Entertainment and Design (TED) talks, and NPR reports. As Cabell gave voice to a life experience that was, in many ways, so different from my own, I found that I was able to listen more openly and empathetically and to see more shades of gray in the so often polarized terrain of contemporary surveillance and war. This is, after all, one of the most valuable abilities of theatrical performance: to create communal space for empathetic reflection on human challenges. As David Krasner posited in his essay "Empathy and Theatre" (2006), empathy functions in theatrical performance as a means of bridging radical differences in order to facilitate deeper, though no less critical, understandings of complicated social and political matters. Empathy "allows us to cross boundaries between us, boundaries that are especially evident in this moment in history. . . . Empathy entails grasping the values inherent in the other's experience without blindly endorsing that experience or action."[89]

The radical power of empathy to transcend even the most divisive human differences shaped the play's narrative and fueled the Pilot's final dramatic dissent/descent. Moments of empathy began to ambush her with increasing frequency. While in a J. C. Penney dressing room, the Pilot mused about other people around the world who, like her, provide remote, unseen labor within globalized surveillance networks. The people watching the department store's surveillance cameras could be half a world away, she imagined, the corporate surveillance outsourced to India. She went on to envision what it would be like for them to visit the faraway place they surveil.

> What if these Indians watching us eventually come here for a vacation but find themselves drawn to JC Penney they don't know why but they are and when they get there they go right past the sale racks right past the shoes they head straight to the changing room they don't know why they have nothing to change they walk in they close the door and they suddenly know why they've come and they wave they wave to all of their friends back home and then they don't know why but they start to cry.[90]

The Pilot's compassionate fantasy raised the possibility that empathy can function as an antidote to divisions between disparate places and people. Perhaps, Brant seemed to suggest, surveillance networks have the capacity not only to divide but also to link the watchers to the watched, the foreign to the familiar, the virtual to the material.

In the climactic moment of the performance, the fragile barrier between the Pilot's civilian life and her military mission finally imploded on the drone's gray screen. Exhausted from weeks of following a leading terrorist who was now in her sights, the Pilot found herself unable to decouple her own family from that of her enemy target. Convinced that it was her own daughter Sam, proudly wielding a My Little Pony Pegasus in flight, running into the arms of the terrorist, she refused to fire, turning the drone away from its deadly mission. However, her desperate heroics, misdirected as they were through her fractured perception, were overcome by another system of surveillance: her commanding officers had noticed "the warning signs" of her distress and had defensively positioned another drone above the Pilot's to deliver a fatal strike.[91] The impact of this drone strike, which destroyed the man and her/his daughter, vibrated through the Pilot's body, collapsing the distances between the Afghan desert, the military trailer in Nevada, and our theater in lower Manhattan.

In the end, *Grounded* extended the themes of interconnectedness—along with attendant imperatives to responsibility—to include the audience. The final moments after the devastating climax found the Pilot calm again and speaking to the audience from a military detention site. We in the theater were no longer ancillary onlookers in a narrative that did not include us but part and parcel of the forces that landed the

Pilot in this final resting place, grounded far from her family, her Blue. "You who watch me / Who observe me watch my every move here and I know you watch me . . . for Everything is Witnessed / . . . Know That You Are Not Safe."[92] No longer simply a site of leisurely entertainment and innocent voyeurism, the theater itself became a space of surveillance and judgment. On one level, her chilling warning included the audience in the diegetic world of her story, reminding us that we, too, were subject to the complex web of global surveillance and power that had ensnared her. On another, metatheatrical level, her words held up for scrutiny the power dynamics of our own spectatorship, so familiar in the theater that they typically escape critical recognition. Our spectatorship was conflated with the disciplinary surveillance under which she had been placed; we had, after all, come to the theater "to observe [her], to watch [her] every move." There was, she seemed to alert us, a burden of responsibility that comes with witnessing a play like *Grounded*. "None of the Guilty Will Be Spared," she continued prophetically, implying that responsibility for the devastating impacts of this war belonged not only to military superpowers and terrorists in the Middle East but also to soldiers like herself and witnesses like us.[93] The final word of the play—"boom"— delivered in little more than a whisper, was aimed not at the enemy targets at which the Pilot had directed it before but instead at us, the audience.[94] The protective distance we may have felt, sitting safe in the theater, was a mirage; far as we may have been from drone strikes in the Afghan desert, we were, after all, quite close to the ground zero that first motivated them. Recalling the communitas of the tragic drama of 9/11 that brought Americans together in shock and mourning, *Grounded* proposed that the ongoing wars in the Middle East and intensifications in global surveillance—long echoes of the events of 9/11—likewise offer opportunities, imperatives even, to recognize our interconnectedness and collective responsibility for human suffering of many kinds.

Flying Forward

For better or worse, the popularity of drones in social, political, and artistic arenas shows no signs of diminishing. The FAA expects the number of regulated drones in use domestically to increase to over thirty thousand by 2020, expanding broadly into commercial spheres and fueling what some predict could become a ninety-billion-dollar industry.[95] While the jury is still out on what the future of drone use will look like in domestic markets and foreign wars, there will undoubtedly continue to be competing benefits and drawbacks to the myriad uses of drones. The drone artworks we have seen so far—and no doubt we can expect to see many more—have at once expanded, pushed back on, and refocused the discourses on drones and their place in our global society. While they do not necessarily provide answers, they pose important ethical and aesthetic questions that challenge the presiding arbiters of drone use in military, state, and commercial realms. These challenges have come in the form of cautionary representations of and defensive strategies against the violence wrought by drone strikes; aerial videos, dance performances, and interactive installations, which show that drones can serve as tools with which to chart alternative spatial practices that are creative rather than destructive, oppositional and resistant rather than oppressive; and narratives that approach even the most violent and divisive uses of drones with empathy and careful consideration for people involved in all aspects of their use. As we hover over this new frontier of surveillance, artists from around the world must continue to use drones to create vital new forms of activism, mobility, storytelling, empathy and ethical witnessing.

Coda

A Small History of Surveillance Art

———— ✺ ————

To offer a conclusion for a genre of performance and activism that is growing at the rate of surveillance art would be not only difficult but disingenuous. For one thing, I have no doubt that by the time this book is being read, many of the examples and technologies herein will be considered outdated, outstripped by slicker, smarter, and more sophisticated technologies and techniques of surveillance. My hopeful prediction is that, in tandem with this inevitable progress, volumes of new and diverse surveillance art and performance works will have come into being as well. Just as the artists gathered in this book have appropriated available technologies of surveillance and staged them within frames of theatrical performance, so, too, must the artists and activists of the coming years seize emergent technologies of surveillance and submit them to critical aesthetic, social, and political abilities to creative and critical experimentation. Surveillance art has become a critical and invaluable genre of performance within surveillance society that necessitates more formal attention from scholars as well. As illustrated by "Surveillance Technologies in Performance," a special issue of the *International Journal for Performing Arts and Digital Media*,[1] as well as by James Harding's forthcoming book, *The Sixties, Center Stage* (University of Michigan Press, 2017) on this topic, there is diverse and politically important work being produced by visual and performance art scholars on the subject of surveillance art. I am confident that far more work of this kind is on the way.

I thus conclude this book with a forward-looking gaze. I employ the tone of a commencement, with its simultaneous goals of honoring the work that has been done thus far and pointing towards the efforts that will be required to meet the changes and challenges that lie ahead. We are, after all, already embarking on the next era of surveillance society and art, as drones, biometric surveillance, (meta)dataveillance, and locative media and biodata sensors embedded in personal digital devices, vehicles, and even people have become increasingly commonplace. These forms of surveillance will only continue to push legal and social boundaries of privacy, mobility, access, and personal rights, even as they seek to guard them.

The importance of vibrant, creative, and diverse surveillance art practices around the world is likewise growing in urgency. Surveillance art and performance works must continue to serve a vital purpose: to help audiences visualize the risks of and imagine potential alternatives to a surveillance society that is increasingly determined by large-scale state and corporate interests. A recurrent theme in my analyses of the surveillance artworks in this book has been to emphasize the value of representing and addressing the human faces and individual identities on both sides of surveillant apparatuses. If, as David Lyon, among others, has argued, surveillance has now become so pervasive, dispersed, and constant that we are living in a postprivate society, then "postprivate strategies" that bring individual players to visibility, accountability, and perhaps even trustworthiness are not only appropriate but imperative.[2] To counter the goals of homogenization, uniformity, and universality within dominant, disciplinary surveillance, surveillance artists relentlessly reassert the individual, exceptional, abnormal, and marginalized in radically contingent detail. Through the "performative spaces" they create, whether in virtual or material space, surveillance artists can submit totalizing, automated, and networked surveillance systems to the interconnected and experiential proximity of a face-to-face, human encounter.[3] The framework of theatrical performance can thereby remind the watchers and watched alike that surveillance and its effects are, in fact, made up of particular instances in discreet times and places in which people interact through tools of perception and communication. The strategies of so many of the performance artists examined in this book reflect this goal: Steve Mann, with his strategy of sousveillance, which, through "humans being clerks can make clerks be human"; Jill Magid as she chronicled her time under surveillance in Liverpool through a series of intimate love letters to her "Dear Observer"; Leo Selvaggio, open sourcing his own identity and face for use by friends and strangers; Erica Scourti, dramatizing the effects of consumer dataveillance on her body, psyche, and personal life; Hannah Price, photographing the faces of men who catcalled her on the streets of Philadelphia; and Wafaa Bilal, as he tattooed the location of each Iraqi and American death in the ongoing war in Iraq on his own back. By asserting the personal, the detailed, the idiosynchratic, surveillance artists bring attention to the normalizing tendencies of disciplinary surveillance and illustrate, in often heartbreaking detail, all that is overlooked by such approaches. Through their attention to the details of individual desire and imagination, they illuminate the possibilities for empathy, interconnectivity, and creative collaboration across surveillant interfaces. They enact a pervasive desire to bring damages and abuses of surveillance society to visibility and justice and, in their place, to "make something beautiful."[4]

In Defense of a Small History of Surveillance

As I have done periodically throughout the book, I will here again look back to an earlier moment in techno-cultural history as a means of framing the cultural import of the work of surveillance artists going forward. Walter Benjamin's 1931 essay "A Small History of Photography," though written long before most of the technological inventions discussed in this book, provides a resonant conceptual framework through which to explain the ongoing historiographic import of surveillance art and performance. Much like his later "Work of Art in the Age of Mechanical Reproduction," here Benjamin took up the enduring and complex question of the relationship between representational technologies and the making of history. For him photography could be put to positive or negative cultural uses; the medium could be used to monumentalize objects and moments, securing history as a series overarching, naturalized, and even fascist events. Or, in the hands of photographers he admired, such as Eugène Atget, the camera could be used to "pass by the great sights and the so-called landmarks" to focus instead on the details of everyday living—what Benjamin referred to as the "secrets" in the monuments—that are often overlooked and forgotten in the making of history.[5] In other words, photography has a split capacity: to reproduce scenes that are already culturally legible, adhering to the dictates of social and political norms; or to capture and reveal the radically specific details that can "puncture" the placid surface of normalized vision and behavior.[6]

The historical moment in which Benjamin was analyzing the uses of photography holds important parallels with the contemporary conditions under which surveillance artists are working today. In 1931, with the invention of modern photography nearly a century old and a range of "snapshot" cameras, such as the Kodak Brownie, firmly in the grasp of thousands of amateur photographers, Benjamin's essay acknowledged the simultaneous gifts and threats posed by the medium of photography to the recording of social and political histories. His bitter critiques of the induction of photography into the sphere of commerce, advertising, and political propaganda were driven by his political opposition to uses of photography that supported and legitimized large-scale fascist politics. Conversely, his approval of Atget's attention to a row of unlaced boots, an empty Paris courtyard, or dinner tables empty save for the yet to be cleared dishes, was motivated by his belief that photography could make visible the political value of representing minute, idiosyncratic human actions and small, individual details of everyday life. Now, well into the second decade of the twenty-first century, surveillance technologies have become commonplace in a range of quotidian transactions. Automated systems of dataveillance track and analyze consumers' browsing histories, purchases, and travels; smart phones unlock at the sight of their owner's face. In place of the Kodak Brownie, amateur surveillance practitioners now pilot drones, attach GPS tracking devices to their pets, cars, and children, track their fitness and mood with biosurveillance devices, and monitor their homes with personal security cameras. The risks of corporate and state control through digital surveillance systems that track and monitor movements and transactions are tempered or even eclipsed by the benefits many see in the conveniences and pleasures of social and consumer surveillance.

A particular word in Benjamin's title, commonly assumed to be an explanation of the brevity of his essay (indeed, it has often been translated as "short" or "brief" rather than "small"), insistently points out the importance of *scale* in the making of history, and, moreover, in the *scale of the history* being made. On one hand there is large, capital *H* History—the History of Bentham's Panopticon and Hitler's Third Reich; on the other, small, lowercase *h* histories record alternative, multiple, and subversive accounts of human interactions, memories, and experiences.[7] Benjamin's "*Small* History of Photography" argues that, while the camera could function as an agent of large, Fascist History, it could also function as a tool with which to stubbornly and creatively carve out *small*, alternative versions of history being written in the pedestrian spaces of everyday

life. Amid poetic lamentations over the loss of aura within processes of mechanical reproduction, Benjamin thus articulated his profound hope that photography could, in fact, have a *small history*. To build this theory Benjamin applied the theories of his friend and fellow socialist Bertolt Brecht, advocating for Marxist materialist tactics in photography that, through "the illumination of detail," could set a scene of "estrangement between man and his surroundings."[8] A small history of photography, and photography deployed in the interests of a small history, Benjamin implied, could thus represent and enact vital social critique and political resistance. Authors of these small histories could combat the totalizing force of large-scale Histories and, as Benjamin put it, "bring about a real state of emergency . . . [which] will improve our position in the struggle against Fascism."[9]

Benjamin's message was a cautionary one that presaged the introduction of technologies of capture into ever expanding capitalist structures of economic and political power. In place of fascist governments, we are facing what Jay Stanley of the ACLU calls the "surveillance industrial complex."[10] State and corporate entities alike (and, increasingly, in tandem) employ surveillance technologies to capture and hold that which will be included in capital *H* History. They collect data that will determine what and who is visible, marketable, patriotic, and normal or criminal, invisible, dangerous, and abnormal. As the art and performance works in this book illustrate, surveillance technologies can also be employed in the services of a *small history*, functioning as tools with which to document a multitude of alternative and individuated experiences, memories, and perspectives. While I stop short of invoking Benjamin's "state of emergency" to describe the (albeit alarming) conditions of our current surveillance society, I have come to think of surveillance art as a means of writing and enacting a vital *small history of surveillance*. Artists who record, represent, and create small histories of surveillance (and they are, importantly, multiple) destabilize the stronghold on Truth and History sought by large-scale governments and sprawling consolidations of capitalist power. Small histories of surveillance bring to visibility individual experiences, memories, and desires within monumentalized systems of security and commerce, even as they critique the large-scale, dehumanizing effects of dominant surveillance systems. Surveillance artists are not the only ones working to construct these small histories of surveillance. Groups such as CopWatch, and Witness for Peace use video and photography to document incidents of police and military brutality against everyday subjects and bring the perpetrators to justice.[11] Sizable social movements such as Occupy Wall Street and its many regional counterparts in 2011–12, the Arab Spring revolutions in 2010–11, and the currently unfolding Black Lives Matter movement that has documented endemic police brutality against African American civilians in US cities in recent years illustrate the power of motivated amateurs to mobilize social surveillance systems to politically impactful ends.

In order to facilitate and support small histories of surveillance, surveillance art functions like the shutter of a camera, stilling a scene in order to facilitate critical inspection of it. Through performative "citizen arrests," as I refer to them in chapter 2, the "user-*un*friendly" technologies of chapter 3, or the resistant spatial practices and feminist strategies of representation that I have tracked throughout, artists catch the attention of passersby—pedestrian users-consumers of surveillance technologies—and stop them, however momentarily, in their tracks. They halt the routines in which the ubiquitous surveillance technologies are passed by without notice, without a glance, or used uncritically. In that stilled moment of heightened attention, they hold the surveillant exchange up for critical examination and creative reconsideration. These strategies have the capacity to reveal what Benjamin described as the "secret in the monument" of dominant, hegemonic, capitalist (and for him, fascist) culture. For Benjamin the secret that can be revealed through photography is the "optical unconscious," made visible through the camera's capacity to slow and enlarge. Drawing on theories of the unconscious in psychoanalysis, Benjamin proposed that a scene, stilled by the camera, could reveal to a careful eye details of a trauma that was holding a subject or society prisoner to a violent or unjust past.[12] This capacity to reveal underlying traumas and injustices was, for Benjamin, the ethical duty of photography. Within the sprawling flows of networked surveillance—monuments to state and corporate power and knowledge—there also lies a secret. Surveillance technologies used in service of discovering and representing small, histories have the capacity to reveal to the astute spectator the traumas, injustices, and possibilities for change secreted within the architecture of surveillance society. In the hands of artists, activists, and amateurs—the fugitive "anyones" of the contemporary Panopticon—surveillance technologies have the potential to uncover and make visible traumas and injustices and to ameliorate the ills of contemporary surveillance society with empathy and humanity.

Toward a Small Future of Surveillance Art and Performance

Performance theorists and practitioners, such as Brecht, Benjamin, and the many feminist and avant-garde artists that I have referenced throughout the book, continue to serve as models for the work of surveillance artists. They provide valuable historical and tactical precedents from which we can draw inspiration to meet our current social and political challenges. The examples of surveillance art and performance gathered in this book will likewise, I trust, provide models and inspiration for politically engaged and aesthetically innovative works of the future. Taking cues from the user-*un*friendly technologies of Mann, Dominguez, and the IAA, the aerial *derives* practiced by drone pilot–cyborg flaneurs, the DIY signboards of the SCP, the emergent dramaturgies of CCTV filmmaking, feminist explicit body performances of/under surveillance, and data masks that represent and protect vulnerable populations from the wordless violence of biometric surveillance, I encourage readers of this book to construct their own surveillance art practices. Creative, ethically conscious, and politically resistant histories (and futures) of surveillance are needed everywhere. It is my hope that artists, activists, scholars, hobbyists, and entrepreneurs will repeat, revise, update, transpose, and reimagine the possibilities of surveillance art within an ever expanding range of contexts and spaces.

Moving forward from the performance works and techno-social circumstances explored in this book, it will be advantageous to define some future objectives for surveillance art as a politically engaged performance form. As concerns are only growing over the sociopolitical effects of invisible processes of "panoptic sorting" and "differential mobilities" in dataveillance and biometric surveillance, as well as shadowy connections among military, state, and corporate surveillance systems, surveillance artists will need to do more to make visible hidden agendas and effects of state and corporate surveillance. Going forward, surveillance artists will need to further emphasize the need for corporate transparency and individual accountability for people at all levels of state and corporate surveillance. They will need to critically explore the risks of surveillance in public space, particularly in relation to less regulated technologies such as private UAVs and biometric surveillance technologies such as mechanized facial recognition. They will need to represent injustices and abuses of power that occur in private and semiprivate spaces of work, leisure, and virtual communication. And, as surveillance technologies become increasingly available to a broad range of consumers, they will need to imagine and model alternative, disruptive, and resistant modes of participation and usership.

There is a great deal more work to be done in the area of gender-focused surveillance art in particular: to challenge assumptions about the gender-neutrality of state, corporate, and institutional surveillance systems; to reassert feminism as an important lens through which to analyze and critique any scene of surveillance; to trouble habits of representation in surveillance culture that uncritically conflate fetishes of sex and security; and to bring attention to systemic discrimination and inequalities based on gender and sexuality that are routinely propagated through social and political surveillance systems. Although many cultural and political gains have been made in the name of feminism and civil rights over the last half century and more, patriarchal ideologies of control and discipline continue to shape social relations, behaviors, and narratives throughout contemporary cultures around the world. Symptoms of sexism, racism, homophobia, and economic elitism continue to plague large and small systems of surveillance, in spaces that range from national border controls to social media sites. It is therefore of great importance that feminist artists and performers continue to appropriate technologies of surveillance and re-vision them as tools for critical self-representation, savvy mimicry, explicit body performance, and a multitude of resistant, hysteric, feminist subjectivities.

Small histories of surveillance will begin to add up, creating a constellation of alternative, humane, and intersubjective pathways within surveillance society. Strengthened by their mobility, diversity, and fugitivity, these in turn can provide important counterbalances to the capital *H* Histories of discipline and control that steer dominant discourses and practices of surveillance. While it would be too simple to argue that surveillance art will overturn the vast empire of the "surveillance industrial complex," such work is needed to augment and ground the robust yet often limited critical discourses of surveillance in mainstream media, politics, and academia. By enacting the dangers and opportunities of surveillance society in a range of performative spaces, surveillance artists provide audiences with vital opportunities to better see and reflect on—and, more important, to imagine and rehearse alternatives to—dominant models of surveillance. Each moment that shows that another, smaller, more humane and connected world is possible constitutes a step *out* of current models of discipline and control and *toward* a world in which other ways of being, seeing, and relating are possible.

Notes

———⚮———

Introduction

1. Joshua Kopstein, "Street Artist behind Satirical NYPD 'Drone' Posters Arrested," *The Verge*, December 2, 2012, accessed August 26, 2013, http://www.theverge.com/2012/12/2/3718094/street-artist-nypd-drone-posters-arrested-surveillance

2. Matt Harvey and Aymann Ismail, "Wanted 'Drone' Poster Artist Discusses How He Punked the NYPD," *Animal New York*, September 24, 2012, accessed August 26, 2013, http://animalnewyork.com/2012/wanted-drone-poster-artist-discusses-how-he-punked-the-nypd/

3. Online forums such as freeessam.com were created to show support for his commitment to arts activism and his critique of state and military drone use. All of Attia's charges were eventually dropped by a New York district court in March 2014.

4. See Manuel De Landa's *War in the Age of Intelligent Machines* (New York: Zone Books, 1991).

5. In "The Surveillance Society: The Threat of 1984-Style Techniques," Marx warned, "Today's surveillance society can prod even deeper into physical, social and personal areas. It hears whispers and penetrates walls, windows, clouds, and darkness. The categorical monitoring associated with video cameras, metal detectors, . . . and the computer are creating a society in which everyone, not just a few suspects, is a target for surveillance." Gary T. Marx, "The Surveillance Society: The Threat of 1984-Style Techniques," *The Futurist* (June 21–26, 1985): 22–24.

6. See Christian Parenti's *The Soft Cage: Surveillance in America from Slavery to the War on Terror* (New York: Basic Books, 2003).

7. David Murakami Wood and Stephen Graham use the term *differential mobility* to describe these disparities in access and mobility based on surveillance. See their "Permeable Boundaries in Soft-Ware Sorted Society: Surveillance and Differentiations of Mobility," in *Mobile Technologies of the City*, ed. Mimi Sheller and John Urry (London: Routledge, 2006), 177–91.

8. See James B. Rule, *Private Lives and Public Surveillance* (London: Allen Lane,

1973); Gary T. Marx *Undercover: Police Surveillance in America* (Berkeley: University of California Press, 1988); and David Lyon, *The Electronic Eye: The Rise of Surveillance Society* (Minneapolis: Polity Press, 1994).

9. Rachel Dubrofsky and Shoshana Amielle Magnet, eds., *Feminist Surveillance Studies* (Durham: Duke University Press, 2015), 4. Dubrofsky and Magnet make reference to prison populations, people with disabilities living in institutions, immigrants, and refugees as examples of groups to which privacy tends not to apply. Instead, they argue, the question of privacy needs to include certain considerations: "[W]ho is considered to have a right to privacy? Whose privacy is not a concern and why?" (4). Moreover, as the feminist surveillance theorist Rachel Hall argues in that book, an overburdened emphasis on privacy in fact may exacerbate situations of domestic violence or sexual abuse, in which the violence often occurs in the "private" space of the home or out of the public eye and is secreted through cultural traditions of shaming (Rachel Hall, "Terror and the Female Grotesque: Introducing Full Body Scanners to U.S. Airports," 146–47).

10. See, for example, Jay Stanley, *The Surveillance-Industrial Complex: How the American Government Is Conscripting Businesses and Individuals in the Construction of a Surveillance Society* (New York: American Civil Liberties Union, 2004). As Stanley, of the ACLU, chronicles, companies such as BAE Systems in Europe and Acxiom, ChoicePoint, and Lexis-Nexis in the United States have developed profit-driven systems that trade in the construction and analysis of identities; these "are largely invisible to the average person, but make up an enormous, multi-billion-dollar industry" (25). See also Paolo Singer, *Corporate Warriors: The Rise of the Privatized Military Industry* (Ithaca, NY: Cornell University Press, 2003).

11. Angel Nevarez and Alex Rivera, "Lowdrone," accessed August 29, 2013, http://lowdrone.com

12. Electronic Disturbance Theater/b.a.n.g. lab, "Transborder Immigrant Tool," Micha Cardenas, Amy Sara Carroll, Ricardo Dominguez, Elle Mehrmand, and Brett Stalbaum, artists, accessed May 9, 2016, https://faculty.washington.edu/michamc/wordpress-bang/

13. Philip Auslander's *Liveness: Performance in a Mediatized Culture* (London: Routledge, 1999), Jay Bolter and Richard Grusin's *Remediation* (Cambridge: MIT Press, 2000), Gabriella Giannacchi's *Virtual Theatres* (London: Routledge, 2004), Matthew Causey's *Theater and Performance in Digital Culture* (London: Routledge, 2006), Steve Dixon's *Digital Performance* (Cambridge: MIT Press, 2007), Greg Giesekam's *Staging the Screen: The Use of Film and Video in Theatre* (London: Palgrave, 2007), Sarah Bay-Cheng's *Mapping Intermediality in Performance* (Amsterdam: Amsterdam University Press, 2010), Jennifer Parker-Starbuck's *Cyborg Theatre: Corporeal/Technological Intersections in Multimedia Performance* (Houndmills, Basingstoke, Hampshire: Palgrave Macmillan, 2011), and Jason Farman's *Mobile Interface Theory: Embodied Space and Locative Media* (London: Routledge, 2012), among others, have richly cataloged and analyzed the increasingly popular practice of incorporating emergent technologies of sound and music, virtual reality, video and digital media, webcasting, and e-mail dialogue into theater and performance.

14. As techno-social performance theorists have been careful to note, the inclusion of new technologies and forms of media in theater is not a new phenomenon. Artistic creators from the fields of dance, theater, film, and digital media have long experimented with overlapping methods and technologies in order to build innova-

tive performance forms and experiences. See Dixon, *Digital Performance*, 37–46; and Giesekam, *Staging the Screen*, 5–6.

15. Dixon, *Digital Performance*, 3.

16. Ibid., 3–4.

17. As Harding notes, the term *total performance*, branded by BAE Systems in the United Kingdom, should also be read as a means of protecting the company's profit margin: "[I]t means cultivating an enduring need for CCTV surveillance technologies as part of a strategy for maximizing profits. . . . Ultimately, 'total performance' means the opposite of eliminating threat. It means sustaining the need for and hence increasing the profits reaped by what activists like Jay Stanley of the ACLU have called the 'surveillance industrial complex.'" James Harding, "Outperforming Activism: Reflections on the Demise of the Surveillance Camera Players," in "Surveillance Technologies in Performance," ed. Elise Morrison, special issue, *International Journal of Performance Arts and Digital Media* 11:2 (2015): 131–47.

18. "While disciplinary institutions and mechanisms forged Western Europe's industrial revolution and its system of colonial empires, those of performance are programming the circuits of our postindustrial, postcolonial world. . . . [S]uch technologies as electronic media and the Internet allow discourses and practices from different geographical and historical situations to be networked and patched together, their traditions to be electronically archived and played back, their forms and processes to become raw materials for other productions." Jon McKenzie, *Perform or Else: From Discipline to Performance* (London: Routledge, 2001),18.

19. Mark Andrejevic, *Reality TV: The Work of Being Watched.* (Oxford: Rowman and Littlefield, 2004). Andrejevic locates this trend in relation to the reality TV boom of the late 1990s and early 2000s: "[P]roducers [of reality TV] can deploy the offer of participation as a means of enticing viewers to share in the production of a relatively inexpensive and profitable entertainment product. In this respect, reality TV anticipates the exploitation of what this book describes as the work of being watched, a form of production wherein consumers are invited to sell access to their personal lives in a way not dissimilar to that in which they sell their labor power" (6).

20. Harding, "Outperforming Activism," 19–20.

21. Harding, "Outperforming Activism," 21.

22. Eugenio Barba, in his theory of "theatre anthropology," developed the term *extra-daily* to describe the special attention paid by actors to their bodies, minds, and the representational space around them. See Eugenio Barba, "Theatre Anthropology—Research," International School of Theatre Anthropology, accessed July 16, 2015, http://www.odinteatret.dk/research/ista/theatre-anthropology.aspx

23. Parker-Starbuck, *Cyborg Theatre*, 8.

24. See Michel Foucault, *Discipline and Punish: The Birth of the Prison* (New York: Vintage Books, 1995) and Giles Deleuze, "Postscript on the Societies of Control," *October* (1992: 3–7).

25. See Andrejevic, *Reality TV*. For an interesting study on Twitter, surveillance, and gender, see Rachel Dubrofsky and Megan Wood, "Gender, Race, and Authenticity: Celebrity Women Tweeting for the Gaze," in *Feminist Surveillance Studies*, edited by Rachel Dubrofsky and Shoshana Amielle Magnet (Durham: Duke University Press, 2015), 93–106.

26. Mark Andrejevic, "The Work of Watching One Another: Lateral Surveillance, Risk, and Governance," *Surveillance & Society* 2:4 (2005): 485.

27. See Lisa Nakamura, *Race after the Internet* (London: Routledge, 2012); and Shoshana Amielle Magnet, *When Biometrics Fail: Gender, Race, and the Technology of Identity* (Durham: Duke University Press, 2011).

28. This process of theatricality has been defined by what performance theorist Erika Fischer-Lichte has called the production of "signs of signs" in her "Theatricality: A Key Concept in Theatre and Cultural Studies," *Theatre Research International* 20:2 (1995): 85. Similarly, Janelle Reinelt has pointed out that the play of signs is a fundamental process of theatricality: "[S]pectators must perceive that the process of using signs as signs prevails over their customary semiotic function in order for the process to be theatrical." Janelle Reinelt, "The Politics of Discourse: Performativity Meets Theatricality," in "Theatricality," ed. Josette Féral, special issue, *Substance* 31:2 (2002): 208.

29. John McGrath, *Loving Big Brother: Performance, Privacy, and Surveillance Space* (London: Routledge, 2004) 141.

30. Ibid., 141. McGrath argued that surveillance, as a two-way visual process in which the watcher and the watched are constituted through a mutual awareness of the processes of surveillance, produces a unique kind of performative space (141–49). To build his theory of "performative space," McGrath invoked Henri Lefebvre's theory of the production of space, which Lefebvre describes according to three strands: spatial practice, representations of space, and representational space or "the perceived, the conceived, and the lived." See Henri Lefebvre, *The Production of Space*, trans. Donald Nicholson-Smith (London: Blackwell, 1991), 39.

31. I use the term *materialist* for two reasons: first, as a means of distinguishing the approaches of surveillance artists from "deterministic" approaches to technology, which assume that technologies can and should only be used for the purposes for which they were originally designed; and, second, as a means of referring to the representational strategies of theater makers from Bertolt Brecht to Caryl Churchill, who utilized theories drawn from Marxist materialism to critique social and political issues through theatrical production. See Jill Dolan, *The Feminist Spectator as Critic* (Ann Arbor: University of Michigan Press, 1988), 14–15.

32. Ibid., 14.

33. Critical Art Ensemble, *Digital Resistance: Explorations in Tactical Media* (Brooklyn: Autonomedia, 2001), 8. The group has also explored the generative aspects of digital age hackers in both *Digital Resistance* and *Electronic Civil Disobedience and Other Unpopular Ideas* (Brooklyn: Autonomedia, 1996). It deems attacks waged by surveillance artist-engineers against state- and corporate-dominated technological systems to be valuable acts of digital and electronic resistance, advocating the form of hacking and "reengineering" that it calls "digital resistance."

34. CAE, *Digital Resistance*, 98–99, 105–12.

35. Ibid., 104.

36. The term *defamiliarization* was coined in 1917 by Viktor Shklovsky in his essay "Art as Technique" to describe a literary strategy by which artful or poetic language can be made to appear strange and unfamiliar to the reader; as he put it, "Art exists that one may recover the sensation of life; it exists to make one feel things, to make the stone *stony*. The purpose of art is to impart the sensation of things as they are perceived and not as they are known." Viktor Shklovsky, "Art as Technique," in *Russian Formalist Criticism: Four Essays*, trans. Lee T. Lemon and Marion J. Reis (Lincoln: University of Nebraska Press, 1965) 12. By using defamiliarization as a tactic of representation, artists can thereby challenge habits, expectations, and "overautomatization" in

the reception of literature. Theater practitioners and theorists, such as Erwin Piscator and Bertolt Brecht, soon applied this theory to theater making, using formalist, materialist strategies to reframe familiar gestures, scenes, and narratives as new and unfamiliar, thus opening a cognitive space for refreshed consideration and critique. See Bertolt Brecht, "Alienation Effects in Chinese Acting," in *Brecht on Theatre: The Development of an Aesthetic*, trans. John Willet (New York: Hill and Wang, 1964), 91–99.

37. David Lyon, *Surveillance Society: Monitoring in Everyday Life* (Philadelphia: Open University Press, 2001), 20.

38. Laura Mulvey, "Visual Pleasure and the Narrative Cinema," in *Visual and Other Pleasures* (Bloomington: Indiana University Press, 1989), originally published in *Screen* 16:3 (1975): 6–18.

39. See Hille Koskela "Video Surveillance, Gender, and the Safety of Public Urban Space: 'Peeping Tom' Goes High Tech?" *Urban Geography* 23:3 (2002), 257–78.

40. McGrath, *Loving Big Brother*, 56–98.

41. Kirstie Ball et al., "Editorial: Surveillance Studies Needs Gender and Sexuality," in "Gender, Sexuality and Surveillance," ed. Kirstie Ball, Nicola Green, Hille Koskela, and David J. Phillips, special issue, *Surveillance & Society* 6:4 (2009): 352.

42. For example, "In the Anglo-American north, the politics of what is hidden and what is revealed are imbued with gendered and sexualised politics of heteronormativity and shame, and of vulnerability and fear." Ball et al., *Surveillance and Society*, 353. See also Terri Kapsalis, *Public Privates: Performing Gynecology from Both Sides of the Speculum* (Durham: Duke University Press, 1997).

43. Magnet, *When Biometrics Fail*.

44. Hall, "Terror and the Female Grotesque," 128; Dubrofsky and Wood, "Gender, Race, and Authenticity."

45. Marxist materialist feminism is also championed by authors Kevin Walby and Seantel Anais in Dubrofsky and Magnet's *Feminist Surveillance Studies*. They build on feminist sociologist Dorothy Smith's theory of "institutional ethnography" to suggest that Marxist materialist feminism can help provide a methodology for surveillance studies, writing, "[T]he work people do with texts when conducting surveillance is a point of entry for understanding how the material relations of surveillance are organized." Kevin Walby and Seantel Anais, "Research Methods, Institutional Ethnography, and Feminist Surveillance Studies," in *Feminist Surveillance Studies*, edited by Rachel Dubrofsky and Shoshana Amielle Magnet (Durham: Duke University Press, 2015), 220.

46. Jill Magid, "Surveillance Shoe," accessed August 26, 2010, http://www.jill-magid.net/SurveillanceShoe.php

47. Rebecca Schneider, *The Explicit Body in Performance* (London: Routledge, 1997), 23.

48. Dubrofsky and Magnet, *Feminist Surveillance Studies*, 16. For examples of alternative communities of feminists online, see Nakamura's work on feminist digital-gaming activism, in which user-driven blogs, Tumblr sites, and Twitter hash tags "appropriate the social media tools that we already have to exercise forms of countersurveillance that are noncoercive in nature." Lisa Nakamura, "Blaming, Shaming, and the Feminization of Social Media," in *Feminist Surveillance Studies*, edited by Rachel Dubrofsky and Shoshana Amielle Magnet (Durham: Duke University Press, 2015), 225.

49. As Nakamura argues in the conclusion to *Feminist Surveillance Studies*, female users and users from other sexually marginalized and stigmatized groups are over-

whelmingly the subjects of social and political surveillance and online harassment and victimization ("Blaming," 224). See also Dubrofsky and Wood's analysis of the cultural surveillance of images of female celebrities on Twitter in "Gender, Race, and Authenticity."

50. Donna Haraway, Margaret Morse, Judith Wajcman, Sue-Ellen Case, Shoshana Magnet, Tori Monahan, Lisa Nakamura, and Rachel Dubrofski, among others, have offered valuable analyses of gender in relation to technological changes brought about by the digital age, posing provocative questions about how the body is destabilized in the overlapping regimes of information in virtual space.

51. See R. Claire Snyder, "What Is Third-Wave Feminism? A New Directions Essay," *Signs* 34:1 (Autumn 2008): 175–96.

52. Ednie Kaeh Garrison, "Are We on a Wavelength Yet?" In *Different Wavelengths: Studies of the Contemporary Women's Movement,* ed. Jo Reger. (London: Routledge, 2005), 243–45.

53. Judith Butler, "Performative Acts and Gender Constitution: An Essay in Phenomenology and Feminist Theory," *Theatre Journal* 40:4 (1988): 519–20. In this work and others, including *Gender Trouble: Feminism and the Subversion of Identity* (New York: Routledge, 1990); *Bodies That Matter: On the Discursive Limits of "Sex"* (New York: Routledge, 1993); and *The Psychic Life of Power: Theories in Subjection* (Stanford: Stanford University Press, 1997), Butler has argued that, while gender identity can never be separated from the political and cultural systems in which it is produced and maintained, one's gender is actively constructed by and through repetition and iterability, making it simultaneously performed and performative. While, like Foucault, she contests the degree of agency inherent in subjects whose identities are reflexively imbricated in powerful social systems and institutions that discipline them, Butler suggests the possibility of insubordination within the performativity of gender.

54. For de Lauretis, technologies of gender include dominant apparatuses of representation in visual culture, such as Hollywood films and mainstream literature, that condition and discipline gender formations on social and individual levels. Teresa de Lauretis, *Technologies of Gender: Essays on Theory, Film, and Fiction* (Bloomington: Indiana University Press, 1987), 2–3.

55. Butler, "Performative Acts," 519–20.

56. Michel Foucault, *Discipline and Punish: The Birth of the Prison,* trans. Alan Sheridan (New York: Vintage Books, 1995), 207.

57. Amateur participation is advocated by CAE because "amateurs have the ability to see through the dominant paradigms, . . . [and] are not invested in institutionalized systems of knowledge production and policy construction, and hence do not have irresistible forces guiding the outcome of their process such as maintaining a place in the funding hierarchy . . . or prestige capital" (Critical Art Ensemble, *Digital Resistance,* 9). Similarly, surveillance theorist David Brin has argued that the active participation of amateurs in contemporary networks of surveillance ensures that information flows not only through the hands of high-level executives, corporations, and state departments but also through those of a multiplicity of well-informed citizens using increasingly available technologies of digital communication and information gathering (such as online social software networks). Brin uses the biological metaphor of T cells to support his position; he argues that the social body, like the corporeal body, needs cellular entities that function as "deputies" to detect a myriad of potential threats or the odd behaviors of other native cells. Alternative media groups, political blogs, and grassroots groups such as CopWatch provide T-cell-like forms of

protection as they search for and report less visible abuses of power and attacks on civil liberties. See David Brin, *The Transparent Society: Will Technology Force Us to Choose Between Privacy and Freedom?* (Reading, MA: Addison-Wesley, 1998), 134.

58. See Elise Morrison, "User-*un*friendly: Surveillance Art as Participatory Performance." *Theater* 43:3 (Fall 2013): 5–22.

59. See McGrath, *Loving Big Brother*, 8; and Clive Norris and Gary Armstrong, *The Maximum Surveillance Society: The Rise of CCTV* (New York: Berg, 1999).

60. See David Lyon, "9/11, Synopticon and Scopophilia: Watching and Being Watched," in *The New Politics of Surveillance and Visibility*, ed. Kevin Haggerty and Richard Ericson (Toronto: University of Toronto Press, 2006), 36–53.

61. Michel de Certeau, *The Practice of Everyday Life* (Berkeley: University of California Press, 1988), 91.

62. Ibid.

63. Richard Schechner, "9/11 as Avant-Garde Art?," in "War," special issue, *PMLA* 124:5 (2009): 1820–29.

64. Ibid., 1823.

65. Ibid.

66. Ibid., 1826.

67. See Louis Althusser, "Ideology and Ideological State Apparatuses (Notes towards an Investigation)," in *Lenin and Other Philosophies* (New York: Monthly Review Press, 1971): 85-126. See also de Lauretis, *Technologies of Gender*, 6–13, for a feminist application of Althusser's theory of interpellation and ideology.

68. De Certeau positions his theory of the unscripted spatial practice of walking in ambiguous relation to Foucault's theory of panopticism. Panoptic surveillance depends upon the management of space, visibility, and mobility; as de Certeau puts it, the mechanisms of panoptic power "draw their efficacy from a relationship between procedures and the space that they redistribute in order to make an 'operator' out of it" (de Certeau, *Practice*, 96).

69. Ibid.

70. Ibid.

71. Cultural theorists such as Gilles Deleuze and David Lyon have argued that panoptic surveillance, with its love of enclosures and containment, was already becoming a thing of the past by the dawn of the twenty-first century.

72. Mimi Sheller and John Urry, "The New Mobilities Paradigm." *Environment and Planning A* 38:2 (2006): 211. Mobility studies blends sociological, geographic, media, and transportation research to better understand how the "spatialities of social life presuppose (and frequently involve conflict over) both the actual and imagined movement of people" (208). Tim Cresswell, a leading mobilities scholar, has described a "new mobilities paradigm" that prioritizes mobility and fluidity over fixity and stability; in contrast to a "sedentarist" worldview, mobilities scholarship seeks to make visible "nomadic" experiences that are increasingly the norm in contemporary society. Cresswell has cautioned that the "general celebration of the nomadic in contemporary theory too often levels out agency so that . . . differences in the experience of mobility disappear." Tim Cresswell, *On the Move: Mobility in the Modern Western World* (London: Routledge, 2006), 255. Feminist geographers in particular have cautioned that mobility is frequently romanticized, grounded in a white, western, masculine, economically secure subjectivity that "pays little heed to the struggles inherent in many people's everyday practices of mobility." Dydia DeLyser, "Flying: Feminisms and Mobilities; Crusading for Aviation in the 1920s," in *Geographies of Mobilities*, ed. Tim

Cresswell (Surrey: Ashgate, 2011), 85. David Murakami Wood and Stephen Graham make similar arguments in "Permeable Boundaries," 177–78.

73. See Sarah Elwood and Katharyne Mitchell, "Another Politics Is Possible: Neogeographies, Visual Spatial Tactics, and Political Formation," *Cartographica* 48:4 (2013): 275–92. See also Jason Farman, *Mobile Interface Theory: Embodied Space and Locative Media* (London: Routledge, 2012); and Karen O'Rourke, *Walking and Mapping: Artists as Cartographers* (Cambridge: MIT Press, 2013).

74. Robin Bernstein, *Racial Innocence: Performing American Childhood from Slavery to Civil Rights* (New York: New York University Press, 2011), 71.

75. Ibid., 12.

76. See Manu Luksch, "Manifesto for CCTV Filmmakers" (2006), ambienttv.net, accessed July 19, 2015, http://www.ambienttv.net/content/?q=dpamanifesto

77. Amy Siciliano, "Swinging at the State: Media, Surveillance, and Subversion," *Aether: The Journal of Media Geography* 1 (October 2007): 55.

78. McGrath, *Loving Big Brother*, 142. "For surveillance art, the link to daily spatial practices is particularly apparent. We still do not see a surveillance camera in a gallery without thinking of surveillance cameras in the street" (4).

79. Bernstein, *Racial Innocence*, 13.

Chapter 1

1. Author's notes taken during a performance by Theater of the Eighth Day of *The Files* at the Yale Repertory Theatre's No Boundaries Festival, January 20, 2014 (hereafter cited as "Author's Notes").

2. Program notes, "About *The Files*," Yale Repertory Theater, January 20–22, 2014, 5 (hereafter cited as "Program Notes").

3. "Author's Notes."

4. Ibid.

5. Ibid. Presumably this meant the right to hold gatherings (rehearsals, meetings, performances) under the title of a theatrical company.

6. Company member Ewa Wojciak, quoted in "Program Notes," 6.

7. Jay David Bolter and Richard Grusin, "Remediation," *Configurations* 4:3 (1996): 345.

8. Bolter and Grusin, *Remediation*, 59–60.

9. Ibid., 15. Bolter and Grusin do invest to some degree in developmental genealogies of reform and thus overlook significant ways in which existing "older" representational media, such as theater, have integrated and critically reframed newer forms of media. As they put it, "[N]ew media [present] themselves as refashioned and improved versions of other media" (14–15). This is because "the assumption of reform is so strong that a new medium is now expected to justify itself by improving on a predecessor" (59). Bolter and Grusin extend this cultural expectation for "reform" beyond contemporary digital media, writing that photography "was seen as the reform of illusionistic painting and the cinema as the reform of the theatre" (60).

10. In *Digital Performance*, Dixon chronicles a genealogical history of "digital performance," citing early theatrical devices of the Greek deus ex machina and moving through Wilhelm Richard Wagner's concept of the total artwork (*Gesamtkunstwerk*) to early dance and technology experiments by Loïe Fuller in the late nineteenth century and by the Bauhaus artist Oskar Schlemmer in the 1920s. Giesekam's *Staging the Screen* importantly counters formulations of remediation that posit new media as

distinct from theater or theatricality, as Giesekam argues that theater has substantially shaped film, video, and television since the mid-nineteenth century: "Recent alarms over theatre remediating film, television, and video are ironic, given that these media themselves originally borrowed considerably from the theatre, before they developed more distinctive conventions and concerns. As the newer media evolved critics attempted to demarcate their specific qualities and conventions, often rejecting work that seemed too 'theatrical' for failing to acknowledge the distinctiveness of the particular medium" (*Staging the Screen*, 5–6).

11. Adam Sonstegard, "Performing Remediation: Minstrelsy, Photography, and *The Octoroon*," *Criticism* 48:3 (2006): 375.

12. The play, which took on the controversial subject of miscegenation, navigated diverse political positions with two different endings. When it played in England, *The Octoroon* ended with Zoe, the mixed-race heroine, united in marriage with her (white) lover and able to retain her land and inheritance. In America the play was performed with a tragic ending in which Zoe poisoned herself, dying in her lover's arms. The latter, tragic ending was the only one permitted to be performed in the United States in order to avoid showing a mixed-race marriage (illegal at that point in history) onstage.

13. Sonstegard, "Performing Remediation," 376. He went on, "[A]n analysis of the play today dramatizes, as it were, the extent to which Americans have accepted—indeed, have become saturated with—that very culture of photographic surveillance" (376). See also Harley Erdman's essay "Caught in the 'Eye of the Eternal': Justice, Race, and the Camera from *The Octoroon* to Rodney King." *Theatre Journal* 45:3 (1993): 333–48.

14. See John Tagg, *The Burden of Representation: Essays on Photographies and Histories* (Minneapolis: University of Minnesota Press, 1993).

15. See D. J. Hopkins and Shelley Orr, Performance review of *Measure for Measure*, directed by Simon McBurney, *Theatre Journal* 57:1 (2005): 97–100.

16. Builders Association, "*Super Vision* Project Description," accessed July 19, 2015, http://www.thebuildersassociation.org/prod_supervision_info.html

17. Sarah Bay-Cheng, "Ready for My Close Up," *Theater* (2014): 88–89.

18. See Shklovsky, "Art as Technique"; and Brecht, "Alienation Effects."

19. Foucault, *Discipline and Punish*, 200.

20. Lyon, "9/11," 41–43.

21. See Foucault, *Discipline and Punish*, particularly part 3, "Discipline"; *Power/Knowledge: Selected Interviews and Other Writings, 1972–1977* (New York: Pantheon Books, 1980), particularly "Truth and Power" and "The Eye of Power"; and *The History of Sexuality, vol. 1* (1978), particularly part 2, "The Repressive Hypothesis."

22. Tagg, *Burden of Representation*, 66.

23. As Althusserian and Foucauldian theories posit, recognition of a preinterpellated state would seem impossible, as the subject is always already interrelated into an ideological regime (society); they argue that there is no subject (as causal agent or substance/essence) outside of machines/systems of interpellation or ideology. Likewise, Jacques Lacan argues that there is no (speaking) subject outside the symbolic order of language.

24. McGrath, *Loving Big Brother*, 3.

25. See Pannill Camp, "Theatre Optics: Enlightenment Theatre Architecture in France and the Architectonics of Husserl's Phenomenology," *Theatre Journal* 59:4 (2007): 615–33. Camp points out that common architectural layouts in eighteenth-

and nineteenth-century theaters (in France and elsewhere in Europe) were constructed according to the representation of space that dominated Enlightenment natural philosophy. That is to say, Enlightenment models of knowledge and power (which arguably continue today) conditioned the spectatorial and spatial relationship between theater audiences and the stage.

26. Marilyn Frye, *The Politics of Reality: Essays in Feminist Theory* (Freedom, CA: Crossing Press, 1983), 155 (emphasis added).

27. See Oscar Brockett and Franklin Joseph Hildy, *History of the Theatre*, 9th ed. (Boston: Allyn and Bacon, 2003). Censoring bodies and government regulations were formed at various points in theater history; for example, the term *obscene* derived its meaning from bodies or acts that, due to graphic, immoral, or violent characteristics, were deemed improper to be shown on the Greek stage (in a scene). The master of revels (117–88) and various licensing acts (214–15) regulated what could and could not be shown in theaters in Renaissance England. Regulations of this kind continue to be enacted through government funding organizations such as the National Endowment for the Arts (NEA). In a controversial decision that showed the conservative politics and cultural power of the NEA in 1990, chairman John Frohnmayer vetoed the grants of four performance artists (Karen Finley, Tim Miller, John Fleck, and Holly Hughes, known as the NEA Four) even after they had successfully passed through a peer review process.

28. As Foucault put it, the panoptic principle provided a clear model of an efficient and sustainable form of discipline based on a visible yet unverifiable site of power: "Bentham laid down the principle that power should be visible and unverifiable. Visible: the inmate will constantly have before his eyes the tall outline of the central tower from which he is spied upon. Unverifiable: the inmate must never know whether he is being looked at any one moment; but he must be sure that may always be so" (*Discipline and Punish*, 201).

29. Gilles Deleuze was one of the first to radically update Foucault's schema of a disciplinary society, developing instead a theory of "societies of control." Societies of control are characterized by continually modulating and interconnected networks of digitized information that track and control the behavior of individuals across a range of markets and spheres of interaction. In place of the institutions and individuals that defined Foucault's disciplinary society, societies of control feature "'dividuals,' and masses, samples, data, markets, or 'banks,'" which amass and interact digitally across space and time (Gilles Deleuze, "Postscript on the Societies of Control," *October* 59 (Winter, 1992): 4–5). In societies of control, the human subject becomes destabilized as a corporeal entity, appearing instead as pieces of personal data that are abstracted from distinct locales and bodies and sorted into a series of informational flows; these flows of personal data coalesce into distinct "data doubles," correlating to individual subjects that are tracked and targeted by state and corporate entities. Kevin Haggerty and Richard Ericson, eds., *The New Politics of Surveillance and Visibility* (Toronto: University of Toronto Press, 2006, 606.

30. Diderot was most influential in the theater world for his advice to the actor to imagine the fourth wall and behave as if he or she was not "performing." In 1758 he wrote, "When you write or act, think no more of the audience than if it had never existed. Imagine a huge wall across the front of the stage, separating you from the audience, and behave exactly as if the curtain had never risen." Denis Diderot, "On Dramatic Poetry," in *Diderot's Selected Writings*, ed. Lester G. Crocker, trans. Derek Coltman (New York: Macmillan, 1966), 206.

31. Peggy Phelan, *Unmarked: The Politics of Performance* (London: Routledge, 1993), 150–51.

32. Andrew Sofer's *Dark Matter: Invisibility in Drama, Theater, and Performance* (Ann Arbor: University of Michigan Press, 2013) speaks eloquently of the matrix of visibility and invisibility that characterizes theatrical performance and spectatorship, and of the power of the invisible onstage. Sofer places particular import on what he calls theater's "dark matter" or "the invisible dimension of theater that escapes visual detection, even though its effects are felt everywhere in performance" (3).

33. Phelan, *Unmarked*, 192.

34. For many avant-garde theorists and practitioners, notably Erwin Piscator and Bertolt Brecht, this distance from the *real* is an integral part of the efficacy and artistry of theater, allowing for critical reflections on and reimaginings of social and political life through theatrical representation. See Bertolt Brecht, *Brecht on Theatre: The Development of an Aesthetic*, trans. John Willet (New York: Hill and Wang, 1964); and C. D. Innes, *Erwin Piscator's Political Theatre* (Cambridge: Cambridge University Press: 1977). Antitheatrical perspectives, offered by theorists as diverse as Plato and Michael Fried, have criticized theatrical representation as a process of copying, or doubling, which blurs and debases an object's *ideal*, or *real,* status once it is incorporated in a theatrical frame. See Plato, "Allegory of the Cave," book VII of *The Republic* (360, BCE), in *The Republic of Plato*, trans. Allan Bloom (New York: Basic Books, 1968); and Michael Fried, "Art and Objecthood" (1967), in *Art and Objecthood* (Chicago: University of Chicago Press, 1998). In contemporary performance theory, theatricality continues to be championed and problematized as a process that blends truth and falsity, reality and representation. The conscious construction of theatrical events has led theorists such as Erika Fischer-Lichte to suggest that theater is a process of representation and refraction that positions the *theatrical* at a considerable distance from the *real* (Fischer-Lichte, "Theatricality," 85–90). See also Josette Feral, "Introduction," in "Theatricality," ed. Josette Féral, special issue, *Substance* 31:2 (2002): 3–16.

35. Tagg, *Burden of Representation*, 66.

36. The modernist fascination with candid photography was articulated most pointedly in a popular theory that emerged in the mid-1930s, not long after handheld cameras were developed and came to be widely used among the middle and upper classes. "New Objectivity," or to its German originators "Neue Sachlichkeit," posited that brutal, universal reality could only be captured by candid, documentary photography. The theories of New Objectivity were embodied most memorably in the Mass Observation movement of the mid-1930s in Britain, a marriage between social science and documentary photography. For August Sander and the other practitioners of mass observation, when the camera could be concealed or ignored, subjects caught on film were seen as all the more real or truthful for their lack of attention to posterity. Profoundly influenced by New Objectivity, the movement embodied a utopian, antidisciplinary moment in the history of surveillance photography. The founders of the movement aimed to conduct an anthropology of their own society, believing that through the exact documentation of life as it was really lived in England at that time they could counterbalance the presentational, social veneer of late Victorian England. See Deborah Frizzell, *Humphrey Spender's Humanist Landscapes: Photo-Documents, 1932–1942* (New Haven: Yale Center for British Art, 1997), 18. Sander espoused the belief that the candid photograph "would 'fix and hold fast history' and 'express the whole brutal inhuman spirit of the time in universally comprehensible form'" (11). In other words, it was through the concealment of the camera-eye that

he felt he could be most successful in the project of mass observation. Furthermore, he believed that a candid photographic image could reveal universal truths that could be read by anyone, from anywhere, at any point in history.

37. Nicholas Ridout, *Stage Fright, Animals, and Other Theatrical Problems* (New York: Cambridge University Press, 2006), 31–32. Ridout calls this the "failure of relation" that lies at the heart of theater, a facet he finds most exciting about theater making and spectatorship.

38. Ibid., 9.

39. "Point Blank," PS122, accessed November 9, 2008, http://www.ps122.org/performances/point_blank.html

40. See Tom Sellar, "In *An Octoroon*, Branden Jacobs-Jenkins Knocks Us Flat on Our Preconceptions," *Village Voice*, May 7, 2014, accessed July 20, 2015, http://www.villagevoice.com/2014–05–07/theater/an-octoroon-soho-rep/full/

41. Barthes called the "'photographic referent' not the *optionally* real thing to which an image or sign refers but the *necessarily* real thing which has been placed before the lens." Roland Barthes, *Camera Lucida: Reflections on Photography*, translated by Richard Howard (New York: Hill and Wang), 76.

42. Ibid., 76.

43. Łukasz Drewniak, "'POSITIVISM MAKES SENSE': Conversation with Ewa Wójciak," *Dziennik Gazeta Prawna*, no. 5 (2010), accessed January 25, 2014, http://osmego.art.pl/t8d/main/en/

44. Ibid. A firm believer in the power of documentary representation, Wojciak argued, "A documentary movie has a greater power of influence than a feature movie. The same with photography. . . . Documentary is the fascination of the time of my maturity. . . . I am deeply moved by actually every story about human fates" (ibid.).

45. Rebecca Schneider, *Performing Remains: Art and War in Times of Theatrical Reenactment* (London: Routledge) 35, 43.

46. See Elise Morrison, "Witness Protection: Surveillance Technologies in Theatrical Productions," in *Bastard or Playmate? Adapting Theatre, Mutating Media, and Contemporary Performing Arts*, ed. R. Vanderbeeken, B. De Backere, and C. Stalpaert, (Amsterdam: University of Amsterdam Press, 2012), 122–43.

47. Alice Jones, "*Contains Violence*, Lyric Hammersmith Roof Top Terrace," *The Independent*, April 9, 2008, accessed October 10, 2008, http://www.independent.co.uk/arts-entertainment/theatre-dance/reviews/contains-violence-lyric-hammersmith-roof-terrace-london-806273.html

48. Susannah Clap, "The Good, the Bad, and the Photocopier," *The Guardian*, April 6, 2008, accessed October 10, 2008, http://www.guardian.co.uk/stage/2008/apr/06/theatre2

49. Donald Hutera, "*Contains Violence* at the Lyric, Hammersmith," *The Times Online*, April 4, 2008, accessed October 10, 2008, http://entertainment.timesonline.co.uk/tol/arts_and_entertainment/stage/theatre/article3672054.ece

50. Azma Dar, "Peeping Toms: Monday 5 May, 2008," *Smudgeyink* (blog), May 5, 2008, accessed October 10, 2008, http://smudgeyink.blogspot.com/

51. Robin McKie, "What the Punters Saw . . . ," *The Observer*, March 16, 2008, accessed October 10, 2008, http://www.guardian.co.uk/stage/2008/mar/16/theatre1

52. See Sigmund Freud, *Three Essays on the Theory of Sexuality*, trans. James Strachey (London: Hogarth Press, 1955); and Victor Burgin, "Jenni's Room: Exhibitionism and Solitude," in *ctrl [space]: Rhetorics of Surveillance from Bentham to Big Brother*, ed.

Thomas Levin, Ursula Frohne, and Peter Weibel (Leipzig: ZKM, MedienKunstNetz, 2002).

53. Lyn Gardner, "Contains Violence," *The Guardian*, April 5, 2008, accessed October 10, 2008, http://www.guardian.co.uk/stage/2008/apr/05/theatre2 (emphasis added).

54. Clap, "The Good, the Bad."

55. Paul Arendt, "Another View: Private Investigator Michael Colacicco on *Contains Violence*," *The Guardian*, April 8, 2008, accessed October 10, 2008, http://www.guardian.co.uk/artanddesign/2008/apr/08/art.dance

56. Bernstein, *Racial Innocence*, 12.

57. Andrew Sofer, *The Stage Life of Props* (Ann Arbor: University of Michigan Press, 2003). Sofer argues that the prop can "become a concrete vehicle for confronting dramatic convention and revitalizing theatrical practice" (vii).

58. Ibid., vi.

59. Ibid., viii.

60. Bernstein, *Racial Innocence*, 11.

61. Clap, "The Good, the Bad."

62. Dar, "Peeping Toms."

63. Clap, "The Good, the Bad."

64. Gardner, "Contains Violence."

65. Hutera, "*Contains Violence.*"

66. McKie, "What the Punters Saw."

67. Arendt, "Another View."

68. Clap, "The Good, the Bad."

Chapter 2

1. Jill Magid, "Evidence Locker" (2004), accessed August 25, 2010, http://www.evidencelocker.net/story.php

2. Evidence lockers are housed in the Liverpool Police Department's CCTV control system's main IBM computer. In the end, Magid's "evidence locker" included twelve hours, thirty-three minutes, and thirty-three seconds of video footage filmed entirely by the police, along with the thirty-one letters that Magid sent to the police on the day of her departure. The CCTV video records of Magid are time stamped and stored as "traces" in Police Log #2887 (ibid.).

3. *Evidence Locker* has appeared as a collection in the Liverpool biennial festival and several museums and is publicly available as an online exhibit. Together the CCTV footage and Magid's thirty-one letters make up an online representation of an "evidence locker," which she has made available to "third-party witnesses." Once a visitor has registered as a witness, he or she receives the entries in Magid's locker in thirty-one installments. These entries, which include links to the visual "traces" of Magid captured via CCTV, are sent directly to a personal e-mail address at the frequency of either once an hour for thirty-one hours or once a day for thirty-one days (ibid.).

4. Liverpool *Echo*, September 1, 2000, quoted in Roy Coleman, "Reclaiming the Streets: Closed Circuit Television, Neoliberalism, and the Mystification of Social Divisions in Liverpool, UK," *Surveillance & Society* 2:2–3 (2004): 293.

5. "Iain Bundred's whole life is a movie. Every step he takes is captured on unseen cameras as secret watchers see his life unfold. It may seem like a plot for Jim

Carey's Hollywood hit *The Truman Show*. But this is the reality in Liverpool today, not just for Iain but for all of us. . . . The watchers do not care how we live our lives, as long as we stay within the law. But the pickpocket, the mugger, the armed robber, or the drunken driver knows that those hidden eyes are out there. Today the *Echo* takes you behind the scenes to show you a day in the life of an ordinary [Liverpool] citizen, through the eyes of the closed circuit television" (Liverpool *Echo*, quoted in Coleman, "Reclaiming the Streets," 293).

6. Coleman, "Reclaiming the Streets," 293.

7. Norris and Armstrong, *Maximum Surveillance Society*, 91. Coleman, writing about the politics of visibility and neoliberal strategies of policing public space, cited the city of Liverpool's decision to ban skateboarding in public spaces as an example of using surveillance technologies to determine what and who can and cannot be done or seen in public space: "As a key tool in the politics of vision, cameras in the cities of the UK are helping to put into effect what can and cannot be seen on the streets. As cameras aid the strategic balance between aesthetics and function, any notion of the city as a space of cultural expression for younger people continues to be highly circumscribed. In Liverpool, skateboarders can be fined from between £250 to a £1000 if they break a bylaw banning skating passed by city councilors in July 2002. Liverpool council claimed that skateboarding should be an offense as it is giving the city a bad image in terms of scaring off tourists and shoppers, as well as damaging statues and memorials" (Coleman, "Reclaiming the Streets," 301). The leisurely but nonconsumerist activities of young people (skateboarders) were disproportionately targeted as undesirable in urban space. Homelessness and poverty likewise tended to be removed from view within downtown urban centers in order to construct and maintain the picture of a friendly, safe "theme-park city" that invites the participation of economically stable and socially normative consumers (302).

8. Coleman, "Reclaiming the Streets," 306.

9. This was President Barack Obama's proposal following the grand jury's decision not to indict white officer Darren Wilson following the accusation that he used excessive force in the death of a young black man, Michael Brown, in Ferguson, Missouri, in 2014. The Obama administration has since provided funding for local police departments to purchase and implement body cameras as routine procedure. See Julia Edwards, "Obama Administration Says to Provide $20 Million for Police Body Cameras," Reuters, May 1, 2015, accessed July 20, 2015, http://www.reuters.com/article/2015/05/01/us-usa-police cameras idUSKBN0NM3PL20150501

10. See Elise Morrison, "Citizen Arrest: Surveillance Art and the Passerby." *International Journal of Performance Arts and Digital Media*, 7:2 (2011): 239–57.

11. Bolter and Grusin, "Remediation," 345.

12. SCP, "Ten Year Report," accessed August 25, 2010, http://www.notbored.org/10-year-report.html

13. Quoting e-mail correspondence with SCP founder Bill Brown, Harding wrote, "Bill Brown has suggested that the changes ultimately were geared toward a much larger public audience that could only be reached through a cultivated relationship with the media. He notes that 'the SCP didn't simply perform or, rather, it didn't simply perform in front of surveillance cameras and the passersby who might happen to see the performance in action. It also quite deliberately performed in front of the mass media: writers, radio broadcasters, TV crews'" (Harding, "Outperforming Activism," 8). Indeed, a few years into their work, the SCP amended its founding documents to read, "Please note that since the group's founding, the Surveillance Camera

Players have changed quite a bit. The SCP no longer consider their primary audience to be the police officers and security guards who monitor the surveillance cameras installed in public places. Today, the SCP concentrate on the people who happen to walk by and see one of their performances" (SCP, "SCP Founding," Accessed May 11, 2016) http://www.notbored.org/scp-founding.html

14. Harding, "Outperforming Activism," 6.

15. Brecht, *Brecht on Theatre*, 79.

16. The situationists, led by Guy Debord, developed a visual tactic known as the *detourne*, which involved the creation of new, often critical meanings through the strategic rearrangement of popular sign systems. To *detourné* elements of visual culture, the Situationists would rescript popular comic strips, inserting their own captions or thought bubbles into widely circulated sketches. Culture jammers in the 1990s, such as AdBusters, took on this tactic, rescripting popular advertising logos with critical text—such as the McDeath logo, which played on the McDonald's internationally recognizable font, layout, and coloring. Nato Thompson, ed., *The Interventionists: A Users' Manual for the Creative Disruption of Everyday Life.* (North Adams, MA: MASS MoCA, 2004), 16–17.

17. Ibid., 86.

18. Performance theorists have argued that placing embodied critiques within a frame of play can allow for greater departures from the normalized rules or conventions of social life while at the same time obliquely referring to and critiquing those rules. Erving Goffman's *Frame Analysis: An Essay on the Organization of Experience* (New York: Harper and Row, 1974) describes cognitive frames that encompass formal, as well as everyday, performative situations within which participants "play" by a set of commonly understood rules and signals. Gregory Bateson, in his earlier theorization of play and metacommunication, argued that within such a frame a rhetorical substitution can be applied, one in which, for example, an animal's playful nip connotes a more serious bite, while not actually being the bite itself. Gregory Bateson, "A Theory of Play and Fantasy," *Psychiatric Research Reports* 2 (1955): 39–51.

19. SCP, "God's Eyes," accessed August 25, 2010, http://www.notbored.org/god%27s-eyes.html

20. SCP, "It's OK, Officer," accessed August 25, 2010, http://www.notbored.org/its-ok-officer.html

21. SCP, "We Know You Are Watching," accessed August 25, 2010, http://www.notbored.org/jay-day-both.jpg

22. SCP, "Amnesia," accessed August 25, 2010, http://www.notbored.org/amnesia.html. See also Harding's analysis of the piece in which he reads the performance as "a reminder of the extent to which CCTV systems have made amnesiacs of us all with regard to our own identities" ("Outperforming Activism," 29).

23. Norris and Armstrong, *Maximum Surveillance Society*, 91. Norris and Armstrong significantly critique assumptions that public CCTV surveillance can be theorized as a model of panopticism; they argue that CCTV surveillance and the subjects it seeks to police are too fluid and dispersed. Instead, they assert that there is less impact on crime prevention than on a general norming of the population (92–93). These findings, in particular the lack of evidence to support CCTV as a crime deterrent, have been consistently supported in more recent research. See, for example, William Webster, "CCTV Policy in the UK: Reconsidering the Evidence Base," *Surveillance & Society* 6:1 (2009): 10–22.

24. William Webster has argued that the focus of CCTV law enforcement shifted

from crime prevention to the identification and removal of "antisocial and undesirable behaviour" (ibid., 13).

25. Jacques Ranciere, "Ten Theses on Politics," *Theory & Event* 5:3 (2001): 5.

26. Drawing on the research of Norris and Armstrong, Harding has rightly argued that the SCP pushed back against cultural assumptions that publicly installed CCTV cameras were meant only to affect the criminal element of society and should therefore not be considered a risk or concern for the "ordinary" citizen: "[T]he panoptic effect on those who view themselves as law-abiding citizens presumably would be minimal since they need not internalize once again a set of values that they believe they already possess—values like those presumably cultivated within church communities like St. Patrick's in New York" (Harding, "Outperforming Activism," 14–15). Harding goes on to explore a seeming conflict between the messages of SCP performances such as *God's Eyes Here on Earth*, which "tended to reinforce the popularized notions of panopticism that underlie the idea that surveillance cameras deter crime," and their political critiques of such assumptions, which have tended to follow Norris and Armstrong's findings on the inefficacy of CCTV as a crime deterrent (15–16).

27. Gabriella Giannachi, *The Politics of New Media Theatre* (New York: Routledge, 2007), 47.

28. In Deleuze's description of contemporary "societies of control," "dividuals" replace "individuals" and, as such, are transformed into abstract fragments of personal data that are sorted into series of discrete informational flows within a massive system of networked surveillance (Deleuze *Postscript*, 2). These flows of personal data— referred to as "data doubles"—correlate with individual subjects but only insofar as they allow individuals to be digitally tracked and targeted by state and corporate entities. As facial and gait recognition and other modes of biometric surveillance become increasingly popular in civic surveillance systems, the trend toward depersonalization will only increase.

29. Faye Ginsberg, "Rethinking the Digital Age," in *Global Indigenous Media*, ed. Pam Wilson and Michelle Stewart (Durham: Duke University Press, 2008), 287–88.

30. Pointing to the SCP's use of Orwell's *1984* narrative, Harding argues that the group's focus on the state as the consolidated seat of power (and evil) was misplaced and in fact was one reason why it eventual disbanded. He insists that such a focus misses the far more worrisome reality, which is that private companies such as Axiom have amassed far more consolidated power in the arena of gathering, storing, and trading personal information (Harding, "Outperforming Activism," 139–41).

31. Yes Men, "Identity Corrections," accessed January 21, 2015, http://theyesmen.org/

32. Yes Men, "World Trade Organization," accessed January 21, 2015, http://www.gatt.org/

33. Yes Men, "Tampere Hijinks," accessed August 19, 2010, http://theyesmen.org/hijinks/tampere

34. Thompson, *Interventionists*, 106.

35. Critical Art Ensemble, *Digital Resistance*, 98–99, 104.

36. See ibid., 105–12.

37. See the documentary *Yes Men*, film, 2003, directed by Dan Ollman, Sarah Price, and Chris Smith. In the footage that Servin and Vamos include of news reports of the Barbie/GI Joe switch, the boys and girls interviewed thought it was hilarious and gleefully played with the dolls.

38. Yes Men, "Yes Lab: Get Involved," accessed January 23, 2015, http://www.yeslab.org/get-involved

39. From surrealism to the civil rights movement in the 1960s and 1970s, men have dominated the activist stage, pushing women's voices and concerns to the margins. See Rudolph Kuenzli, "Surrealism and Misogyny," in *Surrealism and Women*, ed. Mary Ann Caws, Rudolph Kuenzli, and Gwen Raaberg (Cambridge: MIT Press, 1991), 17–26; and Ann Standley, "The Role of Black Women in the Civil Rights Movement," in *Women in the Civil Rights Movement: Trailblazers and Torchbearers, 1941–1965*, ed. Vicki L. Crawford, Jacqueline Anne Rouse, and Barbara Woods (Athens: University of Georgia Press, 1990), 183–202. The "second wave" of feminism arose largely in response to these exclusions, as women activists gathered together to articulate a set of women's concerns and rights. Even within female-led activism, however, there continues to be unequal treatment of women. In a notable recent case, members of the feminist activist group Pussy Riot received especially severe punishment for their activist performances in public spaces around Moscow. In their trials, the prosecution focused on their "loose sexuality" and improper behavior as young women rather than their articulate criticisms of President Vladimir Putin's government. In fact some scholars have noted that male-dominated activism is more easily incorporated within mainstream political action, as activist men are more readily seen to be lobbying, networking, and debating rather than protesting or performing as "activists." See Jeff Hearn, "The Problems Boys and Men Create," in *From Boys to Men: Social Constructions of Masculinity in Contemporary Society*, ed. Tamara Shefer. (Lansdowne: University of Cape Town Press, 2007), 13–14.

40. See Ball et al. "Editorial," 353.

41. Koskela critically compares gendered violence and fear with voyeuristic uses of surveillance, exposing shared ground between cultural models of the desirous voyeur "Peeping Tom" and the protective disciplinarian, "Big Brother" (Koskela, "Video Surveillance," 257–78).

42. Magid, "Evidence Locker."

43. As Anuja Madan, writing about Godard's filmic style, described it, "Through the use of jump cuts, non conventional angles, natural settings, non-stylized acting and free wheeling, elliptical dialogues, the scene before our eyes becomes less of a scene." Anuja Madan, "The Language of Emotion in Godard's Films," *Cine Action*, no. 80 (2010), accessed March 30, 2015, http://cineaction.ca/issue80sample.htm

44. As Godard put it, "All great fiction films tend towards documentary, just as all great documentaries tend toward fiction. . . . [E]ach word implies a part of the other. And he who opts wholeheartedly for one, necessarily finds the other at the end of his journey." Jean-Luc Godard, *Godard on Godard: Critical Writings by Jean-Luc Godard*, ed. Jean Narboni and Tom Milne (New York: Da Capo, 1986), 132–33.

45. For example, feminist film theorists have noted that cinematic techniques of the 180-degree rule (a basic guideline for establishing the spatial relationship between two figures on screen), eyeline match (which matches the audience's viewpoint with that of the onscreen character), and 30-degree rule (which recommends that the camera should move at least 30 degrees between successive shots capturing the same subject) make editing invisible, smooth, and "natural" and the act of consuming the image seem to require no interpretive labor.

46. Mulvey, "Visual Pleasure," 14.

47. De Lauretis drew attention to the differences between *women* and *Woman* as a

means of examining the relationship between gender positions and the power strategies that constitute them (such as cinema as a technology of gender). Teresa de Lauretis, *Alice Doesn't: Feminism, Semiotics, Cinema* (Bloomington: Indiana University Press, 1984), 5.

48. Doane's notion of a feminist spectator identifying with her onscreen likeness as a masquerade drew on Joan Riviere's 1929 essay "Womanliness as Masquerade," although Doane employed the concept of masquerade as a feminist strategy to create a critical distance between woman as spectator and woman as image. Mary Ann Doane, "Film and the Masquerade: Theorizing the Female Spectator." *Screen* 23:3 (1982): 74–88; Joan Riviere, "Womanliness as Masquerade," in *Formations of Fantasy*, edited by Victor Burgin, James Donald, and Cora Kaplan (London and New York: Methuen, 1986), 35–44.

49. In *The Feminist Spectator as Critic*, Jill Dolan promotes a materialist approach to theater making and spectatorship, employing materialist feminist criticism "to denaturalize the psychological identification processes implicit in representation," arguing that "when the representational apparatus is foregrounded, its once mystified ideology becomes clear" (14–15). She describes "materialist feminism" as an "apparatus-based theory and practice," thus emphasizing the need to focus on the traditional architecture of representation and reception in theater in order to show its repressive and exclusionary production of gender.

50. In short, Diamond states, "Brecht insisted on *more mimesis* not less." Elin Diamond, *Unmaking Mimesis: Essays on Feminism and Theater* (London: Routledge, 1997), 38–39. See also her introduction to the volume (viii). While his theater did not aim to deny referentiality, Brecht aimed "to expunge the ahistorical referent." She continues, "A gestic feminist criticism would 'alienate' or foreground those moments in a playtext when social attitudes about gender and sexuality conceal or disrupt patriarchal ideology . . . focus[ing] on historical material constraints in the production of images" as well as in their reception (54).

51. Ibid., 368.

52. Magid "Evidence Locker."

53. Ibid.

54. Ibid.

55. Ibid.

56. Ibid.

57. See Annette Kuhn, *Women's Pictures: Feminism and Cinema* (London: Routledge, 1982).

58. Kaja Silverman, *The Threshold of the Visible World* (New York: Routledge, 1996), 205–27.

59. Sophie Calle, with Paul Auster, *Double Game* (London: Violette Limited, 1999), 122–23.

60. Ibid., 126.

61. Ibid., 131.

62. Other pieces, such as *The Hotel* (1983), *Suite Vénitienne* (1980), *Appointment with Sigmund Freud* (1999), *Exquisite Pain* (2004), and *Take Care of Yourself* (2007), chart Calle's ongoing fascination with cultural constructions of gender, authorship, evidence, and embodiment.

63. See Leslie Camhi, "PS 1 Hosts 'Wack!—Real Women Have Oeuvres': A Retrospective Look at the Roots of Feminist Art," *Village Voice*, February 26, 2008, accessed

July 10, 2010, http://www.villagevoice.com/2008–02–26/art/p-s-1-hosts-wack-mdash-real-women-have-oeuvres/

64. Calle, *Double Game*, 126.

65. See Shoshona Felman, *The Scandal of the Speaking Body* (Ithaca, NY: Cornell University Press, 1983). See also D. Soyini Madison, "Performing Theory/Embodied Writing," *Text and Performance Quarterly* 19:2 (1999): 107–24.

66. See Roland Barthes, *Image/Text/Music*, trans. Stephen Heath (New York: Hill and Wang, 1977). Feminist theorists Silverman and Felman notably criticized and at the same time appropriated the concept of voiced writing in their respective analyses of the female voice in cinema and literature. Silverman's criticism stemmed from Barthes's alignment of the authorial body as it is refigured within the text of voiced writing with his post-structuralist proclamation of the "death of the author," a claim that ironically came at precisely the moment when feminist writers were claiming space for distinctively feminist voices in order to stake out linguistic power for female authors. See Kaja Silverman "The Female Authorial Voice," in *The Acoustic Mirror: The Female Voice in Psychoanalysis and Cinema* (Bloomington: Indiana University Press, 1988), 190–92, for her critique of Roland Barthes's "Death of the Author," *Aspen* 5-6 (Fall-Winter, 1967), accessed March 7, 2010, www.ubu.com/aspen/aspen5and6/threeEssays.html#barthes

67. Felman, *Scandal*, 65.

68. Ibid., 5.

69. J. L. Austin, *How to Do Things with Words* (Cambridge: Harvard University Press, 1962), 6–7.

70. Felman, *Scandal*, 5 (emphasis in original). This is the "scandal" of which Felman writes, "the incongruous but indissoluble relation between language and the body; the scandal of the *seduction* of the human body insofar as it speaks" (5).

71. Ibid., 55–56. In Austin's description of the *performative speech act*, the *true/false* binary is replaced with a criterion he calls "felicitous" or "infelicitous"; by this he means that *performatives* are parts of language that cannot be logically true or false; rather they can be "successful" or "unsuccessful" according to the action that they do or do not engender (Austin, *How to Do Things*, 9–11).

72. In *Appointment with Sigmund Freud*, Calle incorporated her own personal objects into the Freud Museum's permanent collection, pairing the objects with stories about the psychological roles they played in her life. She included, among other things, a red shoe she was caught stealing as a child, a love letter she ordered from a professional letter writer (because she had never received a real one), and a stuffed cat, which, when alive, had been strangled by a jealous lover when she preferred to share her bed with it rather than him. Sophie Calle, *Appointment with Sigmund Freud* (London: Thames and Hudson, 2004).

73. Calle, *Double Game*, 140–85.

74. Ibid., 122.

75. Petra Gördüren, "On the Trail of the Ego: Sophie Calle's Pursuits," in *ctrl [space]: Rhetorics of Surveillance from Bentham to Big Brother*, ed. Thomas Levin, Ursula Frohne, and Peter Weibel (Leipzig: ZKM, McdienKunstNetz, 2002).

76. Building on second-wave feminist discourse and conflict, third wavers have tended to take multivocality and difference as a starting point, not seeking to collapse the notion of feminist (or even women) into a definition. As R. Claire Snyder put it, "[T]hird-wave feminism makes three important tactical moves that respond

to a series of theoretical problems within the second wave. First, in response to the collapse of the category of 'women,' the third wave foregrounds personal narratives that illustrate an intersectional and multiperspectival version of feminism. Second, as a consequence of the rise of postmodernism, third-wavers embrace multivocality over synthesis and action over theoretical justification. Finally, in response to the divisiveness of the sex wars, third-wave feminism emphasizes an inclusive and nonjudgmental approach that refuses to police the boundaries of the feminist political. In other words, third-wave feminism rejects grand narratives for a feminism that operates as a hermeneutics of critique within a wide array of discursive locations, and replaces attempts at unity with a dynamic and welcoming politics of coalition" (Snyder, "What Is Third-Wave Feminism?," 176).

77. Rosecrans Baldwin, "My Harassers: Hannah Price." *Morning News,* October 14, 2013, accessed March 7, 2014, http://www.themorningnews.org/gallery/my-harassers

78. Kat Chow, "A Photographer Turns Her Lens on Men Who Catcall," *National Public Radio: Code Switch,* October 17, 2013, accessed March 7, 2014, http://www.npr.org/sections/codeswitch/2013/10/17/235413025/a-photographer-turns-her-lens-on-men-who-cat-call

79. Ibid.
80. Ibid.
81. Ibid.
82. Ibid.

83. Laura Mulvey, *Fetishism and Curiosity* (London: British Film Institute, 1996), 62.

84. Ibid., 59. In the myth, Pandora is famous because she is beautiful and desirable to men and feared because she is a woman who broke the rules and looked where she was not supposed to, namely, inside her "box," which metaphorically describes the interior of the female body and the attendant horrors it supposedly holds for male viewers (60–61).

85. Ibid. 59.
86. Magid "Evidence Locker."
87. Ibid. (italics in original).
88. Ibid. (italics in original).
89. Ibid. (italics in original).
90. Ibid.

91. T. Maureen, "Invisibility/Hypervisibility: The Paradox of Normative Whiteness," *Transformations* 9:2 (1998): 55–64.

92. These criticisms echo similar accusations within the second-wave feminist movement, as black feminists such as Audre Lorde and bell hooks criticized feminists such as Betty Friedan and groups such as the National Organization for Women for assuming that the particular experiences, values, and modes of expression of white, heterosexual, middle-class women were universal to all women. Lorde actively challenged white feminists with her writing, confronting issues of racism in feminist thought. She maintained that a great deal of the scholarship of white feminists served to augment the oppression of black women, a conviction that led to angry confrontations, most notably in the scathing open letter addressed to radical lesbian feminist Mary Daly. See Audre Lorde, "Open Letter to Mary Daly," in *Sister Outsider* (Berkeley, CA: Crossing Press, 1984), 66. Similarly, in her essay "The Master's Tools Will Never Dismantle the Master's House" (in the same volume), Lorde attacked the underlying

racism of feminism, describing it as unrecognized dependence on the patriarchy. Written in a similar vein, bell hooks's *Ain't I a Woman? Black Women and Feminism* (Boston: South End Press, 1981) examined the historical impact of sexism and racism on black women, devaluation of black womanhood in media representations and the education system, and the disregard for issues of race and class within feminism. See also bell hooks, *Reel to Real: Race, Sex, and Class at the Movies* (London: Routledge, 1996).

93. Chow, "A Photographer." While it is difficult to agree on such statistics, multiple studies have suggested that black men are between three and ten times more likely than white men to be watched by security cameras or searched or detained by police officers. A 2012 Princeton study suggested that black men are six times more likely to be targeted by police officers. See Merrell Noden, "Racial Surveillance: How One Prevalent Form of Inequality Affects the Lives of African-Americans," *Princeton Alumni Weekly*, July 9, 2014, accessed May 3, 2015, https://paw.princeton.edu/issues/2014/07/09/pages/7630/index.xml

94. David Lyon, *Surveillance after 9/11* (Cambridge: Polity Press, 2003), 27.

95. Coleman, "Reclaiming the Streets," 304–5.

Chapter 3

1. Wafaa Bilal, "Domestic Tension" (2007), accessed July 10, 2010, http://www.wafaabilal.com/html/domesticTension.html. The project, along with its backstory and Bilal's reflections after it concluded, was written up in detail in a book-length publication by Bilal and Kari Lydersen, *Shoot an Iraqi: Art, Life, and Resistance under the Gun* (San Francisco: City Lights, 2008).

2. Bilal's project went "viral" to the degree that it was mentioned on digg.com, a website that tracks and advertises the websites with the most hits on a given day. Bilal and Lydersen, *Shoot an Iraqi*, 79.

3. Foucault, *Discipline and Punish*, 200.

4. See Theodor Adorno and Walter Benjamin, *The Complete Correspondence, 1928–1940* (Cambridge: Harvard University Press, 1999); and Walter Benjamin, "The Work of Art in the Age of Mechanical Reproduction," in *Illuminations: Walter Benjamin Essays and Reflections*, ed. Hannah Arendt, trans. Harry Zohn (New York: Pantheon, 1968). In a presentation given at Yale University in April 2014, Thomas Stubblefield made a point along these lines that also influenced my thinking on Benjamin's position on cinema, its onslaught on the senses, and its relationship to the various forms of participatory surveillance today.

5. Wendy Hui-Kyong Chun, *Control and Freedom: Power and Paranoia in the Age of Fiber Optics* (Cambridge: MIT Press, 2006), 44. In *Domain Matrix*, Sue-Ellen Case theorizes the portrayal and construction of user/consumer identities within the contexts of queer theory and virtual technologies, posing provocative questions about how the body is situated and destabilized in competing and overlapping regimes of print, the screen, and virtual space. Sue-Ellen Case *Domain Matrix: Performing Lesbian at the End of Print Culture* (Bloomington: Indiana University Press, 1996).

6. Ranciere, "Ten Theses," 5.

7. Deleuze, *Postscript*.

8. Oscar H. Gandy, *The Panoptic Sort: A Political Economy of Personal Information* (Boulder: Westview Press, 1993), 15–18. David Lyon calls this "social sorting" (*Surveillance Society*, 51, 61). See also Brin, *Transparent Society*, 13–15.

9. Wood and Graham, "Permeable Boundaries," 188.

10. Global Entry is a program developed by US Customs and Border Protection that allows preapproved, low-risk travelers, identified through fingerprint and facial recognition technology, to enter the country through an expedited system. Developed as a replacement for the Immigration and Naturalization Service Passenger Accelerated Service System (INSPASS), which was dissolved in 2002, Global Entry is used in over thirty international airports in the United States and Canada. Japan, Australia, New Zealand, Hong Kong, and Taiwan have similar systems, which use biometric passports and "smart" national identification cards to fast-track preapproved citizens. For details, see the Global Entry website, www.globalentry.gov

11. Wood and Graham, "Permeable Boundaries," 177–78.

12. Ibid., 179.

13. Members of the IAA, along with a number of other visual and performance artists working in public space, were gathered together by curator and theorist Nato Thompson in a 2004 exhibit at MASS MoCA (Massachusetts Museum of Contemporary Art) titled *The Interventionists*.

14. Diana Taylor, *Disappearing Acts: Spectacles of Gender and Nationalism in Argentina's "Dirty War"* (Durham: Duke University Press, 1997), 122–23.

15. IAA, "Mission," Institute for Applied Autonomy, accessed August 25, 2010, http://www.appliedautonomy.com/mission.html

16. The computing software trade has also adopted the term *Trojan horse* to describe a kind of malicious software—known as malware—that appears to perform a desirable function but in fact gives computer hackers unauthorized access to the host machine.

17. David Lyon (*Surveillance Society*), Manuel de Landa (*War*), and James Rule (*Private Lives*), among others, have explicated the ontology of surveillance technologies as they have been developed historically in service of military operations, crime prevention, judicial evidence, and national security.

18. IAA, "Terminal Air," Institute for Applied Autonomy, accessed August 25, 2010, http://www.appliedautonomy.com/terminalair/index.html

19. IAA, "Defensive Surveillance: Lessons from the Republican National Convention," in *Surveillance and Security*, ed. Torin Monahan (London: Routledge, 2006), 172.

20. IAA, *Engaging Ambivalence: Interventions in Engineering Culture* (Brooklyn: Autonomedia, 2005), 97.

21. Erich W. Schienke, "On the Outside Looking Out: An Interview with the Institute for Applied Autonomy," *Surveillance & Society* 1:1 (2002): 107.

22. IAA, "Defensive Surveillance," 167.

23. Ibid., 172.

24. Ibid.

25. Ibid., 170.

26. The Situationist tactic of the *dérive* was influenced by the situationist theory of "psychogeography" and involved a meandering walk through urban space in which the walker chose a path according to his or her interest, distraction, and desire rather than the commerce and control-oriented design of most urban centers. With the *dérive*, the Situationists proposed that ways of physically and psychically engaging with public space were in fact political acts that could either maintain or challenge the capitalist status quo. A contemporary example of *dérive*-inspired interventionism is Alex Villar's 2001 project "Temporary Occupations." Villar hopped over,

crawled through, and slipped past walls, fences, railings, and gates designed to manage and control pedestrian movement in urban centers. He used trespassing as a way to highlight and challenge aspects of built environments and the ways in which boundaries between public and private are maintained. See Alex Villar, "Temporary Occupations," accessed August 25, 2010, http://www.de-tour.org/series/temp_occupations/index.html; and Thompson, *Interventionists*, 16.

27. IAA, "iSEE," Institute for Applied Autonomy, accessed August 25, 2010, http://www.appliedautonomy.com/isee.html

28. IAA, *Engaging Ambivalence*, 98. Surveillance theorists such as Oscar H. Gandy have likewise asserted that invisible and dispersed processes of sorting and dividing social subjects, discussed earlier, are the product of the engineering and programming of surveillance software systems, suggesting that the ethical burden should fall on programmers and engineers (Gandy, *Panoptic Sort*, 18–20). Indeed, evidence of programming bias is apparent even in studies that support the effects of such systems. For example, although the report "Automatic Detection of Abnormal Behavior and Threats in Crowded Spaces," or ADABTS, which the European Union commissioned in 2007, claims that, unlike "human police officers," automated data processing avoids being influenced by "personal interest" or "prejudices." It also acknowledges that "programmers may have a bias which leads to biased programming or training." CORDIS [Community Research and Development Information Service], "Final Report Summary—ADABTS (Automatic Detection of Abnormal Behavior and Threats in Crowded Spaces)" (2011), accessed June 26, 2015, http://cordis.europa.eu/result/rcn/153868_en.html

29. Thompson, *Interventionists*, 105.

30. Mann defines the term as follows: "Sousveillance: the recording of an activity from the perspective of a participant in the activity; the recording or monitoring of real or apparent authority figures by others, particularly those who are generally the subject of surveillance; watchful vigilance from underneath; a situationist critique of surveillance." Steve Mann, "Sousveillance," accessed August 25, 2010, http://wearcam.org/sousveillance.htm

31. Steve Mann, "Existential Technology," *LEONARDO* 36:1 (2003): 21–22.

32. Mann's WearComp (wearable computer), which has been under development since the 1980s, presaged Google Glass, introduced on the consumer market in 2014; both superimpose e-mails and a live web browser on the wearer's field of vision and allow the wearer to record what he or she sees. Steve Mann, "Wear Comp," accessed August 25, 2010, http://wearcam.org/wearcompdef.html. However, while Google claims that Google Glass was created in order to make technology less of an impediment to everyday life, Mann intended his WearComp to make visible his goals of inverse surveillance. Astro Teller, "Why We Developed Google Glass," *CNN online*, June 4, 2014, accessed June 5, 2014, http://www.cnn.com/2014/06/04/opinion/teller-google-glass/

33. Mann, "Existential Technology," 24.

34. Ibid.

35. Similarly, in another ongoing project that challenges the sociopolitical hierarchy through sousveillance, Mann requires identification scans of police officers in order to access his own information, since his ID wallet will literally not open unless another ID is scanned (Mann, "Existential Technology," 21–22).

36. See Gary T. Marx, "Ethics for the New Surveillance," *Information Society* 14:3 (1998): 171–85; and "Electric Eye in the Sky: Some Reflections on the New Surveil-

lance and Popular Culture," in *Computers, Surveillance, and Privacy*, ed. David Lyon and Elia Zureik (Minneapolis: University of Minnesota Press, 1996).

37. Lorde, "Master's Tools," 110–14.

38. Kirsty Robertson, "'Try to Walk with the Sound of My Footsteps': The Surveillant Body in Contemporary Art," *Communication Review* 11:1 (2008): 25.

39. Butler, "Performative Acts," 519–20.

40. See Guy Debord, "Report on the Construction of Situations and on the International Situationist Tendency Conditions of Organization and Action," translated by Ken Knabb. *Situationist International Online*, accessed August 25, 2010, http://www.cddc.vt.edu/sionline/si/report.html, the founding manifesto of the situationist movement, wherein he discusses the risks of recuperation. Situationist scholar Tom McDonough notes that *recuperation* is tactically and theoretically very close to *detournement*, possibly even identical were it not for Debord's insistence on aligning *recuperation* with dominating practices of bourgeois capitalist culture. While Debord termed *recuperation* a tactic that threatened the revolutionary aims of the situationists by mining them for potential capitalist profits, McDonough notes that "there is irony in the use of the idea of recuperation to bolster the alleged purity of the situationist avant-garde, for what is recuperation other than a strategy of mixing, blending?" Tom McDonough, *Guy Debord and the Situationist International: Texts and Documents* (Cambridge: MIT Press, 2004), xiii. He goes on to posit that "*detournement*, the situationist strategy of diverting elements of affirmative bourgeois culture to revolutionary ends . . . [is] the exact corollary of recuperation," suggesting that we "can only assume that the bourgeoisie was as adept at *detournement* as the situationists themselves, that, in fact, recuperation and *detournement* were one and the same, a shared cultural strategy" (xiv). The blurred boundaries between—or similar tactics of—dominant culture and revolutionary tactics that McDonough describes undermine situationist claims to a position of pure opposition.

41. A classic example is the Gap's "1969" design line, which, at least initially, mimicked the styles of hippie protesters of the Vietnam War era—bellbottoms with holes and so on.

42. In the document "Now, the SI," Debord wrote, "[I]t is quite natural that our enemies manage to partially use us . . . [for] just like the proletariat, we cannot claim to be unexploitable within the given circumstances" (quoted in McDonough, xiii).

43. Steve Mann, Jason Nollman, and Barry Wellman, "Sousveillance: Inventing and Using Wearable Computing Devices for Data Collection in Surveillance Environments," *Surveillance & Society* 1:3 (2003): 331–55.

44. See Mann, "Sousveillance."

45. "Patrol the Border from Home!," Live Leak, accessed April 1, 2015, http://www.liveleak.com/view?i=68b_1323233391. The Texas Border Sherriff's Coalition also encourages users to set up their own neighborhood watches by providing access to locally installed CCTV camera networks. Organizations such as this have been critiqued and challenged by projects such as *Lowdrone*, created by Angel Nevarez and Alex Rivera, discussed in the "Introduction" and chapter 6 of this book.

46. Mann, Nollman, and Wellman, "Sousveillance," 333.

47. Critical Art Ensemble, *Electronic Civil Disobedience*, 18.

48. In November 2009 Alex Dunbar interviewed Dominguez and published "Follow the GPS, ÉSE: The Transborder Immigrant Tool Helps Mexicans Cross Over Safely," *Vice*, November 2009, accessed August 10, 2010, http://www.viceland.com/int/v16n11/htdocs/follow-the-gps-225.php?page=2

49. Dominguez described the intersecting investigations and the pressures they caused in an interview with Zach Blas in 2012, published on the *Reclamations* blog. Zach Blas, "On Electronic Civil Disobedience: Interview with Ricardo Dominguez," *Reclamations (blog),* January 17, 2012, accessed August 30, 2012, http://www.reclamationsjournal.org/blog/?ha_exhibit=interview-with-ricardo-dominguez

50. See "Critics Blast Transborder Immigrant Tool," *Fox News,* March 10, 2010, accessed August 10, 2010, http://www.foxnews.com/us/2010/03/10/critics-blast-transborder-immigrant-tool-irresponsible-use-technology/. The project's cultural and political controversy build on those of Dominguez's previous "disturbances" with EDT, such as the FloodNet system, a participatory website-jamming network that allowed anyone with an Internet connection to overuse, or jam, the official sites of the US Border Patrol, White House, G8 (Group of 8, a meeting of the most economicaly powerful industrialized nations), and Mexican embassy, among others, rendering them inaccessible. FloodNet attracted a Department of Justice investigation and the deployment of an "informational war weapon" by the US government (Dunbar, "Follow the GPS," 1–2).

51. In Blas, "On Electronic Civil Disobedience," Dominguez credited this terminology to Laura Borràs Castanyer and Juan B. Gutiérrez.

52. Electronic Disturbance Theatre/b.a.n.g. lab, "Transborder Immigrant Tool."

53. Ranciere, "Ten Theses," 6.

54. Ibid. Ranciere writes of this process as "the manifestation of dissensus" or "the presence of two worlds in one," defining *dissensus* "not [as] the confrontation between interests or opinions" but rather "the manifestation of a distance of the sensible from itself" (6).

55. Electronic Disturbance Theatre/b.a.n.g. lab, "Transborder Immigrant Tool."

56. Taylor, *Disappearing Acts,* 123. Taylor described the politically repressive and violent conditions of Argentina's "Dirty War" in which the military enacted public spectacles of violence that the civilian population had to witness but pretend to not see: "The triumph of the atrocity was that it forced people to look away—a gesture that undid their sense of personal and communal cohesion even as it seemed to bracket them from their volatile surroundings. Spectacles of violence rendered the population silent, deaf, and blind. . . . The military violence could have been relatively invisible, as the term 'disappearance' suggests. The fact that it wasn't indicates that the population as a whole was the intended target, positioned by means of the spectacle. People had to deny what they saw and, by turning away, collude with the violence around them. . . . To see, without being able to do, disempowers absolutely. But seeing, without even admitting that one is seeing, further turns the violence on oneself. Percepticide blinds, maims, kills through the senses" (122–23).

57. To combat the blinding strategies of contemporary percepticide, activist groups have formulated tactics to make visible and audible the processes, spaces, and people that have been silenced and made invisible by various political strategies and oversights. Groups such as CopWatch, Witness for Peace, or School of the Americas Watch pointedly bear witness to and report on acts and/or social conditions that military, corporate, or state entities around the world attempt to erase, overlook, and silence. Online blogs and alternative news groups such as these use the capacity of communications and surveillance technologies to build new models of visibility and transparency through which to broadcast and critique political situations around the world. See www.soaw.org, www.copwatch.org, and www.witnessforpeace.org for more

information on these politically independent, national and international grassroots organizations.

58. See Coco Fusco, *Dolores*, accessed July 10, 2010, http://www.thing.net/~cocofusco/video/dolores/dolores1.htm. See also Coco Fusco, *The Bodies That Were Not Ours* (London: Routledge. 2001).

59. See Coco Fusco, *English Is Broken Here: Notes on Cultural Fusion in the Americas* (New York: New Press, 1995).

60. While *Dolores* has been her most direct engagement with surveillance technologies, many of Fusco's performance artworks deal in some way with the politics of sight, oversight, and individual agency. One of her best-known pieces, *The Couple in the Cage* (1993), was a parody of ethnographic museum dioramas and historical world's fair exhibits in which Fusco and Mexican performance artist Guillermo Gómez-Peña toured internationally as caged specimens of primitive, "savage" humans displayed as exotic curios. The piece critiqued cultural institutions for their histories of displaying exotic bodies for the gaze of medical and cultural knowledge and created live situations in which viewers had to confront their own position as spectators of human captivity and objectification. See Fusco, *Bodies*, 233–36. See also Coco Fusco and Guillermo Gómez-Peña, *The Couple in a Cage: A Guatinaui Odyssey*, film version by Coco Fusco and Paula Herdia (1993), accessed July 10, 2010, http://www.thing.net/~cocofusco/subpages/videos/subpages/couple/couple.html.

61. See Hasan Elahi, *Tracking Transience*, accessed July 10, 2010, http://tracking-transience.net/

62. "TED Speaker: Hasan Elahi," October 2011, accessed October 9, 2014, http://www.ted.com/speakers/hasan_elahi

63. Hasan Elahi, "Giving the FBI What It Wants," *New York Times*, October 30, 2011, accessed October 9, 2014, http://www.nytimes.com/2011/10/30/opinion/sunday/giving-the-fbi-what-it-wants.html?pagewanted=all&_r=0

64. Ibid.

65. Ibid.

66. Ibid.

67. Emily Rosamund gives an engaging analysis of Elahi's project, arguing that his strategies perform the "self as [data] set" in a way that reflects and resists changing modes of surveillance analysis in the early twenty-first century. Emily Rosamond, "Technologies of Attribution: Characterizing the Citizen-Consumer in Surveillance Performance," in "Surveillance Technologies in Performance," ed. Elise Morrison, special issue, *International Journal of Performance Arts and Digital Media* 11:2 (2015): 148–64.

68. Elahi, "Giving the FBI What It Wants."

69. See Bilal, "Domestic Tension."

70. Embodied, durational performance has long been Bilal's favored modality as a means of materializing large political issues across the space of his own body. As I discuss at greater length in chapter 5, several of Bilal's other works have featured his own body as an artistic/political canvas. In *and Counting . . .* Bilal had his back tattooed with a map of Iraq on which a dot was placed for each American and Iraqi death—the Iraqi deaths were marked with an ink that was invisible unless viewed under a black light. See Wafaa Bilal, "and Counting . . . ," accessed September 24, 2014, http://wafaabilal.com/and-counting/. In his best-known project, *3rdi*, Bilal had a small digital camera surgically implanted on the back of his head; the camera

was programmed to take a picture every minute of every day, creating an "objective" and "automatic" record-keeping device for Bilal's daily activities for two years. See Wafaa Bilal, "3rdi," accessed September 24, 2014, http://wafaabilal.com/thirdi/

71. For another example of immersive gaming created for political purposes see Lindsay Brandon Hunter, "This Is Not a Threat: Conspiracy for Good," in "Surveillance Technologies in Performance," ed. Elise Morrison, special issue, *International Journal of Performance Arts and Digital Media* 11:2. (2015): 185–201. See also Jennifer R. Whitson and Bart Simon, "Game Studies Meets Surveillance Studies at the Edge of Digital Culture: An Introduction to a Special Issue on Surveillance, Games, and Play," in "Surveillance, Gaming and Play," ed. Jennifer R. Whitson and Bart Simon, special issue, *Surveillance & Society* 12:3 (2014): 309–19.

72. Bilal and Lydersen, *Shoot an Iraqi*, 79.

73. Ibid., 78–79.

74. Ibid.

75. Bilal described one scenario that occurred midway through the project, which showed how his presence as a metaphorical target and individual interlocutor intervened in the anonymity, distance, and dehumanization that can plague online interactions: "For the past two nights three young women from the UK who heard me on the BBC had been online until 4 a.m., teasing me, telling cute jokes and talking about flying to Chicago for a visit. They were all in different towns, but they were having a party together in my chat room. One of them was crazy or maybe drunk. She kept saying 'KILL KILL MAIM KILL.' Then 'Yr a hadsome bloke! Don't b coy.' I wanted to cut through the ridiculous banter and talk to her as a normal human being. Finally, when I told her about my brother's and father's deaths I was able to engage her in real conversation" (ibid., 74). Although in that case the details of Bilal's personal mourning led the women to apologize and extend their sympathies to Bilal, exchanging personal stories was not a sure-fire antidote to the carelessness and anonymity of online interchanges. Bilal observed that male visitors were often far more interested in shooting than talking; one even figured out how to hack the controls of the gun, setting it to fire nonstop like a machine gun. In other cases, even when visitors chatted with him, Bilal observed that they seemed to be "entering a discussion just because they want to win an argument, trying to hijack someone else's platform just so they can show off their intellect, but not contributing to anything" (75).

76. Clio Unger, "'SHOOT HIM NOW!!!' Anonymity, Accountability, and Online Spectatorship in Wafaa Bilal's *Domestic Tension*," in "Surveillance Technologies in Performance," ed. Elise Morrison, special issue, *International Journal of Performance Arts and Digital Media* 11:2 (2015): 202–18.

77. Bilal and Lydersen, *Shoot an Iraqi*, xix.

78. Blast Theory, "Rider Spoke," accessed September 24, 2014, http://www.blast-theory.co.uk/projects/rider-spoke/

79. Andrejevic, *Reality TV*, 15.

80. Ibid.

81. Jason Farman, "Mobile Media Performances as Asynchronous Embodiment," *International Journal of ScreenDance* 2:1 (2012): 49.

82. Ibid., 48–49.

83. See Michael Goodchild, "NeoGeography and the Nature of Geographic Expertise," *Journal of Location Based Services* 3:2 (June 2009): 82–96. "Neogeography combines the complex techniques of cartography and GIS and places them within

reach of users and developers." Andrew Turner, *Introduction to Neogeography* (2006), O'Reilly Media, accessed April 24, 2015, http://highearthorbit.com/neogeography/book.pdf

84. Elwood and Mitchell. "Another Politics."

85. Rowan Wilken, "Proximity and Alienation: Narratives of City, Self, and Other in the Locative Games of Blast Theory," in *The Mobile Story*, ed. Jason Farman (London: Routledge, 2014), 182.

86. Farman, *Mobile Interface Theory*, 105.

87. Wilken, "Proximity," 177.

88. Ibid., 182.

89. Alan Chamberlain, quoted in ibid.

90. Ibid., 183.

91. Blast Theory, "Rider Spoke."

92. An AOL spokesperson, Andrew Weinstein, explained the misguided reasoning behind the disclosure in a public apology in the days following the data leak. Michael Arrington, "AOL: 'This Was a Screw-Up,'" *Tech Crunch*, August 7, 2006, accessed April 14, 2014, http://techcrunch.com/2006/08/07/aol-this-was-a-screw-up/

93. Michael Barbaro and Tom Zeller Jr., "A Face Is Exposed for AOL Searcher No. 4417749," *New York Times*, August 9, 2006, accessed April 14, 2014, http://www.nytimes.com/2006/08/09/technology/09aol.html?pagewanted=all&_r=0

94. Lernert Engleberts and Sander Plug, *I Love Alaska* (2009), MiniMovies, accessed April 14, 2014, http://www.minimovies.org/documentaires/view/ilovealaska

95. Thomas Stubblefield, "'Moving' Images: Film, Dataveillance, and the Labor of the Visual." Paper presented at the conference Fields of Vision: Observation, Surveillance, Voyeurism, Whitney Humanities Center, Yale University, February 21, 2014, presentation draft supplied to the author, p. 2.

96. Ibid.

97. Ibid., 7.

98. Ibid.

99. Engleberts and Plug, *I Love Alaska*.

100. Irigaray and Cixous emphasized that women, historically limited to being sexual objects for men—as virgins or prostitutes, wives or mothers—have been prevented from expressing or authoring their female sexuality, desires, and pleasures to men, other women, or even themselves. Irigaray referred to this linguistic prison as "phallogocentric language." See Luce Irigaray, *This Sex Which Is Not One*, trans. Catherine Porter, with Carolyn Burke (Ithaca, NY: Cornell University Press, 1985).

101. Hélène Cixous, "The Laugh of the Medusa," *Signs* 1:4 (1976): 875.

102. I discuss this strategy at length in chapter 4, drawing on Sjogren's theorization of the voice off. She distinguishes between the voice-over and the voice off as a means of avoiding the connotation that sound is merely *layered over*—and thus relegated to the same processes of subjection as—the filmic image: "Whereas 'over' suggests a top 'layer' or cloak of some kind, 'off' connotes otherness—a distinctness that moves alongside, 'elsewhere.' In this sense, 'off' best evokes the tension of a dialectic to the image, a vital relationship to preserve in descriptions of the voice." Britta Sjogren, *Into the Vortex: Female Voice and Paradox in Film* (Urbana: University of Illinois Press, 2006), 6.

103. Nate Anderson, "2006 AOL Search Data Snafu Spawns 'I Love Alaska' Short

Films," *Ars Technica,* January 27, 2009, accessed June 16, 2015, http://arstechnica. com/business/2009/01/aol-search-data-spawns-i-love-alaska-short-films/

Chapter 4

1. De Lauretis, *Alice Doesn't,* 36.

2. Mann designed this incarnation of his wearcam devices in 2001. See Steve Mann, "HeartCam," accessed August 25, 2010, http://wearcam.org/domewear/ HeartCam.htm

3. Mann, "Existential Technology," 21.

4. As Laura Mulvey put it, "In their traditional exhibitionist role women are simultaneously looked at and displayed, with their appearance coded for strong visual and erotic impact so that they can be said to connote to-be-looked-at-ness" ("Visual Pleasure," 19).

5. Firepile, "Steve Mann," *Hyper-textual Ontology Blog,* August 10, 2004, accessed Dec. 30, 2009. http://wearcam.org/tv04/hyper-textual_ontology.htm

6. As Butler, Foucault, and many others have argued, the cultural construction and maintenance of gender binaries as a naturalized fact of social life have long been used to produce norms of heterosexual structures of desire that in turn support certain hegemonic socioeconomic and political structures. Building on Foucault, Butler has argued, "[T]he association of a natural sex with a discrete gender and with an ostensibly natural 'attraction' to the opposing sex/gender is an unnatural conjunction of cultural constructs in the service of reproductive interests." Gender operates in service of social organizations, kinship bonds, and economic stability at the level of the family unit; these organizations "require taboos and a punitive regulation of reproduction to effect that end" (Butler, "Performative Acts," 523).

7. Ibid., 519.

8. Ibid., 526.

9. Koskela, "Video Surveillance," 257–78.

10. Mulvey, "Visual Pleasure," 16.

11. Mulvey, "Visual Pleasure," 19.

12. Dolan, *Feminist Spectator,* 1.

13. John Berger, *Ways of Seeing* (London: Penguin, 1972), 45.

14. In *Technologies of Gender,* Teresa de Lauretis reformulated Foucault's concept of "technologies of sex" in his *History of Sexuality* in order to address the shortcomings in his theory of cultural discipline, arguing that he did not pay enough attention to the ways in which technologies of sex address men and women differently (de Lauretis, *Technologies of Gender,* 2, 12–13).

15. Mulvey, *Fetishism,* 6. From a Freudian psychoanalytic perspective, surveillance technologies become fetishes similarly constructed against the loss of power and control. They cover over an anxious reliance on patriarchal power and latent fears regarding the possibility of a space outside the reach of the law: law of the state, law of the father, law of language. See Althusser, "Ideology"; Foucault, *Power/Knowledge;* Jacques Lacan, "The Mirror Stage as Formative of the Function of the I as Revealed in Psychoanalytic Experience," in *Ecrits,* translated by Alan Sheridan (New York: Norton, 1977); and Luce Irigaray, *Speculum of the Other Woman,* translated by Gillian C. Gill (Ithaca, NY: Cornell University Press, 1985. In the visual medium of surveillance art, surveillance equipment itself is often figured as both agent and object of a fetishizing gaze.

16. Schneider argued that such practices could unsettle traditional constructions of the feminine as "emblematic of the given to be seen, . . . virgin territory made passive before a veiled masculine gaze" (*Explicit Body*, 71). She describes women who "look back" in this way as valuable troublemakers: "The political whore, the object who doesn't wait to be 'invested' in order to look back, is a trouble-making whore" (108).

17. Ibid., 72.

18. Ibid., 122.

19. Mann, "Existential Technology," 21.

20. Ibid., 22.

21. Ibid.

22. Elin Diamond, "Mimesis, Mimicry, and the 'True-Real,'" *Modern Drama* 32:1 (1989): 58–72.

23. Doane, "Film," 75–76, 78. This collapse was meant to be exhibited on the bodies of female spectators. In films that were marketed as "women's pictures," "weepies," or "chick flicks," tears of empathy are expected of the female spectator; identification and reception are collapsed onto the body of the spectator.

24. Doane, "Film," 81. Doane argued that the problem for the female spectator lay in the lack of a critical distance between the female audience member and the Woman as image onscreen (80). Her notion of a feminist spectator identifying with her onscreen likeness as a masquerade drew on Joan Riviere's 1929 essay "Womanliness as Masquerade." Riviere, who had worked for several years with Freud and his daughter Anna, theorized an area of sexual development wherein women—intellectual, career-minded women in particular—developed an exterior representation of "femininity," which they "put on" as a defensive mask with which to hide their masculinity.

25. Sue-Ellen Case, "Towards a Butch-Femme Aesthetic," in *The Lesbian and Gay Studies Reader*, ed. Henry Abelove, Michèle Aina Barale, and David M. Halperin (New York: Routledge, 1993), 291. See also Jill Dolan, "Desire Dressed in a Trenchcoat," in *The Drama Review* 33.1 (1989): 59–67.

26. After the Amsterdam police department's initial refusal to allow Magid to bedazzle surveillance cameras in the name of "art," Magid reframed her project as a commercial venture that utilized untapped aesthetic potential within contemporary cityscapes: "When I presented myself as an artist, no one would speak to me. . . . So I invented a company, System Azure Security Ornamentation. I called them up and said, 'I'm a security ornamentation professional.' The title made all the difference, and soon I was meeting with police administrators to discuss the public's relationship with surveillance." Jill Magid, "System Azure," last modified October 8, 2008, accessed August 25, 2010, http://www.jillmagid.net/SystemAzure.php

27. Jill Magid, "Monitoring Desire," MA thesis, MIT, 2000, accessed December 16, 2009, http://jillmagid.net/MIT-Thesis.php

28. Magid, "System Azure."

29. Schneider, drawing on Benjamin's theorization of the dialectic of prostitutes, wrote, "[T]he prostitute appeared to embody a paradox: as both commodity and seller she embodied a bizarre and potentially terroristic collapse of active and passive, subject and object, into a single entity" (*Explicit Body*, 24). She goes on to read the figure of the prostitute according to Marxist materialist theory as "both emblematic of and threatening to some of the operative tenets of commodity capitalism. The

prostitute is not only commodity and seller, but laborer," embodying human labor and the commodity in one form (24).

30. See Susan Sontag, "Notes on Camp," in *Against Interpretation* (New York: Farrar, Straus & Giroux, 1966).

31. Goli Mohammadi, "Interview with Artist and Roboticist Giles Walker," *Make*, April 25, 2013, accessed April 25, 2015. http://makezine.com/2013/04/25/maker-faire-uk-interview-with-artist-giles-walker/

32. Giles Walker, "Peepshow" (2007), accessed August 25, 2010, http://www.gileswalker.org/gileswalker.org/PEEPSHOW/Pages/pole_dancers.html

33. Craig Owens, "Posing," in *Beyond Recognition: Representation, Power, and Culture* (Berkeley: University of California Press, 1994), 204.

34. Using the process of posing for a photograph as a quotidian example, Owens posits that the body "freezes" in a pose in order to somehow resist the power of the immobilizing technology of capture itself: "If, posing for a photograph, I freeze, it is not in order to assist the photographer, but in some sense to resist him, to protect myself from his immobilizing gaze" (ibid., 211).

35. Ibid., 214.

36. Adam Frucci, "Pole Dancing Robots Ruin Both Robots and Strippers Simultaneously," *gizmodo* , December 4, 2008, accessed August 25, 2010, http://gizmodo.com/5101838/pole-dancing-robots-ruin-both-robots-and-strippers-simultaneously

37. Adario Strange, "Pole Dancing Robots Make CCTV Surveillance Sexy," *DVICE*, December 5, 2008, accessed August 25, 2010, http://dvice.com/archives/2008/12/pole_dancing_ro.php c

38. Geekologie, "Tipping with TNT: Pole Dancing Stripper-Bots," December 5, 2008, accessed April 25, 2015, http://geekologie.com/2008/12/stripper-robots-make-me-questi.php

39. Silverman, *Threshold*, 205–27.

40. Ibid., 214.

41. Owens, "Posing," 212.

42. Schneider described Diamond's theory of hysteria and "feminist mimicry" through a strategy she terms "showing the show," a style of performance that "shows the show of realism" (*Explicit Body*, 116).

43. Michelle Starr, "Watch Robotic Pole Dancers Shake Their Actuators," *CNET*, March 12, 2014, accessed February 10, 2015, http://www.cnet.com/news/watch-robotic-pole-dancers-shake-their-actuators/

44. Schneider, *Explicit Body*, 20.

45. Magid, "Monitoring Desire."

46. As Jacqueline Rose described representations of women in classic cinema, "[W]oman is constructed . . . as a negative to the man, [and] woman becomes a total object of fantasy (or an object of total fantasy), elevated into the place of the Other and made to stand for its truth." Jacqueline Rose, *Sexuality in the Field of Vision* (London: Verso, 1986), 47–50. See also Kaja Silverman, *The Acoustic Mirror: The Female Voice in Psychoanalysis and Cinema* (Bloomington: Indiana University Press, 1988), 4–5, 8.

47. Magid, "Monitoring Desire."

48. Schneider, *Explicit Body*, 22.

49. Ibid., 23.

50. Magid, "Monitoring Desire"; Diamond, *Unmaking Mimesis*, 52.

51. Magid, "Surveillance Shoe."

52. Schneider, *Explicit Body*, 21.

53. Hatoum explored similar medical surveillance technologies and internal imaging in *Corps Étranger* (1994). See Lisa Cartwright, *Screening the Body: Tracing Medicine's Visual Culture* (Minneapolis: University of Minnesota Press, 1995); and Kapsalis, *Public Privates* for histories of science and medicine and the use of visual technologies (x-rays, etc.) to view the body's "interior."

54. Like performance artists Carolee Schneemann, Linda Montano, Cindy Sherman, and Annie Sprinkle, Hatoum used her body—and, in particular, the interior of her body—as a stage on which to complicate traditions of constructing the female body as a signifier of medical knowledge. Hatoum's use of her own body parts (fluids, nail clippings, hair, etc.) carved her mark in the feminist art world. Janine Antoni, "Mona Hatoum," *BOMB* 63 (Spring 1998), accessed April 25, 2015, http://bombmagazine.org/article/2130/

55. Ibid.

56. Schneider, *Explicit Body*, 72.

57. The problem, as de Lauretis famously put it, is that the female form is problematically "unrepresentable except as representation" (*Technologies of Gender*, 20).

58. Schneider, *Explicit Body*, 23.

59. Ibid., 116 (emphasis added).

60. Diamond, *Unmaking Mimesis*, 13. Diamond cannily studies Charcot's "theatre of hysteria" and Freud's consequent treatments of female hysterics in order to build a theory of what she calls "realism's hysteria." Finding an uncanny mirror in Freud's emphasis on "confession" as a means of converting hysterics, Diamond traces the archetypal transformation of a hysterical, sexually overexpressive woman in melodrama and realist theater into a socially acceptable, docile picture of femininity (or a forever pathologized fallen woman) through the process of confession.

61. Ibid., 14.

62. See Irigaray, *Speculum*, 144–45; and, Kapsalis, *Public Privates*.

63. James Parry, "Finding the Essence: Mona Hatoum," *Canvas: Art and Culture from the Middle East and Arab World* 6:1 (2010): 128.

64. Like many of her works, *Deep Throat* employed furniture as a means of inviting the viewer into the scene: "The sculptures based on furniture are very much about the body too, they encourage the viewer to mentally project themselves onto the objects" (Antoni, "Mona Hatoum").

65. While Hatoum has dismissed the idea that her work is a product of her cultural background—"As if I have a recipe and I can actually isolate the Arab ingredient, the woman ingredient, the Palestinian ingredient. People often expect tidy definitions of otherness, as if identity is something fixed and easily definable"—she has also reflected that her experience of exile has driven her to create works that represent and physicalize "a sense of dislocation" and overlapping identities. For example, she titled *Corps Étranger*, which means "foreign body," to invoke multiple meanings: alien object of endoscopic camera or body of a foreigner (Antoni, "Mona Hatoum").

66. Ibid.

67. Although it was hosted by an art gallery, *Eyes of Laura* was created to be exhibited and viewed online in private domestic and work spaces rather than art institutions. On this basis, it has been part of two online exhibitions: *Subversive Souvenirs*, produced by the Toronto-based Gallery TPW with the Virtual Museum of Canada in 2006; and *revolutionsonline*, part of the Sydney Biennale in Australia in 2008. See DOCAM Research Alliance, "Janet Cardiff: *Eyes of Laura*, 2004," accessed July 10,

2010, http://www.docam.ca/en/component/content/article/351-janet-cardiff-eyes-of-laura-2004.html

68. Janet Cardiff, "Eyes of Laura," accessed August 26, 2010, http://www.eyesoflaura.org/

69. See the technological specifications involved in DOCAM (Documentation and Conservation of the Media Arts Heritage), "Janet Cardiff."

70. *Eyes of Laura* stayed current for a number of years by resetting after each cycle of diary entries was complete. According to its designers, "[T]he website was launched on September 1, 2004. . . . The blog postings run for a nine-month period; the website then sits dormant for three months until it is restarted with the first posting" (ibid.).

71. Cardiff, "Eyes of Laura."

72. Ibid.

73. Irigaray referred to this linguistic prison as "phallogocentric language" in *This Sex Which Is Not One.*

74. Silverman, *Acoustic Mirror,* 31.

75. Cixous, "Laugh," 875.

76. Silverman, *Acoustic Mirror,* 38.

77. Ibid., 186. Consequently, Silverman and Doane both developed taxonomies of the female voice in film; these taxonomies, though slightly different in aim, each correlated the degree to which a female voice can resist patriarchal control to its degree of (dis)embodiment. See Mary Ann Doane, "The Voice in the Cinema: The Articulation of Body and Space," in *Film Sound: Theory and Practice,* ed. Elisabeth Weis and John Belton (New York: Columbia University Press, 1985), 40–43; and Silverman *Acoustic Mirror,* 46–54, 58–65.

78. Sjogren, *Into the Vortex,* 2. Sjogren argues that Doane and Silverman mapped the female voice in film in ways that foreclosed the possibility of agency for it within the image structure of film.

79. Sjogren chose the term "voice-off" to avoid the connotation that sound is merely *layered over*—and thus relegated to the same processes of subjection as—the filmic image: "Whereas 'over' suggests a top 'layer' or cloak of some kind, 'off' connotes otherness—a distinctness that moves alongside, 'elsewhere.' In this sense, 'off' best evokes the tension of a dialectic to the image, a vital relationship to preserve in descriptions of the voice" (ibid., 6).

80. In "When the Woman Looks," Williams argued that when viewing scenes of terror onscreen "little boys and men make it a point of honor to look, while little girls and grown women cover their eyes. . . . [T]here are excellent reasons for this refusal of women to look—not least of which that she is often asked to bear witness to her own powerlessness in the face of rape, mutilation and murder." Linda Williams, "When the Woman Looks," in *(Re)Vision: Essays in Feminist Film Criticism,* ed. Mary Ann Doane, Patricia Mellencamp, and Linda Williams (Los Angeles: American Film Institute, 1984), 83. Doane, writing in the same edited volume, put it similarly, observing that "the woman's exercise of an active investigating gaze can only be simultaneous with her own victimization." Mary Ann Doane, "The 'Woman's Film': Possession and Address," in *(Re)Vision: Essays in Feminist Film Criticism,* ed. Mary Ann Doane, Patricia Mellencamp, and Linda Williams (Los Angeles: American Film Institute, 1984), 72. See also Barbara Creed, *The Monstrous-Feminine: Film, Feminism, Psychoanalysis* (London: Routledge, 1993).

81. Cardiff, "Eyes of Laura."

82. Ibid.

83. Ibid.

84. Sarah Boxer, "When Seeing Is Not Always Believing," *New York Times*, July 11, 2005, accessed July 10, 2010, http://www.nytimes.com/2005/07/11/arts/design/11laur.html

85. See Public Art Fund, "Janet Cardiff: Her Long Black Hair," accessed July 10, 2010, http://www.publicartfund.org/pafweb/projects/04/cardiff_J_04.html

86. Boxer, "When Seeing."

87. Ibid.

88. Cardiff has installed audio walks in cities around the world, including New York, Washington, DC, Montreal, Berlin, San Francisco, and London. For a list see Janet Cardiff, "Walks," accessed July 10, 2010, http://www.cardiffmiller.com/artworks/walks/index.html

89. Robertson, "Try to Walk," 36.

90. See Julia Kristeva, "Women's Time," translated by Alice Jardin, *Signs* 7:1 (Autumn 1981): 13–35; and Emily Apter, "'Women's Time' in Theory," *Differences* 21:1 (2010): 1–18.

91. This idea of surveillance drag takes its inspiration from Elizabeth Freeman's notion of "temporal drag," which plays with associations of retrogression, delay, and the pull of the past on the present (and vice versa) in the term *drag*. See Elizabeth Freeman, "Packing History, Count(er)ing Generations," *New Literary History* 31:4 (2000): 727–44.

92. Carolyn Christov-Bakargiev, *Janet Cardiff: A Survey of Works* (New York: P.S.1 Contemporary Arts Center, 2002).

93. Monica Biagioli, "Janet Cardiff the Missing Voice (Case Study B): An Audio Walk," *Artfocus* 68 (2000): 12–14. In a conversation with Canadian filmmaker Atom Egoyan, Cardiff revealed her aim to unsettle familiar habits of spectatorship: "I want the pieces to be disconcerting in several ways so that the audience can't just forget about their bodies for the duration of their involvement like we do in a film." Atom Egoyan, "Janet Cardiff," *BOMB* 79 (Spring, 2002), accessed July 10, 2010, http://bombsite.com/issues/79/articles/2463. By many accounts, she is successful, as the dominance of vision typical of filmic spectatorship is often overwhelmed by auditory stimuli on Cardiff's walks. As one reviewer of her London walk noted, "[S]uch disjunction between video and audio in some cases and correlation in others . . . [creates] a bleed-over effect: what is heard influences what is seen and vice versa" (Biagioli, "Janet Cardiff," 13). Participant responses have included terms such as *panic attack, paranoia, surreal,* and even *schizophrenic* to describe their experiences of Cardiff's walks (Christov-Bakargiev, *Janet Cardiff*; Biagioli, "Janet Cardiff").

94. Diamond, *Unmaking Mimesis*, 13–19. Irigaray has argued that "hysterical mimicry," as opposed to the "imposed mimicry" that patriarchal society expects a woman to exhibit, can become a critical tactic by means of which women can exhibit symptoms of patriarchal oppression (*Speculum*, 54). Diamond similarly described an explicitly "feminist mimesis" in which female bodies reflexively and intentionally perform the "symptoms of femininity," thereby revealing, however ironically, the ways in which the symbols of femininity are mimicked into seeming reality ("Mimesis, Mimicry," 68–70). See also Schneider, *Explicit Body*, 116–17. In *The Hysteric's Guide to the Future Female Subject*, MacCannell posited that psychoanalytic models of the hysteric and the sadomasochistic pervert quite accurately describe the masks of femininity described by Joan Riviere in 1929, which are forcibly imposed on the bodies of girls

as they are taught to become proper female subjects. Juliet Flower MacCannell, *The Hysteric's Guide to the Future Female Subject* (Minneapolis: University of Minnesota Press, 2000), 50. MacCannell argued that, as the hysteric and pervert are conditions that place women outside the law and logic of mainstream patriarchal society, these seeming pathologies can lay the groundwork for a critical and empowered femininity (42).

95. Hall, "Terror," 136.

96. Dubrofsky and Wood, "Gender."

97. Ibid., 94.

98. Dubrofksy and Wood update Mulvey's analysis of the "hermetically sealed world" of cinema into which the voyeuristic, male-coded gaze peers (Dubrofksy and Wood, "Gender," 97). They argue that Twitter is far from sealed, as "users bring others—in real time—into their private (ostensibly "real") worlds"; instead there is far more fluidity between watcher and watched, as the social media platform enables users to move easily between posting their own images and viewing the posts of others (98).

99. Dubrofksy and Wood, "Gender," 96.

100. See, for example, Magnet's *When Biometrics Fail*.

101. Dubrofksy and Wood, "Gender," 97.

Chapter 5

1. Charlie Brooker, "Be Right Back," *Black Mirror* (television Series), Channel 4, BBC, produced by Zeppotron, aired February 11, 2013.

2. See Lisa Bode, "Digital Doppelgangers," *M/C: A journal of media and culture* 8:3 (July 2005), accessed July 22, 2015, http://journal.media-culture.org.au/0507/07-bode.php. Websites (such as www.digital-double.com) educate users about "organisations whose interests range from marketing to national security . . . [that] build up a profile of who you are based on your online activity" and facilitate searches by which an individual might "discover [his or her] own digital double" (Digital-Double, accessed July 22, 2015 http://www.digital-double.com/digital-double/)

3. Nakamura, "Blaming," 221.

4. Wood and Graham, "Permeable Boundaries," 179.

5. Nakamura, "Blaming," 221.

6. Magnet, *When Biometrics Fail*, 11.

7. Ibid.

8. See Tagg, *Burden of Representation*, 66.

9. Dubrofksy and Wood, "Gender," 98.

10. As Christopher Innes defined it in "[N]aturalism tries to offer a photographic reproduction of reality in order to emphasize the material aspects of human existence." Christopher Innes, "Naturalism," in *Modern Theatre in Context*, ed. Christopher Innes, March 2003, accessed July 22, 2015, http://moderndrama.ca/crc/chrono/sup.php?id=36&print. Naturalism's paternity is often ascribed to the late-eighteenth-century literary and theatrical theorist, novelist, and playwright Émile Zola. In deep admiration of his contemporary, Édouard Manet, along with other impressionist painters, Zola espoused the artistic ideals of faithfully observing and aesthetically rendering scenes of everyday life. Émile Zola, "Preface to Therese Raquin" (1873), translated by Kathleen Boutall, in *Theatre/Theory/Theatre: The Major Critical Texts from Aristotle and Zeami to Soyinka and Havel*, edited by Daniel Gerould (New York: Applause Theatre and Cinema Books, 2000), 352.

11. In the preface to *Therese Raquin*, which he adapted from the novel, Zola wrote, "[I] tried to stress the ordinary occupations of my characters so that they shall not appear to be 'acting' but 'living' before the public" ("Preface," 355). Zola defended his theatrical work's "definite purpose of helping in the theatre the broad movement of truth and experimental knowledge which in the last century has been growing and spreading throughout the whole field of human intelligence. The impulse has been given by the new scientific methods. Because of them, naturalism has had an effect on criticism and history by submitting man and his works to an exact analysis, taking into account circumstances, environments and physical attributes" (353–54). He called the new "naturalist" movements in painting, novel writing, and, he hoped, theater, revelatory of the "newborn babe of truth," which brings with it "the power of reality" (354).

12. Émile Zola, "Naturalism in the Theatre" (1881), translated by Jane House, in *Theatre/Theory/Theatre: The Major Critical Texts from Aristotle and Zeami to Soyinka and Havel*, edited by Daniel Gerould (New York: Applause Theatre and Cinema Books, 2000),365. To foreground the relationship between the individual and his or her environment, stage director André Antoine, who directed Zola, Strindberg, Ibsen, and many other playwrights in the naturalist and realist styles in his Theatre Libre, used the stage to reproduce reality in as great and accurate detail as possible. In a particularly infamous example, when directing a production of *The Butchers* (1888) Antoine hung real, bloody meat from hooks onstage; for his production of *A Doll's House* (1889), he imported Norwegian cedar to build the set. Gabrielle Cody and Evert Sprinchorn, eds., *The Columbia Encyclopedia of Modern Drama* (New York: Columbia University Press, 2007), 474. These examples of naturalist uses of theatrical scenery, along with a strict adherence to the notion of a "fourth wall," which had simply been removed to allow the audience to peer into the onstage proceedings, express what Zola called a "continuous description" of nature.

13. Surveillance scholars Margit Sutrop and Katrin Laas-Mikko claim that "second generation biometric systems are focused on more intricate behavioral patterns, as indicated by gait or movement of the body or by biological traits, states, and conditions of the body (e.g., heat, smell, electrocardiogram, or DNA), with the aim of profiling people on the basis of prediction of their actions and behaviors," whereas earlier forms of biometric surveillance focused on "characteristics readily visible to the naked eye or ear such as the iris, face, hand geometry, shape of the ear, and voice." Margit Sutrop and Katrin Laas-Mikko, "From Identity Verification to Behavior Prediction: Ethical Implications of Second Generation Biometrics," *Review of Policy Research* 29:1 (2012): 22.

14. According to the inaugural paper introducing the system, "DeepFace: Closing the Gap to Human-Level Performance in Face Verification," presented by the developers in 2014, human facial recognition averages 97.5 percent accuracy; DeepFace has nearly achieved the same, at 97.35 percent accuracy. Yaniv Taigman et al., "DeepFace: Closing the Gap to Human-Level Performance in Face Verification," paper delivered at the conference Computer Vision and Pattern Recognition, June 24, 2014, accessed May 19, 2015, https://research.facebook.com/publications/480567225376225/deepface-closing-the-gap-to-human-level-performance-in-face-verification/. In contrast, the FBI's Next Generation Identification, which launched officially in September 2014, has an accuracy rating of 85 percent. "FBI Next Generation Identification," FBI.gov, accessed April 25, 2015, http://www.fbi.gov/about-us/cjis/fingerprints_biometrics/ngi

15. The automatic tagging feature was implemented for Facebook users in the United States in early 2015, although the program currently remains blocked by European Union regulations for users in Europe. See Victoria Woollaston, "Facebook Can Tag You in Photos AUTOMATICALLY: Social Network Starts Rolling Out DeepFace Recognition Feature," *Daily Mail*, February 9, 2015, accessed April 25, 2015, http://www.dailymail.co.uk/sciencetech/article-2946186/Facebook-soon-tag-photos-AUTOMATICALLY-Social-network-starts-rolling-DeepFace-feature.html; and John Bohannon, "Facebook Will Soon Be Able to ID You in Any Photo," *Science*, February 5, 2015, accessed April 25, 2015, http://news.sciencemag.org/social-sciences/2015/02/facebook-will-soon-be-able-id-you-any-photo

16. DeepFace is not alone in the race to augment human vision and knowledge with machine vision and interconnected data networks; another facial recognition software program called NameTag, which is being developed by the US firm Facial-Network, has proposed partnerships with wearable devices like Google Glass that could identify passersby on the street, supplying not only their names but also other information that can be gleaned from social media sites, dating websites, and criminal databases. See Bohannon, "Facebook."

17. Kathryn Conrad, "Surveillance, Gender, and the Virtual Body in the Information Age," *Surveillance & Society* 6:4 (2009): 381.

18. Magnet, *When Biometrics Fail*, 4.

19. Ibid., 5.

20. Ibid. With regard to the expansion of biometrics to border control and national security, Magnet notes that the United States' "9/11 Commission Report" of 2004 recommended biometrics as the key technology in which the state should invest as a means of defending its borders (9). Private corporations have followed suit, promoting biometrics as the primary means of assessing risk and preventing loss.

21. For an example that proves the widespread assumption that data are more reliable than the individual self-report or observation, see the report "Automatic Detection of Abnormal Behavior and Threats in Crowded Spaces," or ADABTS, which the European Union commissioned in 2007 (CORDIS, "Final Report Summary"). James Harding speculates that the study, little of which has been declassified, likely used ethnic and cultural markers to identify potential threats: "Since for 'security reasons' very little of the actual ADABTS study has been declassified, one can't help but speculate that the supposed indicators of abnormal behavior and threat also include ethnic and cultural markers that the EU decided were too politically controversial to publish openly" (Harding, "Outperforming Activism," 24).

22. The CPD received an initial grant of over two million dollars to develop a two-phase experimental program in predictive policing. As Matt Stroud wrote in *The Verge*, Chicago's "combination of headline-making homicide rates and already established data- and tech-focused policing made it a perfect fit." Matt Stroud, "The Minority Report: Chicago's New Police Computer Predicts Crimes, but Is It Racist?" *The Verge*, February 19, 2014, accessed April 25, 2015, http://www.theverge.com/2014/2/19/5419854/the-minority-report-this-computer-predicts-crime-but-is-it-racist

23. Garry F. McCarthy, "Custom Notifications in Chicago—Pilot Program," Chicago Police Department, July 2013, accessed April 25, 2015, http://directives.chicagopolice.org/directives-mobile/data/a7a57bf0–13fa59ed-26113-fa63–2e1d9a10bb-60b9ae.html?ownapi=1

24. The thrust of the program is preventative: "The custom notification will iden-

tify those at-risk individuals and reach out to advise them of the risks and consequences of their actions should they engage in criminal conduct" (ibid.). While the CPD has not shared the criteria for selection, the experts with whom it has worked assure the public that the people who end up on the "heat list" are there for a statistically defensible reason: "These are persons who the model has determined are those most likely to be involved in a shooting or homicide, with probabilities that are hundreds of times that of an ordinary citizen" (e-mail from an NIJ press liaison, published in Stroud, "Minority Report").

25. Miles Wernick, quoted in Stroud, "Minority Report."

26. Stroud, "Minority Report."

27. Simone Browne, "Digital Epidermalization: Race, Identity, Biometrics," *Critical Sociology* 36:1 (2010): 131. Although Gilroy suggested that biometric technologies (such as ultrasounds or neuroimaging) examine the body at such microscopic and intimate scales that they produce a "postracial humanism," he, too, has argued that the effects of these technologies are far from "postracial" in their interpretation and sociopolitical impact. Paul Gilroy, *Against Race: Imagining Political Culture beyond the Color Line* (Cambridge: Harvard University Press, 2000). Gilroy's concept of "epidermal thinking," which Browne employs, links epistemologies of sight and the racialized body.

28. Browne, "Digital Epidermalization," 135.

29. Lewis Gordon, "Is the Human a Teleological Suspension of Man? Phenomenological Exploration of Sylvia Wynter's Fanonian and Biodicean Reflections," in *After Man, towards the Human: Critical Essays on the Thought of Sylvia Wynter*, ed. Anthony Bogues (Kingston, Jamaica: Ian Randle, 2006), 237–57.

30. Samir Nanavati, Michael Thieme, and Raj Nanavati. *Biometrics: Identity Verification in a Networked World* (New York: Wiley & Sons, 2002): 36–37.

31. Ibid., 37.

32. Magnet, *When Biometrics Fail*, 9. See also her chapter "Criminalizing Poverty: Adding Biometrics to Welfare," 69–90.

33. Ibid., 11.

34. CORDIS, "Final Report Summary," quoted in Harding, "Outperforming Activism," 25.

35. Harding, "Outperforming Activism," 25–26.

36. Ibid.

37. Bertolt Brecht, "A Short Organum for the Theatre," in *Brecht on Theatre: The Development of an Aesthetic*, trans. John Willet (New York: Hill and Wang, 1964):.188–89. Brecht criticized naturalist pieces such as *The Weavers*, in which, he argued, the "old habits" of catharsis and passive spectatorship are maintained: "This deadweight . . . is also needed for plays like *Ghosts* and *The Weavers*, although there the social structure, in the shape of a 'setting,' presents itself as more open to question. The feelings, insights and impulses of the chief characters are forced on us, and so we learn nothing more about society than we can get from the 'setting'" (189–90).

38. Ibid., 190.

39. André Breton, *Manifestos of Surrealism*, trans. Richard Seaver and Helen R. Lane (Ann Arbor: University of Michigan Press, 1969), 6.

40. Ibid., 9.

41. Ibid., 36–38.

42. Surrealist artists such as Salvador Dali, Marcel Duchamp, Claude Cahun, and Hannah Hoch employed masks to highlight or downplay sexuality (building a kind of

androgyny that was particularly interesting to many surrealist artists) and/or to reject oppressive aspects of western culture (anything from the war to bourgeois ideals). See Louise Tythacott, *Surrealism and the Exotic* (London: Routledge, 2003).

43. Zach Blas, "Face Cages," accessed April 25, 2015, http://www.zachblas.info/projects/face-cages/

44. Ibid.

45. Ibid.

46. Artists such as Salvador Dali, Marcel Duchamp, Claude Cahun, Hannah Hoch, and Roland Penrose employed masks in their photography and painting, even wearing them at a few documented dinner parties. See David Bates, *Photography and Surrealism: Sexuality, Colonialism, and Social Dissent* (London: I. B. Tauris, 2004).

47. This aspect of surrealism has been debated for decades. In *Surrealism and the Exotic*, Louise Tythacott argued that "the movement's original anti-war stance led members to disavow nationalism, imperialism and racism, to value colonized cultures over European colonizing powers. . . . Inverting Social Darwinist hierarchies, they elevated the primitive to the top of their ladder of human creative achievement." At the same time, she concedes that "such strategies may be criticized for their romantic naivety—as a form of inverse racism." (12). David Bates, in *Photography and Surrealism*, likewise praises the surrealist critiques of colonialist practices while at the same time putting pressure on their ambivalent use of orientalism in their imagery.

48. Blas, "Facial Weaponization," accessed April 25, 2015, http://www.zachblas.info/projects/facial-weaponization-suite/

49. Ibid.

50. Ibid.

51. Blas created this series in response to several recent scientific studies showing that sexual orientation can be determined through rapid facial recognition techniques.

52. Kirstie Ball and her colleagues argued, "In the Anglo-American north, the politics of what is hidden and what is revealed are imbued with gendered and sexualised politics of heteronormativity and shame, and of vulnerability and fear" (Ball et al., "Editorial," 353).

53. Blas, "Facial Weaponization."

54. Adam Harvey, "CV Dazzle," CV Dazzle, accessed September 25, 2014, https://cvdazzle.com/

55. Ibid.

56. See Kuenzli, "Surrealism."

57. Young's blog invites anyone to host their own version of the party, for which she supplies makeup and hairstyle tips and resources. Stephanie Young, "Participate," in "Antirecognition.tumblr" (blog), accessed May 10, 2015. http://antirecognition.tumblr.com/participate. Monica McClure, a Brooklyn-based poet, hosted another Anti-surveillance Feminist Poet Hair & Makeup Party. The event was documented by Emily Raw, a photographer living and working in Brooklyn. Emily Raw, "Anti-surveillance Feminist Hair and Makeup Party," accessed May 10, 2015, http://emily-raw.com/albums/anti-surveillance-feminist-poet-hair-makeup-party/

58. Stephanie Young, *SOME NOTES ON THE ANTI-SURVEILLANCE FEMINIST POET HAIR & MAKEUP PARTY* (Oakland, CA: Dusie Press, 2014). As Ana Cecilia Alvarez wrote of the project, "More than using the gal pal party as means to challenge the omnipresent state watch, these women organised the meet to address how women police one another." Ana Cecilia Alvarez, "How to Hide from Big Brother Sur-

veillance," *Dazed,* July 2014, accessed April 15, 2015, http://www.dazeddigital.com/artsandculture/article/19131/1/artists-writers-show-how-to-hide-from-big-brother-government-surveillance

59. Young, *SOME NOTES,* 5.

60. Young's decision to throw a "hair and makeup party" draws on "traditional femme grooming rituals and female bonding" reminiscent of neighborhood gatherings of housewives, typically around themes of domesticity and feminine beauty. Young admits, "I keep wanting to say 'like a Tupperware party!' and stopping myself" (ibid., 12).

61. Ibid., 4.

62. See Snyder, "What Is Third-Wave Feminism?"

63. Nicole Lyn Pesce, "Young Women Poets Like Camille Rankine, Trisha Low, and Lisa Marie Basile Bring New Energy to World of Words," *New York Daily News,* December 20, 2013, accessed April 15, 2015, http://www.nydailynews.com/entertainment/music-arts/young-women-poets-shaking-world-words-article-1.1553019

64. Young, *SOME NOTES,* 9.

65. Ibid., 11.

66. Ibid., 9.

67. Leonardo Selvaggio, "URME Surveillance: Performing Privilege in the Face of Automation," in "Surveillance Technologies in Performance," ed. Elise Morrison, special issue, *International Journal of Performance Arts and Digital Media* 11:2 (2015): 165–84. His experiments with open sourcing identity first took the form of a project called YouAreMe.net, in which users could log on and use Selvaggio's identity to send e-mails, perform as an avatar, appear in pictures, or "friend" people on Facebook.

68. The URME Surveillance Identity Prosthetic resin mask is available through Selvaggio's partners at ThatsMyFace.com, the website of a company that creates three-dimensional models of a person's face from a single image and then prints that face as a wearable mask. As the resin version retails for two hundred dollars, Selvaggio also made a paper version that users can download and print for a dollar. Although the paper version is not as successful a means of "passing" as Leo Selvaggio, as human passersby will be able to see clearly that it is a two-dimensional mask, facial detection software will still identify the user as Leo Selvaggio (ibid.).

69. Ibid.

70. Ibid.

71. Martin Esslin, *The Theatre of the Absurd* (London: Penguin Books, 1961), 23.

72. Describing the work of absurdist practitioners such as Eugène Ionesco, Samuel Beckett, and Jean Genet, Esslin wrote, "Theatre of the Absurd strives to express its sense of the senselessness of the human condition and the inadequacy of the rational approach by the open abandonment of rational devices and discursive thought" (ibid., 24).

73. Ionesco, quoted in ibid., 138.

74. Selvaggio, "URME Surveillance." As Selvaggio describes in this essay, URME Mirror was another early experiment with grafting his face onto another person's body.

75. Ibid.

76. Esslin, *Theatre of the Absurd,* 132.

77. Selvaggio, "URME Surveillance."

78. Luksch, "Manifesto."

79. "Data Protection Act, 1998." UK Government Legislation. Accessed April 15, 2015. http://www.legislation.gov.uk/ukpga/1998/29/section/1

80. Luksch's work has helped to pioneer a genre known as surveillance cinema, named for the artists' uses of publicly installed surveillance cameras. There are several works I discuss elsewhere—namely, *Eyes of Laura,* discussed in chapter 4, *I Love Alaska* featured in chapter 3, and *Evidence Locker* in chapter 2—that also fit within this category, as they utilize cinematic referents and conventions to tell stories about surveillance in daily life. Surveillance cinema draws on representational strategies of the more established practice of "found footage filmmaking." See Martin Zeilinger, "Appropriation and the Authoring Function of Camera Surveillance in Manu Luksch's *Faceless,*" in *Eyes Everywhere: The Global Growth of Camera Surveillance,* ed. Aaron Doyle, Randy Lippert, and David Lyon (London: Routledge, 2012). See also Christopher Heron, "Surveillance Camera Cinema (*Faceless, Der Riese, Influenza*), Video Essay (Issue 1)," *The Seventh Art: Worth Viewing,* February 4, 2012. Accessed February 24, 2015, http://www.theseventhart.org/main/surveillance-camera-cinema-faceless-der-riese-influenza-video-essay-issue-1/

81. Manu Luksch, *Faceless,* film (2007), produced by Amour Fou Film Produktion and Ambient Information Systems, accessed February 24, 2014, http://www.ambienttv.net/content/?q=facelessthemovie

82. Drawing on theories of epic poetry by Goethe and Schiller, Brecht aligned himself with the epic narrative, through which events can be portrayed as totally past and therefore evaluated with more critical distance. See Bertolt Brecht, "The Modern Theatre is the Epic Theatre" in *Brecht on Theatre: The Development of an Aesthetic,* trans. John Willet (New York: Hill and Wang, 1964): 33–42). Willett translated the German *Verfremdungseffekt* as "alienation," although it has also been translated as the "estrangement" effect.

83. Brecht, "Short Organum," 190.

84. Ibid.

85. Ibid., 198–201.

86. Thomas Stubblefield theorized the participatory labor of *Faceless,* along with *I Love Alaska,* in "'Moving' Images." I discuss his perspective on this in chapter 3.

87. See Zeilinger, "Appropriation"; and Heron, "Surveillance Camera Cinema."

88. *Readymade* is a term used at the time to distinguish between manufactured and handmade items available to consumers. Although Duchamp resisted defining *readymade art* as a practice, several definitions that circulated in dadaist and surrealist publications of the time have been attributed to him, including "an ordinary object elevated to the dignity of a work of art by the mere choice of an artist" (first published in André Breton and Paul Éluard's *Dictionnaire abrégé du Surréalisme*). See Hector Obalk, "The Unfindable Readymade," *Tout-fait: The Marcel Duchamp Studies Online Journal* 1:2 (May 2000), accessed April 25, 2015, http://www.toutfait.com/issues/issue_2/Articles/obalk.html

89. The theory behind the readymade was explained in an article, anonymous but almost certainly by Duchamp himself, in the May 1917 issue of the avant-garde magazine *The Blind Man,* which was published by Duchamp and several friends: "Whether Mr Mutt with his own hands made the fountain or not has no importance. He CHOSE it. He took an ordinary article of life, and placed it so that its useful significance disappeared under the new title and point of view—created a new thought for that object." Tate Museum Online Resources, "Readymade," accessed April 25, 2015, http://www.tate.org.uk/learn/online-resources/glossary/r/readymade

90. Browne, "Digital Epidermalization," 136.

91. For an engaging description and analysis of how artists, scientists, and military entities are experimenting with "brain surveillance" devices such as the Emotiv headset, see Ellen Pearlman, "The Brain as Site Specific Surveillant Performative Space," in "Surveillance Technologies in Performance," ed. Elise Morrison, special issue, *International Journal of Performance Arts and Digital Media* 11:2 (2015): 219–34.

92. Users enter data about their body type, hairstyle, eye color, and so on to create an avatar that can be used to try on clothes and glasses, visualize weight loss or breast enhancements, and serve as a representative on social networking sites. See, for example, corpo.myvirtualmodel.com. There are numerous permutations of this service, through which users can model weight loss, different haircuts and eye colors, or even what their unborn son or daughter might look like. See modelmydiet.com; joyofclothes.com/my-account/model-me; and myvirtualchild.com, accessed April 10, 2015.

93. Conrad, "Surveillance," 382.

94. By tracking the keywords that individuals input into the Google search engine, the websites they browse, and the content of personal e-mails, Google developed AdWords as a systematic means of providing its advertisers with real time data that would help them identify and contact potential customers. Google, "AdWords," accessed April 10, 2015, https://support.google.com/adwords/answer/1704410?hl=en

95. Erica Scourti, "Life in AdWords" (2012–13), accessed April 10, 2015, http://ericascourti.com/art_pages/life_in_adwords.html

96. In its description of AdWords, Google entices advertisers with the logic of targeted advertising: "A few important things set AdWords apart from other kinds of advertising. Using AdWords, you can: Reach people at the precise moment they're searching for what you offer. Your ad is displayed to people who are already searching for the kinds of products and services you offer" (Google, "AdWords"). See also Jason Mick, "Google: Yes, We 'Read' Your Gmail," *Daily Tech*, August 15, 2013, accessed April 25, 2015, http://www.dailytech.com/Google+Yes+we+Read+Your+Gmail/article33184.htm

97. Nakamura, "Blaming," 224. She argues also that female users and users from other sexually marginalized and stigmatized groups are overwhelmingly the subjects of social and political surveillance and online harassment and victimization.

98. Breton, *Manifestos*, 26.

99. Ibid., 24.

100. Scourti, "Life in AdWords."

101. Ibid.

102. John Cheney-Lippold refers to developments in algorithmic identity production by companies such as Google and Quantcast as a form of "soft biopolitics." John Cheney-Lippold, "A New Algorithmic Identity: Soft Biopolitics and the Modulation of Control," *Theory, Culture, and Society* 28:6 (2011): 164–81.

103. As Emily Rosamond observed of the piece, Scourti illustrates the "self as product." Using Scourti's piece, along with SWAMP's *McService* (2003) and Hasan Elahi's *Tracking Transience* (2005–), Rosamond traces a trajectory in the processes by which surveillance technologies "characterize" individuals throughout the years between two watershed moments—the 9/11 terrorist attacks in 2001 and the Edward Snowden–NSA revelations in 2013—from "self as threat, to self as set, to self as product" (Rosamond, "Technologies," 148).

104. The UK "cookie law" was revised in 2012, taking effect in early 2013. "In line

with recent changes in European legislation, UK law now requires website operators to ask for a website user's permission when placing certain kinds of cookies on their devices for the first time. Where consent is required, the law states that it should be "informed consent." This increases the onus on website operators to ensure that visitors understand what cookies are and why website operators and others want to use them." International Chamber of Commerce, United Kingdom, "ICC UK Cookie Guide," November 2012, accessed April 25, 2015, http://www.cookielaw.org/media/1096/icc_uk_cookiesguide_revnov.pdf. As a result, services such as Google could no longer track a user's keywords without his or her informed consent (previously it had been an "opt-out" arrangement).

105. Scourti, "Life in AdWords."

106. Erica Scourti, *(End of) Life in AdWords,* video (2013), recorded by Emily Candela, accessed April 10, 2015, https://vimeo.com/59354268

107. See Bilal and Lydersen (*Shoot an Iraqi*), as well as the artists' descriptions on Bilal's website, wafaabilal.com.

108. Antonin Artaud "The Theater and Cruelty" (1933), trans. Mary Caroline Richards, in *Theatre/Theory/Theatre: The Major Critical Texts from Aristotle and Zeami to Soyinka and Havel, ed.* Daniel Gerould (New York: Applause Theatre and Cinema Books, 2000): 435.

109. Ibid.

110. For a detailed analysis of Artaud's investments in masses, crowds, and spectacles in theatrical performance (and the relationship of these strategies to the politics and aesthetics of fascism), see Kimberly Jannarone, *Artaud and His Doubles* (Ann Arbor: University of Michigan Press, 2012), in particular "Section II: Audience, Mass, Crowd," 75–188.

111. Artaud, "Theater and Cruelty," 437.

112. Quoted in Daniel Gerould, "Antonin Artaud," in *Theatre/Theory/Theatre: The Major Critical Texts from Aristotle and Zeami to Soyinka and Havel,* ed. Daniel Gerould. (New York: Applause Theatre and Cinema Books, 2000): 433.

113. The piece was commissioned as part of the exhibition *Told/Untold/Retold,* which inaugurated the Mathaf: Arab Museum of Modern Art in Doha (Bilal, "3rdi").

114. Ashley Rawlings, "Remote Repercussions: Wafaa Bilal," *ArtAsiaPacific,* no. 72 (2011), accessed September 25, 2014, http://artasiapacific.com/Magazine/72/RemoteRepercussionsWafaaBilal

115. "It's a bit ironic to be told by the photography department not to take photographs," Bilal says, "but NYU is a private institution and they are entitled to protect the privacy of their students. It's a difficult line for them to tread" (ibid.).

116. Bilal, "3rdi."

117. Artaud, "Letters on Language" (1933), trans. Mary Caroline Richards, in *Theatre/Theory/Theatre: The Major Critical Texts from Aristotle and Zeami to Soyinka and Havel,* ed. Daniel Gerould (New York: Applause Theatre and Cinema Books, 2000): 441.

118. Louise Tythacott described this as a kind of "inverse racism" (*Surrealism,* 12). See also Olga Taxidou, *The Mask: A Periodical Performance by Edward Gordon Craig* (London: Routledge, 2013), 82–85.

119. Antonin Artaud, "The Theater and Its Double" (1938), trans. Mary Caroline Richards, in *Theatre/Theory/Theatre: The Major Critical Texts from Aristotle and Zeami to Soyinka and Havel,* ed. Daniel Gerould (New York: Applause Theatre and Cinema Books, 2000), 438.

120. Ibid., 440.

121. Gerould, "Antonin Artaud," 433.
122. Rawlings, "Remote Repercussions."
123. Brockett and Hildy, *History of the Theatre*, 420–21.
124. Bilal, "3rdi."
125. Rawlings, "Remote Repercussions."
126. Technologies such as the Go-Pro, a series of hardy, wearable cameras, have been marketed as a means of "life-logging" and amateur documentary filmmaking. The tag lines for advertising have included "Be a Hero" and "Share your world." See the company's website, *www.gopro.com.*
127. Walter Benjamin, "Theses on the Philosophy of History," in *Illuminations: Walter Benjamin Essays and Reflections*, ed. Hannah Arendt, trans. Harry Zohn (New York: Pantheon, 1968), 249.
128. For a discussion of naturalism as part of the avant-garde, modernist movement, see Dan Rabellato's essay "Naturalism and Symbolism: Early Modernist Practice," in *Routledge Drama Anthology and Sourcebook: From Modernism to Contemporary Performance*, ed. Maggie Gale and John Deeney (Abingdon, UK: Routledge, 2010), 6–24. Rabellato seeks to recuperate naturalism as part of the avant-garde, experimental theater movement of the early twentieth century.
129. James Harding, *Ghosts of the Avant-Garde(s): Exorcising Experimental Theater and Performance* (Ann Arbor: University of Michigan Press, 2013), 26.
130. See Schecher, "9/11," and my discussion of it in the "Introduction" to this book.
131. Selvaggio, "URME Surveillance."
132. Linking the simple tactics of the SCP performance of *Amnesia* (2002) to the complex conditions of biometric surveillance, Harding writes, "[A]cts that, without our consent, cast each and every one of us into sorted categories over which we have little if any control, those systems literally establish who we are and assign us identities of which we can have no recollection because those identities are stored in memory—in data banks—to which we have not been granted access. This is the new amnesia" ("Outperforming Activism," 29).

Chapter 6

1. De Certeau, *Practice*, 92.
2. Pilobolus Dance Theater, *Seraph* (2010), video of performance, published May 14, 2013, accessed May 20, 2014, https://www.youtube.com/watch?v=pT0K8yJhHpo
3. In fact drones have been employed in military missions throughout the history of aviation, but the twenty-first century marks a sharp increase in their technological capabilities and the military's investment in them. While drones have a longer history than is commonly known, with the first ones having taken flight in the early 1900s as part of early experiments in aviation, their use by the military increased by several orders of magnitude in the decade after 9/11. In 2011, the *New York Times* reported, "The Pentagon now has some 7,000 aerial drones, compared with fewer than 50 a decade ago. Within the next decade the Air Force anticipates a decrease in manned aircraft but expects its number of "multirole" aerial drones like the Reaper—the ones that spy as well as strike—to nearly quadruple, to 536. Already the Air Force is training more remote pilots, 350 this year alone, than fighter and bomber pilots combined." Elisabeth Bumiller and Thom Shanker, "War Evolves with Drones, Some

Tiny as Bugs," *New York Times*, June 19, 2011, accessed May 5, 2014, http://www.
nytimes.com/2011/06/20/world/20drones.html?pagewanted=all&_r=0)

4. See Medea Benjamin, *Drone Warfare: Killing by Remote Control* (London: Verso,
2012); and P. W. Singer, "Robots at War: The New Battlefield," *Wilson Quarterly* 33:1
(2009): 30–48, accessed October 9, 2012, http://www.jstor.org/stable/40262238

5. However, the potential, and likelihood, that domestic drones could soon be
armed is already evident in the legal discourses framing their use. According to a Customs and Border Protection report obtained by the Electronic Frontier Foundation
through a Freedom of Information Act lawsuit, the Customs and Border Protection
agency has actively considered adding weapons to Predator drones currently used on
the US-Mexico border to search for illegal immigrants and drug trafficking. A section of the heavily redacted 107-page report that deals with the equipment mounted
on the drones states, "Additional payload upgrades could include expendables or
non-lethal weapons designed to immobilize [targets of interest]." Electronic Frontier
Foundation, "Customs and Border Protection 2010 Drone Concept of Operations
Report for Congress" (2010), accessed August 29, 2013, https://www.eff.org/docu-
ment/customs-border-protection-2010-drone-concept-operations-report-congress

6. On May 9, 2014, the television network CNN reported a near crash between a
commercial airliner and a small, camouflaged UAV flying at 2,300 feet (a height currently illegal for unregistered UAVs). Jim Williams, the head of the FAA's Unmanned
Aircraft Systems (UAS) office, reported, "The pilot said that the UAS was so close
to his jet that he was sure he had collided with it. . . . Thankfully, inspection to the
airliner after landing found no damage. But this may not always be the case." Greg
Botelho, "FAA Official: Drone, Jetliner Nearly Collided over Florida," *CNN*, May 11,
2014, accessed May 28, 2014, http://www.cnn.com/2014/05/09/travel/unmanned-
drone-danger/. Lawmakers, cultural theorists, and technology experts have imagined the myriad possibilities for drone hacking, predicting a range of scenarios from
coordinated terrorist attacks to mischievous commandeering of delivery drones. See
Katia Moskovitch, "Are Drones the Next Target for Hackers?," *BBC*, February 6, 2014,
accessed May 28, 2014, http://www.bbc.com/future/story/20140206-can-drones-be-
hacked

7. See Jason Reagan, "Drone Sales Figures for 2014," *Dronelife, January 24, 2015*
accessed June 24, 2015, http://dronelife.com/2015/01/24/drone-sales-figures-
2014-hard-navigate/

8. Speculations about where drone regulations are headed, particularly in the
commercial realm, are frequent. See, for example, David Morgan, "FAA Expects to
Clear U.S. Commercial Drones within a Year," Reuters, June 17, 2015, accessed July
24, 2015, http://www.reuters.com/article/2015/06/17/us-usa-drones-congress-
idUSKBN0OX1P020150617

9. "Law Enforcement Agencies Using Drones List, Map," *Governing Data*,
accessed May 13, 2013, http://www.governing.com/gov-data/safety-justice/drones-
state-local-law-enforcement-agencies-license-list.html; Jason Mick, "Dept. of Homeland Sec Brings War Blimps to the Mexican Border," *Daily Tech*, August 15, 2012,
accessed August 29, 2013 http://www.dailytech.com/Dept+of+Homeland+Sec+Brin
gs+War+Blimps+to+the+Mexican+Border/article25415.htm

10. Matt Smith, "Flying Drone Peers into Japan's Damaged Reactors," *CNN*,
April 10, 2011, accessed 11 June 2014, http://www.cnn.com/2011/WORLD/asiap-
cf/04/10/japan.nuclear.reactors/

11. Dave Powell, "UK Aerial Photography Law and CAA rules for drone use," Aerial Photography Wales, December 16, 2014, accessed 11 May 2016, http://aerialphotographywales.com/uk-aerial-photography-law-and-caa-rules-for-drone-use/; Nick Hopkins, "Revealed: Who Can Fly Drones in UK Airspace," *The Guardian,* January 25, 2013, accessed August 24, 2013, http://www.guardian.co.uk/world/2013/jan/25/who-can-fly-drones-uk-airspace;

12. Jason Koebler, "Google to Fund Anti-poaching Drones in Asia, Africa," *U.S. News & World Report,* December 7, 2012, accessed July 11, 2014, www.usnews.com/news/articles/2012/12/07/google-to-fund-anti-poaching-drones-in-asia-africa

13. See, for example, Bigad Shaban, "Drone Degrees: Universities Train Students for Future of Flight," *CBS News,* February 5, 2014, accessed February 17, 2015, http://www.cbsnews.com/news/drone-degrees-universities-train-students-for-high-tech-future-of-flight/; and Timothy Reuter, "Participate in an Upcoming Drone Art Show with the DC Area Drone User Group," *DIY Drones (blog),* March 25, 2013, accessed May 13, 2013, http://diydrones.com/profiles/blogs/participate-in-the-drone-art-show-from-the-dc-area-drone-user

14. Jason Gilbert, "Tacocopter Aims to Deliver Tacos Using Unmanned Drone Helicopters," *Huffington Post,* March 23, 2012, accessed May 13, 2013, http://www.huffingtonpost.com/2012/03/23/tacocopter-startup-delivers-tacos-by-unmanned-drone-helicopter_n_1375842.html. See also the company website, www.tacocopter.com.

15. Amazon representatives acknowledged that it will take several years for such a service to be approved by the FAA, but this did not prevent them from publicizing their cutting-edge plans. See "Amazon Prime Air," Amazon, accessed May 9, 2014, http://www.amazon.com/b?node=8037720011

16. See the *Drone Wars* and *Stop Drones* blogs at www.dronewars.net and www.stopdrones.com, accessed August 29, 2013. Josh Begley has been tweeting the location of every reported drone strike in Iraq since 2002 through his Twitter feed, "@Dronestrike" (www.twitter.com/dronestream). British visual artist James Bridle began posting images of drone strikes in the Middle East on the popular social media platform Instagram in 2012. He calls this project Dronestagram. James Bridle, "Dronestagram" (2012–), accessed August 29, 2013, http://dronestagram.tumblr.com/

17. Jason Koebler, "City in Virginia Becomes First to Pass Anti-drone Legislation," *US News & World Report,* February 5, 2013, accessed May 13, 2013, http://www.usnews.com/news/articles/2013/02/05/city-in-virginia-becomes-first-to-pass-anti-drone-legislation-. However, these local laws may be more symbolic than practical, as they do not prohibit federal and state drones from flying in city air space.

18. M. Ryan Calo, "The Drone as Privacy Catalyst," *Stanford Law Review Online,* 64:29 (2011): 30, accessed May 15, 2013, http://www.stanfordlawreview.org/online/drone-privacy-catalyst. The "Internet age" has certainly hosted its share of privacy debates and civil liberties concerns; however, concerns over potential privacy violations in Internet data mining, facial recognition technology, GPS enabled cell phones, and networked databases of personal financial and medical information have not galvanized any similar level of legislative reform. Calo suggests that, in contrast, drones may once again provide the highly visible and tangible violations of personal privacy that could motivate more comprehensive privacy legislation reforms (30).

19. Oliver Wainwright, "Spraycopter: The Drone That Does Graffiti," *The Guardian,* April 21, 2014, accessed April 24, 2014, http://www.theguardian.com/artand-

design/architecture-design-blog/2014/apr/21/drone-does-graffiti-street-art; "German Railways to Test Anti-graffiti Drones," *BBC News,* May 27, 2013, accessed April 24, 2014, http://www.bbc.com/news/world-europe-22678580

20. Dylan Love, "British Criminals Are Using Drones to Steal Marijuana," *Business Insider,* April 23, 2014, accessed April 23, 2014, http://www.businessinsider.com/british-using-drones-to-steal-marijuana-2014-4

21. Nevarez and Rivera, "Lowdrone."

22. James Bridle, "Drone Shadow," accessed May 7, 2013, http://shorttermmemoryloss.com/portfolio/project/drone-shadows/. The project was restaged in Istanbul in October 2012 for the Adhocracy and Istanbul Design Biennial.

23. Josh Begley, "Metadata," accessed September 24, 2014, http://metadata.joshbegley.com/

24. Christina Bonnington and Spencer Ackerman, "Apple Rejects App That Tracks U.S. Drone Strikes," *Wired,* August 30, 2012, accessed September 24, 2014, http://www.wired.com/2012/08/drone-app/

25. Robinson Meyer, "A New iPhone App Catalogues and Maps U.S. Drone Killings," *The Atlantic,* February 11, 2014, accessed September 24, 2014, http://www.theatlantic.com/technology/archive/2014/02/a-new-iphone-app-catalogues-and-maps-us-drone-killings/283713/

26. Bonnington and Ackerman, "Apple."

27. Asher J. Kohn, "An Architectural Defense from Drones," *Fraser—Extreme Architecture,* Spring 2012, accessed August 25, 2013, http://www.scribd.com/doc/104135119/An-Architectural-Defense-From-Drones

28. Ibid., 2.

29. Kohn cites as one of his influences Safdie's design of Building 67 in Canada, which is notorious for its chaotic design (ibid., 4), as well as the work of several Dutch designers.

30. Ibid.

31. Dana Priest, "Government Surveillance Spurs Americans to Fight Back," *Washington Post,* August 14, 2013, accessed June 2, 2014, http://www.washingtonpost.com/lifestyle/style/government-surveillance-spurs-americans-to-fight-back/2013/08/14/edea430a-0522-11e3-a07f-49ddc7417125_story_1.html

32. Adam Harvey, "Stealth Wear: New Designs for Counter-Surveillance," *ah projects,* accessed May 9, 2013, http://ahprojects.com/projects/stealth-wear/

33. Ibid.

34. Adam Harvey, "Off Pocket," *ah projects* accessed June 15, 2014, http://ahprojects.com/projects/off-pocket/

35. Harvey, "Stealth Wear."

36. De Certeau, *Practice,* 93.

37. Hijabs occupy a particularly vexed place in feminist and cultural discourses. The act of covering up in public has raised a great deal of controversy in both Islamist countries (such as Iran, Saudi Arabia, and Afghanistan) and countries that host a diaspora of Muslims. Many women who choose to wear hijabs do so for reasons of modesty, which, they argue, allows them to enter public society without the burden of sexualization that frequently accompanies female bodies. Judith Lorber, "Heroes, Warriors, and *Burqas*: A Feminist Sociologist's Reflections on September 11," *Sociological Forum* 17:3 (2002): 389. However, in places like Iran after the 1979 revolution and Afghanistan under Taliban rule after 1996, wearing a hijab has also entailed great social, political, and economic sacrifices for the women who wear them, although

some have argued that wearing hijabs has raised the social status of typically poorer and less educated religious women. Shahin Gerami and Melodye Lehnerer, "Women's Agency and Household Diplomacy: Negotiating Fundamentalism," *Gender and Society* 15 (2001): 556–73.

38. As Gerami, writing about new models of masculinity and heroism that emerged after the Iranian revolution, described it, "In the visual culture that flourished after the revolution, a new genre appeared, devoted to the war efforts and the martyrs. The martyr is a young, unmarried (virgin, innocent) man, fearless and strong. He is depicted with eyes cast forward to *jihad* and the blessed state of martyrdom. His hair is dark and held back with a bandana with Qur'anic inscriptions. If depicted in full figure, he wears white, the color of a coffin, while holding a gun. Sometimes he is depicted in the foreground, leading a group of women and older male martyrs; or he is depicted in the foreground of fully veiled women and young girls, protecting them and the country's honor." Shahin Gerami, "Mullahs, Martyrs, and Men: Conceptualizing Masculinity in the Islamic Republic of Iran," *Men and Masculinities* 5:3 (2003): 267.

39. Harvey, "Stealth Wear."

40. Harvey has been caught before in the economic and cultural gap between art-house high fashion and everyday consumer markets, and he has made an effort to make other of his countersurveillance devices more available to a broad base of consumers. For example, he has worked to meet high levels of demand for the Off Pocket through a kick-starter campaign; the product, which currently retails for eighty dollars, has repeatedly sold out through his online "privacy gift shop" (see http://privacygiftshop.com/products/off-pocket, accessed June 15, 2014).

41. Margot Badran, "Islamic Feminism," *Al-Ahram Weekly Online*, January 17–23, 2002, accessed July 19, 2014, http://weekly.ahram.org.eg/2002/569/cu1.htm

42. *Zoologic* was performed in April 2015 as part of the First Works Providence arts festival in Providence, Rhode Island. The piece dramatized Thalia Field's text Zoologic (2004) and was devised by Artistic Director Jamie Jewett, composer/media artist R. Luke DuBois, and myself in collaboration with performers Shura Baryshnikov, Sydney Skybetter, Kathryn McNamara, and Ali Brodsky. For more on this work, see http://lostwax.org/work/zoologic/

43. Jason Koebler, "Dances with Drones," *US News & World Report*, May 15, 2013, accessed April 23, 2014, http://www.usnews.com/news/articles/2013/05/15/dance-company-incorporates-drones-into-performance

44. Robin James, "Music for Drones," *It's Her Factory (blog)*, February 26, 2013, accessed May 29, 2014, http://www.its-her-factory.com/2013/02/music-for-drones-introduction/

45. Their "ensemble" will include "four toy drones that mimic the composition of a traditional string quartet: two smallish 'violins,' a medium-sized 'viola,' and a large 'cello'" (ibid.).

46. Assor chose to name his work *Ophan*, a Hebrew word meaning "spoked wheel," which also refers to a kind of angel. Nadav Assor, "Ophan" (2014), accessed October 28, 2014, http://www.nadassor.net/2014/10/ophan/

47. Ars Electronica Futurelab, *49 Quadcopters in the Night*, Voestalpine Klangwolke festival, Linz, Austria, 2012, video of performance, accessed May 9, 2013, http://www.youtube.com/watch?feature=player_embedded&v=ShGl5rQK3ew

48. James, "Music for Drones." She went on, "Industrial music is built on the idea of making pop music with and from the means of military-industrial production, and

especially the apparently non-musical noises they generate. How might quadcopter drone sounds be the basis of an industrial/EBM [elecronic body music] track? How can we put our use of drones in postmillennial industrial music in conversation with the use of machine gun sounds in 90s industrial music (e.g., sampled sounds from film, or mimicked by blast drumming)?"

49. Conceived by Rajeev Basu, the fifteen drones were conceived by invited guest artists, including eBoy, Supermundane, Adhemas Batista, Kyle Platts, Robin van Wijk, Michael Willis, Simon Thompson, Craig & Karl, Ian Stevenson, Antonio Ladrillo, and Saiman Chow. Rajeev Basu, *Drones of New York* (2013), created for the Museum of the Moving Image, New York, accessed May 7, 2013, http://www.dronesofnewyork.com/

50. See, for example, the website of Skydrone, a leading high-end brand, which offers an FPV package. www.skydrone.aero/fpv

51. According to the rules of the Academy of Model Aeronautics (AMA) for "Radio Controlled Model Aircraft Operation," users utilizing FPV systems are required to have an "AMA FPV spotter next to him/her maintaining VLOS [visual line of sight] with the FPV aircraft throughout its flight." Academy of Model Aeronautics, "Radio Controlled Model Aircraft Operation: Utilizing 'First Person View' Systems," January 2014, accessed May 15, 2014, http://www.modelaircraft.org/files/550.pdf. However, word on the street is that the majority of FPV pilots disregard this dictum and choose to fly solo and/or beyond the line of sight.

52. Tretch5000, *Detroit Mix FPV*, June 22, 2012, YouTube video, accessed May 17, 2014, https://www.youtube.com/watch?v=LkMiIT1VG98

53. Walter Benjamin, *Charles Baudelaire: A Lyric Poet in the Era of High Capitalism*, trans. Harry Zohn (London: Verso, 1983), 54.

54. Charles Baudelaire, *The Painter of Modern Life* (New York: Da Capo Press, 1964). Baudelaire referred to the flaneur as "the painter of modern life," a description that Susan Sontag to a pedestrian photographer: "The photographer is an armed version of the solitary walker reconnoitering, stalking, cruising the urban inferno, the voyeuristic stroller who discovers the city as a landscape of voluptuous extremes. Adept of the joys of watching, connoisseur of empathy, the flâneur finds the world 'picturesque.'" Susan Sontag, *On Photography* (London: Penguin Books, 1977), 55.

55. Benjamin, *Charles Baudelaire*, 54.

56. Alexis Madrigal, "Detroit 'Ruin Porn' from a Drone," *The Atlantic*, July 17, 2012, accessed May 9, 2014, http://www.theatlantic.com/technology/archive/2012/07/detroit-ruin-porn-from-a-drone/259944/

57. Donna Haraway, "A Cyborg Manifesto: Science, Technology, and Socialist-Feminism in the Late Twentieth Century," in *Simians, Cyborgs and Women: The Reinvention of Nature* (New York: Routledge, 1991), 149.

58. De Certeau, *Practice*, 92. For de Certeau, the "lust to be a viewpoint" is ascribed to the position of panoptic power situated atop the World Trade Center and gazing down at the streets in which life happens at a separate and invisible level. He critiques this viewpoint as a "fiction of knowledge."

59. Ibid., 102–3.

60. Nadav Assor, *Lessons on Leaving Your Body*, film (2014), accessed May 24, 2015, http://www.nadassor.net/2014/10/lessons-leaving-body-2014/

61. These nonviolent civilian drone practices resonate with de Certeau's description of a "proliferating illegitimacy," which is practiced in such a way as to constitute "everyday regulations and surreptitious creativities" under the radar of "the observational organization" (de Certeau, *Practice*, 96).

62. Angel Nevarez and Alex Rivera, "Tijuana Calling—Lowdrone," accessed 16 July 2015, http://www.marktribe.net/curatorial/tijuana-calling/low-drone/

63. See Mick, "Dept. of Homeland Sec."

64. Nevarez and Rivera. "Tijuana Calling."

65. Debord, "Report."

66. Ian Steadman, "Artist Imagines a Drone with Self-Consciousness That Feels Bad about Its Job," Wired, March 7, 2013, accessed May 21, 2014, http://www.wired.co.uk/news/archive/2013–03/07/self-aware-drone-art-george-barber

67. George Barber, The Freestone Drone, film, 2013, courtesy of Waterside Contemporary Art Gallery, London, accessed May 7, 2013, http://waterside-contemporary.com/exhibitions/the-freestone-drone/. See also the trailer on the Vimeo website, accessed May 7, 2013, https://vimeo.com/56444355

68. Barber, The Freestone Drone.

69. Steadman, "Artist."

70. Ibid.

71. The production featured Hannah Cabell as the Pilot and was directed by Ken Rus Schmoll. See my review of this production in Elise Morrison, "Ambushed by Empathy: George Brant's Grounded," TDR/The Drama Review 58:4 (2014): 163–69.

72. George Brant, Grounded (London: Oberon Modern Plays, 2013), 23.

73. Ibid., 25.

74. Ibid., 27.

75. "Grounded: A Review by Eduardo Ramirez," Military Experience and the Arts, October 30, 2013, accessed March 10, 2014, http://militaryexperience.org/2013/10/30/grounded-a-review-by-edwardo-ramirez/

76. Brant, Grounded, 23.

77. In "Flying," Dydia DeLyser examines the history of women aviators in the 1920s as a means of articulating a feminist practice during a period of time that has been largely overlooked in feminist history. Women aviators such as Amelia Earhart and Louise Thaden "helped reconfigure the gendered moral geographies of their time" (87). As Thaden put it in a 1938 memoir, "We felt the responsibility of doing a good job, for upon our shoulders rested the fate of future employment of women pilots" (quoted in ibid., 91).

78. A rare exception is Turkey, where Sabiha Gökçen became the first female fighter pilot in history in 1936. In the 2000s and 2010s, Israel, Germany, Poland, South Korea, Pakistan, and China began to allow women to fly fighter planes.

79. See NPR, "First Female Fighter Pilot: 'Attention Wasn't What I Wanted,'" The Sunday Conversation, May 12, 2013, National Public Radio, accessed April 25, 2014, http://www.npr.org/2013/05/12/183315464/first-female-fighter-pilot-attention-wasnt-what-i-wanted

80. Brant, Grounded, 31.

81. Ibid.

82. Ibid., 34–35.

83. Ibid., 38, 41.

84. Ibid., 44.

85. Ibid., 45–46.

86. Ibid., 43, 46.

87. Ibid., 36.

88. Ibid., 56.

89. David Krasner, "Empathy and Theater," In *Staging Philosophy: Intersections of Theater, Performance, and Philosophy*, ed. David Krasner and David Saltz (Ann Arbor: University of Michigan Press, 2006), 256.

90. Brant, *Grounded*, 48–49.

91. Ibid., 69.

92. Ibid., 70.

93. Ibid.

94. Ibid., 71.

95. Richard M. Thompson II, "Drones in Domestic Surveillance Operations: Fourth Amendment Implications and Legislative Responses," *Congressional Research Service*, April 2013, accessed August 29, 2013, http://www.fas.org/sgp/crs/natsec/R42701.pdf

Coda

1. "Surveillance Technologies in Performance," ed. Elise Morrison, special issue, *International Journal for Performing Arts and Digital Media* 11:2 (2015).

2. Lyon, *Surveillance after 9/11*, 27.

3. McGrath, *Loving Big Brother*, 141.

4. This phrase occurs in several of the artists' statements about their own work. See, for example, the discussion of Jill Magid and Hannah Price in chapter 2.

5. Walter Benjamin, "A Small History of Photography," in *'One-Way Street' and Other Writings*, trans. Edmund Jephcott and Kingsley Shorter (London: New Left Books, 1979), 250.

6. Benjamin's construction of the hegemonic scene (recognizable for its adherence to cultural norms and the dictates of large-scale policies) versus the detail (that which stands out as radically specific and contradictory) in photography is echoed in Roland Barthes's notion of the "studium" and the "punctum." See Barthes, *Camera Lucida*, 25–28.

7. As Susan Sontag astutely notes in her 1975 essay "Fascinating Fascism," the aesthetics and architecture of fascism involve huge, larger than life structures that dwarf and overwhelm the individual human subject in order to exert total control. Susan Sontag, "Fascinating Fascism," *New York Review of Books*, February 6, 1975, republished in Susan Sontag, *Under the Sign of Saturn: Essays* (New York: Picador, 1980), 86–88.

8. Benjamin, "Small History," 251.

9. Benjamin, "Theses," 257. In his 1940 "Theses on the Philosophy of History," Benjamin describes a "state of emergency" that must be recognized and recorded by individual citizens in order to fight fascism, the horrors of which, "in the name of progress," were being treated "as a historical norm." He insisted that the (capital *H*) History being produced and naturalized by fascist governments must be countered by individuals and small collectives committed to using alternative history-making techniques.

10. Stanley, *Surveillance-Industrial Complex*.

11. See Laura Huey, "Cop Watching in the Downtown Eastside," in *Surveillance and Security*, ed. Torin Monahan (Routledge: New York, 2006), 149–66.

12. Benjamin "Small History," 243–44.

Bibliography

Academy of Model Aeronautics. "Radio Controlled Model Aircraft Operation: Utilizing 'First Person View' Systems," January 2014. Accessed May 15, 2014. http://www.modelaircraft.org/files/550.pdf

Adorno, Theodor, and Walter Benjamin. *The Complete Correspondence, 1928–1940*. Cambridge: Harvard University Press, 1999.

Al-Ali, Nadje, and Deborah Al-Najjar. *We Are Iraqis: Aesthetics and Politics in a Time of War.* Syracuse, NY: Syracuse University Press, 2012.

Althusser, Louis. "Ideology and Ideological State Apparatuses (Notes towards an Investigation)" In *Lenin and Other Philosophies, 85–126.* New York: Monthly Review Press, 1971.

Alvarez, Ana Cecilia. "How to Hide from Big Brother Surveillance." *Dazed,* July 2014. Accessed April 15, 2015. http://www.dazeddigital.com/artsandculture/article/19131/1/artists-writers-show-how-to-hide-from-big-brother-government-surveillance

"Amazon Prime Air." Amazon. Accessed May 9, 2014. http://www.amazon.com/b?node=8037720011

Anderson, Nate. "2006 AOL Search Data Snafu Spawns 'I Love Alaska' Short Films." *Ars Technica,* January 27, 2009. Accessed June 16, 2015. http://arstechnica.com/business/2009/01/aol-search-data-spawns-i-love-alaska-short-films/

Andrejevic, Mark. *Reality TV: The Work of Being Watched.* Oxford: Rowman and Littlefield, 2004.

Andrejevic, Mark. "The Work of Watching One Another: Lateral Surveillance, Risk, and Governance." *Surveillance & Society* 2:4 (2005): 479–97.

Antoni, Janine. "Mona Hatoum." *BOMB* 63, (Spring 1998). Accessed April 25, 2015. http://bombmagazine.org/article/2130/

Apter, Emily. "'Women's Time' in Theory." *Differences* 21:1 (2010): 1–18.

Arendt, Paul. "Another View: Private Investigator Michael Colacicco on *Contains Violence.*" *The Guardian,* April 8, 2008. Accessed October 10, 2008. http://www.guardian.co.uk/artanddesign/2008/apr/08/art.dance

Arrington, Michael. "AOL: 'This Was a Screw-Up.'" *Tech Crunch,* August 7, 2006. Accessed April 14, 2014. http://techcrunch.com/2006/08/07/aol-this-was-a-screw-up/

Ars Electronica Futurelab. *49 Quadcopters in the Night.* Voestalpine Klangwolke festival, Linz, Austria, 2012. Video of performance. Accessed May 9, 2013. http://www.youtube.com/watch?feature=player_embedded&v=ShGl5rQK3ew

Artaud, Antonin. "Letters on Language" (1933), Translated by Mary Caroline Richards. In *Theatre/Theory/Theatre: The Major Critical Texts from Aristotle and Zeami to Soyinka and Havel,* edited by Daniel Gerould, 440–43. New York: Applause Theatre and Cinema Books, 2000.

Artaud, Antonin. "The Theater and Cruelty" (1933). Translated by Mary Caroline Richards. In *Theatre/Theory/Theatre: The Major Critical Texts from Aristotle and Zeami to Soyinka and Havel, edited by* Daniel Gerould, 435–40. New York: Applause Theatre and Cinema Books, 2000.

Assor, Nadav. *Lessons on Leaving Your Body.* Film, 2014. Accessed May 24, 2015. http://www.nadassor.net/2014/10/lessons-leaving-body-2014/

Assor, Nadav. "Ophan" (2014). Accessed October 28, 2014. http://www.nadassor.net/2014/10/ophan/

Astro Teller. "Why We Developed Google Glass." *CNN Online,* June 4, 2014. Accessed June 5, 2014. http://www.cnn.com/2014/06/04/opinion/teller-google-glass/

Auslander, Philip. *Liveness: Performance in a Mediatized Culture.* London: Routledge, 1999.

Austin, J. L. *How to Do Things with Words.* Cambridge: Harvard University Press, 1962.

Badran, Margot. "Islamic Feminism." *Al-Ahram Weekly Online,* January 17–23, 2002. Accessed July 19, 2014. http://weekly.ahram.org.eg/2002/569/cu1.htm

Baldwin, Rosecrans. "My Harassers: Hannah Price." *Morning News,* October 14, 2013. Accessed March 7, 2014. http://www.themorningnews.org/gallery/my-harassers

Ball, Kirstie, Nicola Green, Hille Koskela, and David J. Phillips. "Editorial: Surveillance Studies Needs Gender and Sexuality." In "Gender, Sexuality and Surveillance," edited by Kirstie Ball, Nicola Green, Hille Koskela, and David J. Phillips. Special issue, *Surveillance & Society* 6:4 (2009): 352–56.

Barba, Eugenio. "Theatre Anthropology—Research." International School of Theatre Anthropology. Accessed July 16, 2015. http://www.odinteatret.dk/research/ista/theatre-anthropology.aspx

Barbaro, Michael, and Tom Zeller Jr. "A Face Is Exposed for AOL Searcher No. 4417749." *New York Times,* August 9, 2006. Accessed April 14, 2014. http://www.nytimes.com/2006/08/09/technology/09aol.html?pagewanted=all&_r=0

Barber, George. *The Freestone Drone.* Film, 2013. Courtesy of Waterside Contemporary Art Gallery, London. Accessed May 7, 2013. http://waterside-contemporary.com/exhibitions/the-freestone-drone/. Trailer. Accessed May 7, 2013. https://vimeo.com/56444355

Barthes, Roland. *Camera Lucida: Reflections on Photography.* Translated by Richard Howard. New York: Hill and Wang, 1981.

Barthes, Roland. "Death of the Author." *Aspen* 5–6 (Fall-Winter, 1967). Accessed March 7, 2010. www.ubu.com/aspen/aspen5and6/threeEssays.html#barthes

Barthes, Roland. *Image/Text/Music.* Translated by Stephen Heath. New York: Hill and Wang, 1977.

Basu, Rajeev. *Drones of New York* (2013). Created for the Museum of the Moving Image, New York. Accessed May 7, 2013. http://www.dronesofnewyork.com/

Bates, David. *Photography and Surrealism: Sexuality, Colonialism, and Social Dissent.* London: I. B. Tauris, 2004.

Bateson, Gregory. "A Theory of Play and Fantasy." *Psychiatric Research Reports* 2 (1955): 39–51.

Baudelaire, Charles. *The Painter of Modern Life.* New York: Da Capo Press, 1964.

Bay-Cheng, Sarah. "Ready for My Close Up." *Theater 44.3* (2014): 86–93.

Bay-Cheng, Sarah, Chiel Kattenbelt, Andy Lavender, and Robin Nelson, eds. *Mapping Intermediality in Performance.* Amsterdam: Amsterdam University Press, 2010.

Begley, Josh. "@Dronestrike" (2002–). *Twitter.* Accessed August 29, 2013. https://twitter.com/dronestream

Begley, Josh. "Metadata." Accessed September 24, 2014. http://metadata.joshbegley.com

Benjamin, Medea. *Drone Warfare: Killing by Remote Control.* London: Verso, 2012.

Benjamin, Walter. *Charles Baudelaire: A Lyric Poet in the Era of High Capitalism.* Translated by Harry Zohn. London: Verso, 1983.

Benjamin, Walter. "A Small History of Photography." In *'One-Way Street' and Other Writings.* Translated by Edmund Jephcott and Kingsley Shorter, 240–57. London: New Left Books, 1979.

Benjamin, Walter. "Theses on the Philosophy of History." In *Illuminations: Walter Benjamin Essays and Reflections.* Edited by Hannah Arendt, translated by Harry Zohn, 253–64. New York: Pantheon, 1968.

Benjamin, Walter. "The Work of Art in the Age of Mechanical Reproduction." In *Illuminations: Walter Benjamin Essays and Reflections.* Edited by Hannah Arendt, translated by Harry Zohn, 217–52. New York: Pantheon, 1968.

Berger, John. *Ways of Seeing.* London: Penguin, 1972.

Bernstein, Robin. *Racial Innocence: Performing American Childhood from Slavery to Civil Rights.* New York: New York University Press, 2011.

Biagioli, Monica. "Janet Cardiff the Missing Voice (Case Study B): An Audio Walk." *Artfocus* 68 (2000): 12–14.

Bilal, Wafaa. "and Counting . . ." (2010). Accessed September 24, 2014. http://wafaabilal.com/and-counting/

Bilal, Wafaa. "Domestic Tension" (2007). Accessed July 10, 2012. http://www.wafaabilal.com/html/domesticTension.html

Bilal, Wafaa. "3rdi" (2010–11). Accessed September 24, 2014. http://wafaabilal.com/thirdi/

Bilal, Wafaa. "Virtual Jihadi" (2008). Accessed September 24, 2014. http://wafaabilal.com/virtual-jihadi/

Bilal, Wafaa, and Keri Lydersen. *Shoot an Iraqi: Art, Life, and Resistance under the Gun.* San Francisco: City Lights, 2008.

Blas, Zach. "On Electronic Civil Disobedience: Interview with Ricardo Dominguez." *Reclamations* (blog), January 17, 2012. Accessed August 30, 2012. http://www.reclamationsjournal.org/blog/?ha_exhibit=interview-with-ricardo-dominguez

Blas, Zach. "Face Cages." Accessed April 25, 2015. http://www.zachblas.info/projects/face-cages/

Blas, Zach. "Facial Weaponization." Accessed April 25, 2015. http://www.zachblas.info/projects/facial-weaponization-suite/

Blast Theory. "Rider Spoke" (2007). Accessed September 24, 2014. http://www.blast-theory.co.uk/projects/rider-spoke/

Bode, Lisa. "Digital Doppelgangers." *M/C: A journal of media and culture* 8:3 (July

2005). Accessed July 22, 2015. http://journal.media-culture.org.au/0507/07-bode.php.

Bohannon, John. "Facebook Will Soon Be Able to ID You in Any Photo." *Science,* February 5, 2015. Accessed April 25, 2015. http://news.sciencemag.org/social-sciences/2015/02/facebook-will-soon-be-able-id-you-any-photo

Bolter, Jay David, and Richard Grusin. *Remediation.* Cambridge: MIT Press, 2000.

Bolter, Jay David, and Richard Grusin. "Remediation." *Configurations* 4:3 (1996): 311–58.

Bonnington, Christina, and Spencer Ackerman. "Apple Rejects App That Tracks U.S. Drone Strikes." *Wired,* August 30, 2012. Accessed September 24, 2014. http://www.wired.com/2012/08/drone-app/

Bornstein, Kate. *Gender Outlaw: On Men, Women, and the Rest of Us.* New York: Vintage Books, 1994.

Bornstein, Kate. *My Gender Workbook: How to Become a Real Man, a Real Woman, the Real You, or Something Else Entirely.* New York: Routledge, 1998.

Botelho, Greg. "FAA Official: Drone, Jetliner Nearly Collided over Florida." *CNN,* May 11, 2014. Accessed May 28, 2014. http://www.cnn.com/2014/05/09/travel/unmanned-drone-danger/

Boxer, Sarah. "When Seeing Is Not Always Believing." *New York Times,* July 11, 2005. Accessed July 10, 2010. http://www.nytimes.com/2005/07/11/arts/design/11laur.html

Boyko, Brian. "Interview: Wafaa Bilal Casts Himself as Terrorist in Virtual Jihadi." *Geeks Are Sexy,* Accessed May 11, 2016. https://www.geeksaresexy.net/2008/03/03/interview-wafaa-bilal-casts-himself-as-terrorist-in-virtual-jihadi/.

Brant, George. *Grounded.* London: Oberon Modern Plays, 2013.

Brecht, Bertolt. "Alienation Effects in Chinese Acting." In *Brecht on Theatre: The Development of an Aesthetic.* Translated by John Willet, 91–99. New York: Hill and Wang, 1964.

Brecht, Bertolt. "A Short Organum for the Theatre." In *Brecht on Theatre: The Development of an Aesthetic.* Translated by John Willet, 179–208. New York: Hill and Wang, 1964.

Brecht, Bertolt. "The Modern Theatre is the Epic Theatre." In *Brecht on Theatre: The Development of an Aesthetic.* Translated by John Willet, 33–42. New York: Hill and Wang, 1964.

Breton, André. *Manifestos of Surrealism.* Translated by Richard Seaver and Helen R. Lane. Ann Arbor: University of Michigan Press, 1969.

Bridle, James. "Drone Shadow" (2012). Accessed May 7, 2013. http://shorttermmemoryloss.com/portfolio/project/drone-shadows/

Bridle, James. "Dronestagram" (2012–). Accessed August 29, 2013. http://dronestagram.tumblr.com/

Brin, David. *The Transparent Society: Will Technology Force Us to Choose between Privacy and Freedom?* Reading, MA: Addison-Wesley, 1998.

Brockett, Oscar, and Franklin Joseph Hildy. *History of the Theatre.* 9th ed. Boston: Allyn and Bacon, 2003.

Brooker, Charlie. "Be Right Back." *Black Mirror.* Television series, Channel 4, BBC. Produced by Zeppotron. Episode aired February 11, 2013.

Browne, Simone. "Digital Epidermalization: Race, Identity, Biometrics." *Critical Sociology* 36:1 (2010): 131–50.

Builders Association. "*Super Vision* Project Description." Accessed July 19, 2015. http://www.thebuildersassociation.org/prod_supervision_info.html

Bumiller, Elisabeth, and Thom Shanker. "War Evolves with Drones, Some Tiny as Bugs." *New York Times,* June 19, 2011. Accessed May 5, 2014. http://www.nytimes.com/2011/06/20/world/20drones.html?pagewanted=all&_r=0

Burgin, Victor. "Jenni's Room: Exhibitionism and Solitude." In *ctrl [space]: Rhetorics of Surveillance from Bentham to Big Brother,* edited by Thomas Levin, Ursula Frohne, and Peter Weibel, 228–35. Leipzig: ZKM, MedienKunstNetz, 2002.

Butler, Judith. *Bodies That Matter: On the Discursive Limits of "Sex"* New York : Routledge, 1993.

Butler, Judith. *Gender Trouble: Feminism and the Subversion of Identity.* New York : Routledge, 1990.

Butler, Judith. "Performative Acts and Gender Constitution: An Essay in Phenomenology and Feminist Theory." *Theatre Journal* 40:4 (1988): 519–31.

Butler, Judith. *The Psychic Life of Power: Theories in Subjection.* Stanford: Stanford University Press, 1997.

Calle, Sophie. *Appointment with Sigmund Freud.* London: Thames and Hudson, 2004.

Calle, Sophie, with Paul Auster. *Double Game.* London: Violette Limited, 1999.

Calo, M. Ryan. "The Drone as Privacy Catalyst." *Stanford Law Review Online* 64:29 (2011). Accessed May 15, 2013. http://www.stanfordlawreview.org/online/drone-privacy-catalyst

Camhi, Leslie. "PS 1 Hosts 'Wack!—Real Women Have Oeuvres': A Retrospective Look at the Roots of Feminist Art." *Village Voice,* February 26, 2008. Accessed July 10, 2010. http://www.villagevoice.com/2008-02-26/art/p-s-1-hosts-wack-mdash-real-women-have-oeuvres/

Camp, Pannill. "Theatre Optics: Enlightenment Theatre Architecture in France and the Architectonics of Husserl's Phenomenology." *Theatre Journal* 59:4 (2007): 615–33.

Cardiff, Janet. "Eyes of Laura." Accessed August 26, 2010. http://www.eyesoflaura.org/

Cardiff, Janet. "Walks." Accessed July 10, 2010. http://www.cardiffmiller.com/artworks/walks/index.html

Carroll, Lewis. *Alice in Wonderland and Through the Looking Glass.* New York: Grosset and Dunlap, 1994.

Cartwright, Lisa. *Screening the Body: Tracing Medicine's Visual Culture.* Minneapolis: University of Minnesota Press, 1995.

Case, Sue-Ellen. *Domain Matrix: Performing Lesbian at the End of Print Culture.* Bloomington: Indiana University Press, 1996.

Case, Sue-Ellen. "Towards a Butch-Femme Aesthetic." In *The Lesbian and Gay Studies Reader,* edited by Henry Abelove, Michèle Aina Barale, and David M. Halperin, 294–306. New York: Routledge, 1993.

Causey, Matthew. *Theater and Performance in Digital Culture: From Simulation to Embeddedness.* London: Routledge, 2006.

Cheney-Lippold, John. "A New Algorithmic Identity: Soft Biopolitics and the Modulation of Control." *Theory, Culture, and Society* 28:6 (2011): 164–81.

Chow, Kat. "A Photographer Turns Her Lens on Men Who Catcall." *National Public Radio: Code Switch,* October 17, 2013. Accessed March 7, 2014. http://www.npr.org/sections/codeswitch/2013/10/17/235413025/a-photographer-turns-her-lens-on-men-who-cat-call

Christov-Bakargiev, Carolyn. *Janet Cardiff: A Survey of Works.* New York: P.S.1 Contemporary Arts Center, 2002.

Chun, Wendy Hui-Kyong. *Control and Freedom: Power and Paranoia in the Age of Fiber Optics.* Cambridge: MIT Press, 2006.

Clap, Susannah. "The Good, the Bad, and the Photocopier." *The Guardian,* April 6, 2008. Accessed October 10, 2008. http://www.guardian.co.uk/stage/2008/apr/06/theatre2

Clark, Andy. *Natural Born Cyborgs.* Oxford: Oxford University Press, 2003.

Clark, Ross. *The Road to Big Brother: One Man's Struggle against the Surveillance Society.* New York: Encounter Books, 2009.

Cixous, Hélène. "The Laugh of the Medusa." *Signs* 1:4 (1976): 875–93.

Cixous, Hélène, and Catherine Clement, eds. *The Newly Born Woman.* Minneapolis: University of Minnesota Press, 1975.

Cody, Gabrielle, and Evert Sprinchorn, eds. *The Columbia Encyclopedia of Modern Drama.* New York: Columbia University Press, 2007.

Coleman, Roy. "Reclaiming the Streets: Closed Circuit Television, Neoliberalism, and the Mystification of Social Divisions in Liverpool, UK." *Surveillance & Society* 2:2–3 (2004): 293–309.

Conrad, Kathryn. "Surveillance, Gender, and the Virtual Body in the Information Age." *Surveillance & Society* 6:4 (2009): 380–87.

CORDIS [Community Research and Development Information Service]. "Final Report Summary: ADABTS (Automatic Detection of Abnormal Behavior and Threats in Crowded Spaces)" (2011). Accessed June 26, 2015. http://cordis.europa.eu/result/rcn/153868_en.html

Creed, Barbara. *The Monstrous-Feminine: Film, Feminism, Psychoanalysis.* London: Routledge, 1993.

Cresswell, Tim. *On the Move: Mobility in the Modern Western World.* London: Routledge, 2006.

Cresswell, Tim, and Peter Merriman, eds. *Geographies of Mobilities: Practices, Spaces, Subjects.* Surrey: Ashgate: 2011.

Crispin, Sterling. "Data Masks: Biometric Surveillance Masks Evolving in the Gaze of the Technological Other." MA thesis, University of California, Santa Barbara, December 2014. Accessed February 25, 2015. http://www.sterlingcrispin.com/Sterling_Crispin_Data-masks_MS_Thesis.pdf

Critical Art Ensemble. *Digital Resistance: Explorations in Tactical Media.* Brooklyn: Autonomedia, 2001.

Critical Art Ensemble. *Electronic Civil Disobedience and Other Unpopular Ideas.* Brooklyn: Autonomedia, 1996.

Critical Art Ensemble. *Flesh Machine: Cyborgs, Designer Babies, Eugenic Consciousness.* Brooklyn: Autonomedia, 1998.

"Critics Blast Transborder Immigrant Tool." *Fox News,* March 10, 2010. Accessed August 10, 2010. http://www.foxnews.com/us/2010/03/10/critics-blast-transborder-immigrant-tool-irresponsible-use-technology/

Dar, Azma. "Peeping Toms: Monday 5 May, 2008." *Smudgeyink* (blog), May 5, 2008. Accessed October 10, 2008. http://smudgeyink.blogspot.com/

"Data Protection Act, 1998." UK Government Legislation. Accessed April 15, 2015. http://www.legislation.gov.uk/ukpga/1998/29/section/1

Debord, Guy. "Report on the Construction of Situations and on the International Situationist Tendency Conditions of Organization and Action." Translated by Ken

Knabb. *Situationist International Online.* Accessed August 25, 2010. http://www. cddc.vt.edu/sionline/si/report.html

Debord, Guy. *The Society of Spectacle.* New York: Zone Books, 1994.

De Certeau, Michel. *The Practice of Everyday Life.* Berkeley: University of California Press, 1988.

De Landa, Manuel. *War in the Age of Intelligent Machines.* New York: Zone Books, 1991.

De Lauretis, Teresa. *Alice Doesn't: Feminism, Semiotics, Cinema.* Bloomington: Indiana University Press, 1984.

De Lauretis, Teresa. *Technologies of Gender: Essays on Theory, Film, and Fiction.* Bloomington: Indiana University Press, 1987.

Deleuze, Gilles. "Postscript on the Societies of Control." *October, 59.*(Winter, 1992): 3–7.

DeLyser, Dydia. "Flying: Feminisms and Mobilities; Crusading for Aviation in the 1920s." In *Geographies of Mobilities,* edited by Tim Cresswell, 83–98. Surrey: Ashgate, 2011.

Diamond, Elin. "Brechtian Theory/Feminist Theory: Toward a Gestic Feminist Criticism." *TDR/The Drama Review* 32:1 (1988): 82–94.

Diamond, Elin. "Mimesis, Mimicry, and the 'True-Real.'" *Modern Drama* 32:1 (1989): 58–72.

Diamond, Elin. *Unmaking Mimesis: Essays on Feminism and Theater.* London: Routledge, 1997.

Diderot, Denis. "On Dramatic Poetry." In *Diderot's Selected Writings,* edited by Lester G. Crocker, translated by Derek Coltman, 202–30. New York: Macmillan, 1966.

"Digital-double.com." Accessed July 22, 2015. http://www.digital-double.com/digital-double/

Dixon, Steve. *Digital Performance.* Cambridge: MIT Press, 2007.

Doane, Mary Ann. "Film and the Masquerade: Theorizing the Female Spectator." *Screen* 23:3 (1982): 74–88.

Doane, Mary Ann. "The Voice in the Cinema: The Articulation of Body and Space." In *Film Sound: Theory and Practice,* edited by Elisabeth Weis and John Belton, 162–76. New York: Columbia University Press, 1985.

Doane, Mary Ann. "The 'Woman's Film': Possession and Address." In *(Re)Vision: Essays in Feminist Film Criticism,* edited by Mary Ann Doane, Patricia Mellencamp, and Linda Williams, 67–82. Los Angeles: American Film Institute, 1984.

DOCAM (Documentation and Conservation of the Media Arts Heritage) Research Alliance. "Janet Cardiff: *Eyes of Laura,* 2004." Accessed July 10, 2010. http://www. docam.ca/en/component/content/article/351-janet-cardiff-eyes-of-laura-2004. html

Dolan, Jill. "Desire Dressed in a Trenchcoat." In *The Drama Review* 33.1 (1989): 59–67.

Dolan, Jill. *The Feminist Spectator as Critic.* Ann Arbor: University of Michigan Press, 1988.

Drewniak, Łukasz. "'Positivism Makes Sense: Conversation with Ewa Wójciak." *Dziennik Gazeta Prawna,* no. 5 (2010). Accessed January 25, 2014. http://osmego.art. pl/t8d/main/en/

Dubrofsky, Rachel, and Shoshana Amielle Magnet, eds. *Feminist Surveillance Studies.* Durham: Duke University Press, 2015.

Dubrofsky, Rachel, and Megan Wood. "Gender, Race, and Authenticity: Celebrity Women Tweeting for the Gaze." In *Feminist Surveillance Studies,* edited by Rachel

Dubrofsky and Shoshana Amielle Magnet, 93–106. Durham: Duke University Press, 2015.

Dunbar, Alex. "Follow the GPS, ÉSE: The Transborder Immigrant Tool Helps Mexicans Cross Over Safely." *Vice*, November 2009. Accessed August 10, 2010. http://www.viceland.com/int/v16n11/htdocs/follow-the-gps-225.php?page=1

Edwards, Julia. "Obama Administration Says to Provide $20 Million for Police Body Cameras." Reuters, May 1, 2015. Accessed July 20, 2015. http://www.reuters.com/article/2015/05/01/us-usa-police-cameras-idUSKBN0NM3PL20150501

Egoyan, Atom. "Janet Cardiff." *BOMB* 79 (Spring, 2002). Accessed July 10, 2010. http://bombsite.com/issues/79/articles/2463

Elahi, Hasan. "Giving the FBI What It Wants." *New York Times*, October 30, 2011. Accessed October 9, 2014. http://www.nytimes.com/2011/10/30/opinion/sunday/giving-the-fbi-what-it-wants.html?pagewanted=all&_r=0

Elahi, Hasan. *Tracking Transience*. Accessed July 10, 2010. http://trackingtransience.net/

Electronic Disturbance Theater/b.a.n.g. lab. "Transborder Immigrant Tool." Micha Cardenas, Amy Sara Carroll, Ricardo Dominguez, Elle Mehrmand, and Brett Stalbaum, artists. Accessed May 9, 2016. https://faculty.washington.edu/michamc/wordpress-bang/

Electronic Frontier Foundation. "Customs and Border Protection 2010 Drone Concept of Operations Report for Congress" (2010). Accessed August 29, 2013. https://www.eff.org/document/customs-border-protection-2010-drone-concept-operations-report-congress

Elwood, Sarah, and Katharyne Mitchell. "Another Politics Is Possible: Neogeographies, Visual Spatial Tactics, and Political Formation." *Cartographica* 48:4 (2013): 275–92.

Engleberts, Lernert, and Sander Plug. *I Love Alaska* Film, 2009. MiniMovies. Accessed April 14, 2014. http://www.minimovies.org/documentaires/view/ilovealaska

Erdman, Harley. "Caught in the 'Eye of the Eternal': Justice, Race, and the Camera from *The Octoroon* to Rodney King." *Theatre Journal* 45:3 (1993): 333–48.

Farman, Jason. "Mobile Media Performances as Asynchronous Embodiment." *International Journal of ScreenDance* 2:1 (2012): 48–51.

Esslin, Martin. *The Theatre of the Absurd*. London: Penguin Books, 1961.

Evans, Christine. *You Are Dead. You Are Here.* New York: Indie Theater Now, 2014.

Farman, Jason. *Mobile Interface Theory: Embodied Space and Locative Media*. London: Routledge, 2012.

"FBI Next Generation Identification." FBI. Accessed April 25, 2015. http://www.fbi.gov/about-us/cjis/fingerprints_biometrics/ngi

Federal Aviation Administration. "Umanned Aircraft Systems—News." Accessed July 16, 2015. https://www.faa.gov/uas/news/

Felman, Shoshona. *The Scandal of the Speaking Body*. Ithaca, NY: Cornell University Press, 1983.

Feral, Josette. "Introduction." In "Theatricality," editor Josette Féral. Special issue, *Substance* 31:2 (2002): 3–16.

Fiebach, Joachim. "Theatricality: From Oral Traditions to Televised 'Realities.'" In "Theatricality," editor Josette Féral. *Substance* 31: 2 (2002): 17–41.

Firepile. "Steve Mann." *Hyper-textual Ontology* (blog), August 10, 2004. Accessed December 30, 2009. http://wearcam.org/tv04/hyper-textual_ontology.htm

Fischer-Lichte, Erika. "Theatricality: A Key Concept in Theatre and Cultural Studies." *Theatre Research International* 20:2 (1995): 85–90.

Foucault, Michel. *Discipline and Punish: The Birth of the Prison.* Translated by Alan Sheridan. New York: Vintage Books, 1995.

Foucault, Michel. *The History of Sexuality.* Vol. 1. New York: Random House, 1978.

Foucault, Michel. *Power/Knowledge: Selected Interviews and Other Writings, 1972–1977.* New York: Pantheon Books, 1980.

France, Marie. "Sadomasochism and Feminism." *Feminist Review* 16 (1984): 35–42.

Franklin Institute. "The Kodak Brownie." Accessed August 25, 2010. http://www.fi.edu/learn/sci-tech/kodak-brownie/kodak-brownie.php?cts=photography-recreation

Freeman, Elizabeth. "Packing History, Count(er)ing Generations." *New Literary History* 31:4 (2000): 727–44.

Freud, Sigmund. "Fetishism." In *Standard Edition of the Complete Psychological Works,* vol. 21. London: Hogarth Press, 1961.

Freud, Sigmund. *Three Essays on the Theory of Sexuality.* Translated by James Strachey. London: Hogarth Press, 1955.

Fried, Michael. "Art and Objecthood." In *Art and Objecthood,* 148–72. Chicago: University of Chicago Press, 1998.

Frizzel, Deborah. *Humphrey Spender's Humanist Landscapes: Photo-Documents, 1932–1942.* New Haven: Yale Center for British Art, 1997.

Frucci, Adam. "Pole Dancing Robots Ruin Both Robots and Strippers Simultaneously." *gizmodo (blog),* December 4, 2008. Accessed August 25, 2010. http://gizmodo.com/5101838/pole-dancing-robots-ruin-both-robots-and-strippers-simultaneously

Frye, Marilyn. *The Politics of Reality: Essays in Feminist Theory.* Freedom, CA: Crossing Press, 1983.

Fuchs, Elinor. *The Death of Character: Perspectives on Theater after Modernism.* Bloomington: Indiana University Press, 1996.

Fusco, Coco. *The Bodies That Were Not Ours.* London: Routledge. 2001.

Fusco, Coco. *Dolores.* Accessed July 10, 2010. http://www.thing.net/~cocofusco/video/dolores/dolores1.htm

Fusco, Coco. *English Is Broken Here: Notes on Cultural Fusion in the Americas.* New York: New Press. 1995.

Fusco, Coco, and Guillermo Gómez-Peña. *The Couple in a Cage: A Guatinaui Odyssey.* Film version by Coco Fusco and Paula Herdia (1993). Accessed July 10, 2010. http://www.thing.net/~cocofusco/subpages/videos/subpages/couple/couple.html

Gandy, Oscar H. *The Panoptic Sort: A Political Economy of Personal Information.* Boulder: Westview Press, 1993.

Gardner, Lyn. "Contains Violence." *The Guardian,* April 5, 2008. Accessed October 10, 2008. http://www.guardian.co.uk/stage/2008/apr/05/theatre2

Garrison, Ednie Kaeh. "Are We on a Wavelength Yet?" In *Different Wavelengths: Studies of the Contemporary Women's Movement,* edited by Jo Reger, 237–56. London: Routledge, 2005.

Geekologie. "Tipping with TNT: Pole Dancing Stripper-Bots." December 5, 2008. Accessed April 25, 2015. http://geekologie.com/2008/12/stripper-robots-make-me-questi.php

Gerami, Shahin. "Mullahs, Martyrs, and Men: Conceptualizing Masculinity in the Islamic Republic of Iran." *Men and Masculinities* 5:3 (2003): 257–74.

Gerami, Shahin, and Melodye Lehnerer. "Women's Agency and Household Diplomacy: Negotiating Fundamentalism." *Gender and Society* 15 (2001): 556–73.

"German Railways to Test Anti-graffiti Drones." *BBC News*, May 27, 2013. Accessed April 24, 2014. http://www.bbc.com/news/world-europe-22678580

Gerould, Daniel. "Antonin Artaud." In *Theatre/Theory/Theatre: The Major Critical Texts from Aristotle and Zeami to Soyinka and Havel*, edited by Daniel Gerould, 433–34. New York: Applause Theatre and Cinema Books, 2000

Giannachi, Gabriella. *The Politics of New Media Theatre.* New York: Routledge, 2007.

Giannacchi, Gabriella. *Virtual Theatres.* London: Routledge, 2004.

Giesekam, Greg. *Staging the Screen: The Use of Film and Video in Theatre.* London: Palgrave, 2007.

Gilbert, Jason. "Tacocopter Aims to Deliver Tacos Using Unmanned Drone Helicopters." *Huffington Post*, March 23, 2012. Accessed May 13, 2013. http://www.huffingtonpost.com/2012/03/23/tacocopter-startup-delivers-tacos-by-unmanned-drone-helicopter_n_1375842.html

Gilroy, Paul. *Against Race: Imagining Political Culture beyond the Color Line.* Cambridge: Harvard University Press, 2000.

Ginsberg, Faye. "Rethinking the Digital Age." In *Global Indigenous Media*, edited by Pam Wilson and Michelle Stewart, 127–44. Durham: Duke University Press, 2008.

Godard, Jean-Luc. *Godard on Godard: Critical Writings by Jean-Luc Godard.* Edited by Jean Narboni and Tom Milne. New York: Da Capo, 1986.

Goffman, Erving. *Frame Analysis: An Essay on the Organization of Experience.* New York: Harper and Row, 1974.

Goodchild, Michael. "NeoGeography and the Nature of Geographic Expertise." *Journal of Location Based Services* 3:2 (June 2009): 82–96.

Google. "AdWords." Accessed April 10, 2015. https://support.google.com/adwords/answer/1704410?hl=en

Gordon, Lewis. "Is the Human a Teleological Suspension of Man? Phenomenological Exploration of Sylvia Wynter's Fanonian and Biodicean Reflections." In *After Man, towards the Human: Critical Essays on the Thought of Sylvia Wynter*, edited by Anthony Bogues, 237–57. Kingston, Jamaica: Ian Randle, 2006.

Gördüren, Petra. "On the Trail of the Ego: Sophie Calle's Pursuits." In *ctrl [space]: Rhetorics of Surveillance from Bentham to Big Brother*, edited by Thomas Levin, Ursula Frohne, and Peter Weibel. Leipzig: ZKM, MedienKunstNetz, 2002. Accessed May 11, 2016. http://hosting.zkm.de/ctrlspace/e/texts/10

"*Grounded:* A Review by Eduardo Ramirez." *Military Experience and the Arts*, October 30, 2013. Accessed March 10, 2014. http://militaryexperience.org/2013/10/30/grounded-a-review-by-edwardo-ramirez/

Haggerty, Kevin, and Richard Ericson, eds. *The New Politics of Surveillance and Visibility.* Toronto: University of Toronto Press, 2006.

Hall, Rachel. "Terror and the Female Grotesque: Introducing Full Body Scanners to U.S. Airports." In *Feminist Surveillance Studies*, edited by Rachel Dubrofsky and Shoshana Amielle Magnet, 127–149. Durham: Duke University Press, 2015.

Haraway, Donna. "A Cyborg Manifesto: Science, Technology, and Socialist-Feminism in the Late Twentieth Century." In *Simians, Cyborgs, and Women: The Reinvention of Nature*, 149–82. New York: Routledge, 1991.

Harding, James. *Ghosts of the Avant-Garde(s): Exorcising Experimental Theater and Performance.* Ann Arbor: University of Michigan Press, 2013.

Harding, James. "Outperforming Activism: Reflections on the Demise of the Surveillance Camera Players." In "Surveillance Technologies in Performance," edited by Elise Morrison. Special issue, *International Journal of Performance Arts and Digital Media* 11:2 (2015): 131–47

Harvey, Adam. "CV Dazzle." Accessed September 25, 2014. https://cvdazzle.com/

Harvey, Adam. "Off Pocket." *Ahprojects.* Accessed June 15, 2014. http://ahprojects.com/projects/off-pocket/

Harvey, Adam. "Stealth Wear: New Designs for Counter-Surveillance." *Ahprojects.* Accessed May 9, 2013. http://ahprojects.com/projects/stealth-wear/

Harvey, Matt, and Aymann Ismail. "Wanted 'Drone' Poster Artist Discusses How He Punked the NYPD." *Animal New York,* September 24, 2012. Accessed August 26, 2013. http://animalnewyork.com/2012/wanted-drone-poster-artist-discusses-how-he-punked-the-nypd/

Hearn, Jeff. "The Problems Boys and Men Create." In *From Boys to Men: Social Constructions of Masculinity in Contemporary Society,* edited by Tamara Shefer, 13–32. Lansdowne: University of Cape Town Press, 2007.

Heron, Christopher. "Surveillance Camera Cinema (*Faceless, Der Riese, Influenza*). Video Essay (Issue 1)." *The Seventh Art: Worth Viewing,* February 4, 2012. Accessed February 24, 2015. http://www.theseventhart.org/main/surveillance-camera-cinema-faceless-der-riese-influenza-video-essay-issue-1/

Hopkins, D. J., and Shelley Orr. Performance review of *Measure for Measure,* directed by Simon McBurney. *Theatre Journal* 57:1 (2005): 97–100.

Hopkins, Nick. "Revealed: Who Can Fly Drones in UK Airspace." *The Guardian,* January 25, 2013. Accessed August 24, 2013. http://www.guardian.co.uk/world/2013/jan/25/who-can-fly-drones-uk-airspace

Hopkins, Patrick D. "Rethinking Sadomasochism: Feminism, Interpretation, and Simulation." *Hypatia* 9:1 (1994): 116–41.

hooks, bell. *Ain't I a Woman? Black Women and Feminism.* Boston: South End Press, 1981.

hooks, bell. *Reel to Real: Race, Sex, and Class at the Movies.* London: Routledge, 1996.

Houston, Kerr. "Remote Control: Distance in Two Works by Emily Jacir and Wafaa Bilal.'" *Southeastern College Art Conference Review* 16:2 (2014): 189–96.

Huey, Laura. "Cop Watching in the Downtown Eastside." In *Surveillance and Security,* edited by Torin Monahan, 149–66. Routledge: New York, 2006.

Hunter, Lindsay Brandon. "This Is Not a Threat: Conspiracy for Good." In "Surveillance Technologies in Performance," edited by Elise Morrison. Special issue, *International Journal of Performance Arts and Digital Media* 11:2 (2015): 185–201.

Hutera, Donald. "*Contains Violence* at the Lyric, Hammersmith." *The Times Online,* April 4, 2008. Accessed October 10, 2008. http://entertainment.timesonline.co.uk/tol/arts_and_entertainment/stage/theatre/article3672054.ece

IAA [Institute for Applied Autonomy]. "Defensive Surveillance: Lessons from the Republican National Convention." In *Surveillance and Security,* edited by Torin Monahan, 167–74. London: Routledge, 2006.

IAA. *Engaging Ambivalence: Interventions in Engineering Culture.* Brooklyn: Autonomedia, 2005.

IAA, "iSEE." Institute for Applied Autonomy. Accessed August 25, 2010. http://www.appliedautonomy.com/isee.html

IAA. "Mission." Institute for Applied Autonomy. Accessed August 25, 2010. http://www.appliedautonomy.com/mission.html

IAA. "Terminal Air." Institute for Applied Autonomy. Accessed August 25, 2010. http://www.appliedautonomy.com/terminalair/index.html

Ilnytzky, Ula. "Wafaa Bilal, NYU Artist, Gets Camera Implanted in Head." *Huffington Post,* January 23, 2011. Accessed September 25, 2014. http://www.huffingtonpost.com/2010/11/23/wafaa-bilal-nyu-artist-ge_n_787446.html

Ingram, Alan. "Experimental Geopolitics: Wafaa Bilal's *Domestic Tension.*" *Geographical Journal* 178:2 (2012): 123–33.

Innes, Christopher. *Erwin Piscator's Political Theatre.* Cambridge: Cambridge University Press, 1977.

Innes Christopher. "Naturalism." In *Modern Theatre in Context,* edited by Christopher Innes, March 2003. Accessed July 22, 2015. http://moderndrama.ca/crc/chrono/sup.php?id=36&print

International Chamber of Commerce, United Kingdom. "ICC UK Cookie Guide," November 2012. Accessed April 25, 2015. http://www.cookielaw.org/media/1096/icc_uk_cookiesguide_revnov.pdf

Internet Encyclopedia of Philosophy. "Interventionism." Accessed August 25, 2010. http://www.iep.utm.edu/interven/

Irigaray, Luce. *Speculum of the Other Woman.* Translated by Gillian C. Gill. Ithaca, NY: Cornell University Press, 1985.

Irigaray, Luce. *This Sex Which Is Not One.* Translated by Catherine Porter, with Carolyn Burke. Ithaca, NY: Cornell University Press, 1985.

James, Robin. "Music for Drones." *It's Her Factory* (blog), February 26, 2013. Accessed May 29, 2014. http://www.its-her-factory.com/2013/02/music-for-drones-introduction/

Jannarone, Kimberly. *Artaud and His Doubles.* Ann Arbor: University of Michigan Press, 2012.

Jones, Alice. "*Contains Violence,* Lyric Hammersmith Roof Top Terrace." *The Independent,* April 9, 2008. Accessed October 10, 2008. http://www.independent.co.uk/arts-entertainment/theatre-dance/reviews/contains-violence-lyric-hammersmith-roof-terrace-london-806273.html

Jones, Amelia. "Presence in Absentia: Experiencing Performance as Documentation." *Art Journal* 56:4 (1997): 11–18.

Kapsalis, Terri. *Public Privates: Performing Gynecology from Both Sides of the Speculum.* Durham: Duke University Press, 1997.

Kodak. "Brownie Camera Features." Accessed August 25, 2010. http://www.kodak.com/US/en/corp/features/brownieCam/

Koebler, Jason. "City in Virginia Becomes First to Pass Anti-drone Legislation." *US News & World Report,* February 5, 2013. Accessed May 13, 2013. http://www.usnews.com/news/articles/2013/02/05/city-in-virginia-becomes-first-to-pass-anti-drone-legislation-

Koebler, Jason. "Dances with Drones." *US News & World Report,* May 15, 2013. Accessed April 23, 2014. http://www.usnews.com/news/articles/2013/05/15/dance-company-incorporates-drones-into-performance

Koebler, Jason. "Google to Fund Anti-poaching Drones in Asia, Africa." *U.S. News & World Report,* December 7, 2012. Accessed July 11, 2014. www.usnews.com/news/articles/2012/12/07/google-to-fund-anti-poaching-drones-in-asia-africa

Kohn, Asher J. "An Architectural Defense from Drones." *Fraser—Extreme Archi-*

tecture, Spring 2012. Accessed August 25, 2013. http://www.scribd.com/doc/104135119/An-Architectural-Defense-From-Drones

Kopstein, Joshua. "Street Artist behind Satirical NYPD 'Drone' Posters Arrested." *The Verge*, December 2, 2012. Accessed August 26, 2013. http://www.theverge.com/2012/12/2/3718094/street-artist-nypd-drone-posters-arrested-surveillance

Koskela, Hille. "'Cam Era': The Contemporary Urban Panopticon." *Surveillance & Society* 1:3 (2003): 292–313.

Koskela, Hille. "Video Surveillance, Gender, and the Safety of Public Urban Space: 'Peeping Tom' Goes High Tech?" *Urban Geography* 23:3 (2002): 257–78.

Krasner, David. "Empathy and Theater." In *Staging Philosophy: Intersections of Theater, Performance, and Philosophy*, edited by David Krasner and David Saltz, 255–77. Ann Arbor: University of Michigan Press, 2006.

Kristeva, Julia. "A New Type of Intellectual: The Dissident." In *The Kristeva Reader*. Edited by Toril Moi, 292–300. New York: Columbia University Press, 1986.

Kristeva, Julia. "Women's Time." Translated by Alice Jardin. *Signs* 7:1 (Autumn 1981): 13–35.

Kuenzli, Rudolph. "Surrealism and Misogyny." In *Surrealism and Women*, edited by Mary Ann Caws, Rudolph Kuenzli, and Gwen Raaberg, 17–26. Cambridge: MIT Press, 1991.

Kuhn, Annette. *Women's Pictures: Feminism and Cinema*. London: Routledge, 1982.

Lacan, Jacques. "The Mirror Stage as Formative of the Function of the I as Revealed in Psychoanalytic Experience." In *Ecrits*. Translated by Alan Sheridan, 3–9. New York: Norton, 1977.

"Law Enforcement Agencies Using Drones List, Map." *Governing Data*. Accessed May 13, 2013. http://www.governing.com/gov-data/safety-justice/drones-state-local-law-enforcement-agencies-license-list.html

Lawrence, Amy. *Echo and Narcissus: Women's Voices in Classic Hollywood Cinema*. Berkeley: University of California Press, 1995.

Lefebvre, Henri. *The Production of Space*. Translated by Donald Nicholson-Smith. London: Blackwell, 1991.

Levin, Thomas, Ursula Frohne, and Peter Weibel, eds. *ctrl [space]: Rhetorics of Surveillance from Bentham to Big Brother*. Leipzig: ZKM, MedienKunstNetz, 2002.

Lorber, Judith. "Heroes, Warriors, and Burqas: A Feminist Sociologist's Reflections on September 11." *Sociological Forum* 17:3 (2002): 377–96.

Lorde, Audre. "The Master's Tools Will Never Dismantle the Master's House." In *Sister Outsider*, 110–14. Berkeley, CA: Crossing Press, 1984.

Lorde, Audre. "Open Letter to Mary Daly." In *Sister Outsider*, 66. Berkeley, CA: Crossing Press, 1984.

Love, Dylan. "British Criminals Are Using Drones to Steal Marijuana." *Business Insider*, April 23, 2014. Accessed April 23, 2014. http://www.businessinsider.com/british-using-drones-to-steal-marijuana-2014-4

Luksch, Manu. *Faceless*. Film, 2007. Produced by Amour Fou Film Produktion and Ambient Information Systems. Accessed February 24, 2014. http://www.ambienttv.net/content/?q=facelessthemovie

Luksch, Manu. "Manifesto for CCTV Filmmakers." 2006. ambienttv.net. Accessed July 19, 2015. http://www.ambienttv.net/content/?q=dpamanifesto

Lyon, David. *The Electronic Eye: The Rise of Surveillance Society*. Minneapolis: Polity Press, 1994.

Lyon, David. *Surveillance after 9/11*. Cambridge: Polity Press, 2003.

Lyon, David. *Surveillance Society: Monitoring in Everyday Life.* Philadelphia: Open University Press, 2001.

Lyon, David. "9/11, Synopticon and Scopophilia: Watching and Being Watched." In *The New Politics of Surveillance and Visibility*, edited by Kevin Haggerty and Richard Ericson, 36–53. Toronto: University of Toronto Press, 2006.

MacCannell, Juliet Flower. *The Hysteric's Guide to the Future Female Subject.* Minneapolis: University of Minnesota Press, 2000.

Madan, Anuja. "The Language of Emotion in Godard's Films." *Cine Action, no.* 80 (2010). Accessed July 20, 2015. http://cineaction.ca/issue80sample.htm

Madison, D. Soyini. "Performing Theory/Embodied Writing." *Text and Performance Quarterly* 19:2 (1999): 107–24.

Madrigal, Alexis. "Detroit 'Ruin Porn' from a Drone." *The Atlantic*, July 17, 2012. Accessed May 9, 2014. http://www.theatlantic.com/technology/archive/2012/07/detroit-ruin-porn-from-a-drone/259944/

Magid, Jill. "Evidence Locker" (2004). Accessed August 25, 2010. http://www.evidencelocker.net/story.php

Magid, Jill. "Monitoring Desire." MA thesis, MIT, 2000. Accessed December 16, 2009. http://jillmagid.net/MIT-Thesis.php

Magid, Jill. "Surveillance Shoe." Accessed August 26, 2010. http://www.jillmagid.net/SurveillanceShoe.php

Magid, Jill. "System Azure." Last modified October 8, 2008. Accessed August 25, 2010. http://www.jillmagid.net/SystemAzure.php

Magnet, Shoshana Amielle. *When Biometrics Fail: Gender, Race, and the Technology of Identity.* Durham: Duke University Press, 2011.

Mann, Steve. "Existential Technology." *LEONARDO* 36:1 (2003): 19–25.

Mann, Steve. "HeartCam." Accessed August 25, 2010. http://wearcam.org/domewear/heartcam.htm

Mann, Steve. "Sousveillance." Accessed August 25, 2010. http://wearcam.org/sousveillance.htm

Mann, Steve. "Wear Comp." Accessed August 25, 2010. http://wearcam.org/wearcompdef.html

Mann, Steve, Jason Nollman, and Barry Wellman. "Sousveillance: Inventing and Using Wearable Computing Devices for Data Collection in Surveillance Environments." *Surveillance & Society* 1:3 (2003): 331–55.

Marx, Gary T. "Electric Eye in the Sky: Some Reflections on the New Surveillance and Popular Culture." In *Computers, Surveillance, and Privacy*, edited by David Lyon and Elia Zureik, 193–236. Minneapolis: University of Minnesota Press, 1996.

Marx, Gary T. "Ethics for the New Surveillance." *Information Society* 14:3 (1998): 171–85.

Marx, Gary T. "The Surveillance Society: The Threat of 1984-Style Techniques." *The Futurist* 6 (June 1985): 21–26.

Marx, Gary T. *Undercover: Police Surveillance in America.* Berkeley: University of California Press, 1988.

Maureen, T. "Invisibility/Hypervisibility: The Paradox of Normative Whiteness." *Transformations* 9:2 (1998): 55–64.

McCarthy, Garry F.. "Custom Notifications in Chicago—Pilot Program." Chicago Police Department, July 2013. Accessed April 25, 2015. http://directives.chicago-police.org/directives-mobile/data/a7a57bf0-13fa59ed-26113-fa63-2e1d9a10bb-60b9ae.html?ownapi=1

McDonough, Tom. *Guy Debord and the Situationist International: Texts and Documents.* Cambridge: MIT Press, 2004.

McGrath, John. *Loving Big Brother: Performance, Privacy, and Surveillance Space.* London: Routledge, 2004.

McKenzie, Jon. *Perform or Else: From Discipline to Performance.* London: Routledge, 2001.

McKie, Robin. "What the Punters Saw . . ." *The Observer,* March 16, 2008. Accessed October 10, 2008. http://www.guardian.co.uk/stage/2008/mar/16/theatre1

Meyer, Robinson. "A New iPhone App Catalogues and Maps U.S. Drone Killings." *The Atlantic,* February 11, 2014. Accessed September 24, 2014. http://www.theatlantic.com/technology/archive/2014/02/a-new-iphone-app-catalogues-and-maps-us-drone-killings/283713/

Mick, Jason. "Dept. of Homeland Sec Brings War Blimps to the Mexican Border." *Daily Tech,* August 15, 2012. Accessed August 29, 2013. http://www.dailytech.com/Dept+of+Homeland+Sec+Brings+War+Blimps+to+the+Mexican+Border/article25415.htm

Mick, Jason. "Google: Yes, We 'Read' Your Gmail." *Daily Tech,* August 15, 2013. Accessed April 25, 2015. http://www.dailytech.com/Google+Yes+we+Read+Your+Gmail/article33184.htm

Mohammadi, Goli. "Interview with Artist and Roboticist Giles Walker." *Make.* April 25, 2013. Accessed April 25, 2015. http://makezine.com/2013/04/25/maker-faire-uk-interview-with-artist-giles-walker/

Monahan, Torin, ed. *Surveillance and Security: Technological Politics and Power in Everyday Life.* London: Routledge, 2006.

Morgan, David. "FAA Expects to Clear U.S. Commercial Drones within a Year." Reuters, June 17, 2015. Accessed July 24, 2015. http://www.reuters.com/article/2015/06/17/us-usa-drones-congress-idUSKBN0OX1P020150617

Morrison, Elise. "Ambushed by Empathy: George Brant's *Grounded.*" *TDR/The Drama Review 58:4* (2014): 163–69.

Morrison, Elise. "Citizen Arrest: Surveillance Art and the Passerby." *International Journal of Performing Arts and Digital Media* 7:2 (2011): 239–57.

Morrison, Elise. "User-*un*friendly: Surveillance Art as Participatory Performance." *Theater* 43:3 (Fall 2013): 5–22.

Morrison, Elise. "Witness Protection: Surveillance Technologies in Theatrical Productions." In *Bastard or Playmate? Adapting Theatre, Mutating Media, and Contemporary Performing Arts,* edited by R. Vanderbeeken, B. De Backere, and C. Stalpaert, 122–43. Amsterdam: University of Amsterdam Press, 2012.

Morrison, Elise, ed. "Surveillance Technologies in Performance." Special Issue. *International Journal for Performing Arts and Digital Media* 11:2 (2015).

Morse, Margaret. "Sunshine and Shroud: Cyborg Bodies and the Collective and Personal Self." In *Cyborg Bodies,* edited by Jennifer John and Yvonne Volkart. Leipzig: ZKM, MedienKunstNetz, 2005. Accessed May 11, 2016. http://www.medienkunstnetz.de/source-text/117/

Moskovitch, Katia. "Are Drones the Next Target for Hackers?" *BBC,* February 6, 2014. Accessed May 28, 2014. http://www.bbc.com/future/story/20140206-can-drones-be-hacked

Mulvey, Laura. *Fetishism and Curiosity.* London: British Film Institute, 1996.

Mulvey, Laura. "Pandora: Topologies of the Mask and Curiosity." In *Sexuality and Space,* edited by Beatriz Colomina, 53–72. Princeton: Princeton Architectural Press, 1992.

Mulvey, Laura. "Visual Pleasure and the Narrative Cinema." In *Visual and Other Pleasures*. Bloomington: Indiana University Press, 1989: 14–29. Originally published in *Screen* 16:3 (1975): 6–18.

Museum of the History of Science. "Cameras: The Technology of Photographic Imaging." Accessed August 25, 2010. www.mhs.ox.ac.uk/cameras/index.htm?overview

Nakamura, Lisa. "Blaming, Shaming, and the Feminization of Social Media." In *Feminist Surveillance Studies,* edited by Rachel Dubrofsky and Shoshana Amielle Magnet, 221–28. Durham: Duke University Press, 2015.

Nakamura, Lisa. *Race after the Internet.* London: Routledge, 2012.

Nanavati, Samir, Michael Thieme, and Raj Nanavati. *Biometrics: Identity Verification in a Networked World.* New York: Wiley & Sons, 2002.

Nevarez, Angel, and Alex Rivera. "Lowdrone." Accessed August 29, 2013. http://lowdrone.com.

Nevarez, Angel, and Alex Rivera. "Tijuana Calling—Lowdrone." Accessed July 16, 2015. http://www.marktribe.net/curatorial/tijuana-calling/low-drone/

Noden, Merrell. "Racial Surveillance: How One Prevalent Form of Inequality Affects the Lives of African-Americans." *Princeton Alumni Weekly,* July 9, 2014. Accessed April 25, 2015. https://paw.princeton.edu/issues/2014/07/09/pages/7630/index.xml

Norris, Clive, and Gary Armstrong. *The Maximum Surveillance Society: The Rise of CCTV.* New York: Berg, 1999.

NPR. "First Female Fighter Pilot: 'Attention Wasn't What I Wanted.'" *Sunday Conversation,* May 12, 2013. *National Public Radio.* Accessed April 25, 2014. http://www.npr.org/2013/05/12/183315464/first-female-fighter-pilot-attention-wasnt-what-i-wanted

Obalk, Hector. "The Unfindable Readymade." *Tout-fait: The Marcel Duchamp Studies Online Journal* 1:2 (May 2000). Accessed April 25, 2015. http://www.toutfait.com/issues/issue_2/Articles/obalk.html

O'Rourke, Karen. *Walking and Mapping: Artists as Cartographers.* Cambridge: MIT Press, 2013.

Ovid. "Echo and Narcissus." In *Metamorphoses,* book IV. Translated by John Dryden (1717). Accessed August 25, 2010. http://personal.centenary.edu/~dhavird/Echo.html

Owens, Craig. "Posing." In *Beyond Recognition: Representation, Power, and Culture.* Berkeley: University of California Press, 1994.

Parenti, Christian. *The Soft Cage: Surveillance in America from Slavery to the War on Terror.* New York: Basic Books, 2003.

Parker-Starbuck, Jennifer. *Cyborg Theatre: Corporeal/Technological Intersections in Multimedia Performance.* Houndmills, Basingstoke, Hampshire: Palgrave Macmillan, 2011.

Parry, James. "Finding the Essence: Mona Hatoum." *Canvas: Art and Culture from the Middle East and Arab World* 6:1 (2010): 114–29.

"Patrol the Border from Home!" Live Leak. Accessed April 1, 2015. http://www.liveleak.com/view?i=68b_1323233391

Pearlman, Ellen. "The Brain as Site Specific Surveillant Performative Space." In "Surveillance Technologies in Performance," edited by Elise Morrison. Special issue, *International Journal of Performance Arts and Digital Media* 11:2 (2015): 219–34.

Pesce, Nicole Lyn. "Young Women Poets Like Camille Rankine, Trisha Low, and Lisa Marie Basile Bring New Energy to World of Words." *New York Daily News,* December 20, 2013. Accessed April 15, 2015. http://www.nydailynews.com/entertain-ment/music-arts/young-women-poets-shaking-world-words-article-1.1553019

Phelan, Peggy. *Unmarked: The Politics of Performance.* London: Routledge, 1993.

Pilobolus Dance Theater. *Seraph* (2010). Video of performance. Published May 14, 2013. Accessed May 20, 2014. https://www.youtube.com/watch?v=pT0K8yJhHpo

Plato. "Allegory of the Cave." Book VII of *The Republic* (360 BCE). In *The Republic of Plato*, translated by Allan Bloom, 193–220. New York: Basic Books, 1968.

"Point Blank." PS122. Accessed November 9, 2008. http://www.ps122.org/perfor-mances/point_blank.html

Powell, Dave. "UK Aerial Photography Law and CAA rules for drone use." *Aerial Photography* Wales. December 16, 2014. Accessed 11 May 2016. http://aerialphotog-raphywales.com/uk-aerial-photography-law-and-caa-rules-for-drone-use/

Priest, Dana. "Government Surveillance Spurs Americans to Fight Back." *Washington Post*, August 14, 2013. Accessed June 2, 2014. http://www.washington-post.com/lifestyle/style/government-surveillance-spurs-americans-to-fight-back/2013/08/14/edea430a-0522-11e3-a07f-49ddc7417125_story_1.html

Program Notes. "About *The Files*." Yale Repertory Theatre, January 20–22, 2014.

Public Art Fund. "Janet Cardiff: *Her Long Black Hair*." Accessed July 10, 2010. http://www.publicartfund.org/pafweb/projects/04/cardiff_J_04.html

Rabellato, Dan. "Naturalism and Symbolism: Early Modernist Practice." In *Routledge Drama Anthology and Sourcebook: From Modernism to Contemporary Performance*, edited by Maggie Gale and John Deeney, 6–24. Abingdon, UK: Routledge, 2010.

Ranciere, Jacques. "Ten Theses on Politics." *Theory & Event* 5:3 (2001): 1–9.

Raw, Emily. "Anti-surveillance Feminist Hair and Makeup Party." Accessed May 10, 2015. http://emilyraw.com/albums/anti-surveillance-feminist-poet-hair-make-up-party/

Rawlings, Ashley. "Remote Repercussions: Wafaa Bilal." *ArtAsiaPacific*, no. 72 (2011). Accessed September 25, 2014. http://artasiapacific.com/Magazine/72/RemoteRepercussionsWafaaBilal

Reagan, Jason. "Drone Sales Figures for 2014." *Dronelife. January 24, 2015*. Accessed August 24, 2014. http://dronelife.com/2015/01/24/drone-sales-figures-2014-hard-navigate/

Reinelt, Janelle. "The Politics of Discourse: Performativity Meets Theatricality." In "Theatricality," editor Josette Féral. *Substance* 31:2 (2002): 201–15.

Reuter, Timothy. "Participate in an Upcoming Drone Art Show with the DC Area Drone User Group." *DIY Drones (blog)*, March 25, 2013. Accessed May 13, 2013. http://diydrones.com/profiles/blogs/participate-in-the-drone-art-show-from-the-dc-area-drone-user

Ridout, Nicholas. *Stage Fright, Animals, and Other Theatrical Problems*. New York: Cambridge University Press, 2006.

Riviere, Joan. "Womanliness as Masquerade." In *Formations of Fantasy*, edited by Victor Burgin, James Donald, and Cora Kaplan, 35–44. London and New York: Methuen, 1986.

Roach, Joseph. *Cities of the Dead: Circum Atlantic Performance*. New York: Columbia University Press, 1996.

Robertson, Kirsty. "'Try to Walk with the Sound of My Footsteps': The Surveillant Body in Contemporary Art." *Communication Review* 11:1 (2008): 24–41.

Rosamond, Emily. "Technologies of Attribution: Characterizing the Citizen-Consumer in Surveillance Performance." In "Surveillance Technologies in Performance," edited by Elise Morrison. Special issue, *International Journal of Performance Arts and Digital Media* 11:2 (2015): 148–64.

Rose, Jacqueline. *Sexuality in the Field of Vision*. London: Verso, 1986.

Rosenthal, Emerson. "Japanese Dance Company Choreographs Performance with Drones." *The Creators Project*, May 22, 2014. Accessed May 25, 2014. http://thecreatorsproject.vice.com/blog/daito-manabe-dance-company-eleven-play

Rule, James B. *Private Lives and Public Surveillance*. London: Allen Lane, 1973.

Schechner, Richard. *Between Theatre and Anthropology*. University of Pennsylvania Press: 1985.

Schechner, Richard. "9/11 as Avant-Garde Art?" In "War." Special issue, *PMLA* 124:5 (2009): 1820–29.

Scher, Julia. *Tell Me When You're Ready: Works, 1990–1995*. Introduced and curated by Anna Indych. Somerville, MA: PFM Publishers, 2002.

Schienke, Erich W. "On the Outside Looking Out: An Interview with the Institute for Applied Autonomy." *Surveillance & Society* 1:1 (2002): 102–19.

Schneider, Rebecca. *The Explicit Body in Performance*. London: Routledge, 1997.

Schneider, Rebecca. "Archives: Performance Remains." *Performance Research* 6:2 (2001): 100–108.

Schneider, Rebecca. *Performing Remains: Art and War in Times of Theatrical Reenactment*. London: Routledge, 2011.

Scourti, Erica. *(End of) Life in AdWords*. Video, 2013. Recorded by Emily Candela. Accessed April 10, 2015. https://vimeo.com/59354268

Scourti, Erica. "Life in AdWords" (2012–13). Accessed April 10, 2015. http://ericascourti.com/art_pages/life_in_adwords.html

SCP [Surveillance Camera Players]. "Amnesia." Accessed August 25, 2010. http://www.notbored.org/amnesia.html

SCP. "Being Watched." Accessed August 25, 2010. http://www.notbored.org/being-watched.html

SCP. "God's Eyes." Accessed August 25, 2010. http://www.notbored.org/god%27s-eyes.html

SCP. *How to Stage Your Own "Surveillance Camera Theater" in 10 Easy-to-Follow Steps!* Accessed August 25, 2010. http://www.notbored.org/scp-how-to.html

SCP. "It's OK, Officer." Accessed August 25, 2010. http://www.notbored.org/its-ok-officer.html

SCP. "SCP Founding." Accessed May 11, 2016. http://www.notbored.org/scp-founding.html

SCP. "Something Interesting." August 25, 2010. http://www.notbored.org/something-interesting.html

SCP "Ten Year Report." Accessed August 25, 2010. http://www.notbored.org/10-year-report.html

SCP. "We Know You Are Watching." Accessed August 25, 2010. http://www.notbored.org/jay-day-both.jpg

Sellar, Tom. "In *An Octoroon*, Branden Jacobs-Jenkins Knocks Us Flat on Our Preconceptions." *Village Voice*, May 7, 2014. Accessed July 20, 2015. http://www.villagevoice.com/2014-05-07/theater/an-octoroon-soho-rep/full/

Selvaggio, Leonardo. "URME Surveillance: Performing Privilege in the Face of Automation." In "Surveillance Technologies in Performance," edited by Elise Morrison. Special issue, *International Journal of Performance Arts and Digital Media* 11:2 (2015): 165–84.

Shaban, Bigad. "Drone Degrees: Universities Train Students for Future of Flight." *CBS News*, February 5, 2014. Accessed February 17, 2015. http://www.cbsnews.com/news/drone-degrees-universities-train-students-for-high-tech-future-of-flight/

Shank, Theodore. "Squat Theatre" *Performing Arts Journal* 3:2 (1978), 61–69.

Sheller Mimi, and John Urry. "The New Mobilities Paradigm." *Environment and Planning A* 38:2 (2006): 207–26.

Shklovsky, Victor. "Art as Technique." In *Russian Formalist Criticism: Four Essays*. Translated by Lee T. Lemon and Marion J. Reis, 3–24. Lincoln: University of Nebraska Press, 1965.

Siciliano, Amy. "Swinging at the State: Media, Surveillance, and Subversion." *Aether: The Journal of Media Geography* 1 (October 2007): 53–55.

Silverman, Kaja. "The Female Authorial Voice." In *The Acoustic Mirror: The Female Voice in Psychoanalysis and Cinema, 187–234*. Bloomington: Indiana University Press, 1988.

Silverman, Kaja. *The Threshold of the Visible World*. New York: Routledge, 1996.

Singer, Paolo. *Corporate Warriors: The Rise of the Privatized Military Industry*. Ithaca, NY: Cornell University Press, 2003.

Singer, P. W. "Robots at War: The New Battlefield." *Wilson Quarterly* 33:1 (2009): 30–48. Accessed October 9, 2012. http://www.jstor.org/stable/40262238

Sjogren, Britta. *Into the Vortex: Female Voice and Paradox in Film*. Urbana: University of Illinois Press, 2006.

Smith, Matt. "Flying Drone Peers into Japan's Damaged Reactors." *CNN*, April 10, 2011. Accessed June 11, 2014. http://www.cnn.com/2011/WORLD/asiapcf/04/10/japan.nuclear.reactors/

Snyder, R. Claire. "What Is Third-Wave Feminism? A New Directions Essay." *Signs* 34:1 (Autumn 2008): 175–96.

Sofer, Andrew. *Dark Matter: Invisibility in Drama, Theater, and Performance*. Ann Arbor: University of Michigan Press, 2013.

Sofer, Andrew. *The Stage Life of Props*. Ann Arbor: University of Michigan Press, 2003.

Solove, Daniel J. *The Digital Person: Technology and Privacy in the Information Age*. New York: New York University Press, 2004.

Sonstegard, Adam. "Performing Remediation: Minstrelsy, Photography, and *The Octoroon*." *Criticism* 48:3 (2006): 375–95.

Sontag, Susan. "Fascinating Fascism." *New York Review of Books*, February 6, 1975. Republished in Susan Sontag, *Under the Sign of Saturn: Essays*, 73–105. New York: Picador, 1980.

Sontag, Susan. "Notes on Camp." In *Against Interpretation, 275–92*. New York: Farrar, Straus & Giroux, 1966.

Sontag, Susan. *On Photography*. London: Penguin Books, 1977.

Stahl, Roger. *Militainment, Inc.: War, Media, and Popular Culture*. New York: Routledge, 2010.

Stahl, Roger. *Returning Fire: Interventions in Video Game Culture*. Northampton, MA: Media Education Foundation, 2011.

Standley, Ann. "The Role of Black Women in the Civil Rights Movement." In *Women in the Civil Rights Movement: Trailblazers and Torchbearers, 1941–1965*, edited by Vicki L. Crawford, Jacqueline Anne Rouse, and Barbara Woods, 183–202. Athens: University of Georgia Press, 1990.

Stanley, Jay. *The Surveillance-Industrial Complex: How the American Government Is Conscripting Businesses and Individuals in the Construction of a Surveillance Society*. New York: American Civil Liberties Union, 2004.

Starr, Michelle. "Watch Robotic Pole Dancers Shake Their Actuators." *CNET*, March 12, 2014. Accessed February 10, 2015. http://www.cnet.com/news/watch-robotic-pole-dancers-shake-their-actuators/

States, Bert. *Great Reckonings in Little Rooms*. Berkeley: University of California Press, 1985.

Steadman, Ian. "Artist Imagines a Drone with Self-Consciousness That Feels Bad about Its Job." *Wired*, March 7, 2013. Accessed May 21, 2014. http://www.wired.co.uk/news/archive/2013–03/07/self-aware-drone-art-george-barber

Strange, Adario. "Pole Dancing Robots Make CCTV Surveillance Sexy." *DVICE*, December 5, 2008. Accessed August 25, 2010. http://dvice.com/archives/2008/12/pole_dancing_ro.php

Stroud, Matt. "The Minority Report: Chicago's New Police Computer Predicts Crimes, but Is It Racist?" *The Verge*, February 19, 2014. Accessed April 25, 2015. http://www.theverge.com/2014/2/19/5419854/the-minority-report-this-computer-predicts-crime-but-is-it-racist

Stubblefield, Thomas. "'Moving' Images: Film, Dataveillance, and the Labor of the Visual." Paper presented at the conference Fields of Vision: Observation, Surveillance, Voyeurism, Whitney Humanities Center, Yale University, February 21, 2014.

Sutrop, Margit, and Katrin Laas-Mikko. "From Identity Verification to Behavior Prediction: Ethical Implications of Second Generation Biometrics." *Review of Policy Research* 29:1 (2012): 21–36.

Tagg, John. *The Burden of Representation: Essays on Photographies and Histories*. Minneapolis: University of Minnesota Press, 1993.

Taigman, Yaniv, Ming Yang, Marc'Aurelio Ranzato, and Lior Wolf. "DeepFace: Closing the Gap to Human-Level Performance in Face Verification." Paper delivered at the conference Computer Vision and Pattern Recognition, June 24, 2014. Accessed May 19, 2015. https://research.facebook.com/publications/480567225376225/deepface-closing-the-gap-to-human-level-performance-in-face-verification/

Tate Museum Online Resources. "Readymade." Accessed April 25, 2015. http://www.tate.org.uk/learn/online-resources/glossary/r/readymade

Taxidou, Olga. *The Mask: A Periodical Performance by Edward Gordon Craig*. Routledge: 2013.

Taylor, Diana. *The Archive and the Repertoire: Performing Memory in the Americas*. Durham: Duke University Press, 2003.

Taylor, Diana. *Disappearing Acts: Spectacles of Gender and Nationalism in Argentina's "Dirty War."* Durham: Duke University Press, 1997.

"TED Speaker: Hasan Elahi." October 2011. Accessed October 9, 2014. http://www.ted.com/speakers/hasan_elahi

Thompson, Nato, ed. *The Interventionists: A Users' Manual for the Creative Disruption of Everyday Life*. North Adams, MA: Massachusetts Museum of Contemporary Art,, 2004.

Thompson, Richard M., II. "Drones in Domestic Surveillance Operations: Fourth Amendment Implications and Legislative Responses." *Congressional Research Service*, April 2013. Accessed August 29, 2013. http://www.fas.org/sgp/crs/natsec/R42701.pdf

Tretch5000. *Detroit Mix FPV,* June 22, 2012. YouTube video. Accessed May 17, 2014. https://www.youtube.com/watch?v=LkMiIT1VG98

Turner, Andrew. *Introduction to Neogeography* (2006). O'Reilly Media. Accessed April 24, 2015. http://highearthorbit.com/neogeography/book.pdf

Tythacott, Louise. *Surrealism and the Exotic.* London: Routledge, 2003.

Unger, Clio. "'SHOOT HIM NOW!!!': Anonymity, Accountability, and Online Spectatorship in Wafaa Bilal's *Domestic Tension.*" In "Surveillance Technologies in Performance," edited by Elise Morrison. Special issue, *International Journal of Performance Arts and Digital Media* 11:2 (2015): 202–18.

US Congress, Office of Technology Assessment. *Electronic Surveillance in a Digital Age.* Washington, DC: Government Printing Office, 1995.

Vaneigem, Raoul. *The Revolution of Everyday Life.* Translated by Donald Nicholson-Smith. London: Rebel Press, 1983.

Villar, Alex. "Temporary Occupations." Accessed August 25, 2010. http://www.de-tour.org/series/temp_occupations/index.html

Wainwright, Oliver. "Spraycopter: The Drone That Does Graffiti." *The Guardian,* April 21, 2014. Accessed April 24, 2014. http://www.theguardian.com/artanddesign/architecture-design-blog/2014/apr/21/drone-does-graffiti-street-art

Wajcam, Judith. *TechnoFeminism.* Cambridge: Polity Press, 2004.

Walby, Kevin, and Seantel Anais. "Research Methods, Institutional Ethnography, and Feminist Surveillance Studies." In *Feminist Surveillance Studies,* edited by Rachel Dubrofsky and Shoshana Amielle Magnet, 208–20. Durham: Duke University Press, 2015.

Walker, Giles. "Peepshow" (2007). Accessed August 25, 2010. http://www.gileswalk-er.org/gileswalker.org/PEEPSHOW/Pages/pole_dancers.html

Webster, William. "CCTV Policy in the UK: Reconsidering the Evidence Base." *Surveillance & Society* 6:1 (2009): 10–22.

Wilken, Rowan. "Proximity and Alienation: Narratives of City, Self, and Other in the Locative Games of Blast Theory." In *The Mobile Story,* edited by Jason Farman, 175–91. London: Routledge, 2014.

Williams, Linda. "When the Woman Looks." In *(Re)Vision: Essays in Feminist Film Criticism,* edited by Mary Ann Doane, Patricia Mellencamp, and Linda Williams, 83–99. Los Angeles: American Film Institute, 1984.

Wood, David Murakami, and Stephen Graham. "Permeable Boundaries in Soft-Ware Sorted Society: Surveillance and Differentiations of Mobility." In *Mobile Technologies of the City,* edited by Mimi Sheller and John Urry, 177–91. London: Routledge, 2006.

Woollaston, Victoria. "Facebook Can Tag You In Photos AUTOMATICALLY: Social Network Starts Rolling Out DeepFace Recognition Feature." *Daily Mail,* February 9, 2015. Accessed April 25, 2015. http://www.dailymail.co.uk/sciencetech/article-2946186/Facebook-soon-tag-photos-AUTOMATICALLY-Social-network-starts-rolling-DeepFace-feature.html

Whitson, Jennifer R., and Bart Simon. "Game Studies Meets Surveillance Studies at the Edge of Digital Culture: An Introduction to a Special Issue on Surveillance, Games and Play." In "Surveillance, Gaming and Play," edited by Jennifer R. Whitson and Bart Simon. Special issue, *Surveillance & Society* 12:3 (2014): 309–19.

Yes Men. Film, 2003. Directed by Dan Ollman, Sarah Price, and Chris Smith.

Yes Men. "Identity Corrections." Accessed January 21, 2015. http://theyesmen.org/

Yes Men. "Tampere Hijinks." Accessed August 19, 2010. http://theyesmen.org/hijinks/tampere.

Yes Men. "World Trade Organization." Accessed January 21, 2015. http://www.gatt. org/

Yes Men. "Yes Lab: Get Involved." Accessed January 23, 2015. http://www.yeslab.org/ get-involved

Young, Stephanie. "Participate." In "Antirecognition.tumblr" (blog). Accessed May 10, 2015. http://antirecognition.tumblr.com/participate

Young, Stephanie. SOME NOTES ON THE ANTI-SURVEILLANCE FEMINIST POET HAIR & MAKEUP PARTY. Oakland, CA: Dusie Press, 2014.

Zeilinger, Martin. "Appropriation and the Authoring Function of Camera Surveillance in Manu Luksch's Faceless." In Eyes Everywhere: The Global Growth of Camera Surveillance, edited by Aaron Doyle, Randy Lippert, and David Lyon, 262–73. London: Routledge, 2012.

Zola, Émile. "Naturalism in the Theatre" (1881). Translated by Jane House. In Theatre/Theory/Theatre: The Major Critical Texts from Aristotle and Zeami to Soyinka and Havel, edited by Daniel Gerould, 358–67. New York: Applause Theatre and Cinema Books, 2000.

Zola, Émile. "Preface to Therese Raquin" (1873). Translated by Kathleen Boutall. In Theatre/Theory/Theatre: The Major Critical Texts from Aristotle and Zeami to Soyinka and Havel, edited by Daniel Gerould, 351–57. New York: Applause Theatre and Cinema Books, 2000.

Index

Photographs are indicated by italicized page numbers.

351

gender, 192, 193, 203, 205–6, 208; gendered issues of, 181; iris scanning technologies, 192; and racial profiling, 199–200; resistance techniques used by artists against, 196; "retraining" of systems, 193–94; second generation focus, 312n13; Violence Reduction Strategy (VRS) program, 191, 313n24; white male privilege of, 192, 193, 206. *See also* facial recognition software

Black Lives Matter movement, 69

Black Mirror (TV program), 183–85

Blas, Zach: *Face Cages*, 197, *198*, 199; *Facial Weaponization Suite*, 199–200, *201, 202*

Blast Theory, *Rider Spoke*, 107, 130–35, *131*

blogs: *Eyes of Laura* (Cardiff), 172, 177; *Tracking Transience* (Elahi), 123–26

"Blow Up" (Cortázar), 176

Blow Up (film), 176

body cameras, 69, 290n9

Bolter, Jay David, 33, 284n9

Bonnano, Mike, 80

Boucicault, Dion, *The Octoroon*, 34, 49

Boxer, Sarah, 177

Brant, George: *Grounded*, 234, 259–66

Brecht, Bertolt: and epic narrative, 317n82; and Marxist materialism, 215, 272; and mimesis, 294n50; on naturalism, 194–95, 314n37; and theatrical interruptions, 73

Brechtian alienation: as anti-surveillance performance technique, 195, 196; and critical spectatorship, 12; in *Faceless* (Luksch), 211, 213–14; in *Life in AdWords* (Scourti), 219, 220

Breton, André, 195, 219

Bridle, James: *Drone Shadows*, 239–241, *240*; Dronestagram project, 322n16

Brin, David, 18, 282n57

Brooker, Charlie, 185

Brown, Michael, 290n9

Browne, Simone, 192, 216

Builders Association, *Super Vision*, 35

Butler, Judith: on gendered bodies, 145; on gender's function, 305n6; on performativity of gender, 18, 282n53;

and performativity of surveillance, 63; and sousveillance, 115

CAA drone legislation, 236

Cabell, Hannah, 260

CAE. *See* Critical Art Ensemble (CAE)

Calle, Sophie: *Appointment with Sigmund Freud*, 91, 294n62, 295n72; desire in works of, 91, 92; *The Detective*, 89–90; "male gaze" in works of, 90, 92; voiced writing in works of, 91

Calo, M. Ryan, 237, 322n18

Camp, Pannill, 285–86n25

candid photographs. *See* photographs, candid

capitalism, 115–16

Cardiff, Janet: *Eyes of Laura*, 172–80, *174*; "sound walks," 178; on unsettling spectatorship, 310n93

Case, Sue-Ellen, 151

catcalling, 93–94. *See also City of Brotherly Love* (Price)

CCTV camera surveillance: as audience, 73–74, 76–77; and crime prevention, 66–67, 291nn23–4, 292n25 discriminatory policies of, 67, 75, 77, 98; *Dolores: From 10 to 10* (Fusco) as mimicking, 122; effect of, 74–75; *Evidence Locker* (Magid), 65, 289nn2–3; *Faceless* (Luksch), 24, 211–16, *213*; fetishism of, 154; Liverpool *Echo* article, 66–67; "Manifesto for CCTV Filmmakers" (Luksch), 23–24; and neoliberalism, 67, 74–75; and "nothing to hide/nothing to fear" concept, 67, 75; and policing of public spaces, 290n7; System Azure project (Magid), 151–52, *153*, 154, *154*; unverifiable surveillance of watchers, 40–41; and visibility/invisibility, 67. *See also* specific projects

cell phones. *See* smart phones; Transborder Immigrant Tool (TBT) project

censorship, 286n27

Central Intelligence Agency (CIA), 108–9

Charcot, Jean-Martin, 169, 308n60

Chicago Police Department (CPD), 191, 313n24